AF484273

TO RIGHT A WRONG

A Transpersonal Framework for Constitutional Construction

Roar A. Mikalsen

To Ellen

FOR THOSE WHO BRING
INTEGRITY TO LAW

CONTENTS

Part Four

A Shifting Paradigm

INTRODUCTION

"[W]hat is government itself but the greatest of all reflections on human nature?"[1]

—James Madison—

SINCE THE AMERICAN CONSTITUTION was enacted more than 200 years ago, a variety of lawyers, justices, political scientists, historians, philosophers, humanists, social scientists, politicians, and concerned citizens have been engaged in pondering what it means, how its more vague and open-ended clauses shall be interpreted, and what its implications are for us as individuals and society. Foremost among these interpreters—as measured by the weight of their impact if not their wisdom—have been the justices at the U.S. Supreme Court. It is they who have had the final word in matters of interpretation and while they have spilt a few words of wisdom, the opposite is equally true. Anyone even remotely familiar with this topic knows that there has been heated controversy among the justices themselves about issues of utmost importance—and that the greater array of scholars have had even more profound disagreements regarding the propriety of the Court's decisions and doctrines.

This book shall not rehearse all the controversy, all the different theories and opinions that have informed the debate to this day. Instead, I aim to bring something new, something that can help remove some of the so-called nebulousness that has been associated with the text itself, something that can separate the wheat from the chaff regarding the appropriateness of the various legal arguments and political theories that have been used to interpret it, and something that can help us see the many disagreements from a more informed perspective. In short, my aim

---

[1] MADISON, HAMILTON & JAY, *THE FEDERALIST PAPERS* (2010) 200

is to offer a new framework for constitutional interpretation, a framework that will add more depth, coherence, stability, and—not least—credibility to the discipline.

These may be big words, but what I hope to provide is nothing more than the logical next step when it comes to constitutional interpretation. As is well known, we already have one framework in place for interpreting the Constitution. This is that of political theory and, as most will agree, one cannot really make sense of the Constitution without its aid; the political theory is the lens through which the text must be read, and yet many scholars—even those who agree on the importance of applying the philosophy of the Founding Fathers—have ended up reaching very different conclusions. Granted, a few have done such a poor job that we are left with a nagging suspicion that their efforts have been less than sincere. For some individuals—especially those in positions of power—it seems to be psychologically impossible to come to terms with rather explicit rules of construction, and whenever the logical implication of the founders' philosophy has been at odds with their own preferences, they will dream up their own idea of what the founders meant and leave it at that.

Without going further into detail on the virtues of these endeavors, this just proves my point, and it should be obvious from the present state of affairs that having a political theory is not enough. To put it in the bluntest terms, a fascist, a socialist, and a libertarian will construe the text in wholly different ways, and this being the case the Constitution can be an accommodating tool for agents of tyranny as well as agents of liberty. There is only one way to solve this problem and it is by adding another factor to the equation, namely human psychology. Psychology, after all, gives birth to politics, just as politics gives birth to law. Human consciousness is the overriding variable that controls everything else, and in drawing on findings from psychology I will therefore present a model that holds great promise for the discipline of law.

The Full-Consciousness and Null-Consciousness Model

The basic premise of the FC/NC model is that the dynamic unfolding between the individual and society is a variable in constant flux and that what changes it is our level of consciousness. That much is obvious. But without going into too much detail, we can, by building on research from psychology, put together a model that describes the defining dynamics between the individual and society at different levels of interaction. As shall be seen there are certain givens which will help us predict the overall effects of certain changes in consciousness, and one of the most important lessons we can draw from this conceptual framework concerns the relationship between the individual and the state.

The reason for this is that the FC/NC model represents a sliding scale of autonomy-fulfilling societal interaction where the NC-end consists of non-autonomous individuals and the FC-end consists of fully autonomous individuals. We all belong somewhere on this scale and while very few fulfill the criteria to be put in either of the extreme ends, I shall for simplicity's sake separate the population into two categories— into those of FC and NC individuals. Considering that most people will exist on the borderline between these two categories, demonstrating FC qualities in one situation and NC qualities in another, this is an oversimplification. But we are here concerned with the bigger picture and for the sake of analysis this generalization works fine.[2]

As we shall see, psychologists will attribute different traits to the different groups, and depending on the autonomy levels present in any society we can predict what government that will result. Freedom and responsibility, as the Founding Fathers knew so well, are inextricably linked. We cannot have one without the other and the more a society is defined by FC traits, the more the state will fulfill its role as a protector and advancer of human rights. The opposite is equally true, and the closer we draw towards the NC-end the state will become an instrument of oppression.

In one end of the model therefore we have those characteristics and dynamics that define the ideal society, while in the other we have those that define less evolved societies. Much more will be said about this. Suffice now to say that the FC/NC model's categorization of societies at different levels of maturity is hardly controversial. Those familiar with

---

[2] As NC traits represent our most unflattering potential, while FC traits represent the opposite, this generalization will also serve another purpose. I have no intention of putting people down on an individual basis, and by applying this generalization—and showing the implications of sticking with either position—I will leave it up to the reader to decide whether he/she, in thoughts, words, and actions, will represent the former or the latter.

Dworkin will notice how this model is loosely applicable to his three models of community,[3] and those familiar with Rawls will recognize the FC society as what he would consider a well-ordered society.[4] The FC society then is no invention of mine. It is simply the kind of society in which we would want to live, where theory and practice is one and the same, and where reason is allowed to guide our ways. Not only that; it is also the kind of society that our leaders will insist that we are: we are already constitutionally committed to those ideals found in FC societies—and to the extent we are weighed and found wanting, it will be due to a failure to practice what we preach.

The implication is a qualitative difference between the reasoning that takes place at the FC and NC level. Most are influenced by both, but in its pure form FC and NC reasoning represent two wholly different ways of perceiving the world. As shall be seen, we are dealing with two different paradigms, one superior to the other, and nowhere is this better exposed than in our system of law. While NC reasoning is revealed to be the result of confused analysis and incomplete understanding—that is, as not being supported by any valid foundation at all—FC reasoning has as its defining trait that it is always harmonious with reason, leading back to first principles. For purposes of constitutional construction this qualitative difference is extremely important. These two types of reasoning form the basis of any dispute on constitutional interpretation and *only FC reasoning* can accurately decipher the Constitution. Because of this, much of this book will be concerned with explaining the difference between FC and NC reasoning and its implications for society.

This book, however, is not only about constitutional construction; it extends further, to its logical conclusion. Having defined the parameters

---

[3] Dworkin describes the attitudes of members of a political community at three different levels of reasoning. The first model, where there is no common bond and understanding and people are driven by selfish pursuits, conforms to the lower end of the FC/NC scale. The second model (the Rulebook Model) represents a more advanced society. At this level, the "members of a political community accept a general commitment to obey rules established in a certain way." Whereas people in the first model have no sense of obligation to each other, here they do. But their obligation is to a certain set of rules and these rules may be unfair, especially to politically weak minorities. It is only at the third level (the Model of Principle) that society has matured to be governed by principled reasoning. Only at this final level is the conditions identified by Dworkin of a true community satisfied, only this type of society has moral legitimacy with integrity of law and legislation. DWORKIN, *LAW'S EMPIRE* (1986) 208-24

[4] RAWLS, *JUSTICE AS FAIRNESS: A RESTATEMENT* (2003) 8-9

of the FC/NC model, we see that not only does it provide us with a frame of reference by which various legal arguments and philosophies can be ordered according to their compatibility with first principles. Having laid out the Spectrum of Consciousness and its implications for social interaction, we have a definite map of the greater moral, legal, political, and psychological landscape, one that provides us with the knowledge needed to assist us in the building of a better future. This being so the FC/NC model is also a unique tool for purposes of social engineering.

As we shall see, there are two kinds of social engineering, one that brings us towards the FC-end and another that takes us towards the NC-end. Both will be discussed, but when it comes to FC-engineering there are two basic tools available, one being consciousness-raising and the other being law.[5] Consciousness being the underlying variable that affects everything else, the extent to which law will fulfill its potential as a tool for these purposes depends on the consciousness of society. And from the dynamics that define societies at various positions on the FC/NC scale, we see that *only societies having reached a certain level of maturity* can begin to apply this discipline for constructive purposes. Societies existing at the lower end of the spectrum will be too informed by special interest groups and short-term priorities to put the science to good use, and so it comes as no surprise that it has yet to be recognized. Even so, the theory is in place for us to apply whenever we are ready, and it is a science no less worthy of recognition than any other.

In looking at this, we find that based on our position on the FC/NC scale we are faced with two choices: progression or regression. When it comes to social engineering this is *the only* map to go by and the choice social engineers must make is what direction. This alone should make the FC/NC model worthy of attention. The law is a powerful tool in the advancement of society towards either end. And considering that the FC-end has been the yardstick against which not only our greatest religious figures but all progressive thinkers throughout history (the Founding Fathers included) have measured the inadequacies of their age,[6] it is not

---

[5] In a previous book I've focused on the former and this work will be concentrating on the latter. For more on consciousness-raising, see MIKALSEN, *REASON IS* (2014)

[6] I use "progressive" in the sense of being oriented towards Wholeness and the ideals, values, and principles that follow. In the FC/NC model all progression is towards this end; towards ever

difficult to see how social engineering naturally connects to the discipline of constitutional construction—and how the FC-end should be the Moral North in any constitutional interpretation.

To fully connect with this greater picture, we must also introduce another lesson from psychology. This is that our psychological development does not stop with adulthood. Psychologists have discovered that we are subjected to growth-conducive and growth-inhibiting potentials throughout our lives and that the extent to which we draw upon the former we will advance cognitively, emotionally, and morally to higher levels of maturity. More shall be said on this important topic. However, psychologists have categorized different stages of growth and based on where we find ourselves certain qualities will be demonstrated.

This knowledge is valuable both for social engineering and constitutional interpretation purposes—which, of course, should amount to the same. It is important for social engineering purposes because the higher levels of growth are synonymous with psychological health, while the lower levels indicate illness. The further towards the lower end we draw, the more we will see the world from a fragmented and isolated perspective and be driven by fear. Depending on their personality, people at this end will exhibit manipulative, immoral, self-centered, and control-oriented traits or they will be more submissive, naïve, and easy to manipulate. In either case, because of their yearning to control others or to be controlled, they will be uncritically embracive of authoritarian systems. The opposite is equally true, and the higher we climb on this scale of psychological well-being, the more we will see ourselves as part of a greater whole and be moved by love. Such people will not only be more resistant to manipulation and opposed to authoritarian systems; they will also be more forgiving, tolerant, honest, and compassionate—in short, more able to integrate and represent those values, ideals, and principles that follow from the Wholeness concept.[7]

---

greater levels of coherence and value-fulfillment, and all regression is towards the opposite—i.e., towards the NC-end.

[7] The tendency of psychological growth towards Wholeness has been aptly described by researchers. Walsh and Grob summarizes the findings: "A common conclusion concerned a fundamental capacity and drive of mind. The mind increasingly came to be seen as a self-organizing, self-optimizing system. Most of these investigators concluded that, given supportive conditions, the mind tends to be self-healing, self-integrating, and self-actualizing. These

Based on this simple chart, we can see that for purposes of social engineering it would be wise to ensure those conditions that promote growth rather than stagnation, for only to the extent that this is done can we become a harmonious and well-ordered society. In this connection one of our greatest challenges is the society in which we live. It is so full of growth-inhibiting factors that the opposite result is ensured. And because we are born into this type of society, development towards higher levels becomes arrested.[8]

This is important knowledge because given more ideal conditions, we would all advance to those levels of psychological health/maturity that define the most "self-actualized" population. The fact that we are more or less "damaged goods," however, does not mean that we must stay that way. Psychologists have developed the tools needed to help people overcome these obstacles; we know what causes regression and what generates growth, and we know that the extent to which we can (1) help individuals "unfreeze" and/or (2) ensure the societal conditions that keep people from freezing in the first place, we can move society forward in the right direction—in the direction of the utopian vision of the Founding Fathers.

---

tendencies of the mind to unfold and develop its potentials had been recognized before in both East and West, psychology and philosophy. Centuries ago, Tibetan Buddhism described the 'self-liberating' nature of mind. More recent recognitions include neuroatomist Kurt Goldstein's 'actualization,' Ken Wilber's 'eros,' and Aldous Huxley's 'moksha drive.' Many psychologists have come to the same conclusion. Examples include Karen Horney's 'self-realization,' Carl Rogers' 'formative tendency,' Carl Jung's 'individuation urge,' Abraham Maslow's 'self-actualization' and 'self-transcendence,' and Erik Erikson's 'self-perfectibility.' These tendencies of mind had been repeatedly recognized throughout history, but they became unavoidably evident with the [research on] psychedelics. Stanislav Grof later coined the term 'holotropism' [movement towards wholeness] to describe the mind's tendency to move towards holotropic or transpersonal experiences and thereby heal and integrate." Walsh & Grob, *Psychological Health and Growth* in WINKELMAN & ROBERTS (EDS), *PSYCHEDELIC MEDICINE* (2007) 215-16

[8] MASLOW, *TOWARD A PSYCHOLOGY OF BEING* (1982) 16 ("What we call 'normal' in psychology is really a psychopathology of the average, so undramatic and so widely spread that we don't even notice it ordinarily. The study of the authentic person and of authentic living helps to throw this general phoniness, this living by illusion and by fear into a harsh, clear light which reveals it clearly as a sickness, even though widely shared."); Walsh, *States and Stages of Consciousness: Current Research and Understandings* in HAMEROFF, KASZNIAK & SCOTT (EDS.), *TOWARD A SCIENCE OF CONSCIOUSNESS* (1998) 684 ("the human condition offers possibilities far beyond those usually recognized. It follows that the condition we have called 'normality' is not the peak of human development but rather may represent an arbitrary, culturally determined form of developmental arrest.")

It should come as no surprise that the stages of developmental growth match perfectly the FC/NC model's sliding scale of autonomy-actualized individuals and the societal interaction that follows. The defining traits of FC societies are exactly those we find in individuals at the highest levels of psychological growth, and the defining traits of NC societies are those found in growth-inhibited individuals.

When it comes to matters of constitutional interpretation this finding is important for two reasons. First, we are constitutionally committed to realizing those values found at the FC-end and it should be reflected in our system of criminal law. *Only* to the extent that this is the case can we say that we are drawing upon the law as a tool for constructive social engineering—and *only* to the extent that this is so can we say that we have a constitutionalized (and just) system of law. The integrity of our legal system, then, depends on the extent to which it coheres with the light of first principles—and this is where our system of law runs into problems.

As we shall see, there are only two kinds of law—the FC and the NC version—and by necessity the former will be a principled system of law while the other will be one of arbitrary law. I say "by necessity" for only FC societies can afford the luxury of having a system of law congruent with its foundation—i.e., the fundamental principles of justice. For this to be the case, society must have evolved to the point where theory and practice is one and the same, and only FC societies have advanced to the point where reason rather than passion defines the parameters for social interaction. In NC societies there will always be a gap between the two; the ruling elites may talk of human rights, common values, the rule of law, human dignity, and so on, but those in positions of power will mean little by it. They will have an agenda of their own, one that is incompatible with the values to which they pay lip-service, and the only thing that can ensure the survival of a system where theory and practice means two different things is a system of arbitrary law.

This is especially important to recognize, as our society does not yet conform to the demands of a just society—of a FC society. While we, on the one hand, celebrate those ideals and principles which would be fully realized and acted upon in the FC society, we fail to live by the very standard to which we hold ourselves, and an honest look reveals that we satisfy the criteria of an *advanced* NC society—no more: (1) we recognize the values of FC societies, (2) we are constitutionally committed to realizing them, but (3) we sometimes fail to do so. The extent to which we fail to live up to the demands of justice will be elaborated upon, as will the nature of the system that maintains the status quo. Suffice now to say that the current American system is a system of arbitrary justice, one that builds on logical contradictions, misconstrued doctrines, and fundamentally flawed analysis—nothing else.

These may be harsh words. However, while FC law will be firmly rooted in first principles, the latter (which may or may not conform to the higher version of law) has nothing but incoherent reasoning and fragmented understanding going for it. To sustain such a system—in order to make it believable—one is dependent on a breed of lawyers and justices who do not really understand (or care) what true law is. In a NC system they are never short in supply, for due to reasons that will be explained later a majority will be too entangled in the mindset that connects them to their day and age to be free from contemporary constraints. Hence, if we conform to the standards of an NC society, these people will adjust to NC standards; they will, in short, become NC individuals and NC individuals do not have the capacity to see beyond the doctrines of the status quo. As mentioned, one of the defining traits that separate FC and NC individuals is that the former are more connected to the implications of Wholeness while the latter see the world from a fragmented and isolated perspective. It is therefore *only* FC individuals who have developed an ability for moral reasoning that transcends time and place—and this explains the major difference between FC and NC jurists.

This also explains the second reason why lessons from psychology should be brought to bear on constitutional interpretation. We need a functional legal/moral compass, and what I have said means that NC individuals lack the basic faculty needed to interpret the U.S. Constitution. As we shall see, the Constitution was an FC document, and the founders were FC individuals. It was their ambition to create a secure foundation upon which a new model of state could be built, one that would secure a maximum amount of liberty and happiness for all, and one that would withstand the attack of those factions that had other ambitions. The *only* thing that could secure such a foundation was fundamental principles, and so it was that state and federal constitutions were enacted that built on these principles.

From this it should be obvious why NC jurists are faced with an impossible task, as they themselves cannot connect with the light of first principles. To do so they must first develop the integrity needed to free themselves from contemporary constraints—and as of yet they have not done so. While this may be a controversial assertion, evidence will be provided. And in this book's part three we shall see that, extrapolating from the reasoning of more than a hundred constitutional challenges to the drug laws, 90 percent of American judges fall into this category.

This does not mean that the higher form of reasoning that qualifies for FC status is out of reach. What is needed, however, is some soul-searching and a crash course in FC law and for us as a society to fully embrace those doctrines that build on first principles. If this foundation is in place, we can expect that most of today's lawyers and jurists will be able to do their job efficiently and competently in a higher evolved system of law—they will, in short, become functional FC lawyers.

Why We Need this Model

On this basis it should be evident why the FC/NC model could help remove some of the so-called nebulousness that has been attributed to the constitutional text; why it could help separate the wheat from the chaff regarding the different arguments and theories that have been used to interpret the text; and why it could help us to see the many disagreements from a more informed perspective. After all, *the only reason* why there has been confusion around these issues is the different worlds of FC and NC reasoning—and where NC individuals see "nebulousness" (or "inkblots") FC individuals see clarity.

To separate reason from madness, then, we need only give FC scholars their due. We must leave it to them to give meaning to the Constitution, for only they know how to interpret it in any coherent fashion; only they can ensure that first principles are cogently applied; and only they can give effect to those barriers that the founders put in place to protect against sinister influences.

When it comes to this, the FC/NC model will provide us with the information we need to understand why this is so. As we shall see, it (1) provides us with a social meter that, based on the autonomy-levels in society, will describe the type of society we are dealing with; (2) it explains the forces that act on us individually and en masse; (3) it enables us to predict the effects that changes in human psychology have on society; (4) it can be applied to any society at any time and place; (5) it provides us with a bigger context, normatively and historically speaking; and (6) it will explain why society operates the way it does—in short, why our system of law is neither better nor worse than it is. In short, it is a map that provides us with a greater, much needed frame of reference— one that should be used by those who want to add more depth, coherence, stability, and credibility to the discipline of law.

Today the Constitution is interpreted without much regard for this bigger picture. As many scholars have noted, the Supreme Court's doctrines have failed to provide us with a reliable direction, and it has no functional moral compass to guide its reasoning. Without it the justices are like shipwrecked lost at sea, paddling their life-raft in whatever direction the winds of public opinion, political expediency, corruption, or personal prejudice may blow, and they need a bigger frame of reference to make sense of the world. The promise of the FC/NC model is that through its application we can find our place in the greater scheme of things. We can gain a firmer foothold and the Court may again, like it did 200 years ago, navigate by the stars—i.e., by the light of first principles.

General Outline of the Book

This book proceeds as follows: In part one we begin by presenting the FC/NC model and framing its bigger-picture implications. We will be given a crash course in social engineering, for in mapping the human psychology we are provided with the tools needed to understand the forces that act upon us individually and en masse. First, we shall study the relationship between the individual and the collective. We shall see that the collective consciousness has a hold on us that is most powerful and how its grip informs our perception. As we shall see, there will always be a distance between theory and practice in those cultures that conform to the criteria of advanced-NC societies and this grip ensures that psychological mechanisms help us "unsee" this distance.

This part of the book may sit uncomfortably with some readers. In fact, to the extent that these defense mechanisms operate to bridge the gap between theory and practice, it can be a bit nauseating. Even so, if we are to have some meaningful frame of reference, we must be willing to confront the disparity head-on. As it stands, this distance can only exist to the extent that we, collectively speaking, are willing to delude ourselves, and if we have any intention of reaching our potential, we must have the courage to face reality. An honest look at the present state of affairs might hurt, but it is also liberating. It is, after all, the only way that we can free ourselves from the restrains that keep the status quo in place. And by recalibrating our worldview so that it conforms to the bigger-picture provisions of the FC/NC model, we are not only provided with a historical and moral context but also a sense of direction. This is the only way of overcoming the challenges we are faced with, and so I hope that readers will bear with me.

Having reviewed all this, we shall see why some individuals are more resistant to manipulation than others, how they effectively have freed themselves from contemporary retrains, and why these people are more intimately connected with the values, ideals, and principles that follow from the Wholeness concept. We shall discuss the qualitative difference between the worldview of FC and NC individuals, and after this bigger-picture review is completed we shall look at its implications for our system of law. In what will be a general introduction, one that lays a foundation of our discussion of the U.S. legal system in part two and three, we shall explore the basic difference between the FC and the NC system of law. We shall see that the former, building on first principles, appeals to human reason while the latter only appeals to arbitrary moral codes, and then we shall discuss the implications for constitutional interpretation. As will be seen, the FC-end must always be the yardstick against which all our laws and regulations must be measured.

In the second part, we shall see what historical evidence can be found in support of this supposition. We shall see that the founders were FC individuals and that the American system of law was a system of principled law. We shall then see how this system, with the progression of time, was corrupted. The aim is not to offer a comprehensive or definitive history, but rather a high-speed and selective tour, focusing on how the inherent tension between the FC and NC paradigm has shaped the evolution of American law. We shall see how American lawyers gradually fell into a habit of NC reasoning as a result of a pressure to conform to the expectations of the status quo. And after discussing how modern doctrines, generally speaking, are flawed and incompatible with first principles, a more in-depth view shall be provided in part three.

In this part we shall get into specifics. We shall discuss how false doctrines and unprincipled reasoning has shaped drug policy and how the courts have failed to properly apply the Constitution when challenges to the drug law have been made. Again, much of the focus will be on the qualitative difference that separates FC from NC reasoning, and again we shall explore the weakness of the latter as compared to the former.

Finally, in part four, we shall return to the bigger picture and see how the tension between the FC and NC paradigm has informed the evolution of society. We shall see how, as society matures, the FC paradigm is gradually being integrated, and how modern trends indicate that it is about to become the dominant influence on our system of law. We shall also say something about social engineering for FC and NC purposes before the implications for American society—and the founders' vision—will be discussed.

The book should be accessible to the common reader as well as specialists in law and I hope you enjoy this journey through the transpersonal framework of perception.

Roar Mikalsen
Bastöy Prison,
July 4, 2016.

PART ONE

FRAMING THE COMING-INTO-BEING OF LAW

1

MAPPING THE HUMAN PSYCHOLOGY

"Men, it has been well said, think in herds; it will be seen that they go mad in herds, while they only recover their senses slowly, and one by one."[1]

—Charles Mackay—

TO SUCCESSFULLY MAP OUT the greater landscape from which law comes into being, we must begin with the forces that act upon us individually and en masse. These forces define behavior at different levels of psychological maturity and depending on the level of maturity different types of society result. It may sound complicated, but it is not. Indeed, as we shall see, it is all remarkably simple, and it is because we as a society have failed to put sufficient weight on a much-neglected variable that problems abound.

This variable is human psychology, the environment of thought which we inhabit, and few pay much attention to it. Like a fish in its element does not see water, we are immersed in an environment of beliefs where fundamental assumptions about reality are rarely questioned or made explicit. Our ideas about ourselves and the world are simply taken for granted. They form our identity, they shape our society, they determine what kind of legal system we shall have—and yet we hardly ever question the premises of our suppositions. We devise clever and ingenious systems of political theory, legal theory, and so on, but we fail to begin where we should—i.e., with a map of human psychology.

---

[1] MACKAY, *EXTRAORDINARY POPULAR DELUSIONS AND THE MADNESS OF CROWDS* (1841)

If we did, we would have seen humanity's problems and challenges in a new light. We would have had a bigger frame of reference from which to measure ourselves and society—and because we need this context to make sense of the world, this is where we begin.

1.1 THE FULL CONSCIOUSNESS &
THE NULL CONSCIOUSNESS MODEL

By building on research from developmental, transpersonal, and social psychology I have put together a map that explains the dynamics that define the relationship between individual and society at different levels of maturity. My first premise, that individuals are at different levels of psychological development, may be seen as controversial—especially from the perspective of those inhabiting the lower-end of the FC/NC model. Indeed, it is in the nature of things that these people cannot even conceive of normative growth. At this level, the world is seen as a value-neutral place, one where fact and value are two different things, and so it will appear self-evident that there can be no "higher" or "lower" human development—and that those who perceive differently must be deluding themselves. Nonetheless, psychologists have studied the issue and based on their findings we can clearly trace individual development from the NC to the FC-end.[2]

First of all, different traits are found at different stages, running from the fear-oriented, isolated, shallow, value-free and fragmented perspective found at the NC-end to the love-oriented, value-laden, holistic, and integrative perspective found at the FC-end. Second, psychologists have found that the NC-end equals mental illness while the FC-end equals health and well-being. And third, they have found that individuals, as a rule, will advance in one direction: they will develop

---

[2] For scholars who have contributed to this research, see Ken Wilber, Jean Gebser, James Mark Baldwin, Jane Loevinger, Clare Graves, Jurgen Habermas, Robert Kegan, Stanislav Grof, Sigmund Freud, Abraham Maslow, Hans Loewald, Jenny Wade, Roberto Assagioli, Michael Washburn, John Battista, William James, R.M. Bucke, James W. Fowler, Roger Walsh, Frances Vaughan, Ellen Langer, Charles Alexander, Charles Grob, Lawrence Kohlberg, Karen Horney, Carl Rogers, Carl Jung, Sri Aurobindo, Indra Sen, Haridas Chaudhuri, Georg Feuerstein, Don Beck, William Damon, Ervin László, Kurt Goldstein, Christopher Cowan, Steve Taylor, and Pierre Teilhard De Chardin.

from the NC towards the FC-end—and not the other way around. Stagnation at one level may be frequent, but it will be attributed to growth-inhibiting factors and when such problems are resolved they progress towards the FC-end.[3]

More shall be said on this, but while some at this point may want to disregard these findings the FC/NC model should be accepted as useful by skeptics alike. Not only does it allow us to predict and understand the interactions between the parts and the whole; it provides us with an idea of what results changes in consciousness will bring, and it helps us, in broad terms, control for different variables in our environment whether they be internal (psychological) or external. In other words, it is a reliable model for social engineering, one that provides us with a testable hypothesis that will work with a 100 percent certainty whether we apply it to ourselves or on a mass-scale. No matter where we would find ourselves on this scale we are provided with a greater context, one that lays out the terrain in either direction. And even though some may take issue with my premise that some types of human characteristics, some types of societal organization, and some types of justice systems are better than others, there is evidence to suggest they are[4]—and I suspect that even moral relativists would prefer a peaceful, loving, harmonious and liberty-oriented society rather than a war torn, fear-ridden, crime-riddled, and hierarchical police state.

Hence, as some human traits and some societies clearly exhibit qualities that are more appealing to reason than others, this premise is difficult to contest.

---

[3] What prevents us from arriving at the FC state of cognition? "In general, all and any of the forces that diminish us, pathologize us, or that make us regress, e.g., ignorance, pain, illness, fear, 'forgetting,' dissociation, reduction to the concrete, neuroticizing, etc. [The level of NC cognition] may be a 'lower,' lesser state, a state in which we are not 'fully functioning,' not at our best, not fully human, not sufficiently integrated. When we are well and healthy and adequately fulfilling the concept 'human being,' then transcendence should in principle be commonplace." MASLOW, *RELIGIONS, VALUES, AND PEAK-EXPERIENCES* (1994) 32

[4] "Clinical experience . . . teaches us that the consequences of making growth choices are 'better' in terms of the person's own biological values, e.g., physical health; absence of pain, discomfort, anxiety, tension, insomnia, nightmares, indigestion, longevity, lack of fear, more happiness, etc., etc. That is, if a person could himself see all the likely consequences of growth and all the likely consequences of coasting or of regression, and if he were allowed to choose between them, he would always (in principle, and under good conditions) choose the consequences of growth and reject the consequences of regression." Ibid. 97-98

That being said, we shall now examine the greater forces that shape law into being, and the relationship between law and the whole can be seen as a Russian nesting doll. According to this analogy, society's body of law represents the innermost doll; this is wrapped inside the bigger sphere of political theory (or societal workings); and this greater body of politics is enveloped by an even greater framework, by the realm of human psychology. To continue this analogy, that to whatever extent we find a dissonance between theory and practice at the level of law or politics we would by necessity be dealing with a schizophrenic nesting doll, because this distance will always have to be traced back to the level of psychology. As this is the most fundamental level, it follows as axiomatic that a dissonance at other levels has its roots in our psyche—or to be more correct, for we are dealing with the nature of mass-events, that it has roots in the *collective* psyche. If we want to understand the status quo, then, we better begin with this mighty variable.

1.2 THE IMPACT OF THE COLLECTIVE CONSCIOUSNESS

The concept of the collective consciousness, while familiar to psychologists and sociologists,[5] has escaped the attention of jurists. However, we have ignored it at our own peril. And to set the stage for a greater frame of reference, one that provides us with an understanding of the context in which law has evolved, we begin with the premise that *a system of law can never be better than that for which the collective consciousness allows.*

As we shall see, our system of law will faithfully mirror the quality of this variable, which in essence is a self-containing multitude. It is the sum of all our minds, and our system of law will at any given time reflect the contemporary legal consciousness of the average citizen. I am not saying that legal scholars have no more wisdom to contribute to the system of law than an uneducated man—some obviously do. I am saying that the system of law as a whole *must* reflect the average consciousness

---

[5] Sociologists have discussed the collective unconscious in how it relates to crime. See GARLAND, *THE CULTURE OF CONTROL* (2001) 135

because it is the sum of all our minds. Therefore, to the extent that positive (FC) qualities such as love, autonomy, understanding, compassion, tolerance, integrity, wisdom, and a sense of community prevails, such qualities will be replicated in the criminal justice system. Indeed, to the extent that such qualities define us we will have little need of such a system at all. It is also axiomatic that to whatever extent negative (NC) qualities such as hatred, intolerance, bitterness, selfishness, irresponsibility, avarice, frustration, and ignorance prevails, this will characterize our system of law (and politics) in the opposite direction.

From this premise it follows that the *only way* we can change things for the better is by making sure that the influence of positive values is strengthened en masse. If we want to live in a world where people are more cooperative and loving, where they respect each other's integrity and autonomy, and where crime is nonexistent, *we have no other choice than to find a way to empower our positive inclinations*. No doubt our current model of criminal justice does a poor job in this regard, no doubt there are ways by which this can be done more effectively—and no doubt doing so necessitates a fundamental review of our most basic assumptions.

We shall have more to say on this but to continue our discussion on the collective psyche, its impact is colossal. Even though most of us never give it much thought, it is there, and we are all in its embrace. From the day we are born we will be shaped in its image. Through our upbringing we absorb the norms of society and are molded. We are like a sponge that not only soaks up society's moral codes but its most commonly held beliefs. This is positive in the sense that, like a magnet, the collective psyche lifts our understanding to the cognitive level of the average citizen. However, it is a negative influence in that, as soon as we have reached this level, it will retard further development. If we want to advance cognitively to higher states of consciousness, we will have to do it on our own and we will constantly feel the pressure of this massive beast to conform to the status quo.

I say "beast," for it has a certain existence of its own and history assures us that it is a dumb and dangerous brute. That is, at the FC level things would be different, but at the NC level it is a group-consciousness slowwitted enough to feed on misconceptions, arrogant enough to ensure that it stays that way, and dangerous enough to take pride in its ignorant ways.

Now, as we live in a NC society, this massive, comatose being (that becomes manifest in the tendencies and instincts of the masses) holds us in its grip. Our unconsciousness, our fears and mediocrity are its lifeblood. It prays on weakness and has no clue of the possibilities and the glory that awaits beyond its event horizon—the FC society. Thus, true to its disposition, it will go out of its way to impede progress. As it remains too obstinate and dimwitted to see beyond the status quo, it has no idea of the retarded, self-defeating, and inhumane creature it has become. Instead, fearing the unknown, its main objective is to preserve its shoddy sense of self. It therefore frustrates any effort to break free and discover a greater reality. Nothing is more threatening to its sense of self than individual integrity and so the status quo preserves itself by rewarding the opposite.

This force is equally present at the micro- and macro level, shaping society in its image. It defines the average citizen's worldview, just as it manifests in the power-balance between the individual and the state and the relationship between states. Depending on time and place, it will be soaked with the masses' irrational tendencies (their repressed fears and their denial of responsibility) and if we want to understand the psychology of mass-movements we must look to the influence of this entity—it is due to its impact that individuals will abandon reason for madness.

What the national psyche cannot admit to, the average individual will predictably deny. It takes integrity to acknowledge that "the emperor wears no clothes," and so many people will go through life failing to see what is right in front of them. On blind faith they will believe that government is fundamentally a force for good; that patriotism equals supporting their government; that the leaders of the nation are the good guys; that they only go to war against the "bad guys"; that wars are fought to protect wholesome values; that military service is honorable; that all is well with the relationship between the individual and the state; that we represent the best of humanity, and so on.

This has been the human condition for millennia. Psychologists are well aware that clear thinking on these issues comes at a psychic cost that few are willing to pay—and when confronted with evidence to the contrary and the distance between fact and fiction rears its head, the impact of this entity makes sure that a majority will repress the natural inclination to try and make sense of the world. It is the weight of this entity that makes the masses embrace any government-sanctioned lie as long as it is widely shared (and the truth is too horrible to accept), and it is due to its influence that well-adjusted citizens will respond with anger and denial whenever others point this out.

History speaks volumes of the misfortune caused by our will to ignorance, our projection of inner fears to the outer world, and our tendencies to follow authority, no matter how incoherent our leaders' reasoning, no matter how corrupt their morals, and no matter how repulsive their behavior. Those in authority need only appeal to our fears and prejudices and like clockwork they reap their harvest. Wars, genocide, persecution of minorities, forced vaccinations, and countless other acts of violence are sure to follow in the wake of this dark alchemy and the masses have no way of stopping this carnage. Being swept up in a greater movement, few have the wits to see the cliff towards which they are heading, and even fewer have the courage to oppose this mindless race to the bottom.

As such dynamics can only persist to the extent that we let unconsciousness govern our lives, this collective consciousness is often referred to as the collective *un*conscious. Consequently, the closer we draw towards the NC-end, the more a society will be subjected to its impact and the more powerful its presence. Hitler's Germany was an example of this force taking over, and it was for this reason that Wilhelm Reich, already before the War, described fascism "in its pure form as the sum total of all the irrational reactions of the average human character."[6] The social dynamics unfolding in Germany at this time is a warning we would do well to remember for the more we let unconsciousness define us, the more hellish will be the result. Nothing good can ever come of it, as this "creature" feeds on darkness. It is the sum of all our repressed fears, all our denial of autonomy and responsibility, and all our childish weaknesses that brings it to life, and it can only be conquered by a willingness of each individual to honour those responsibilities that come with being an adult person.

---

[6] REICH, *THE MASS PSYCHOLOGY OF FASCISM* (1970) xiv

It follows as axiomatic that the further we advance towards the FC-end the more the force of this unconscious will dwindle. Indeed, quite a few have managed to free themselves from its clutches. This will be that percentage which holds FC status and, after a look at the connection between the collective unconscious and the NC State, we shall see why some are more resistant.

1.3 THE NC STATE AND THE COLLECTIVE UNCONSCIOUS

"There is only one political sin: independence; and only one political virtue: obedience. To put it differently, there is only one offense against authority: self-control; and only one obeisance to it: submission to control by authority."[7]

—Thomas Szasz—

We have already been introduced to the link between freedom and responsibility. And just as there is a fundamental antagonism between the state and the individual at the NC level, so there is the same rivalry at play between us and the collective unconscious. Indeed, the NC State is a manifestation of this force, and the further we draw towards the NC-end the more this holds true. The NC State therefore will always equal tyranny, whether by oligarchy, monarchy, or the mob rule of lawless, unrestrained democracy.

To understand why, consider that the further towards the NC-end, the more a society will be under the influence of the psychology of fear and its inhabitants will see the world from an isolated perspective. The more they do, the more the negative qualities of humanity will be encouraged. Self-interest will be seen as diametrically opposed to the interests of others and in the spirit of self-preservation people will begin to see avarice, hostility, mistrust, ruthlessness, and so on, as virtues. This prepares the ground for a dog-eat-dog world, one where the government will be run by factions and individuals eager to pursue selfish ambitions. In the game of NC power-politics, only the most egotistical, merciless,

---

[7] SZASZ, *CEREMONIAL CHEMISTRY* (2003) 175

and cunning individuals can hope to get ahead, and this ensures a dynamic where individuals with these traits will rise to the top.

It goes without saying that the people who are the most eager to play this game will be the people who are *the least* fit to preside over the interests of humanity. They will be the ones that to the greatest extent satisfy NC criteria, those psychologist Philip Zimbardo diagnosed with "the spiritual condition of having an inner black hole so deep within oneself that no amount of power or money can ever fill it."[8] For these people "whatever exists outside of one's self has worth only as it can be exploited by, or taken into one's self,"[9] and as nothing they do will really serve the people, they will have to rely on brute force, propaganda, treachery and misdirection to ensure that they stay in power. Deceit being the name of the game in any society that fails to abide by the principles and ideals to which it pays lip-service, those with a perceived interest in the status quo will deny that this is so. Nonetheless, this dynamic is clearly seen even in our society,[10] and a telltale sign is its overall structure. The only way the NC mindset can ensure its own survival is by depriving a people of their government, and to the extent we are dealing with a hierarchical, control- and competition-oriented structure we can see this force at play.

In societies found at the extreme NC-end, such as Stalin's Soviet Union and Hitler's Germany, this force will be so powerful that FC values, ideals, and principles are not even acknowledged. At this level, the nation is so informed by the psychology of fear that the leaders will openly celebrate strength and ruthlessness as virtues. In more advanced NC states, however, this is not so. Here, the government must honor the standards that follow from the Wholeness perspective, but it will be little more than a ruse. It will be a ploy for officials to look more trustworthy

---

[8] ZIMBARDO, *THE LUCIFER EFFECT* (2009) 4

[9] Ibid.

[10] Jim Kouri, vice president of the National Association of Chiefs of Police, did a study showing that our leaders possess the exact same traits as psychopathic serial killers. These are traits such as superficial charm, an exaggerated sense of self-worth, glibness, lying, lack of remorse and manipulation of others. As he noted: "While many political leaders will deny the assessment regarding their similarities with serial killers and other career criminals, it is part of a psychopathic profile that may be used in assessing the behaviors of many officials and lawmakers at all levels of government." Malcolm, *Oh-oh! Politicians share personality traits with serial killers*, L.A. Times, June 15, 2009

in the eyes of the populace, and they can only hope that their subjects will be sufficiently defined by NC traits for it to work.

If this is so, such a collective state of schizophrenia can carry on for decades, even centuries. At the surface all will be well with the world, but behind the façade powerful forces will be at play to ensure that theory and practice remain separate. These forces will be both psychological and political. At the level of politics, the distance between theory and practice will be maintained by propaganda, violence, a culture of impunity, and a system of arbitrary law, while at the level of psychology, defense mechanisms such as repression, denial, projection, and scapegoating will keep reality from imposing.

The impact of these forces will be discussed. But it is in the nature of things that the FC and the NC worldview are fundamentally opposed and those in charge will see human rights activists and FC individuals as a threat to their powerbase. It is for this reason that the basic antagonism in the NC-realm is not between capitalism or communism or any other government-sanctioned ideology. Instead, it is between individualism and statism. The defining traits of individualism are integrity, autonomy, and responsibility, and it follows that in the NC State these qualities will be deeply despised. Just as the collective unconscious would lose its mighty sweep had people not been seriously lacking in these traits, so the NC State, which owes its existence to the same lack of traits, would be doomed should individuality in any meaningful sense emerge. The NC State therefore can be expected to fight for its own survival, and from this results its *force of inertia*: In order to preserve its own existence, it will advance ruthless, self-serving and fear-driven individuals to positions of power; it will reward obedience and punish integrity; and it will fight our natural drive towards becoming members of the FC community.

I say *natural* drive, as given ideal circumstances we would follow our natural inclination to grow up and become FC individuals. We shall have more to say on this, but history is a testimony to the inherent tendency for growth. From generation to generation, humanity over-comes the obstacles associated with living in a world governed by NC reasoning, and transpersonal theorists have had much to say on how this process applies collectively.[11] Historically speaking, we can therefore see the evolution of society as a progress towards a more and more just order—towards an ever more autonomy-actualizing society with all it entails of an increasingly fine-tuned balance between the individual and the collective. However, as of yet we remain primarily under the influence of those dynamics that define NC societies. And this being so, those who want a career in the upper echelons can expect to be successful only to the extent that they leave all sense of personhood aside.

This is system profiling 101. Just like the collective unconscious the NC system can be said to have an identity of its own, and to ensure its own preservation it will embrace us to the extent we become one with it and reject us to the extent we have a mind of our own. Now, being an *advanced* NC society, our situation is more nuanced, as in the FC State (from which we share some traits) the dynamics will be reversed, and the state will reward those officials with the most integrity to top positions. However, as of yet we have not arrived at this level. We have a way to go until theory and practice becomes one, and the closer a system is to the NC-end the more threatened it will be by human integrity, the more it will be inhabited by "system-zombies," and the more it will be defined by robot-psychology. Always eager to hide its true nature, an advanced NC State will make every effort to praise FC values, but if one wonders what kind of system we are dealing with we need only look at how it treats whistleblowers and conscientious objectors. To the extent society exists at the FC-end, they will be respected and rewarded for their personal courage and vice versa. And looking to people like Edward Snowden, Bradley Manning, Brad Birkenfeld, and Susan Lindauer the diagnosis should be clear.

From this fact alone—never mind all the other symptoms of NC traits we shall discuss—we can conclude that we are not yet the society we pretend to be. And it is for this reason that system representatives, as Reich pointed out, "never orient [themselves] in terms of truth, but in terms of illusions, which usually correspond to the irrational structure of

---

[11] WILBER, *UP FROM EDEN: A TRANSPERSONAL VIEW OF HUMAN EVOLUTION* (1986); AUROBINDO, *THE HUMAN CYCLE, THE IDEAL OF HUMAN UNITY, WAR AND SELF-DETERMINATION* (2012); HALL, *THE SECRET DESTINY OF AMERICA* (1944); GEBSER, *THE EVER PRESENT ORIGIN* (1997)

the masses."[12] Psychologically speaking, they are under great pressure to conform to the expectations of the status quo, and the chasm between theory and practice can only be bridged (on its terms) by rejecting reality. This is therefore what they must do; this is the price they must pay for having a career. It takes its toll psychologically, as there will always be a quiet voice within telling them that they should know better, that they should stand up for what is right. But the pressure of the collective unconscious weighing too heavily, the result is a given: They will do what it takes to fit in, and they will choose NC over FC traits.

This tendency is so common that we cannot really hold it against them. After all, our representatives would not have been under such a pressure to conform unless we all, en masse, every day chose to live the same lie—and if we want to study this dynamic of denial and repression, there is no better arena than the War on Drugs and the War on Terror. If it was not for our eagerness to deny reality, none of these campaigns would be with us today, and they are proof that humanity is still being moved by unconsciousness. As we shall see, the bigger and the more horrible the lie, the more ardently it will be embraced. Psychological defense mechanisms ensure that for NC individuals denial will be the only option—and so the more easily exposed a lie, the more they will attack those who speak truth.

---

[12] REICH, *THE MASS PSYCHOLOGY OF FASCISM* (1970) 210

1.4 The Forces that Keep Theory and Practice Separate

"My inclination to be relieved of having to think, particularly about unpleasant facts, helped me to sway the balance. In this I did not differ from millions of others. Such mental slackness above all facilitated, established, and finally assured the success of the Nationalist Socialist system."[13]

—Albert Speer, Hitler's Minister of Armaments—

As mentioned, the forces that maintain a distance between theory and practice are both psychological and political. At the level of politics, the distance will be maintained by propaganda, violence, a culture of impunity, and a system of arbitrary law, while at the level of psychology defense mechanisms such as repression, denial, projection, and scapegoating will keep reality at bay. The political forces, however, are secondary and psychological incentives will be the primary reason why this state of schizophrenia is allowed to endure.

"Schizophrenia" is not an exaggeration, for in the NC society there will be a tremendous pressure on people to betray their values. Our identity being connected with these values, they cannot be distorted without also undermining and distorting our sense of self, and so the pressure to conform to the status quo will result in a cognitive discord that can only be labeled as a sickness of the mind, no matter how widespread.

First of all, the problem is this. Having established a system that in *name only* represents the ideals and values that follow from Wholeness, what the state actually does must be credited as reflecting these values. The ruling ideology is supposed to equal all things good and decent and so leaders will have to portray everything they do as embodying wholesome traits and qualities. No matter how appalling the state action, no matter how disgraceful the behavior of its representatives, and no matter how loathsome the moral codes of society, they must be praised as conforming to proper ethics.

---

[13] GLOVER, *HUMANITY: A MORAL HISTORY OF THE TWENTIETH CENTURY* (1999) 361

Now, we know that the NC system will necessarily be built on a false foundation. It will be a social order whose authority depends on lies, deception, and false presumptions, and so it will have to spin night into day to ensure its own preservation. Thus, in the NC society a collective state of schizophrenia is slowly induced, for as in Orwell's dystopian novel *Nineteen Eighty-Four* words will have to embody their opposites. Truth being the ultimate enemy, it can no longer be afforded a reality of its own. It can only be whatever the government says it is, and to the degree leaders maintain an aura of respectability (i.e., to the extent they manage to define reality on their terms) this Orwellian process will be complete. The system of values will be broken down and deformed into something wholly different, something satanic, schizophrenic, and spiteful.

In such a society the concept of right and wrong will be deformed into something that no longer makes sense. What serves the state will be promoted as something good, something that is rewarded and worth striving for, and so the qualities attached to the concept of "virtue" will include deceitfulness, avarice, arrogance, ignorance, viciousness, hatefulness, deviousness, ruthlessness, treacherousness, and blind obedience. Furthermore, these negative traits' opposites (righteousness, kindness, truthfulness, critical thinking, helpfulness, autonomy, etc.) will have to be reinterpreted as bad, something to be punished—and thus ashamed of. Such attributes threaten the authority of a despotic order and so they will have to be redefined. Personal strength therefore will be defined as personal weakness, courageous behavior will be described as cowardly, peaceful protesters will be identified as terrorist sympathizers, more forceful agitators for reform will be classified as terrorists, and so on.

The further towards the NC-end, the more pronounced this tendency will be. Even so, we do not need to look hard for the same dynamic at play in our society. We see it when agents of the state label whistleblowers such as Edward Snowden as "arrogant" and a "criminal" for having the integrity to expose the monstrosity of the surveillance-state. We see it in how drug prohibitionists demonize those who fail to abide by their moral codes. We see it in how citizens are taught that telling authorities about their children's drug use is not snitching but helping them understand the consequences of their actions. We see it in how these people describe themselves as crusaders for all that is good and decent while they persecute drug users, force them into prison or "rehabilitation" camps, and break up families. We see it in how the government and mainstream media present warfare as peacekeeping operations. We see it in how they try to project an image of the 9/11-truth movement as terrorist sympathizers. We see it in how conspiracy theorists en masse are being derided as a kooky bunch. We see it in how war is presented as a noble endeavor. And we see it in how soldiers are celebrated and honored for their service in illegal wars.

It all may all seem compelling to individuals whose worldview is defined by the NC Groupmind. Nonetheless, in the sanctuaries of our soul we know better, and we see the psychic costs of clinging to reversed moral codes on American soldiers' psychological problems and suicide rates—many more killing themselves back home than dying in combat.

The latter is exactly what we can expect from such a system. So is the fact that 25 percent of Americans report to have been mentally ill last year, for this tension between reality-in-fact and reality-as-the-government-says-it-is creates a pressure, a dissonance that can only be overcome by self-deception and delusional belief systems. This again is bound to have further corrosive effect on our moral identity and the fabric of society, for truth and moral identity are intimately linked. Thus, as most people do not have the stamina to oppose the state, they must, to preserve their sanity, lay aside their critical faculties and sense of integrity. They also must disengage themselves from any meaningful moral standard, for only in so doing can they accept a dissonance so overwhelming that it, to a thinking person, would be impossible to ignore.

So it is that self-deception feeds on itself. These individuals may be exemplary in the eyes of the state but having lost touch with their inner moral compass, their sense of self is no longer rooted in any meaningful conception of values. For all intents and purposes the FC-world has become the NC-world and vice versa—and so it is that they, in the name of humanism, will trample the very values on which humanism is built. They will become policemen, prison employees, justices, lawyers, academics, soldiers, public officials, and bureaucrats loyal to the status quo. And because they do, the system's force of inertia will continue to take us ever further from that path staked out by the Founding Fathers.

It is a sad story. But if we are to understand the difference between the FC and the NC mindset and the forces that ensure that theory and practice remain separate, it must be told. The first step to recovery, as they say, is admitting that there is a problem. And if we are to understand why people choose madness over reason (for it is a choice, at some level—and it is madness, only commonly shared) we have to recognize the impact of the collective unconscious. It is due to the pressure of this entity that the dynamic unfolds, as the power of group conformity is too enormous. Resistance creates an emotional burden most find impossible to shoulder, and so it is that the bigger the lie, the more eagerly it will be embraced.

When all is said and done it is this, our willingness not to think about things, that makes it possible for theory and practice to remain separate. And as Hannah Arendt discovered after her study of the Nazi psychology, the ideal subject of tyrannical rule is not the person who is convinced of a totalitarian ideology; it is the person for whom the distinction between fact and fiction, truth and falsehood is no longer of any relevance.[14]

Our need to conform to the demands of situational forces has been keenly studied by social psychologists. More than 25,000 experiments including some 8 million people have been done confirming the power of situational and systemic factors in determining our behavior and the findings are astounding. They reveal that most of the population will torture another human being to death as long as certain situational factors (such as the orders being given by a seemingly authorized person) are in place.[15] And they reveal that no matter how horrible their acts, normal people will have little problem rationalizing their behavior. In short, they reveal that people will not really think about things. From this research,

---

[14] ARENDT, *THE ORIGINS OF TOTALITARIANISM* (1966) 474

[15] Psychiatrist Stanley Milgram designed a series of experiments in which people were asked to deliver electrical shocks to a person in another room. The situation was rigged, but the person delivering the shocks did not know this. All he/she was told was that delivering these shocks was necessary for the experiment and a "scientist" would come into the room and ask them to deliver increased voltage.

When 40 psychiatrists were asked to predict the outcome of Milgram's experiments, they estimated that few normal people would go beyond 150 volts and that only the most sadistically inclined (1 percent) would go all the way up to the maximum level of 450 volts. However, 65 percent of the volunteers went all the way, despite desperate pleas to stop. Milgram carried out 19 such experiments across America, they all showed the same: A willingness to go all the way if certain situational factors lined up. ZIMBARDO, *THE LUCIFER EFFECT* (2009) 275-79

our ability to disengage morality and critical thinking whenever situational forces stipulate it is empirically validated.[16] And based on his findings from experiments conducted in 19 American towns, Stanley Milgram (see note 15) concluded that "if a system of death camps were set up in the United States of the sort we had seen in Germany, one would be able to find sufficient personnel for those camps in any medium-sized American town."[17]

1.4.1 THE LURE OF COLLECTIVISM

If we are to take ourselves seriously, then, we must recognize that we are not really that different from the people who were born in Germany in the first half of the 20th century. There was nothing inherently evil that made them embrace the Nazi movement, just as there was nothing about the Nazi regime that was alien to the state. In fact, Hitler's Germany and Stalin's Soviet Union were the logical conclusion of the state project at the NC level of operations. It was the NC State revealing its true nature, as these tyrants merely embraced inherent tendencies.

Truth be told, one of the most important lessons we can draw from history is that if it were not for the distance between theory and practice neither Hitler nor Stalin would have come into power. Nazism may have been an easy lure, given its scapegoating and grandiose vision, but it was because Western democracies falsified their own foundation by openly mocking the values to which they aspired that fuel was given to the dynamic which ensured their arise. It was, after all, easy for fascists and communists to see the duplicity of Western democracies. To anyone who cared to look the liberal principles of self-determination and equality were words bereft of essential meaning and behind the façade was the reality of oppression and inequality. It is little wonder then that a countermovement arose. We see the exact same dynamic at play today in

---

[16] As Zimbardo, the psychiatrist in charge of the Stanford Prison experiment, reminds us: "social psychology offers ample evidence that when [the power of the situation takes control], smart people do stupid things, sane people do crazy things, and moral people do immoral things. . . . A person in the claws of the System just goes along, doing what emerges as the natural way to respond at that time in that place." Ibid. 220, 180

[17] Ibid. 281

the fertile ground for extremist movements such as Islamic State (IS). Drone killings can only increase local hostility. The same is true with open invasion, and only to the extent we represent FC ideals, values, and principles can we fight terrorism and extremist ideologies. The same was true a hundred years ago, and as Normand and Zaidi noted:

> "It should not be forgotten that fascism was primarily a positive ideology that appealed to a shared sense of strength, ethics, and honor based upon service to the community. Under fascism, individual members of a community were mobilized through an idealized version of one destiny by one will under one leader, as opposed to the egoistic self-interest of bourgeois liberalism that set each man against his compatriots: Against liberalism's glorification of the selfish individual they proposed the spirit of self-sacrifice, obedience and communal duty."[18]

The same can also be said of communism: both movements started out as a result of good intentions—as a sincere attempt to deal with the afflictions associated with the NC State. Even so their solution, to do completely away with the notion of individual sovereignty, should have raised eyebrows. The idea of individual rights may have been of little consequence and Western powers may have used it as a ploy to hide a more sinister reality. However, it was all that stood between the people and the oppressive forces intrinsic to NC Government—and if history had not yet provided sufficient lessons, these movements would make it clear that wherever rights are sacrificed for the common good, lives soon will follow. It is estimated that Soviet leaders killed some 60 million people in the seventy-year period after 1917 and the Nazis probably would have outdone them had they not been defeated. No more murderous regimes ever soiled the earth—and in hindsight it should be easy to see that fascists and communists alike mistook the disease (i.e., unrestrained government) for the cure.

At some level it is possible to understand their confusion. After all, the concept of individualism may at first glance be construed as an ideology only selfish and greedy people would endorse—one that, if carried to its logical conclusion, would mean the death of society. The

---

[18] NORMAND & ZAIDI, *HUMAN RIGHTS AT THE UN* (2008) 72-73

lure of collectivism therefore is that it appeals to our good-hearted nature. We naturally want to contribute and to use our powers for the greater good, and it is precisely for this reason that so many people are drawn to collectivist movements. On some level it is liberating to join them, to be inspired by the promise of a glorious future, to fight for a greater cause, and to be swept away by their momentum. However, such movements will always fail to deliver on their promise and the power of the collective unconscious explains why. First of all, it ensures a dynamic that attracts self-serving and control-oriented individuals to positions of power. There will be a totalitarian drive inherent in the NC State and the only thing that can offset this trend is the FC mindset. To the extent this is present the destructive dynamics that follow from the NC mindset will be reversed and a better world can be built. However, mass-movements in NC societies are never grounded on a foundation of respect for individual integrity; they are never all-inclusive; they are never moved by reason; and the psychology of love never feeds the momentum. Instead, we see the opposite: they are collectivist; they are authoritarian; they are exclusive; they are driven by passion; and the psychology of fear feeds the momentum.

Hence, a destructive dynamic takes over. The end-result is always a given, because without a supportive basis in individual integrity the center cannot hold. Psychologically speaking, such movements gain their momentum from nothing but repressed fears—fear of autonomy, fear of responsibility, etc.—and this is why they are so appealing. Their essence is the idea of some supreme authority figure (whether it be in the form of one individual, God, or the state) who will free us from the unbearable affliction of being granted free will; who will remove from our shoulders the responsibility that comes with being autonomous individuals; and who in his/its infinite wisdom will arrange a perfect society—one in which no one is really free but where, at the very least, everyone is "secure" from the burden of autonomy/responsibility.

This is the lie that takes on new forms from century to century. It is passed on by politicians and intellectuals alike, but the truth is that no society can be liberated unless everyone begins to realize inherent FC qualities. It does not matter what ideology the NC State officially embraces, whether it be fascism, communism, socialism, or just plain democracy. The only vision that can help us forward is a truthful embrace of FC traits, for only to the extent that this is done will we be moved by consciousness rather than unconsciousness.

Now some may disagree, thinking that all it takes is for the right leader to emerge (usually having themselves in mind) and then a more perfect world can be realized. However, *without a supportive basis in FC qualities* any collective movement will stray afar. It will be moved by repressed fears rather than reason, and we will be adrift on the great seas of the collective unconscious with no compass or direction, with no hope of reprieve or salvation. It will be the same old story where prejudice and passion will inform the passing of law and ensure its continuance, where oversized enemy images will ravage society, where dominance-oriented factions will be empowered, and where the masses will be moved by unconscious desires rather than conscious choices.

The problem, as always, is that the masses deceive themselves. On one hand, they insist that they want freedom and autonomy, while they fear the responsibility that comes with being a sovereign individual. Hence, they will embrace paternalistic policies and they will want leaders who expose the self-asserting qualities they themselves lack. Thus, the more helpless, shameful, and weak they feel, the more they will promote leaders who display an aura of strength and promise salvation in return for obedience. These leaders, however, will (in any meaningful sense) be just as helpless and weak, for they are no more in charge of themselves than the rest of the citizenry. To the contrary, they will be those who to the greatest extent overcompensate for emotional distress in childhood, seeking to push aside feelings of worthlessness and lack of trust by dominating others. With such individuals in charge and overly submissive citizens at hand to do their bidding, everything is set for disaster. It is the timeless tale of the blind leading the blind, and so the history of NC states is an unending cycle of misfortune and cognitive dissonance.

1.4.2 THE CONNECTION BETWEEN UNCONSCIOUSNESS AND FEAR

History never fails to drive home this lesson: That in the name of all things good, the state will use collectivism as an excuse to destroy the individual, making itself all-powerful in the process. This is not something civil servants strive towards consciously; we do not need a group of sinister plotters in the innermost sanctuaries of government to bring about this dynamic (although it helps). All it takes is that we let our officials do what they normally do—i.e., let the winds of the collective unconscious guide them in whatever direction it might blow.

It is no coincidence that these winds often prove dreadful as there is a powerful connection between unconsciousness and fear. Indeed, the NC mindset draws its very validity from the psychology of fear, and the further we draw towards the NC-end the greater will be its impact. As philosopher Eric Hoffer noted, "it is when power is wedded to chronic fear that it becomes formidable,"[19] and rulers know this. It is a law of NC politics that power will increase only to the extent that they can nourish an atmosphere of fear, as fearless people would never give away control of their lives. Fearful people, on the other hand, do not want responsibility. They want others to save them from themselves (or whatever external threat they fear), and they are looking to authorities to do it. In truth, it is a double blessing for the agents of tyranny: fearing responsibility, people will also fear knowledge, and they will prefer ignorance to inconvenient truths. Hence, for that percentage of the population who thrive in the game of power-politics—those with a spiritual black hole no amount of power or wealth can fill—fear is their mightiest ally.

Now, we cannot know how many of our public servants who suffer from such a condition as they will never admit to it. However, it is certain that those with this condition will be drawn to positions of power and that they will be successful (and plentiful) to the extent society draws near to the NC-end. It is also certain that they will shun no means in their quest for power. We can safely assume that they will join with others like them; that they are intelligent enough to know how to manipulate others as a means to their end; that no war and no machinery of oppression would ever have come into being if wasn't for the presence of such individuals in our governments; and that to the degree they are successful in their quest, the individual citizen will be enslaved. Students of power-politics know this and as H.L. Mencken observed, these people will prosper in

---

[19] Zimbardo, *The Lucifer Effect* (2009) 11

proportion to the extent they "excel in the intervention of imaginary perils and imaginary defenses against them."[20]

It is for this reason that FC individuals are especially watchful when it comes to enemy images. And whether it be a war on communists, terrorists, or drugs that agents of the state will have us embrace, wise people will take care to double-check the validity of the enemy image they are being sold. It is, after all, the energy of these images that keeps war-profiteers afloat; that feeds the authoritarian forces inherent in government; that ensures people will turn on each other; that makes them turn to authority for protection; and that makes them freely give up their rights in exchange for promises of security. Hence, every time FC individuals hear officials embrace the psychology of fear and claim that the interests of the collective (meaning the state) must trump the interests of the individual, they will see the writing on the wall and know that this logic was the foundation of every tyranny ever conceived.

Thus, they will not buy into such reasoning, no matter how well-intentioned. They will know that "collectivism" is just another cry for unrestrained government. They will know that there is no conflict between individualism and the interests of society. And they will know that individualism is in fact *the only* ideology that properly protects the interests of the individual *and* society. History confirms this beyond doubt for every time collectivism is allowed to blossom, we see tragedy follow in its wake. The ideology of individualism, with the value it provides human dignity, the protection it provides against undue infractions, and the limits it puts on state power, is the only ideology that can hold the forces of despotism at bay—and it is for this reason that all FC documents build from this basis.

As we shall see, the U.S. Constitution and modern-day human rights conventions are all such documents. Their purpose is to bar against the tyrannical potential inherent in every government, to maintain the integrity of the fabric of society by putting a leash on authority, and to bring attention to the ever-present dynamics between the individual and the NC State. The social dynamics discussed were well-known to the founders and they did everything in their power to ensure a foundation from which a new type of society could spring into being. They also knew

---

[20] BOWARD, *LOST RIGHTS* (1995) 199

that their work could only be successful to the extent that the people were motivated and guided by FC traits. And if one should wonder why the Constitution today is in shambles and the political philosophy of the founders remains distorted, the answer is simple: It is because we all collectively fail to honor the ideals on which America was built. To this day NC traits are more commonly embraced than FC traits, and James Boward observed the result:

> "[Since the period of the founders, we] have seen the sapping of most restraints on arbitrary government power. American political thinking suffers from a romantic tendency to appraise government by lofty ideals rather than by banal and often grim realities; a tendency to judge politicians by their rhetoric rather than by their day-to-day finagling and petty mendacity; and a tendency to view the expansion of government power by its promises rather than by its results."[21]

As long as unconsciousness continues to guide our ways, this state of affairs will only escalate. The totalitarian aspects of the NC State will become ever more empowered until all pretenses of abiding by the founders' Constitution are gone. Even so, the ultimate authority resides in the people. And to the extent that a population empower themselves—to the extent people take responsibility for their lives and value autonomy—they will have a government responsive to their voice. The dynamics between us and our government fully depends on our sentiments, and while a majority remains unduly influenced by the collective unconscious, there are also those who have not lost touch with the inner compass. This will be that percentage who qualify for FC status, and we shall now see why some refuse to take part in a collective psychosis—why some, indeed, will "walk the talk."

---

[21] Ibid. 5

1.5 INDIVIDUAL DEVELOPMENT

"The empirical fact is that self-actualizing people (fully evolved and developed people) are also our most compassionate, our great improvers and reformers of society, our most effective fighters against injustice, inequality, slavery, cruelty, exploitation (and also our best fighters for excellence, effectiveness, competence). . . . [They are] the most fully human persons."[22]

—Abraham Maslow—

Having been introduced to the influence of the collective consciousness, how it informs thought and behavior, and how the NC State results from the extent to which we fail to take our ideals seriously, it is time to look at our personal development. We have seen that individual development springs from the collective consciousness; that depending on time and place this greater variable will be saturated by different qualities, and that these qualities again will determine how individuals perceive the world. We shall soon see why some are more resistant to its influence, but before we do, let us start with basics.

As mentioned, the dynamic unfolding between the individual and society is a variable in constant flux and what changes it is our level of consciousness. The spectrum of consciousness is wide, and researchers have found that not only individuals but societies tend to evolve from the NC towards the FC-end. Each opposing end is defined by diametrically opposed traits and in one end of the spectrum we will find enlightenment and in the other self-annihilation. The defining traits at the FC-end will be responsibility, autonomy, reason, coherence, expansion, freedom, wholesomeness, rationality, integrity, and wisdom, while those at the NC-end will be slavery, heteronomy, contraction, irresponsibility, inconsistency, dependency, dissipation, confusion, irrationality, passion, infantilism, and lunacy. This is the spectrum from which we must choose: Between wholeness and fragmentation, between light and darkness, between consciousness and unconsciousness, between sanity and mental illness, between value-fulfillment and value-obliteration, between love

---

[22] MASLOW, *RELIGIONS, VALUES, AND PEAK-EXPERIENCES* (1994) xii, 37

and fear, between equality and hierarchy, between autonomy and tyranny.

While most of us will be influenced by both FC and NC traits, this is the continuum of options. We can either feed the forces that move us towards destruction—those of the collective unconscious—or we can wise up, take our inner world seriously, confront our fears, work out our issues, arrive at higher and higher states of consciousness and become ever more enlightened. It is either-or and based on our preferences we will move in either direction on the FC/NC model.

Depending on our choices en masse certain consequences are also bound to follow. If we exhibit NC qualities we will have increasingly control-oriented, competition-oriented, and hierarchical social structures. We will have a social dynamic that punishes positive traits and rewards negative. We will have an atmosphere that breeds enemy images, fear, estrangement, conformity, mental sickness, and tyranny. And we will have self-serving public officials that represent the worst of mankind. This, however, is only one side, and to the extent we choose the other we will have a dynamic that ensures the opposite.

While the choice, put in this perspective, should be easy, it is not always so. Nothing can be more demanding than to accept the responsibility that comes with being an adult and the lure of escape can be tempting. Denial is one of several predictable defense mechanisms when faced with a reality that threatens to overwhelm us and most are very good at ignoring difficult questions. However, to the extent that we do, we are sure to feed the collective unconscious and ensure a dynamic that leaves it to the most fear-ridden and control-oriented individuals to take us all for another hell-ride. We have already seen why this is so, and the reason is that there is a definite relationship between the inner and the outer world. Everything begins with this inner world. There is nothing in the way we organize society that does not have its roots in thought—and the more disorganized our world of thought, the more this inner chaos will manifest.

As a society we have not matured to the point where this is obvious. We tend to take for granted that the world is what it is and that our ideas about it have little bearing on reality. However, truth is the opposite and historically speaking the inherent conflict between the FC and NC mindset explains much of the dynamic that has shaped society. On the one hand we have the voice of reason, the bigger perspective understanding that humanity is really one great organism; that all human beings are equally valuable; that we have a God-given right to life, liberty, and the pursuit of happiness; and that governments are instituted to ensure that this is so. This is the FC perspective. It builds from the perspective of Wholeness, from first principles, and everything follows. On the other hand, we have the world of NC reasoning which sees everything from a fragmented perspective, which sees existence as a constant state of war, and which has little regard for the values that are self-evident as seen from the FC perspective.

All thoughts will be more or less influenced by one or the other perspective. All our thought processes arise from the interplay between the whole and the parts, and to the extent we are colored by one or the other opposite realities will result.

Our problem is that throughout history most have seen the world from the NC perspective. This being so, the world has been governed by its kind of logic and the endless series of misfortunes that have befallen humanity are a testimony to the effect of our beliefs—they do shape our reality. While FC individuals see the world (mainly) through the eyes of love, NC individuals gaze upon it (mainly) through the eyes of fear, and as our thoughts literally create our reality the horrid effects of this mindset have seemed to confirm our worst fears. We have seen wars, deceit, ruthlessness, oppression, and all kinds of mischief as the way of the world, but we have not understood that *we ourselves*—with our mindset—have contributed to the energy that made it so.

It should be obvious that had a greater percentage of humanity seen the world from the FC point of view, the world would have been moved by our positive rather than negative inclinations. We would not have had a political process dominated by self-serving interest groups. We would not have supported deceitful, dishonest, and ruthless politicians who encouraged fears and prejudices, and we would not have had the hierarchical, dominance-oriented, and competitive social order that we have. Understanding that all wars were civil wars, there would be no war. Understanding that the lives of others mattered just as much as ours, we would not be so disrespectful to the interests of others. And understanding that the inner and outer world reflect upon each other, we would not have projected our own fears onto others.

If we really want to get to the roots of our problems, they begin with certain widely shared assumptions about the fundamental nature of reality which are mostly taken for granted. Today, for example, many people embrace the tenets of the Neo-Darwinian worldview or some organized religion. And while the former tells us that existence has no meaning, no value—and that *you*, therefore, have no meaning, no value— the latter tells people that they are born in sin, that God (all that they see as good) is fundamentally different from them, that "he" has made them inadequate and debased, and that he will find a way to punish them.

Whether we are Christians, Muslims, atheists, or simply undecided, many people are colored by such beliefs. The collective unconscious is filled with the deluded debris that results from such massively shared notions and most people are struggling with issues of self-worth. Had we not been besieged by issues of guilt, we would have looked closer at these issues. However, most people imagine the eye of God to be too terrible to bear. Even atheists are afraid of the abyss, and so psychic walls are installed. We will rather cling to an identity on false premises than live naked forever, and so we reject the responsibility of facing our fear. To the extent we do this, we will project our own inner fears and unresolved issues onto our surroundings, and this projection mechanism again turns the world into the horrid place it is.

To put it simple, *if it were not for this all our problems would be over*, and our challenge is to find a way out of this destructive cycle. This is what FC individuals have found, and what they have done is both simple and infinitely difficult: They have taken their inner world seriously, dared to confront their fears, looked at the beliefs behind them, checked them for accuracy, found that these beliefs were deluded, and corrected their thought structure into one of greater harmony and coherence. The most advanced FC individuals have done this over and over—and the more they have searched within, the more they have resolved conflicting belief structures into ones of greater unity with the Wholeness concept. In the process they have attained greater insight into the nature of reality, their analytical powers have increased, and their sense of self has evolved.

This is the essence of the process that psychologists have called self-actualization. It ties the world with spirit, and as this process unfolds people are transcending the dualistic understanding of the NC mindset. High-end FC individuals experience this process as a blending with the

Cosmos at higher and higher levels of completeness. Their old ego dissolves and the apparent paradox is that the more it does the more they build an integrity of their own. Hence, the further they advance towards the FC-end, the more they establish their own moral platform—one that integrates the Wholeness and whatever follows. Every step of the way, they will become more in touch with FC standards; they will become more firmly guided by the light of these values, principles, and ideals; and their quest becomes to represent them to the best of their ability. Consequently, their ultimate mission will be to always—in thought, words, and actions—embody FC values, principles, and ideals, joining them in ever higher union.

For those who are interested in this process, I have written in depth elsewhere.[23] It is validated by psychology, and even if this is a rough outline only, one that ignores a couple variables, we see what separates individuals at the NC and FC level. They both started out from the same position, free-floating on the seas of the collective unconscious. These, however, are treacherous waters. They are a cacophony of disorganized value systems and belief-structures, few of which are fully thought through. Indeed, many of the most commonly shared are fundamentally flawed misconceptions and those adrift on these seas will embrace numerous contradictory beliefs, some more seriously deluded than others.

At the NC level many of these beliefs are accepted as gospel. Indeed, people will retain them even when confronted with evidence of their inaccuracy, usually for reasons of conformity and convenience. Their identity at this stage is simply too dependent on the group consciousness to depart with the old belief-structure. We have already seen the power of group conformity, and so, if they belong to a Church, they may not want to think about dogmas in fear of being ostracized; if they are members of a motorcycle gang, they may not want to reconsider its moral codes in fear of being evicted; and if they work at the DEA, they may not want to question the premises of drug prohibition in fear of losing their job. Examples abound and there are many reasons why people will not want to think about things.

---

[23] MIKALSEN, *REASON IS* (2014)

At some point, however, a normal person will no longer be willing to pay the price of conformity. This price will be growth stagnation, even mental illness, and as we have a natural leaning towards growth most will sooner or later want to make sense of things. It does not take much to figure out that two contradictory beliefs cannot both be true and healthy people will want to avoid the cognitive dissonance that goes with accepting unresolved issues. They will also know that new data cannot be continuously ignored to preserve old beliefs, and they will want to steer clear of the diseased psychological terrain that comes with denying reality. Therefore, sooner or later most people will move on, leave old, disserving, growth-inhibiting and erroneous belief-systems behind and establish new, more coherent frames of reference. The more they do this, the more they will build a platform of their own. They will, in short, begin to build *integrity*, and the more they do, the sooner they will become fully-fledged FC individuals. This integrity is like an island in the sea of collective consciousness. It is the premise from which we evolve, and the more we build our character, the more resistant we become to the ebb and flow of the ideas from the collective consciousness.

Thus, this is the basic difference between FC and NC individuals: They have the courage to question commonly shared beliefs and the ability to process new information. It may not seem like much and we all probably think we share these traits. Even so, when push comes to shove a majority of the population will prefer ignorance to knowledge, illusion to reality, and heteronomy to autonomy—in other words, they will lack the integrity to weather the tides of the collective unconscious.

FC individuals, however, are free from the clutches of this force. Having begun their inner work, (or being naturally endowed with integrity/FC traits in the first place) they are rewarded with a sense of identity which is grounded in something deeper and more profound than the NC Groupmind (that part of the collective unconscious with which most identify). Indeed, the further they evolve towards the high-end, the more their sense of self becomes grounded in the essence of the Cosmos; they realize that they are spiritual beings having a physical experience and their sense of self-worth now comes from their expanded connection.

This deeper sense of self makes it not only possible for them to free themselves from contemporary restraints. But because of this increased connection and their integration of the bigger picture, they also move on to a larger conception of living than self-seeking on NC terms, which is often motivated by personal selfishness and/or obedience to authority. For those who have not severed the connection between their sense of self and the NC Groupmind, it is only natural to think along these lines. However, the inner world of FC individuals has expanded beyond the point where they let collectively shared beliefs and prejudices define perception. Their sense of identity being grounded in something deeper, they no longer identify with the things they own or their social status; they no longer feel compelled to ignore inconvenient truths; and they no longer see self-interest as opposed to the interests of others. Because of their expanded sense of self, their perception of self-interest will be more far-reaching, and while NC individuals think of it in narrow terms, detached from more all-encompassing considerations, FC individuals see it as connected to the bigger picture.[24] As they grow towards the FC-end, their sense of responsibility therefore comes to extend beyond the realm of the physical self (i.e., where psychopaths draw the line), beyond that of friends and family (where most NC individuals draw the line), until it includes humanity, the planet, and the Cosmos as a whole. Their loyalties will, with all that it implies, more and more lie with the ideals, values, and principles that attach to the Wholeness perspective, and this suggests that they are less likely to be manipulated by others, more likely to recognize injustice, and to oppose it.

---

[24] For more on the change of values, see MILLER & DeBACA, *QUANTUM CHANGES* (2001); HOOD, *HANDBOOK OF RELIGIOUS EXPERIENCE* (1995); TAYLOR, *OUT OF THE DARKNESS* (2011); TEASDALE, *THE MYSTIC HEART:* (1999); SMITH, *CLEANSING THE DOORS OF PERCEPTION* (2000); MASLOW, *RELIGIONS, VALUES, AND PEAK-EXPERIENCES* (1994); MURPHY, *THE FUTURE OF THE BODY* (1992); WULFF, *THE PSYCHOLOGY OF RELIGION* (1991); GROF, *PSYCHOLOGY OF THE FUTURE* (2000)

1.6 The FC Society

"The old philosophers taught that physical birth is an accident, for men are born into various races and nationalities according to the laws of generation; but there is a second birth, which is not an accident; it is the consequence of a proper intent. By this second birth man is born by enlightened intelligence out of nation and out of race into an international nation and an international race. It is this larger and coming race that will someday inherit the earth. But unless a man be born again by enlightenment, he shall not be a part of the philosophic empire."[25]

—Manly P. Hall—

Now, few individuals have climbed very high on the FC-end. But based on findings from developmental psychology and transpersonal theory we can estimate that at least ten percent of the population have matured to the point where they have begun to map the relationship between the inner and outer world. The more they excel at this task, the further they advance into FC territory, and it goes without saying that the world will be a vastly different place when the rest of humanity catches up.

It is in the nature of things that more and more people do. As of yet, this group lack the political clout to have a marked systemic effect, but they are increasing in numbers and we are closing in on our status as FC community. A natural question then arises: what will the FC society be like and when do we qualify for this status?

First of all, a society has reached the first level qualifying for FC status when its representative bodies (1) recognize the difference between the social dynamics at work in NC societies as opposed to FC societies; when they (2) understand why this difference exists; and when they (3) have begun to organize their labors in the service of moving us towards greater levels of coherence. In other words, individuals in these bodies must not only recognize basic laws in the operation of consciousness, but they must have enough systemic sway to make policies that complement their insights. When a society has evolved to this point the science of

---

[25] HALL, *THE SECRET DESTINY OF AMERICA* (1944) 11

social engineering will be duly recognized and from there, we can expect things to progress quickly to the betterment of humanity.

To say more on the topic of constructive social engineering, it is autonomy oriented. In the FC society justice is preserving, protecting, and advancing autonomy rights, while injustice is arresting, violating, and transgressing upon autonomy rights. Hence, the task of social engineers will be to preserve and promote as much autonomy as possible. In this sense, FC-engineering is not about generating the greatest amount of happiness per se. It is not about eradicating all perceived vices. Instead, it is about protecting individual boundaries to the greatest extent. It is about ensuring that every individual has the freedom to express herself; to experience whatever pursuits and to realize whatever values that may be within the limits of rational choice.

In this sense social engineers are inspired by what Amartya Sen and others have called *the capability approach*, and their ambition is to ensure that all persons have an equal amount of advantage in terms of opportunities to achieve those things they have a reason to value.

This means that all basic needs must be provided for. The FC society will blossom to the extent that the individual is free to determine what he/she wants to do with his/her life, and so FC engineers a focus on the actual opportunities of living rather than economic improvement per se. The latter, obviously, is an important part of their equations, but they have a wider focus than merely assessing a person's advantage in terms of income, wealth, and resources. One could, after all, easily imagine a society rich in material goods, where everyone had the resources needed to buy everything, but where freedom of choice in the greater sense—in the sense of sexual orientation, information gathering, consciousness experiences, and value pursuits—was very restricted.

Needless to say, this is not the idea that FC engineers have in mind. The point of FC-engineering is not to provide a specific design for a tightly constructed, particular form of society; social engineers have no idea of what the end result will be. They just want to provide the best possible framework for individual and societal growth, one that allows for the greatest possible variety of reasonable value pursuits—one that embraces plurality, not uniformity.

This is the *only* end they have in mind.[26] Knowing that all healthy individuals will want to contribute to the best of their ability, they have no fear that giving individual freedom greatest possible rein will be the death of organized society or that it will be at the expense of the public welfare. On the contrary, FC engineers know that individual-, human-, and societal potential are one and the same, and their foremost concern is providing a basis for sound development. If this structure is in place, all else follows, and so the first task of social engineering will be to raise a generation that has faith in humanity and understands the workings of consciousness. To the extent that this is successfully done the problems that we are so familiar with will not only become history, but the dynamics that make NC societies/individuals come up short will be reversed and a new era will begin.

Now, just as there are different levels of NC societies, the same goes for FC societies. We shall not discuss the evolution of societies at the most advanced FC-end, as this would bring us into realms where we are ill-prepared to go. However, FC societies continually evolve into systems of ever greater coherence and describing the social dynamics inherent in a representative system is easy. On the level of psychology, we will have wholesome, trusting, truthful, responsible, and autonomous individuals. We will have individuals who have gone within, taken their inner world seriously, and shed light on those areas that were engulfed in darkness. Instead of repressing fears and ignoring the inner chaos that shapes and determines NC behavior, these people will know how to balance the inner and the outer world. Hence, they will not be ruled by unconsciousness. Having dealt satisfactorily with their own issues, they will not project unresolved issues onto others; they will not need scapegoats to blame for the perceived ills of society; they will not have to deny reality to get by; they will not have to repress emotional difficulties; and oversized enemy images will not overpower their reasoning. We will, in short, have well-balanced individuals and this will result in a well-balanced society.

---

[26] In this sense, they follow in the tradition of Mill and Wilhelm von Humboldt. As the former quoted the latter: "The end of man, or that which is prescribed by the eternal or immutable dictates of reason, and not suggested by vague and transient desires, is the highest and most harmonious development of his powers to a complete and consistent whole. . . . The grand, leading principle . . . is the absolute and essential importance of human development in its richest diversity." HUMBOLDT, *THE SPHERE AND DUTIES OF GOVERNMENT*, quoted in MILL, *ON LIBERTY* (1978) 55

As we have discussed, the pressure to conform to a narrow and prejudiced "ideal" of citizenship will not exist. Instead, people will be encouraged to realize themselves in their own image, to follow their own lead, and to live as they please. It will hardly be necessary to add the obvious passage "as long as their activities do not directly hurt others," for as these individuals will be psychologically healthier than those of NC societies, they will not have a proclivity to stray afar. Psychologically speaking, every healthy individual will want to contribute to the Whole, and so any pursuit of self-actualization, no matter how uncommon, will be motivated by a yearning to be all they can be for humanity. Consequently, harmonious societies will arise. To summarize their essence, they will be equality-, autonomy-, and liberty-oriented. There will no longer be a perceived dichotomy between self-interest and community interest and at the level of politics there will be no more division into right and left. The only perceived distinction will be between constructive and destructive approaches, the former being those solutions that follow from a reasoning derived from the Wholeness perspective and the latter being that which follows from its opposite— the psychology of fear.

Thus, the FC society will be a world that transcends ideology, one that we can say is capitalist in the sense that freedom of contract and private property rights will be duly respected; one that we can say is socialist in the sense that the government will provide a certain minimum of material support; and one that we can say is communist in the sense that a certain community spirit will prevail. In short, we can say that it represents the best of these ideologies, but most of all we can say that it is libertarian, in the sense that the goal of society will be to advance each individual's liberty and autonomy rights. Because we will be dealing with a nation where the majority qualifies as enlightened human beings, the political process will not be dominated by self-serving factions. As a result, the three branches of government can begin to fulfill their contractual obligations to the people, ensuring that the state discharges its responsibilities as a protector and advancer of human rights. Public servants will therefore be public servants, not wolves in sheep clothing, and a rule of transparency and accountability will ensure that whoever violates the public's trust will be held liable for transgressions.

Having a more responsible citizenry, there will be a social dynamic that rewards integrity, and this will ensure that the best and brightest will be brought forth to positions of service and influence. These officials' analyses and actions will be more harmonious with those that follow from a proper integration of the Wholeness perspective. They will have a deeper understanding of the Wholeness concept and its implications than NC individuals, and as the narrow NC perception of self-interest will not be a problem they will carefully weigh and balance the interests of the individual against those of society in every equation. Considering the complexity of societal interaction, there is still the possibility that human errors occur, but the courts shall make sure that an effective remedy is provided whenever complaints are made.

In other words, the social compact will be effectuated. On the level of law, therefore, the legal system will no longer be another symptom of the factious spirit that defines NC politics. Instead, it will be an instrument of justice, a firm framework that will help us steady the course towards Utopia. There will be a system of principled law, a rule of reason—one where we will give up no more autonomy rights than absolutely necessary for establishing a well-functioning society. Theory and practice will be as one and legal systems around the world, being built on the same principles of law, will mirror each other.

All in all, then, the FC society will be a cooperative venture. The government apparatus will be more finely attuned towards the goal of maximizing the welfare of citizens. It will, in a hitherto unparalleled sense, be a government of the people, by the people, for the people—one where the parts and the Whole constantly will recalibrate each other towards that potential of greatness which is inherent in all things as we together strive to make our world a better place.

1.7 The Difference Between the FC and NC Perspective

"To see things as parts, as incomplete elements, is a lower analytical knowledge. The Absolute is everywhere; it has to be seen and found everywhere. Every finite is an infinite and has to be known and sensed in its intrinsic infiniteness as well as in its surface finite appearance."[27]

—Sri Aurobindo—

As people advance from the NC to the FC-end, we have seen that their belief- and moral structure is constantly being calibrated towards a state of greater harmony with the Wholeness concept. As this process unfolds people are increasingly transcending the dualistic understanding that defines the NC mindset. Thus, to them, the thinking that separates the world into positive and natural law, man and nature, spirit and matter, good and evil, science and religion, sense and sensibility, body and mind, subject and object, life and death, self-interest and community-interest, left and right politics, and so on, is becoming increasingly obsolete.

Individuals found at the very high FC-end claim to have reconciled all such apparent contradictions. They have done their inner work and, in the process, come to know an expanding form of consciousness that makes them ever more one with the Universe. For these individuals therefore, legal theory, political theory, moral theory, social theory, scientific theory, psychological theory, and spiritual theory all merge into one coherent superstructure. It is obvious to them that there can be only one valid law, one valid government, one valid science, and one valid religion, and that they all come together as one for the ready mind.

Now, this assertion will be controversial. Like I said, perhaps 10 percent of the population will qualify for FC status, but only a few have climbed to the point where this appears self-evident. Nevertheless, let us for the sake of argument imagine that there could be something to it: How can it be that the world is perceived so differently from the high-end FC perspective and what does it look like?

---

[27] Capra, *The Tao of Physics* (2010) 486

I have written about this elsewhere,[28] but if we are to emphasize one particular aspect of the high-end FC experience it is that it is deeply spiritual. The reader may have noticed that while the NC-end represents those aspects of our psyche that we would think of as animal-like, the FC-end represents our godlike potentials. And as people more reliably begin to choose the latter, they are rewarded with a more intimate relationship with the Force that sustains existence. As this relationship evolves, human consciousness is transformed into a type of awareness that supersedes the one we know so well.[29] From this perspective consciousness is identified as the Ultimate reality, the one that gives rise to matter. The brain, in other words, is perceived as *a transceiver* rather than a generator of consciousness, and the Universe is seen as a sentient, Super-conscious Organism—one that experiences itself through the play and interaction of its fragments (us).

It bears emphasis that while this is diametrically opposed to most NC individuals' worldview, there is nothing unscientific about it. On the contrary, more and more anomalies in science dictate the need for a fundamental review of basic assumptions and more and more scientists are moving in the direction of the FC paradigm.[30] However, to continue

---

[28] MIKALSEN, *REASON IS* (2014)

[29] See Ibid; MOORJANI, *DYING TO BE ME* (2014); BUCKE, *COSMIC CONSCIOUSNESS* (1961); AUROBINDO, *THE LIFE DIVINE* (1970); GROF, *THE COSMIC GAME* (1998); KRISHNA, *KUNDALINI* (1997); LANGER & ALEXANDER, *HIGHER STAGES OF HUMAN DEVELOPMENT* (1990); TAYLOR, *OUT OF THE DARKNESS* (2011); GROF, *PSYCHOLOGY OF THE FUTURE* (2000); WADE, *CHANGES OF MIND* (1996); UNDERHILL, *MYSTICISM* (1962); TART, *TRANSPERSONAL PSYCHOLOGIES* (1992); WALSH, & VAUGHAN, *BEYOND EGO* (1980); WILBER, *THE EYE OF SPIRIT* (1998); WILBER, *EYE TO EYE* (1996); WILBER, *INTEGRAL SPIRITUALITY* (2006); WILCOCK, *THE ASCENSION MYSTERIES* (2016); WINKELMAN & ROBERTS (EDS.), *PSYCHEDELIC MEDICINE* (2007)

[30] While the basis of the NC paradigm is the matter-creates-consciousness perspective, the FC paradigm builds from the opposite assumption. For a general introduction to the scientific validity of the FC perspective, see MIKALSEN, *REASON IS* (2014); TALBOT, *THE HOLOGRAPHIC UNIVERSE* (2011); MCTAGGART, *THE FIELD* (2008); WILCOCK, *THE SOURCE FIELD INVESTIGATIONS* (2011); SCHWARTZ, *WHAT REALLY MATTERS* (1996)

FC scientists are found in all disciplines. For books on FC physics see DAVIES & GRIBBIN, *THE MATTER MYTH (1992)*; HERBERT, *QUANTUM REALITY:* (1985); GOSWAMI, *THE SELF-AWARE UNIVERSE* (1993); CAPRA, *THE TAO OF PHYSICS* (2010); TALBOT: *MYSTICISM AND THE NEW PHYSICS* (1981); CLOSE, *TRANSCENDENTAL PHYSICS* (2000); ZUKAV, *THE DANCING WU LI MASTERS* (1979). For books on FC biology: LANZA, *BIOCENTRICISM* (2009); LIPTON, *THE BIOLOGY OF BELIEF* (2010); SHELDRAKE, *MORPHIC RESONANCE: THE NATURE OF FORMATIVE CAUSATION* (2009); SHELDRAKE, *THE PRESENCE OF THE PAST* (1995); WATSON, *LIFETIDE* (1979). For books on FC medicine: DOSSEY, *REINVENTING MEDICINE* (1999); PERT, *MOLECULES OF EMOTION* (1999); GERBER, *VIBRATIONAL MEDICINE* (2001). For books on FC psychology: GROF, *PSYCHOLOGY OF THE FUTURE* (2000); TART, *TRANSPERSONAL PSYCHOLOGIES* (1992); DEAN (ED.), *PSYCHIATRY & MYSTICISM* (1979); WINKELMAN, & ROBERTS (EDS.), *PSYCHEDELIC*

our discussion on the high-end FC perspective, another important aspect is that *the evolution of life* is seen as a purposeful unfolding. The trend towards self-actualization, they claim, is not only found in Man but in all things; it is built into the very fabric of existence and we see it all around us. Atoms, molecules, rocks, single-celled organisms, multicellular organisms, plants, animals, man, and Cosmos: All is seen as a movement of this Cosmic Force's inherent drive towards self-actualization at different levels of complexity. Human evolution is viewed as an important part of this movement. It is perceived as a steady drive towards greater and greater levels of coherence, towards greater and greater levels of understanding, towards greater and greater levels of value fulfillment, and towards an ever more transcendental union with the ideational framework upon which everything rests—those principles, values and ideals that follow from the Wholeness.

The question is should we believe them? Is there an objective order of morality that we can appeal to? Is it possible to find a universally valid moral, spiritual, and political theory?

High-end FC individuals absolutely think so. To them it is simply a matter of sufficient psychological growth before it becomes self-evident and, having arrived at another level of being, they will explain it as if they are standing on top of a mountain. For those at the base it will be impossible to gain a proper overview of the mental/moral/legal/ spiritual/political/scientific landscape; therefore, to them it will be impossible to unite all tiers. However, the higher we climb, the more we close in on a single point of perspective, and as seen from its point of view all those aspects of the Wholeness that appear separate at the base ultimately merge into one coherent superstructure—one unified Whole.

It goes without saying that individuals at the base level will be highly skeptical of such notions. To them fact and value remain two completely different things; to them there is no inherent connection between law and morality; to them to be a better and a wiser person is not necessarily the same; to them science and religion is seen as opposing poles; to them the idea that all the world's religions could convey (and unite in) some deeper universal truth is highly suspect; to them reason and emotion remain opposites; to them there is a dichotomy between subject and object; to

---

MEDICINE (2007). For books on FC religion: SMOLEY, *INNER CHRISTIANITY* (2002); TEASDALE, *THE MYSTIC HEART* (1999); STRASSMAN, *DMT AND THE SOUL OF PROPHECY* (2014)

them the mental and the physical are distinctly different worlds; to them the political map is divided into different, conflicting ideologies; to them the link between freedom and responsibility is hardly obvious; to them positive and natural law are fundamentally at odds; to them there is only left and right politics; and to them the idea that all of this diversity, all these conflicting variables, can be transcended into a higher, unified Whole is impossible to fathom.

Even so, according to scientific theory the FC paradigm holds a superior position due to its ability to explain and integrate more data, and the fact that the world is seen so differently from the FC and NC perspective can be explained by the finding that psychological development is integrative. As reason, intuition, and emotion become more aligned, a more refined analytical power is brought to bear and greater depth is provided. Thus, the more we grow, the more parts are unified into wholes, and apparent contradictions at the lower levels will be seen in a new light.

1.7.1 PARALLELS BETWEEN RELIGION AND LAW

In order to give the reader an idea of what this entails I will, in this part, not only discuss its implications for lawyers. The qualitative difference between FC and NC reasoning at the level of law shall be elucidated upon later, but the tendency to integrate more and more variables can best be explained by examining its implications across disciplines. I therefore want to discuss the bigger-picture connotations, as it is here—in the broadening of horizons—that we see the difference between FC and NC reasoning.

That being said, this model of psychological growth (of integration into greater wholes) should be easy enough for lawyers to understand. We see the same integrative process manifested in law, and FC scholars such as Dworkin have connected the ideal of self-government and the idea of legitimacy to the concept of law as integrity.[31] Integrity and coherence obviously connects (even if NC scholars fail to grasp the

---

[31] DWORKIN, *LAW'S EMPIRE* (1986) 189-94

connection), and so we find that a system of FC law is consistent and whole in a manner that NC law is not. In the former, there is not only internal but normative and principled consistency, and the FC system of law integrates all these variables. While NC law, then, operates on only one level, (that of positive/written law) FC law operates on multiple. By ensuring that the positive law is calibrated to conform to a world of ethics *which again* is rooted in first principles it builds a secure foundation for itself, something NC law will never know—or its disciples allow.

Considering the obvious defects of NC law, one could be amazed that rulers still can find lawyers who are willing to practice this trade.[32] However, as seen, one must be at the FC level of cognition to see that there is "a direct connection between integrity and the moral authority of the law,"[33] and lacking sufficient integrity, it is no wonder that NC lawyers will prove their loyalty to power rather than reason. It takes a lawyer of some stature to talk truth to power, just at it takes some stature to connect with the light of first principles, but for those who do the importance of grounding law in reason rather than passion is easily understood. For these people it is also easy to see why all criminal law must conform to principles of fundamental justice. And to the extent that one has a grasp of the interconnectedness of these principles and the logic by which they operate, one can see how the body of criminal law—if it should be worth a damn—must be calibrated towards a state of internal resonance.

Hence, the fact that we have two different systems of constitutional law, one European/international and one American, should be an indication that we have come up short. Imagine, for example, a situation where American and European physicists accepted the same fundamental tenets and yet operated with separate rules of engagement. It would be obvious that leaving cultural inhibitions aside (i.e., adhering to the principles of science and following their lead), would advance our understanding of physics. And as the fundamental principles of law are universally recognized (those found to the extreme NC-end excepted), it

---

[32] More on the defects of NC reasoning applied to law, see Sabo, *The Higher Law Background of the Constitution* (2009) 14-22; Tribe & Dorf, *Levels of Generality in the Definition of Rights* (1990) (Tribe and Dorf sometimes fall short of FC reasoning, but they give a few examples of the fallacies inherent in NC reasoning)

[33] DWORKIN, *LAW'S EMPIRE* (1986) 190

should be clear that the current divide between American and European law is an arbitrary divide; that it is the result of cultural inhibitions; and that leaving prejudices aside, we could arrive at a more harmonious system of law—one that more in tune with the fundamental principles of law.

The same logic also applies to religion: Just as there logically can be only one science of physics and one science of law, there can only be one science of spirituality. Hence, if the world's spiritual traditions had any merit, it could not be found by mindlessly embracing one religion and castigating all others. Instead, as our perspective was the result of cultural inclinations more than reason, the clever thing to do would be to broaden our horizons and to look for the common denominators between different religions. Only in doing so would we have an opportunity to rise above limited perspectives, to separate the wheat from the chaff, and perhaps get some insight into a spiritual reality that transcends time, space, and individual/cultural understanding.

Now, for FC individuals this is self-evident, and it speaks volumes about the power of the collective unconscious that this is controversial. Just like mainstream psychology still fails to include the reality of the soul, so organized religion fails to comprehend it psychologically, even to the simplest degree, and instead of encouraging an experiential approach to spirituality, religious leaders and NC psychologists prefer sticking to hopelessly inadequate scripts.

In regards to psychology, however, a branch has moved beyond the single state fallacy,[34] integrating spirit. This is transpersonal psychology which grew out of the humanistic psychology movement. Also called the Third Force of psychology (Freud and the Behaviorists being the other two), these psychologists studied the *healthy* human mind. And while

---

[34] The single state fallacy is the assumption that all worthwhile cognitive processes reside within normal waking consciousness. However, as transpersonal psychologists, psychedelic therapists, regression therapists, and those familiar with the research on altered states can verify, this is not so. According to people who have experienced unitive states of consciousness they are spiritually, creatively, cognitively, and emotionally enriching, and empirical studies show that they are happier, healthier, and better functioning than non-experiencers. This expanded state of consciousness is often experienced as being "more real" than our ordinary state, and to paraphrase Krupitsky and Kolp, compared to non-experiencers, they "become less anxious and depressed, more responsible and emotionally mature, more self-confident and balanced, and more emotionally open and self-sufficient, with increased ego strength and positive changes in self-concept." (WINKELMAN & ROBERTS, *PSYCHEDELIC MEDICINE* (2007) 83).

mainstream psychologists focused on the normal range and its pathologies, these pioneers would explore the frontiers of human consciousness.

What they found would take them out of the NC paradigm and into the FC paradigm, for as they mapped out the potentials of the human psyche they began to see what the great mystics had always known: That our psyche, individually and collectively speaking, was advancing, and that the process itself seemed to be guided by a Greater Force.[35] Their research would not only merge psychology with disciplines as diverse as religion and quantum physics, but they found that high-end FC individuals had accessed states of consciousness that seemed to indicate another evolutionary leap. These individuals would share the same insights that one may stumble upon in the literature of the mystics. Indeed, research indicated that all organized religions could be traced back to high-end FC individuals and high-end FC experiences; that there was nothing supernatural about the prophetic visions and the lives of history's greatest religious figures; that these were perfectly normal manifestations of those possibilities that existed at the high FC-end; and that, therefore, "all religions are the same in their essence and have always been."[36]

To advanced FC individuals this is all too obvious. And the only reason why this has not been obvious to others is that the institutions that followed in the wake of such high-level FC events were founded and maintained by NC-level individuals. Psychologically speaking, these groups are worlds apart, and as organized religion is the result of NC individuals trying to interpret and make sense of the high-end FC experience it is only natural that the outcome is a confused product. The reason why organized religion is losing membership, therefore, is not that spirituality has outplayed its role. Spirit never will. It is only the old NC

---

[35] Transpersonal psychology has long been the leading edge of psychology. However, as taking its implications seriously would prove the death of the NC paradigm, it has been perceived suspiciously by the establishment, much like libertarianism has been eschewed by the legal establishment. They both undermine fundamental assumptions of the prevailing groupmind and so mainstream scholars will ignore the data rather than follow it to its logical conclusion. Even so, time will honor these FC pioneers. After all, scientific theory holds that the wider application a theory has and the more data it can integrate and explain, the better it is. And to this day, transpersonal theorists' mapping of the psyche (and reality) remains second to none.

[36] MASLOW, *RELIGIONS, VALUES, AND PEAK-EXPERIENCES* (1994) 20

version of spirituality that is struggling to keep up with the times—and one reason why the times are changing is that more and more people are becoming FC individuals.

We see this trend also affecting the discipline of law. As I have said there are basically only two kinds of law—the NC and the FC version—and the fact that the NC version has held sway is no indication of its strength. To the contrary, it is merely an indication of the half-witted reasoning that has passed as "law" to this day, for no better place can one see the qualitative difference between the reasoning that takes place at the FC and NC level. We have already seen that FC individuals are more connected to the implications of the Wholeness concept while NC individuals see the world from a more fragmented and isolated perspective. We have also seen that the more they advance towards the FC-end, the more they build an integrity of their own. The result is that the further they advance towards this end, the more they establish their own moral platform—one that integrates the Wholeness perspective, and one that is connected to and aligned with the light of first principles. As they integrate this perspective, they are rewarded with the ability to see beyond the mental horizon of their contemporaries. They become sufficiently grounded to see through the fog that disables otherwise able minds—the one produced by misconstrued doctrine, aberrant criminal codes, unfounded fears, flawed ideology, insufficient analytical powers, the false authority of precedent.

NC individuals are not that fortunate. They have barely begun to build this platform and so their morals will be basically those of society. This, of course, is no sound measure from which to build a morality, and if these people were born in Germany in the 1920s, they would *with a 100 percent certainty* grow up to become Nazis. It is *only* FC individuals who have developed the ability for moral reasoning that transcends time and place—and this explains the major difference between FC and NC lawyers.

This should also explain the fact that NC individuals lack the basic faculty needed to interpret the U.S. Constitution. As we shall see, the Constitution was an FC document, and the founders were FC individuals. It was their ambition to create a secure foundation upon which a new model of state could be built, one that would secure a maximum of liberty and happiness for all, and one that would withstand the attack of those factions with other ambitions. The only thing that could secure such a foundation was first principles, and the whole point of the Constitution was to anchor the light of these principles.

Thus, it should be apparent why NC lawyers are faced with an impossible task, as they cannot connect with the light of first principles. They may think they do, but NC individuals trying to interpret the Constitution is much like NC individuals trying to interpret or understand the spirituality of high-end FC individuals. We just saw how the result was organized religion, and just as they cannot attempt such an endeavor without making a mockery of spirituality, they cannot attempt to interpret the Constitution without making a mockery of law.[37] The reason why should be obvious, for just as true spirituality will always be animated by the ideals and values that follow from the Wholeness perspective, so true law will always be animated by the fundamental principles of justice. Psychological growth being integrative, we find that at the FC-end the sources of law and religion are interconnected, and that only FC individuals can connect with this firmament. Without this connection one is lost, floating adrift on the seas of the collective unconscious, and so it is that only FC lawyers can we give effect to higher law. Every effort by NC individuals is doomed to fail, as they are in the position of children trying to understand advanced mathematics—it just does not work.

For them to connect with the light of first principles they must first do the inner work. They must recalibrate their mind to the point where it is no longer polluted by the prejudices and moral codes of society, and *then*, to the extent their inner world becomes harmonious with FC values and ideals, they may access the implications of first principles. *There is no other way.* And to provide further example of the extent to which FC reasoning qualitatively differs from NC reasoning, the difference between FC and NC law shall be elaborated upon. It will be a general

---

[37] Because people will interpret any text according to their own personal understanding a book could be written discussing the implications of the FC/NC model for theology. In looking at the world's religions we can find that people at the NC-end will interpret the textual sources of their preferred religion narrowly and in an authoritarian fashion while those at the FC-end, being more directly in contact with spirit (just as FC lawyers are more directly in contact with first principles), will see beyond the textual sources to the essence that forms the basis for all religion. Other researchers have already explored this subject, see FOWLER, *STAGES OF FAITH* (1981); FOWLER, *WEAVING THE NEW CREATION* (1991); WULFF, *PSYCHOLOGY OF RELIGION* (1991); HAGBERG & GUELICH, *THE CRITICAL JOURNEY* (2004)

introduction only, one that lays a foundation of our discussion of the U.S. legal system in part two and three.

2

THE DIFFERENCE BETWEEN FC AND NC LAW

"Reasonable minds can certainly differ, . . . that does not mean that there is no right or correct answer; that there are no clear, eternal principles recognized and put into motion by our founding documents. This was the mistake of the legal realists, and it continues to be the mistake of the critical theorists: law is something more than merely the preferences of the power elites writ large. The law is a distinct, independent discipline, with certain principles and modes of analysis that yield what we can discern to be correct and incorrect answers to certain problems."[38]

—Justice Clarence Thomas—

IN THE FC SOCIETY criminal law is no more extensive than absolutely necessary. The use of this sanction is recognized to come at a great cost not only to the individual but to society alike and every effort is made to ensure that society abides by a minimalist conception of criminal law theory. Of course, as no society will readily admit to any other doctrine, this also applies to NC societies; no matter how oppressive the state and no matter how bad its system of law, its officials will always claim that their actions are no more invasive than absolutely necessary and that everything they do is for the good of society. Therefore, what truly separates FC and NC societies is that the former has principled constraints in place which is not only *intended* to ensure that this is so and that every infringement on individual liberty is justified by objective—rather than subjective—criteria (even more advanced NC

---

[38] Thomas, *Judging* (1996) 6

societies have this), but that these constraints *achieve their proper function* and effectively ensure that their objective is being met.

Now, as Professor Husak has pointed out, to be justified, criminal laws must satisfy each of these four constraints: (1) they must proscribe a nontrivial harm or evil; (2) the hardship and stigma associated with such sanctions may be imposed only for conduct that is wrongful (that violates others rights); (3) violations of criminal laws must result in punishments that are deserved (they must be proportionate to the crime); and (4) the burden of proof must be placed on those who advocate the use of criminal sanctions.[39]

It is important to note that the latter means that the state must be prepared to justify the existence of the criminal law.[40] It is also important to note that even though we live in a NC society this system of law is already in place, at least theoretically. Human rights law, for instance, is there to ensure that all these criteria are being met, just as the U.S Constitution, correctly interpreted, will do the same. The problem, therefore, is the distance between theory and practice and the fact that NC individuals have little regard for the integrity of law.

The reason why is easy to understand as, collectively speaking, the integrity of law will be proportionate to the integrity of self. Identity and truth and integrity and coherence being fundamentally entwined, it goes without saying that an NC system of law will have little to offer on all accounts, for its disciples will be operating on the surface of things where these words have little meaning. For high-end FC individuals it follows as obvious that these words draw their inherent meaning and value from the principles, ideals, and values that attach to the Wholeness perspective—they tie everything together and connect the individual to a greater frame of reference. However, as NC jurists have not yet developed the integrity to connect these terms and to provide them with sufficient depth (i.e., value) to see how they connect, it also follows that they will have no choice but to be satisfied with a system of law that mirrors their own confusion. This will be a system of arbitrary law—one that is rooted in nothing but the authority of the state.

---

[39] HUSAK, *OVERCRIMINALIZATION* (2008) 103

[40] On the idea that a right to justification grounds human rights, see e.g. FORST, *THE RIGHT TO JUSTIFICATION* (2011)

If we want to understand the difference between FC and NC law, this is where it begins. It is as night and day, and if we look at any framework of law it is built on the basis of one of two premises. *Either* its fundamental premise will be that the individual is owned by the government, in the sense that he or she has no rights other than those granted by the state, *or* it will be that the individual has rights independent of whether or not governments recognize them. *All* legal reasoning begins with one or the other proposition. From these first premises two divergent bodies of law originate, and while those who embrace a body of law built on the assumption that the individual is owned by the state will find themselves in the NC category, those who argue coherently from the opposite direction will find themselves in the other.

Legal reasoning must begin with either assumption and two conflicting bodies of law follows. Traditionally, those who subscribe to the NC conception have been called legal positivists[41] while the other brand is represented by natural law theorists/lawyers. Today, the line between natural lawyers and positivists is a blurry one, for as we shall see there is no inherent contradiction between written (positive) law and higher (natural) law. Higher law needs written law to become legalized while written law needs the higher law for its legitimacy, and together they ensure that the system of law is both sufficiently specific and flexible to fulfill its intended function—to see humanity prosper by bringing the light of first principles to earth. Any jurist who knows a thing or two

---

[41] The positivist sees law as a one-way projection of authority and the law is whatever the lawgiver determines. He recognizes no social, ethical, or moral dimension and strictly speaking cannot be a legal theorist. The reason is that a positivist cares not for the philosophy of law—of right and wrong, of legitimate and illegitimate rule, and so on. The more positivistic he views the world, the more narrow-minded his perspective becomes until all that remains is the law *as it is*. To quote Fuller, "the positivist sees the law at the point of dispatch by the lawgiver and again at the point of its impact on the legal subject. He does not see the lawgiver and the citizen in interaction with one another, and by virtue of that failure he fails to see that the creation of an effective interaction between them is an essential ingredient of the law itself." (FULLER, *THE MORALITY OF LAW* (1969) 193)

The flaw of positivism is obvious, as it sees the integrity of the legal system as maintained by authority, not morality. Hence, to a positivist, legality refers to proper procedure, not the function of the law. To him, law and legality is the same and any legal system, no matter how despotic, is entitled to obedience.

about law gets this, and the entire point of the U.S. Constitution (and international human rights law) is to positivize the higher law.[42]

In this sense, therefore, the traditional separation between the two lines of reasoning is officially transcended but NC jurists have made sure that the higher law has not been effectuated. Under cover of a system of principled law they have established a system of arbitrary law and they have done this by falsifying the foundation of the legal system. Instead of thinking things through and ensuring that their argument resonates with the implications of first principles they will, by way of unsound doctrines, jump to conclusions based on their own prejudiced conceptions. And while part two and three will provide more detail, this general introduction shall clarify the flawed foundation of the NC system—which is still in place today.

2.1 THE FC AND NC CONCEPTION OF CONSENT

"Since no man has a natural authority over his fellow, and force creates no right, we must conclude that conventions form the basis of all legitimate authority among men."[43]

—Jean-Jacques Rousseau—

The basic premise of the NC system of law will be that the individual is owned by the state. No matter how much modern lawyers try to veil its foundation behind complex terminology, wonderful words, and highflying aspirations, it all comes down to this. In the NC-world the state, not the individual, is sovereign—and the fact that our leaders talk of "sovereign states" says it all. Furthermore, as the individual has no other rights than those granted by the state, the idea of consent is meaningless. NC leaders, of course, will never admit to this, for as any thinking person will know that "consent is needed to convert a slave

---

[42] See e.g. GERBER, *TO SECURE THESE RIGHTS* (1995); ARKES, *CONSTITUTIONAL ILLUSIONS & ANCHORING TRUTHS* (2010); Rubin, *Judicial Review and the Right to Resist* (2008); Alexy, *Constitutional Rights and Proportionality* (2014)

[43] ROUSSEAU, *THE SOCIAL CONTRACT* (2005) 6

relationship to one that is morally permissible,"[44] they will have to find a way for it to appear otherwise. In Western democracies, the way this is done is simple, and the rulers will either (1) embrace the notion that the legitimacy of the state rests on the original consent of the people, or (2) that it rests on the consent of the people today. In the former case they will say that our forefathers (those who enacted and voted for the original constitution) have consented for us, while in the latter they will say that we, by voting for our politicians, have consented to being governed and have a duty to obey.

However, as Professor Barnett reminds us, "only if persons have a right to refuse their consent can we ever say they have consented,"[45] and so the flawed foundation of these notions of consent becomes apparent.[46] We obviously had no say in a contract that was written 230 years ago and very few people have any direct influence on what goes on in Congress today. Our representatives may not even have been elected by a majority—and even if they were, what they do with the trust given to them is no reliable standard for consent. It is well-known that politicians are much more likely to do the bidding of lobbyists than ordinary citizens and with an approval rating of around 10 percent it is uncontroversial that Congress as a whole has betrayed the American people's trust.

It is evident, then, that these consent theories are worthless—*and this would also be the case even if Congress had a 99 percent approval rating.* Even in that case not everyone would have consented and so, as a 100 percent of the people cannot be expected to consent to everything politicians do all the time, we need another standard of consent.[47]

---

[44] BARNETT, *RESTORING THE LOST CONSTITUTION* (2014) 28

[45] Ibid.

[46] A more elaborate debunking of the stories told to explain how this tacit consent is obtained based on voting, residence, the consent of the founders, and general acquiescence, is found Ibid. 11-52. For analysis of constitutional legitimacy, see also Fallon, *Legitimacy and the Constitution* (2005)

[47] To quote Barnett: "for consent to legitimate governance, it must be actual or real, not hypothetical or metaphorical. That is simply how consent works as a moral principle. One is justified in treating persons in certain ways when they have consented that are impermissible in the absence of their consent. But, for this permission to exist, the person who is affected must have actually manifested or communicated their consent. Although an individual can consent to have sexual relations with another person, imagine a group of three persons in which two vote that the third may be subjected to a sexual assault. No one would suggest that the two can "consent" for the third. It is incumbent on those who adhere to some version of a consent theory of constitutional legitimacy to explain just how and when an actual consent of the governed

This is found by applying the FC standard. If the "consent of the governed" is to have meaning, we must assume that first come rights then comes government, and *only by applying the FC standard* can the people be said to have consented in any meaningful way. In the FC system the individual is the sovereign, and the state is as an aggregate of sovereign individuals. The government is an organizing apparatus put in place by individual sovereigns to ensure that their natural rights are protected, and that goods and burdens are properly allocated. However, given that the government cannot in every instance ask these individual sovereigns their permission to act—and given that universal consent, in any case, would be impossible to obtain—the question becomes: to what kind of system, what kind of rules, is it that an intelligent and reasonably informed individual would give her consent? While "We the People" therefore in the NC system means nothing more than its rulers decrees, it is in the FC system a "We the People" in the abstract: it is a rule by reason; it is *the idea* of what free and equal citizens would consent to.

When it comes to this, there is basically only one kind of system to which all can reasonably agree, and it is one founded upon principles of justice. These principles can all be logically deduced from the first premise, that of individual sovereignty. In the state of nature, we are all born free, equal, and with a natural right to life, liberty, and the pursuit of happiness. However, living as we do in a world where some fail to respect the sovereignty of others, there is a need to organize so that individual rights are protected from the violent onslaught of those who will rape, kill, plunder, and subjugate at will. *Therefore, sovereign individuals unite to form a political society*, and so the question becomes "to what kind of social contract would these sovereign agents give their consent?"[48]

Obviously, they would not accept a deal where they were worse off than in the original state (that before society was formed) and obviously they would not accept a transaction where others got a better deal. The foundation for a just societal order, therefore, is obvious. First, as no one would accept further infringement on self-determination than that which

---

initially did and still does occur." Barnett, *The Misconceived Assumption about Constitutional Assumptions* (2008) 27

[48] The social compact is an imaginary invention, "a device for selecting the best conception of justice in the circumstances of utopian political theory." DWORKIN, *LAW'S EMPIRE* (1986) 192

was necessary to protect the rights of others, there is a presumption of liberty and it is the responsibility of the state to ensure that its intrusion is no more extensive than that which is absolutely necessary for the common welfare. Second, as no one would accept a social contract where they were comparatively disadvantaged, a basic premise is that we all have a fundamental right to be treated with equal respect and concern.

The universal principles of justice follow as a logical conclusion from this outset. We shall have more to say on these, but in essence they dictate that (1) the criminal law must be the option of the last resort; (2) that criminal law's only legitimate goal is the protection of rights; (3) that the state can only proscribe activity that threatens an evident harm to autonomy interests; (4) that harm must be some factual event (rights can only be harmed by means of external conduct, thus ideas and wishes cannot be regulated); (5) that there must be moral blameworthiness for punishment to be inflicted; (6) that the individual remains sovereign even after the formation of society; (7) that all government must be subservient to the public interest (the principle of limited government); (8) that a separation of powers and judicial impartiality shall ensure that this is so; (9) that the state must justify its actions whenever the validity of a law is disputed; (10) that the greater the infringement, the more stringent the criteria and the justification for the infringement must be; and (11) that all laws must conform to standards of equality/non-discrimination, proportionality, and non-arbitrariness.

These principles inform an overlapping whole which shall protect and honor the inherent value of human beings. They are the nucleus around which a body of law must be erected and together they make up that framework which we call the rule of law. Any government worthy of existence ensures that it operates consistently with these principles of justice. And to summarize its implications, the essence of FC-based consent theory is that:

"A particular written constitution should be followed if the substance of what it says is 'good enough' to provide, however imperfectly, the procedural assurances that the laws will respect the rights of the persons on whom they are imposed. A law would be just, and therefore binding in conscience, if its restrictions on a citizen's freedom were (1) necessary to protect the rights of others, and (2) proper insofar as they did not violate the preexisting rights of the persons on whom they were imposed. The second of these requirements dispenses with the need to obtain the consent of the person on whom a law is imposed. After all, if a law has not violated a person's rights, then that person's consent is simply not required.   . . . For example, it does not matter if a murderer has consented to the law prohibiting murder. He cannot complain when a murder statute is imposed upon him because the prohibition on murder does not violate his rights; and he has a duty to obey such a law because it is necessary to protect the rights of others, which he has a duty to respect."[49]

2.2 JUDICIAL REVIEW IN THE FC AND NC SYSTEM OF LAW

Now, even though a constitution may provide a foundation for the social contract, taking care to properly "lock-in and preserve the rights-protecting features of the governing structure" and to "define and limit the power that may properly be exercised,"[50] this is no guarantee that agents of the state will ensure that rights are properly respected. Not everyone in the system of government has humanity's best interest at heart and, even if they did, mistakes could be made.[51] Consequently, as a government "retains legitimacy only so long as it continues to protect

---

[49] Barnett, *We the People: Each and Every One* (2014) 2596; Barnett, *The Misconceived Assumption about Constitutional Assumption*s (2008) 32

[50] Ibid. 49

[51]Professor Kumm identifies four pathologies of the political process: "First, there is the vice of thoughtlessness based on tradition, convention or preference, that give rise to all kinds of inertia to either address established injustices or create new injustices by refusing to make available new technologies to groups which need them most. Second, there are illegitimate reasons relating to the good, which do not respect the limits of public reason and the grounds that coercive power of public authorities may be used for. The first two have in common that they typically address situations in which a dominant majority seeks to make legally compulsory elements of the predominant habits or ways of life. Third, there is the problem of government hyperbole or ideology. Hyperbolic and ideological claims are claims loosely related to concerns that are legitimate. But they fail to justify the concrete measures they are invoked for, because they lack a firm and sufficiently concrete base in reality and are not meaningfully attuned to means-ends relationships. Hyperbole and or ideology serve to increase the discretionary power of public authorities under the guise of ensuring security and tend to undermine effective accountability of office-holders, creating dangers for groups deemed to be suspect by authorities. Fourth there is the problem of capture of the legislative process by rent-seeking special interest groups." Kumm, *Democracy is not enough* (2009) 26-27; See also Rubin, *Bureaucratic Oppression* (2012)

natural rights, its raison d'être,"[52] and the fundamental principles of justice require that a fair balance be struck between the interest of the individual and the protection of society, there must be a measure in place that can provide an effective remedy in those cases where individuals claim that rights violations have taken place. This mechanism is called judicial review. It is the failsafe mechanism that citizens must rely on when the political process fails to perform its proper function and without such a procedure the constitution will be worthless.[53]

This core element of the rule of law—an element that Professor Andenæs described as "one of the West's most important contributions to World Civilization"[54]—is another trait that separates FC and NC states, for while lower-end NC states scoff at the idea and advanced NC states officially endorse it (but make sure to undermine it), only FC states will deliver on their promise. In part three we shall see how the American legal system has deprived citizens of their right to an effective remedy hundreds of times, and the way it is done is by reversing the presumption of liberty.

It bears emphasis that this presumption is the very foundation of the rule of law. Consequently, while FC states will honor the liberty presumption, NC states will abide by the opposite presumption, that of legality. It is impossible to overestimate its implications, as this is the flick switch which separates those states that honor constitutional commitments from those that do not. Faced with a presumption of legality the citizenry will have no legal means to counter an assault on their rights and this is a sure sign that we are dealing with a tyrannical government. It may not be a tyranny of oligarchy or monarchy, but it will be a tyranny nonetheless—and in the case of America we are, at the very least, dealing with the tyranny of unrestrained and lawless democracy. Such a tyranny is not better than other forms of tyranny. It means that a majority of the population (or a smaller portion of politically powerful groups), based on nothing but intolerance and prejudice, will be able to deprive the rest of the population of their rights—and while the FC

---

[52] SIMON, *HUMAN RIGHTS OR AMERICAN PRIVILEGES?* (2007) 9

[53] See Kumm, *Democracy is not enough* (2009); Rubin, *Judicial Review and the Right to Resist* (2008)

[54] ANDENÆS, *ETTER OVERVEIELSE: ARTIKLER I UTVALG* (1992) 170

system will secure individual rights from all totalitarian trends, the NC system will not.

2.3 THE POLICE POWER AND THE
FC AND NC CONCEPTION OF HARM

"In a constitutional regime of criminal law, criminal harm is not simply pain, discomfort, or unease, all of which are phenomena that may be experienced by many creatures. Harm instead is harm to human rights, and in particular to the basic human right to autonomy, which gives rise to human dignity. As Jefferson understood, it is this harm that persons constitute political communities to prevent and, if it cannot be prevented, to punish."[55]

—Markus D. Dubber—

We have seen that to be justified, criminal laws must proscribe a nontrivial harm or evil, and the question then becomes what exactly is a "nontrivial" harm?

One answer could be that the harm must be of proper concern for the public, which means that the reasons for criminalization must be sufficiently weighty. However, this is not saying much. We have merely switched one question with another, and now the query becomes what are "sufficiently weighty" reasons?

This will depend on time and place. Nevertheless, what we can say for sure is that in a FC society the police power is limited to (1) those instances where there is a direct harm to others, or (2) where there is a statistically demonstrated secondary social harm of some significance. If the criminal law applies, these statistically demonstrated secondary harms must outweigh all those concerns that speak in favor of liberty as outlined by modern proportionality analysis. We shall have more to say on this but it consists of a four-prong test that, correctly applied, will balance the interest of the individual against the interests of society. To

---

[55] Dubber, *Toward a Constitutional Law of Crime and Punishment* (2004) 72

pass this test a law must attack a social harm that in some concrete way can be shown to violate the rights of others, either in an individual or collective capacity.

This means that not all social problems are up for grabs. As Joel Feinberg pointed out, "voluntarily risked injuries, deaths, broken backs, and broken hearts, are evils of some kind, [but they are] not violations of rights or grounds for grievance."[56] Consequently, for criminalization to be an option, the purpose of the law must (1) be to prevent the possibility of a direct harm to others that is statistically significant (like drunk driving); (2) it must be directed at harms of some significance (i.e., the indignation experienced by some because they have to live amongst others who do not abide by their moral codes is not itself sufficient reason); and (3) the law must be reasonably calibrated to deal with this social ill. It must, in other words, not be overly harsh or too invasive (not criminalize being drunk at home, in bars, etc.), and in those cases where a law does not attack direct rights violations (like rape, murder, etc.), it should have a proven effect on reducing the asserted evil and the law must not be a greater evil than the mischief it seeks to eradicate. We must always respect the presumption of liberty and keep in mind that an infringement on autonomy rights also counts as harm. The greater the infringement, the greater the harm, and we need good reasons to overcome the presumption of liberty. Therefore, if there is any doubt as to whether a criminal law satisfies the criteria above, the liberty presumption dictates that a criminal law fails the test. In that case the state will still be free to find a way to reduce the alleged evil, but it must do so by other means than the criminal law.

Furthermore, we must keep in mind that the FC conception of the harm principle is, as Professor Richards noted, "a natural consequence of an ethical conception of human rights, in which autonomy is the ultimate good."[57] This means that it is not about avoiding harm at any cost. There is a danger to everything we do, and the idea of clamping down on all possible harms would be the creed of tyrants. Thus, the harm principle, in a FC society, concerns *harms to autonomy*. It is not about maximizing

---

[56] FEINBERG, *HARMLESS WRONGDOING* (1988) 322

[57] RICHARDS, *SEX, DRUGS, DEATH, AND THE LAW* (1982) 7

over-all pleasure but, as Professor Richards put it, "of protecting, on fair terms to all, the higher-order rational interests of persons."[58]

In the FC society therefore, policing is autonomy oriented. The state will be mindful of its role as a protector and advancer of autonomy rights and "crime" will be activity that violates another person's freedom.[59] This means that two consenting adults can do pretty much what they want together, unless society as a whole, in some meaningful sense, can be said to suffer.[60] The implication is that the FC system of law distinguishes between what we can call vices and crimes. Vices will be all those pursuits that may or may not contribute to our happiness but that do not directly harm others. It could be gambling, prostitution, drug taking, TV watching, overeating, etc. Others may not like these activities but if performed by consenting adults, the FC state would not interfere.

Remember the social contract holds that people have a fundamental right to be treated with equal concern and respect. It implies a fundamental respect for their selfhood, which again entails a respect for their freedom to live a life according to their own choosing, to follow their own path, and to learn from their mistakes. It may very well be that the total sum of pleasure, in a weak, pitiful, even meaningless sense of the word, would be maximized in a Matrix-like world where humans were hooked up to machines, put in a drug-induced coma, and forced to live out their lives in a stupor of chemically induced orgasmic bliss. It may be that such an escape from the responsibility and hardships that come with being an autonomous individual would appeal to some. But, then again, everything that makes a life worth living would be taken out

---

[58] Ibid. 17

[59] Dubber, *A Political Theory of Criminal Law* (2004) 36 ("The scope of criminal law is defined by the state's authority to protect the autonomy, or personhood, of its victim-constituents. Autonomy, in other words, helps define the nature of criminal harm—as well as the nature of criminal conduct. . . . Criminal harm is limited to what one might call autonomy harm."); see also BEATTY, *THE ULTIMATE RULE OF LAW* (2004); MÖLLER, *THE GLOBAL MODEL OF CONSTITUTIONAL RIGHTS* (2012); RICHARDS, *SEX, DRUGS, DEATH, AND THE LAW* (1982) 19 ("personal autonomy [should be limited] only where necessary to protect countervailing rights; otherwise, persons should have a general right of personal autonomy.")

[60] Dubber, *A Political Theory of Criminal Law* (2004) 34 ("Not recognizing consent as a defense in the law of punishment amounts violates the prima facie victim's fundamental right to autonomy. It also violates the apparent offender's right to autonomy, at least cases where her facially criminal conduct manifested an agreement between her and the apparent victim (as opposed to merely carrying out the "victim's" orders, say). Punishing the apparent offender therefore would do nothing to vindicate autonomy. On the contrary, it would deny the autonomy of offender and victim alike.")

of the equation. Gone would be the thrill of overcoming obstacles. Gone would be the concept of free will. Gone would be all the challenges and rewards that follow from autonomous living. Gone would be the wisdom that *only experience* of the good *and the bad* can bring.

The problem with the NC conception of the harm principle is that it ignores all this. In the minds of NC individuals even moral disgust counts as some sort of harm to be avoided and, having little regard for the autonomy of others, there is no principled limit to their use of the criminal law. These people therefore think it proper to prohibit every-thing that they themselves do not like or understand. "Witchcraft," sodomy, interracial marriages, contraceptives, music, prostitution, gambling, drugs; whatever they frown upon is up for grabs, and they are even prone to make laws that compel a certain behavior. They may, for instance, demand that you worship a certain god, that you eat certain foods, and take certain drugs—all for "your own good."

The less they know about something, the more fearful they are, and the more keenly they will pursue their mission of eradicating evil. Looking back at history, the religious fervor with which they meddle in the affairs of others has been the cause of almost all human-made suffering. It has been at the heart of every mass-movement gone wrong, but to them this is of little concern. If someone tries to point out the parallels between their crusade and those of earlier days (say the inquisition or Nazism) they will reject them out of hand, for it is impossible to shake their impassioned conviction that they are on the side of good.

More shall be said on this. However, their inability to learn from history is not really a fault of their own, for even though most psychologists are too polite to tell them, their bewilderment is explained by psychological factors they have yet to grasp. First of all, they have no understanding of how their convictions are shaped by the undue influence of exaggerated enemy images, nor do they have any idea of why these images have such an influence in the first place. Second, due to the clogged workings of their minds, NC individuals lack the ability to see their day and age in a historical context. As we have seen, they will be too heavily subdued by the collective unconscious to see the bigger picture, and this is also a reason why they never consider the implications of their argument.

Just to take an example, they always presume that it is *they*—the purveyors of all things good and decent—who have a divine right to dictate to others how to live their lives and if you ask them if others should be allowed to impose their morality onto them, they are quick to reject such a notion. Considering that nobody likes to be deprived of autonomy this is not so strange. But this logical inconsistency will not make them reject their first premise—that they have a right to do this to others.

This feat of self-righteous deception is one of the defining traits of NC individuals. They will hold two conflicting opinions at the same time, and even when the inconsistency is brought to their attention they will continue on as before.

In the history of law, we find many examples of this, one being the prohibition of sodomy. There was a well-known debate on this topic between Lord Devlin and the legal theorists H. L. A. Hart and Ronald Dworkin in 1960s. Devlin argued that the state was in its full right to prohibit homosexuality on account of its duty to protect the moral fiber of society, but Hart and Dworkin made the folly of his position plain. Hart argued coherently why feelings of intolerance and disgust did not represent a moral conviction in any meaningful sense and Dworkin later expanded this argument into a distinction between a sociological and discriminatory sense of the word "morality." To quote Bakalar and Grinspoon:

"In the first sense, morality includes anything that any sufficiently large group considers to be part of its system of ethical beliefs. In the second sense, a conviction is not moral unless the person who holds it is able to give reasons for it—reasons not contaminated by prejudice (for example racism), personal emotion, false factual beliefs, or rationalization, and not dependent solely on the beliefs of other people; for example, 'everyone knows that homosexuality is a sin' is not a discriminating moral statement. A certain degree of sincerity, consistency, and lack of arbitrariness is also necessary; to say that the wrongness of homosexuality is self-evident, like the wrongness of cruelty, would be to fail the test. Dworkin says that Devlin wants the law to ratify morality in the sociological sense, although in fact it should be concerned only with morality in the discriminatory sense. A consensus of prejudices and passions that presents itself as morality deserves no legal respect, and by ignoring it, a legislator or judge vindicates the true implicit morality of the community."[61]

One could, perhaps, be so bold and imagine that no self-respecting scholar would ever again advance Devlin's position after Hart and Dworkin had demolished his argument, pointing out the difference between prejudice and true morality. However, one would be mistaken. As a matter of fact, the U.S. Supreme Court upheld a prohibition on homosexual activities in 1986,[62] and as late as 2003 Justice Scalia, in his dissent in *Lawrence*, argued that laws prohibiting homosexuality (as well as other moral offenses such as masturbation, prostitution, adultery, fornication, etc.) were constitutional for the same reasons as Devlin.

Considering that even to this day there is no shortage of lawyers who share Devlin's and Scalia's position, one can be amazed at the confused reasoning that takes place at the NC level. In the name of all things good, they mete out punishment, while ignorance and prejudice remain valid reasons for visiting upon others the horrors of the criminal law. There is no privacy realm they will not invade, there are no limits to the evils they will inflict upon others, and there is no way to convince them otherwise. FC lawyers may expose the fallacies of their argument, but as NC individuals have not yet matured to the point where they can tell the difference between principled and unprincipled reasoning, between reality and fiction, and between right and wrong, it will be to no avail.

In looking at history, we find that NC individuals are the same people who would persecute heathens in the 1300s, witches in the 1500s, run-away slaves in the 1800s, Jews in the 1940s, and exponents of whatever they find annoying today. It may be prostitution, homosexual activity, drug use, or something else; all that changes is the cultural prejudices and the enemy images which drives them to cruelty. And while FC individuals therefore, with good reason, appreciate the importance of having principled restraints on the police power to ensure that narrow-minded and intolerant bigots cannot dictate to others how to live their lives, we still live in a world where the legal system fails to provide these limits. In fact, as we shall see, the American justice system fails all four

---

[61] BAKALAR & GRINSPOON, *DRUG CONTROL IN A FREE SOCIETY* (1998) 20

[62] *Bowers v. Hardwick*, 478 U.S. 186 (1986)

prongs of the constraint-test identified earlier: (1) it proscribes harms that are trivial to non-existent; (2) it imposes sanctions for conduct that is not wrongful (that does not violate the rights of others); (3) it imposes punishments that cannot be justified (it recognizes no real proportionality restraints); and (4) it places the burden of proof on those who advocate the removal of criminal sanctions.

It should be clear that there is room for improvement. Any theory of law must be measured by the extent to which its application will advance the integrity of the legal system, and as current doctrine clearly fails to honor the principles of fundamental justice the legitimacy of the system is in big trouble. As we shall see, there is no lack of scholars who have pointed out its inherent weaknesses and yet the response of the U.S. Supreme Court has been nil. It consistently ignores all evidence of its failure to provide credible leadership and scholars know this.[63] They have even pointed out the need for impeachment procedures,[64] and as the malfunction of the status quo only becomes more evident, the credibility of the system will continue to fade until (1) the Court awakens to its responsibilities or (2) a new Court is installed.

2.4 THE EVOLUTION OF LAW

Despite the problems discussed thus far, it is not my intention to present a pessimistic outlook. As bad as the present system is, there is not only hope for the future, but it is quite certain that the current state of affairs will be upgraded to FC status.

The reason is that as time has progressed, our legal system has been advancing towards a state of resonance with the principles, ideals, and

---

[63] Dubber, *A Political Theory of Criminal Law* (2004) 7 ("A legitimation gap remains, as a perverse sort of exceptionalism has exempted this, the most extreme, form of state governance from principled scrutiny.")

[64] GERBER, *TO SECURE THESE RIGHTS* (1995) 149, 204 ("The political nature of the impeachment power suggests that a Supreme Court Justice willfully submitting his or her own personal political philosophy for the political philosophy of the Constitution should be impeached. . . . If a more principled approach to government is not adopted, the political philosophy on which the Constitution and this nation are based decrees that revolution and the establishment of a new form of government may be necessary. As it was for the Founders, the choice is ours to make.")

values that follow from the Wholeness perspective.[65] A quick review shows that 400 years ago there were no reliable standards of justice and the most barbarous and cruel punishments were tolerated. Being flayed alive, broken on the wheel, rendered asunder with horses, maimed, mutilated, and scourged to death was common procedure in the Western world; 300 years ago things had improved, but the death penalty was still being applied for most types of "criminal" behavior and few people cared;[66] 200 years ago, the death penalty was still common for violations we would consider minor and laws that treated blacks as property were widely accepted as uncontroversial; 100 years ago much had improved, but laws that restricted rights and freedoms on account of race, gender, and so on, still corresponded to the standards of that time. Things most certainly have picked up since then, but 50 years ago provisions that criminalized sodomy, contraceptives, interracial marriages, and unmarried people living together[67] were all heralded as good law.

To this day therefore, the standard by which we measure the legitimacy of laws has evolved and the past 50 years this standard has become more refined and less ambiguous. As seen from the FC perspective, the reason for this is that the evolution of law has been guided by underlying principles. These are the principles of dignity, autonomy, equality, proportionality, and non-arbitrariness. And even though their application has been diverse—and even though the extent to which they have been allowed to guide the evolution of law has been limited by the prevailing mindset of the age—we find that, as time has passed, these principles have increasingly worked their magic.

This natural progression of the law, from a highly selective, coarse, and incoherent application of these principles towards one that is more consistent, finely tuned, and well-reasoned, is natural. To high-end FC individuals it reflects the journey of the human mind from a state of lesser intelligence towards increasing understanding, and today our system of law has evolved to a point where these principles are clearly defined; where their implications are properly delineated; where their interrelation

---

[65] See MIKALSEN, *HUMAN RISING: THE PROHIBITIONIST PSYCHOSIS AND ITS CONSTITUTIONAL IMPLICATIONS* (2020)

[66] Until the 19th century more than 200 crimes in England were punished with death, and even after 1830 this included sodomy, rape, statutory rape, and certain classes of forgery.

[67] As late as 2012, five U.S. states still criminalized cohabitation.

is acknowledged and understood; where appropriately devised tests are available for balancing purposes; and where the criteria to which all laws must conform are clearly outlined. Hence, from century to century, we have been drawing ever nearer to the FC-end, and current trends suggest that the time when the entire system will be recalibrated towards a state of resonance with FC principles, ideals, and values is imminent. When this happens, our legal system will go from having crime prevention as its focus to one where the ultimate goal is to free the human spirit.[68] Autonomy will be the name of the game,[69] and the legal system can finally begin to serve its proper function as a tool for constructive social engineering.

This will be an awesome achievement; one FC lawyers have been looking forward to for some time. However, as seen from the high-end FC perspective, the evolution of law connects to an even bigger picture, one that unites all tiers of human endeavor in a crowning achievement of the human race. We have already discussed some cross-discipline similarities between fields as diverse as religion and law, and while the next chapter will be of little interest to those firmly entrenched in the NC paradigm, I shall end this section by connecting the bigger picture.

---

[68] Professor Packer noted this difference 50 years ago, when he said that "Crime prevention is not the ultimate aim of the rule of law. Law, including the criminal law, must in a free society be judged ultimately on the basis of its success in promoting human autonomy and the capacity for individual human growth and development. The prevention of crime is an essential aspect of the environmental protection required if autonomy is to flourish. It is, however, a negative aspect and one which, pursued with single-minded zeal, may end up creating an environment in which all are safe but none is free. . . . The ultimate goal of law in a free society . . . is to liberate rather than to restrain." PACKER, *THE LIMITS OF THE CRIMINAL SANCTION* (1968) 65-66

[69] Dubber has written extensively on the difference between the old and the new model of law. As he noted, "[t]he legitimacy of any exercise of the police [power] . . . turn[s] on its compliance with . . . the fundamental principle of political legitimacy: autonomy. The best-ordered society, and the most "expedient" system of criminal police, will be illegitimate if it presumes a qualitative distinction between governor and governed, and thus fails to respect each of its constituents as capable of self-government." Dubber, *A Political Theory of Criminal Law* (2004) 15. See also Dubber, *The Legality Principle in American and German Criminal Law* (2010); Dubber, *New Legal Science: Toward Law as a Global Discipline* (2014)

3

LAW'S RELATION TO THE BIGGER PICTURE

"All life here is a stage or a circumstance in an unfolding progressive evolution of a spirit that has involved itself in Matter and is laboring to manifest itself in that reluctant substance. This is the whole secret of earthly existence."[70]

—Sri Aurobindo—

WE HAVE SEEN THAT to high-end FC individuals legal theory, political theory, moral theory, scientific theory, psychological theory, and spiritual theory all merge into one coherent superstructure. This speaks volumes about the credibility of their position, for where else can we find such a theory of everything, one that bridges the apparent gap between fields as diverse as science and religion?[71]

We also saw that they pictured the evolution of life as guided by an inborn Force, one that drives all things forward, bringing out their inherent potential. And the fact that the framework of the FC/NC model describes a dynamic that runs from the baser/fouler kind of human interaction to the more noble/refined—and that the model itself reflects the historical evolution of society from the NC to the FC-end—may not be so strange to FC lawyers. They already know that law evolves; that throughout history it has become ever more calibrated to meet the demands of justice; and that its evolution mirrors humanity's increasing recognition of the principles of justice.

The evolution of law can be seen as evidence of the process that high-end FC individuals are talking about—and it is *this* process that brings

---

[70] AUROBINDO, *THE HOUR OF GOD* (2009) 111

[71] S*upra* note 30

~ 93 ~

meaning to the old trope "Law works itself pure." *For this is* the alchemy of law: From generation to generation, as humanity evolves, to bring out a more noble form of law latent in the less noble form. We could, however, just as well say that "our Psyche works itself pure," that "Humanity works itself pure," or that "Spirit works itself pure," for according to high-end FC individuals it is the same thing described from different perspectives. Psychologically speaking, they will say that it is the story of our journey from unconsciousness into consciousness, from forgetfulness into remembrance, from being engulfed in the idea of separation to rejoicing in a transcendent understanding of our relationship to the Whole. The FC/NC model mirrors this trajectory and seen in this light human evolution is a much more noble undertaking than those at the NC-end could ever imagine.

The account of human accomplishment, however, does not stop there as, religiously speaking, our journey from the NC to the FC-end is even more profound. As previously discussed, the high-end FC experience is essentially spiritual, and as seen from this perspective human evolution is the process of Spirit working its way through matter, working upon it and refining it until one day the essence of all being can surface. If we are to believe their version of events, there are two sides to this spiritual quest; it is all about the interplay between the fragments (us) and the Whole, and as seen from the perspective of the latter, evolution is the process of the Wholeness *awakening to itself* through our evolving understanding. Hence, the further humanity moves towards the FC-end, the closer we draw to a future point in time when the Oneself, the Face behind all faces (what you may call Source or God), can pierce through and remember itself completely, experiencing Itself in all things *as* all things.

The other side of the story is us, because each of us is this *One*, this One Face behind all faces. And as seen from the perspective of the fragments, evolution is complete when we will all embody a higher form of consciousness—one that psychiatrist R.M. Bucke called the Cosmic. We will then see the world through the eyes of Cosmos.[72] We will become the Galactic Consciousness embodied in man, and we will see ourselves as this One that always has been, always is, always will be.

---

[72] BUCKE, *COSMIC CONSCIOUSNESS* (1961)

This may appear farfetched, but this is the essence of the world's spiritual traditions as seen from the high-end FC perspective. As discussed, organized religion is just the NC-version of spirituality and those who want the FC-version must talk to mystics or other advanced travelers in consciousness. Quite a few are already familiar with this next level of consciousness and having attained states of awareness that transcends time and space (as we know it) some claim to have seen the process unfolding as a whole. They believe that when it comes to this process, there is nothing haphazard about it; that when life was first breathed into matter the Idea itself was always complete; and that the progress of evolution was destined to unfold for this purpose—for us to emerge, strive, falter, despair, collect ourselves, and rise triumphantly.[73]

For those interested, the spiritual quest is detailed elsewhere. It is beyond the scope of this book to elaborate on this process, but Ibn al-Arabi, a 12th century mystic, summarized it beautifully in the following words: "God sleeps in the rock, dreams in the plant, stirs in the animal, and awakens in man." To high-end FC individuals, human consciousness is the bridge that this Greater Force uses to realize itself in the physical—and even if the consciousness of NC individuals has yet to be refined to the point where they can feel this Force becoming manifest, those at the higher FC-end *do feel its presence* in no uncertain terms.

Now, many jurists (but never the good ones) will not want to have their profession sullied by talk of comparison to mysticism. They like to imagine that they are dealing with something much more scientific than mystics in pursuit of spiritual enlightenment, but the truth is far from it. It is only at the NC level that law and religion belong to two different worlds and the further we draw towards the FC-end, the more the two become one.[74] Indeed, only in looking at things at the surface do they

[73] MIKALSEN, *REASON IS* (2014); AUROBINDO, *THE HOUR OF GOD* (2009); AUROBINDO, *THE HUMAN CYCLE* (2012); AUROBINDO, *THE LIFE DIVINE* (1970); AUROBINDO, *ON YOGA: THE SYNTHESIS OF YOGA* (1957); DE CHARDIN, *THE PHENOMENON OF MAN* (1955); TALBOT, *MYSTICISM AND THE NEW PHYSICS* (1981); UNDERHILL, *MYSTICISM* (1962); TEASDALE, *THE MYSTIC HEART* (1999); CAREY, *GOD-MAN: THE WORD MADE FLESH* (1920); WILBER, *UP FROM EDEN* (1986); WILCOCK, *THE SOURCE FIELD INVESTIGATIONS* (2011); BLAVATSKY, *THE SECRET DOCTRINE* (1888); HEINDEL, *THE ROSICRUCIAN COSMO-CONCEPTION* (2012); PURUCKER, *WIND OF THE SPIRIT* (1984)

[74] A look at the founders provides further corroboration, as historically there is a connection between the Enlightenment philosophy and the FC conception of religion. This book has explained why, and many leaders of the French and American Revolution were Deists, which is

appear separate, and as soon as one digs deeper, into their essence, commonalities emerge.

We need only ponder the idea of justice to see that it is so. Any serious deliberation will find that it refuses to be reduced to some positivistic conception which equates justice with law-as-it-is, and the idea of authority is no less mysterious. Only the most hardheaded positivists would argue to the contrary, seeing justice as that which judges do, and the authority of law as being derived from the state. However, very few jurists will honestly subscribe to this notion and FC jurists know better.

Just as children at some point will cease to take the authority of their parents for granted, these jurists have matured to the point where the question "Why" merits a different response than "because our will must be done." To understand this "Why," they must go deeper than the positivists and the simpleminded notion that equates authority with State and its commands with the source of law. They must go beyond this realm of childlike minds. They must enter a world that transcends time and place—and having begun this quest they have joined the mystics in their trade. Just as a mystic wants to experience God more directly, they want to experience the source of Law more directly. And just like a mystic must leave religious dogma behind to reach a deeper understanding of the Divine Mystery, so they, in their search for a true understanding of Law, must open themselves to the Mystery. They must divest themselves of the baggage that comes with their upbringing, education, and prejudices, and trace the interrelationship between Law and Morality to its very source. To find a greater Truth, they must roam beyond the narrow confines of positive law; they must cross over into those territories where political philosophers ruminate, and in pursuit of enlightenment they must go even further; they must go into and even beyond those lands that border on the mystical, into the very essence of Being. It is here that they may connect with the light of first principles. It is here that they may find enlightenment.

No question, then, bona fide jurists are in the business of pursuing a quest no less ambitious than mystics. Like the mystics they are divinely

---

another 18th century name for the FC version of religion. Influential founders in this regard were Benjamin Franklin, Thomas Jefferson, Thomas Paine, James Madison, Alexander Hamilton, Ethan Allen, George Washington, Cornelius Harnett, Governor Morris, and Hugh Williamson.

inspired. Like the mystics they are trying to understand the mind of God. And like the mystics the extent to which their quest will be victorious will mirror how far they have travelled towards the FC-end. The great jurists, therefore, just as the great scientists,[75] have always been mystics at heart. And while they may not have thought of themselves as trailblazers on a spiritual quest, it should be easy enough for FC scholars to recognize that they are dabbling in closely related disciplines. They may not yet be aware of the greater parameters from which human evolution has come into being; they may not know about Out-breath and In-breath, Vishnu's dream, and the Cosmic Play. But we are all, in truth, cosmic dancers and those with eyes to see will know that law does "work itself pure" and that the end-result is a given. As Robert G. Ingersoll, another FC lawyer, observed the greater framework of this process: "As man develops, he places a greater value upon his own rights. Liberty becomes a grander and diviner thing. As he values his own rights, he begins to value the rights of others. And when all men give to all others all the rights they claim for themselves, this world will be civilized."[76]

Now, we are not there yet, and it will be for us to assist in the societal upgrade to FC status. It may seem like an overwhelming task, but historically speaking, we may not be far from this Grand Finale when we shall redeem ourselves and prove victorious. Personally, I believe it is upon us and that the rise of principled law in the past 60 years goes to prove it. What was born out of the Enlightenment era and the efforts of the founders has now arisen in full force. As we shall see, this force was quelled into submission by the increasing dominance of NC lawyers in the 1800s but has survived as an undercurrent. Since the Second World War, it has been steadily gaining momentum, while FC scholars have stripped the Supreme Court's doctrines of all credibility. At long last the alchemy of law nears complete and soon the great work can begin—that of constructive social engineering.

---

[75] FC lawyers join FC physicists in their intuitive embrace of mysticism. See for instance KEN WILBER, *QUANTUM QUESTIONS* for the mystical writings of Einstein, Heisenberg, Schrödinger, de Broglie, Planck, Bohr, Pauli, Eddington, and Jeans. See also CAPRA, *THE TAO OF PHYSICS* (2010); TALBOT: *MYSTICISM AND THE NEW PHYSICS* (1981); CLOSE, *TRANSCENDENTAL PHYSICS* (2000); ZUKAV, *THE DANCING WU LI MASTERS* (1979); DAVIES & GRIBBIN, *THE MATTER MYTH (1992)*; HERBERT, *QUANTUM REALITY:* (1985); GOSWAMI, *THE SELF-AWARE UNIVERSE* (1993)

[76] Ingersoll, *The Liberty Of Man, Woman, And Child* (1877)

4

IMPLICATIONS FOR
CONSTITUTIONAL INTERPRETATION

"How easily men satisfy themselves that the Constitution is exactly what they wish it to be."[77]

—Justice Joseph Story—

FROM WHAT WE HAVE seen, we can understand why people have different opinions about the Constitution. The further a person is drawn towards the NC-end, the more likely he is to see the text as a totalitarian blueprint. The principles of justice that breathe life to its very essence will be hopelessly out of reach, and to fill in the blanks prejudiced conceptions or guesswork does the job.

We see an example in Robert Bork, a judge honest enough to admit his confusion. As he said: "There may be a natural law, but we are not agreed upon what it is, and there is no such law that gives definitive answers to a judge trying to decide a case."[78] Bork gives a voice to a great many scholars. They may agree that the tradition of natural law gave birth to the Constitution and that it in essence is a natural law document (how could they not?), but its implications are lost.

---

[77] Tribe, *On Reading the Constitution* (1986) 12

[78] GERBER, *TO SECURE THESE RIGHTS* (1995) 163. Justice Iredell famously shared Bork's concern in *Calder v. Bull*, when he said that "The ideas of natural justice are regulated by no fixed standard: the ablest and the purest men have differed upon the subject; and all that the Court could properly say, in such an event, would be, that the Legislature (possessed of an equal right of opinion) had passed an act which, in the opinion of the judges, was inconsistent with the abstract principles of natural justice." *Calder v. Bull*, 3 U.S. (3 Dall.) 386 (1798) at 398–99 (Iredell, J., concurring)

Now, as not all natural lawyers are capable of FC reasoning, Bork is correct in asserting that "we are not agreed upon what it is." Historically, there has been no shortage of lawyers who have justified arbitrary legislation by claiming that its authority is derived from a "higher" law. Kings, for instance, famously claimed a divine right to rule based on natural law, and today scholars such as John Finnis and Harry Haffa make the same mistakes. Failing to connect with the light of first principles, such jurists substitute their own prejudices for principled reasoning and argue that homosexuality is unnatural and therefore in violation of natural law. Proponents of this reasoning begin with the presumption that the root of nature is generation and conclude that homosexual acts are punishable by law because they are "unnatural acts, and being unnatural, the very negation of anything that could be called a right according to nature."[79]

Another example is given by Judge Richard Posner. He has stated that "survival of the fittest" could be taken as an example of natural law because it purports to describe a law of behavior that has its source in the "nature" of human beings.[80] Again, however, the mistake is evident. All these people invoke nature to support their case but instead of an argument from first principles, they offer vague generalizations about the way most people *tend* to behave (or, in their mind, should behave).

Examples of such unprincipled, arbitrary natural law reasoning notwithstanding, it is not that common, and we need only listen to those who reason from a FC perspective to learn how it is properly applied. Among those who operate at this level—and can delineate the implications of first principles—there is agreement as to what natural law is and how it applies on a case-by-case basis, and so Bork's criticism only concerns the idea of natural law as it exists at the NC level.

The finding that some people fail to connect with the light of first principles is not a new one. Locke himself spoke to it and also Madison, Jefferson, and Adams subscribed to this view.[81] Applying the lessons from psychology, we can see why this is so, and why we should listen to

---

[79] GERBER, *TO SECURE THESE RIGHTS* (1995) 189. Finnis takes a different view, arguing that homosexual sex cannot involve the union of procreation and emotional commitment that heterosexual sex can, and is therefore an assault on heterosexual union.

[80] ARKES, *CONSTITUTIONAL ILLUSIONS & ANCHORING TRUTHS* (2010) 43

[81] GERBER, *TO SECURE THESE RIGHTS* (1995) 42, 131

those who have this ability rather than those who don't. As we shall see, the Constitution was a FC document, and the leading founders were FC individuals. They wanted to empower the individual by all legal and political means, and this is the very opposite of what NC scholars do. The difference between the two breeds could hardly be greater[82]—and as NC scholars operate within a range where the greater view is lost, they are unfit for the task of constitutional interpretation.

This is all the reason we need to leave these matters to FC scholars, but another is the resulting interpretation. Looking at this, we are in a tight spot today *exactly because* we have left it to NC scholars to make sense of the Constitution.[83] It is because of this that our legal system is skewed in favor of tyranny;[84] it is because of this that voices of reason have been consistently ignored;[85] it is because of this that human rights

---

[82] "Consider the contrast: on the one hand a group of lawyers who have memorized a list of rights, set down in the first eight amendments to the Constitution; on the other hand, a generation of lawyers who had cultivated the art of tracing their judgments back to first principles and anchoring truths." ARKES, *CONSTITUTIONAL ILLUSIONS & ANCHORING TRUTHS* (2010) 8

[83] West, *The Authoritarian Impulse in Constitutional Law* (1988) 539 ("[C]ourts and commentators are presently inclined toward an authoritarian and hence amoral resolution of our constitutional questions in part because modern interpretations of our underlying political theories . . . reflect our anxieties about ourselves, fears about others, and our asocial and even psychopathological tendencies, rather than our social aspirations. The modern judicial impulse toward authoritarian decisionmaking in constitutional cases might in part be a reaction to the sorry self-portrait we have cast in our modern political theory. If we are as we paint ourselves in our political theory—incapable of creative and moral constitutional self-governance—then we are in dire need of authoritarian control."); Sherry, *The Ninth Amendment: Righting an Unwritten Constitution* (1988) 1010 ("A passively textualist approach to the Constitution is itself productive of despair: when we cede the community's moral authority to an external source, we give up a part of our humanity. The desire to appeal to the absolute authority of the historical Constitution is also self-replicating. To the extent that we as a society relieve ourselves of the obligation to make difficult moral decisions, we further undermine our capacity to do so. Moral sensibilities, whether of an individual or of a community, are best developed by making moral choices.")

[84] See e.g. Stuntz, *The Pathological Politics of Criminal Law* (2001) 7 ("the story of American criminal law is a story of tacit cooperation between prosecutors and legislators, each of whom benefits from more and broader crimes, and growing marginalization of judges, who alone are likely to opt for narrower liability rules rather than broader ones."); Materni, *The 100-plus Year old Case for a Minimalist Criminal Law* (2015) 5-6 ("the criminal law is in desperate need of normative and limiting principles beyond the procedural protections that the Supreme Court has recognized over time.")

[85] "For the past generation, virtually everyone who has written about federal criminal law has bemoaned its expansion. But the expansion has continued apace, under very different sorts of Congresses and Presidents. Normative argument does not seem to have mattered. One can put the point more generally: American criminal law's historical development has borne no relation to any plausible normative theory—unless "more" counts as a normative theory. Criminal law

are subject to selective implementation on the basis of power politics;[86] and it is because of this that we have a system of arbitrary justice.

From the scholarly debate we have all the evidence we need that only FC scholars can interpret it in any coherent and consistent fashion and the FC/NC model explains why. As seen, only they are sufficiently free from personal bias to provide the words and values of the Constitution with objective meaning;[87] only they are fit to represent "the ethical tradition that accords respect to the dignity and intrinsic worth of every individual;"[88] and only they can bring integrity to the system of justice. The confusion that takes place at NC level is all too apparent, as it makes no sense to believe in principles of justice and to claim that natural rights are no longer justiciable—or that the enumerated rights warrant a better protection than unenumerated rights. Likewise, it makes no sense to believe in these principles and to support a doctrine of legislative deference, to prioritize procedural over substantive due process, to see the state as sovereign, or to embrace any other consent theory than one founded upon justice. In all cases, the former negates the latter, and only by the unswerving application of FC reasoning can the Constitution represent a coherent political theory.

The consistent application of this principled type of reasoning will also bridge the gap between theory and practice—and if some remain unconvinced why any of this matter, the FC/NC model provides us with good reasons. We can see from this model that to the extent NC individuals are allowed to make sense of the Constitution, we will move society towards the NC-end, and to the extent we leave construction to FC individuals we will move towards the FC-end. In other words, the Constitution can either be used as a tool for agents of tyranny *or* as a tool

---

scholars may be talking to each other (and to a few judges), but they do not appear to be talking to anyone else." Stuntz, *The Pathological Politics of Criminal Law* (2001) 4

[86] NORMAND & ZAIDI, *HUMAN RIGHTS AT THE UN* (2008)

[87] The closer towards the FC-end, the more objective our perception. To quote Maslow: "Perception [at this end] can be relatively ego-transcending, self-forgetful, egoless, unselfish. It can come closer to being unmotivated, impersonal, desireless, detached, not needing or wishing. Which is to say, that it becomes more object-centered [i.e., principle-centered] than ego-centered. The perceptual experience can be more organized around the object itself as a centering point rather than being based upon the selfish ego." MASLOW, *RELIGIONS, VALUES, AND PEAK-EXPERIENCES* (1994) 62

[88] *Hudson v. Palmer*, 468 U.S. 517 (1984) (Stevens, J., dissenting) (quoting *United States ex rel. Miller v. Twomey*, 479 F.2d 701, 712 (7th Cir. 1973)

for agents of liberty; it will have to be either-or, and there is no doubt what the founders advocated. *To their mind the Constitution was to be a solution to the problems that plague NC societies*, and if we consistently choose the FC aspect of interpretation, we will make it so. We will have the moral compass and the tools needed to begin the process of constructive social engineering, and this is all that we can ask of a Constitution. To the extent we do this, we will be honoring its potential—and in honoring its potential we will pay our tribute to the founders.

Add to this that the Constitution is more than a mirror from which people can see whatever reflection they like. As Tribe has pointed out:

> "The authority of the Constitution, its claim to obedience, and the force that we permit it to exercise in our law and over our lives would lose all legitimacy if it really were only a mirror for the readers' ideas and ideals. We have to reject as completely unsatisfactory the idea of an empty, or an infinitely malleable, Constitution. We must find principles of interpretation that can anchor the Constitution in some more secure, determinate, and external reality."[89]

The Constitution, in other words, *must mean something* and to the extent that we can say that the Constitution reflects one single vision and aspiration it must be that we are to strive for the greatest possible amount of autonomy on an individual and collective scale.[90] Its talk of liberty, equality, limited government, due process, privileges and immunities, and the general welfare are certain indicators, and this interpretation is the common denominator found in the Supreme Court's jurisprudence.

---

[89] Tribe, *On Reading the Constitution* (1986) 12

[90] FC scholars identify autonomy as the fundamental principle of political legitimacy. Professor Dubber does it here: "The principle from which the new republican form of government drew, and continues to draw, its legitimacy was 'the consent of the governed.' The consent of the governed in turn mattered not for its own sake, but because republican government is self-government, 'of the people, by the people, for the people,' in Lincoln's memorable phrase. *Ultimately the legitimacy of the state, then, rests on the autonomy of its constituents,* 'the capacity of mankind for self-government,' as Madison put it in the Federalist Papers. All of this is obvious enough. *What's not so obvious, or at least hasn't been so far, is that as a type of state action, criminal law must derive its legitimacy from the same source.*" Dubber, *A Political Theory of Criminal Law: Autonomy and the Legitimacy of State Punishment* (2004) 4-5 (Emphasis mine)

Now, some scholars, like Tribe, are skeptical about reading the Constitution in search for one unifying lofty ideal.[91] Even so, despite a variety of motives and ideological differences among the framers, it is safe to say that the enhancement of autonomy must be its core value. First of all, no single, or more admirable purpose could be found. Autonomy is synonymous with freedom, and the extent to which we can pursue our happiness depends on the extent to which autonomy is restrained. Secondly, even if the framers had conflicting ideas, their vision must conform to this single ambition if we are to take them seriously. As we can see from the FC/NC model, the opposite of autonomy is tyranny. It is therefore safe to say that to the extent the founders were not agents of autonomy, they must have been agents of tyranny, and I have yet to meet a constitutional scholar who would support the notion of the Constitution as an instrument of oppression. It is self-evident that no people would willingly enslave itself, and even though some framers may have entertained an authoritarian agenda this is no reason to stray from the course of liberty. When interpreting the Constitution, we must do so with the best intention, and if we are to fill its words, values, and ideals with meaning, we must see it as a FC document, providing and securing the greatest possible amount of autonomy to individuals in both a personal and collective capacity.[92]

That said, this will not solve all the problems associated with interpreting the Constitution. For one, first principles alone cannot decide anything; they can only lighten our load to the extent a number of variables are known. Being open-ended and abstract, the courts need more rule-like constitutional constructions (what we call doctrines) to put their provisions into effect, and the validity of these doctrines will depend on the extent to which they succeed in channeling the light of first principles. Poor doctrines must result in poor law—and considering that

---

[91] Due to a failure to discriminate between the FC and NC conception of the Constitution Professor Tribe thinks that it "could not possibly express a coherent political theory, however sympathetic and humane I might find its substance. It seems to me almost a contradiction in terms to suppose that one could read a Constitution composed as ours has been as though it were an expression of any unified philosophy." Tribe, *On Reading the Constitution* (1986) 26

[92] The public interest, as Möller has pointed out, "is really only a short form of saying that it serves everyone's autonomy interests." MÖLLER, *THE GLOBAL MODEL OF CONSTITUTIONAL RIGHTS* (2012) 136

current doctrines have been richly criticized for a failure to anchor the light of first principles, it is evident that we need better doctrines.

Secondly, the Constitution is silent on the best way to govern a society. It has nothing to say on race-specific affirmative action, minimum wage laws, drug policy, and so on. Reasonable people may differ as to how one best secures "the blessings of liberty" and it may be impossible to tell which option is the most suitable means of doing so.[93] This will be for humanity to determine according to its best wisdom.[94] However, the FC-end must always be the yardstick against which our laws and regulations must be measured. To the extent they enhance the collective welfare by securing the greatest possible extent of autonomy for all, they will be compatible with the spirit of the Constitution—and likewise, to the extent they fail in this endeavor, they will be unconstitutional.

---

[93] As a FC document, the Constitution supports both libertarian and communitarian versions of autonomy. As the focus traditionally has been on a state's duty to refrain from interfering with our liberties, one can say that the libertarian version has had a strong influence on the justices at the Supreme Court. If autonomy-enhancement is the goal, however, it is logical to conclude that the state has a duty to ensure a certain quality of life for its citizens. The UN's International Covenant on Economic, Social and Cultural Rights are the result of such thinking, and for historical support of this notion, see Heyman, *The First Duty of Government: Protection, Liberty, and the Fourteenth Amendment* (1991)

[94] The level of generality with which the Constitution speaks signifies that the framers intended to leave this issue to successive generations. What were fixed were the fundamental principles of justice; what was not fixed was the way they would inform society. Thus, "as the Constitution endures, persons in every generation can invoke its principles in their own search for greater freedom." *Lawrence*, 539 U.S. at 578–79 (Kennedy J., majority opinion)

PART 2

THE IDEA AND THE DESTRUCTION OF AMERICA

5

THE IDEA OF AMERICA

"A free people [claim] their rights as derived from the laws of nature, and not as the gift of their chief magistrate."[1]

—Thomas Jefferson—

THE FOUNDING OF AMERICA represented a brand-new chapter of civilization building. The founders rejected the idea of a dominion by force, whether it would be by minority or majority rule. Instead, the New Order of the Ages was to be a dominion of reason. As Alexander Hamilton wrote, the United States was to be governed by "reflection and choice" rather than by "accident and force."[2] It was to be a land of the free, a government of wisdom—the ideal state.

Looking to Europe and the countries from which they fled, the founders saw that the old models of government were essentially tyrannies. Whether they were called democracies, republics, or monarchies, the only difference was by what mechanism the few would force their will upon the majority. Not only were these governments internally oppressive. Externally, they were exceedingly fond of war and the only control on imperialist ambitions was the military force of opponents. In short, these states recognized no moral restraints and were unbound by reason.

The fundamental injustice inherent in such a system was obvious to the Founding Fathers. They were not only well-versed in the lessons of history but committed to the ideals of the Enlightenment Era. Chief

---

[1] Thomas Jefferson, *Rights of British America* (1774)

[2] MADISON, HAMILTON & JAY, *THE FEDERALIST PAPERS* (2010) 1

among these was the idea of autonomy, which was an invention of this period. Until that moment in time the idea of sovereign individuals and a government founded on the inherent dignity of man were unheard of. To the thinkers of this era, however, it was evident that if a remedy were to be found, it would have to be in this concept. Inspired by Locke and other theorists therefore, the founders imagined there being a natural state of man. They envisioned that in this natural state, before governments and any kind of organized society, all individuals were born free, of equal worth, and with a set of unalienable rights. It was to protect these rights— the right to life, liberty and the pursuit of happiness—that people formed a government, and from this idea emerged a foundation for the New World.

The Declaration of Independence was the first building block of this foundation.[3] It was in every sense a FC document and several state constitutions followed.[4] The most famous was the Virginia Declaration of Rights, a declaration that has been called "the very birth of what we understand today as modern constitutionalism."[5] It established a firm foundation for the founders' aspirations, one where rights were the basis and foundation of government, and not the other way around.

This is a very important distinction, one that separates FC from NC systems. In the NC conception of rights all powers are transferred to the state at the point where we, from the original state, enter into society. Thus, following this idea, rights can be granted (and withheld) by the government. According to the FC conception, however, the state has no rights to give or to withhold. The state is just a protector of those natural rights that are precursors to all government and "its goal is not to confer

---

[3] See e.g., Gerber, *Liberal Originalism* (2014) 4-5 ("the United States of America was founded to secure the natural rights of the American people. 'To secure these rights,' Thomas Jefferson proclaims in the Declaration of Independence, is the reason that 'governments are instituted among men.' To secure natural rights is, therefore, why the Constitution was enacted, and to secure natural rights is how the Constitution should be interpreted. That is the 'original intent' of the founders.")

[4] The early state constitutions were similarly worded as the Declaration of Independence. The language of the Virginia Constitution was characteristic: all men have "certain inherent rights, . . . namely the enjoyment of life and liberty, with the means of acquiring and possessing property, and pursuing and obtaining happiness and safety." McDonald, *Novus Ordo Seclorum* (1985) 152

[5] Dippel, *Modern Constitutionalism: An Introduction to a History in the Need of Writing* (2005)

any right on the individual, but rather to ensure that others are prevented from harming or destroying already existing rights."[6]

When it comes to this, the FC conception of rights can be logically deduced from natural law doctrine[7] and in the early days of the republic it was recognized by presidents[8] and courts[9] alike. Today the state abides by the NC conception, but there is no shortage of FC scholars to remind us that "our constitutional rights are codifications of those innate rights which exist independent of government,"[10] and that a "discerning constitutional thinker must appreciate the extent to which the constitutional project quintessentially was an effort to codify pre-existing natural law rights."[11]

These scholars see the U.S. Constitution as a FC document, one that naturally connects to the Declaration of Independence.[12] It came into being a decade after the Declaration, much due to the founders' concern that individual rights did not get the protection they were owed. Even

---

[6] Rosenfeld, *The Rule of Law and the Legitimacy of Constitutional Democracy* (2001) 1334

[7] "Men cannot create natural rights, and the government does not grant natural rights to men; men may only create political rights by the consent of those who entered into the same social contract. Men therefore have a duty and an obligation to not infringe on the natural rights of others. Natural law sets the highest good that man should strive towards and sets in place prohibitions which he should not break." Sabo, *The Higher Law Background of the Constitution* (2009) 24

[8] As President John Adams assured the American people, they had "rights antecedent to all earthly governments—rights that cannot be repealed or restrained by human laws—rights derived from the great Legislator of the universe." Sanders, *Ninth Life: An Interpretive Theory of the Ninth Amendment* (1994) 802-03

[9] *Chisholm v. Georgia*, 2 U.S. (2 Dall.) 419 (1793); *Calder v. Bull*, 3 U.S. (3 Dall.) 386 (1798); Sherry, *The Ninth Amendment: Righting an Unwritten Constitution* (1988); Barnett, *We the People: Each and Every One* (2014); Barnett, *Who's Afraid of Unenumerated Rights?* (2006); SIMON, *HUMAN RIGHTS OR AMERICAN PRIVILEGES?* (2007)

[10] O'Scannlain, *The Natural Law in the American Tradition* (2011) 1527

[11] Ibid. 1528. See also BLACK, *A NEW BIRTH FOR FREEDOM* (1999); GERBER, *TO SECURE THESE RIGHTS* (1995); Gerber, *Liberal Originalism* (2014); ARKES, *CONSTITUTIONAL ILLUSIONS & ANCHORING TRUTHS* (2010); Sanders, *Ninth Life* (1994); Rosenfeld, *The Rule of Law and the Legitimacy of Constitutional Democracy* (2001); BLAU & MONCADA, *JUSTICE IN THE UNITED STATES* (2006); SIMON, *HUMAN RIGHTS OR AMERICAN PRIVILEGES?* (2007); Sabo, *The Higher Law Background of the Constitution* (2009)

[12] As Gerber noted, "[t]he particular provisions of the Constitution were written with the founders' background attitudes in mind. The Constitution is not an end in itself; it is the means by which the American political community's ideals—its ends—are ordered. It is therefore necessary to interpret the Constitution in light of those ideals; ideals expressed with unparalleled eloquence by Thomas Jefferson in the Declaration of Independence." Gerber, *Liberal Originalism* (2014) 5

though the ground was extremely fertile for FC reasoning, influential factions preferred the NC system of law. Thus, founders like Madison was alarmed by the transgressions on individual liberty, and the ultimate objective for the framers when they met in Philadelphia in 1787 was to create a system that would do a better job at protecting natural rights than the government had done under the Articles of Confederation.[13] In other words, *these FC individuals sought a way to cope with the dynamics inherent in NC societies*; the purpose of the Constitutional Convention was to find a way to save the system of FC law against the forces that continuously disparaged and sabotaged the elevated ideals from which FC reasoning drew its strength—and the end result was the U.S. Constitution with its Bill of Rights.

5.1 THE UNITED STATES CONSTITUTION

"If men were angels, no government would be necessary. If angels were to govern men, neither external nor internal controls on government would be necessary. In framing a government which is to be administered by men over men, the great difficulty lies in this: you must first enable the government to control the governed; and in the next place, oblige it to control itself."[14]

—James Madison—

In writing a Constitution, the framers sought to create a positive law that would protect pre-existing natural rights. They wanted a mechanism for bringing the higher law down to earth, and in this sense we have a written *and an unwritten* Constitution.[15]

---

[13] GERBER, *TO SECURE THESE RIGHTS*, 100-25; Barnett, *The Ninth Amendment: It Means What It Says* (2006)

[14] MADISON, HAMILTON & JAY, *THE FEDERALIST PAPERS* (2010) 200

[15] "In the abstract, a written constitution can be considered another structural feature of governance, like separation of powers, judicial review, and federalism, whose value lies in its ability to lock-in and preserve the other rights-protecting features of the governing structure, as well as to define and limit the power that may properly be exercised." Barnett, *The Misconceived Assumption about Constitutional Assumptions* (2008) 49. See also AMAR, *AMERICA'S UNWRITTEN CONSTITUTION* (2012); Sherry, *The Founders' Unwritten Constitution* (1987);

The unwritten constitution consists of the principles of natural law as well as the tools and techniques for applying these principles on a case-by-case basis, while the written constitution positivizes the higher, unwritten law. The former proceeds (and gains its authority) from the latter, and even though the Constitution does not explicitly reference natural law, like the Declaration of Independence and several state constitutions, it (1) uses terms that cannot be understood in any other context and (2) it cannot be read in isolation. It must be seen in light of the political theory of the founders, their speeches and diverse writings (especially the Declaration of Independence) and these are replete with references to a higher, unwritten law, accessible to human reason. The Federalist Papers, for instance, frequently rely on "nature," "primary truths," and "reason" to justify general principles of law, and it simply makes no sense to read the Constitution as a NC document.[16]

Even so, this is what many scholars do. Whether it be for reasons of ignorance or convenience, they fail to appreciate the higher law background of the Constitution, and they have managed to get away with it to this day. One reason is that constitutional interpretation did not really evolve to become a fully formed discipline. Until the 1980s little scholarship existed to make sense of the Constitution as a FC document and because a system of NC law had become firmly established precedent, most people assumed that the justices at the Supreme Court knew what they were doing. Today, however, we know that our confidence was misplaced. FC scholars have demolished the credibility of the current system, exposing its flawed foundation for all to see, and whether we look at early jurisprudence, the founders' writings, the debates preceding the Bill of Rights, or the Ninth Amendment scholarship which has accumulated in later years there is too much data

<hr>

Sherry, *The Ninth Amendment: Righting an Unwritten Constitution* (1988); GERBER, *TO SECURE THESE RIGHTS* (1995); Snure, *A Frequent Recurrence to Fundamental Principles* (1992); Grey, *The Uses of an Unwritten Constitution* (1988); Solum, *Originalism and the Unwritten Constitution* (2013); Sanders, *Ninth Life: An Interpretive Theory of the Ninth Amendment* (1994)

[16] As Madison himself wrote: "On the distinctive principles of the [U.S.] Government . . . the best guides are to be found in . . . the Declaration of Independence, as the fundamental Act of Union of these States." Madison, letter to Thomas Jefferson, February 8, 1825

to preserve the prevailing notion of the Constitution as *a source* of our rights.[17]

It is therefore plain wrong when NC scholars talk of "the rights we have *through* the First Amendment", and so on. As Alexander Hamilton described the source of our fundamental rights: "[T]he sacred rights of mankind are not to be rummaged for among old parchments or musty records. They are written as with a sunbeam, in the whole volume of human nature, by the hand of Divinity itself and can never be erased or obscured by mortal power."[18]

The reason why the enumerated rights cannot be the source of our rights should be obvious, as they are secondary to the fundamental principles of justice. The relationship between the two is like that of shadow and light, and the enumerated rights represent the shadow that is cast from these principles into different areas of activity. The First Amendment merely provides *a general outline* of our rights in the area of religion, free speech and the like, just as the Second Amendment's right to bear arms merely details *one* aspect of inviolable rights in the area self-expression and protection. The existence of these rights *does not* depend upon their enumeration any more than the existence of light depends on its shadow. Light creates shadow, not the other way around.

It was this conception of rights that made the American system so unique, for even though the founders were inspired by the British legal system and its leading theorists, this was the crucial difference between the two—one being a system of FC law and the other NC.

We shall later see how doctrines are used to channel the light of first principles into a workable system for determining when we have a rights violation and how this analysis is the same whether or not a right is enumerated. However, to continue our story, it is well-known that the founders were in a quandary as how to prepare a document which would

---

[17] O'Scannlain, *The Natural Law in the American Tradition* (2011) 1516 ("when our founders codified fundamental rights in the Constitution, they did not believe that they were 'creating' those rights, any more than a mathematician 'creates' mathematical principles when he writes the axioms of a formal system."); Sanders, *Ninth Life* (1994) 804 ("the real ideological revolution which occurred over the summer of 1787 lay in the recognition that a constitution could become positive law of a higher level, intended to supplement and give practical force to natural law. The Framers did not . . . intend the Constitution to wholly supplant higher law; rather, they expected natural law to continue to condemn repugnant laws which the Constitution did not expressly prohibit.")

[18] Hamilton, *The Farmer Refuted*, 23 Feb. 1775

be effective in protecting natural rights. Some wanted a Bill of Rights because of the frequent occurrence of undue interference with rights. Others did not want to enumerate *any* rights, precisely for their fear that "an imperfect enumeration would throw all implied power into the scale of the government, and the rights of the people would be rendered incomplete."[19] They knew that a complete enumeration would be impossible[20] and that to enumerate only some would be a dangerous undertaking, one that agents of tyranny would seize upon to deny those rights that were not accounted for.[21] However, Virginia Representative James Madison, the chief architect of the Constitution, thought this problem could be solved by the implementation of an amendment that detailed the rules of construction. His idea was welcomed, and so it was that the Bill of Rights found its form. First, the Founders enumerated eight specific amendments, each focusing on problem areas they sought to remedy. By articulating in general terms protections in those areas deemed most pressing, they provided a rough outline of rights and duties, *and then* came the most important amendment—the Ninth.

---

[19] Pennsylvania representative James Wilson, quoted in Sanders, *Ninth Life* (1994) 765

[20] To quote James Iredell, who became a Justice of the U.S. Supreme Court: "[I]t would be not only useless, but dangerous, to enumerate a number of rights which are not intended to be given up; because it would be implying, in the strongest manner, that every right not included in the exception might be impaired by the government without usurpation; and it would be impossible to enumerate every one. Let anyone make what collection or enumeration of rights he pleases, I will immediately mention twenty or thirty more rights not contained in it." Barnett, *The Ninth Amendment: It Means What It Says* (2006) 28

[21] Alexander Hamilton's argument in The Federalist is well-known: "I . . . affirm that bills of rights, in the sense and in the extent in which they are contended for, are not only unnecessary in the proposed Constitution but would even be dangerous. They would contain various exceptions to powers which are not granted; and on this very account, would afford a colorable pretext to claim more than were granted. For why declare that things shall not be done which there is no power to do? Why for instance, should it be said, that the liberty of press shall not be restrained, when no power is given by which restrictions may be imposed? I will not contend that such a provision would confer a regulating power; but it is evident that it would furnish, to men disposed to usurp, a plausible pretence for claiming that power." The Federalist No. 84 in MADISON, HAMILTON & JAY, *THE FEDERALIST PAPERS* (2010) 329; See also McAffee, *The Original Meaning of the Ninth Amendment* (1990); Sanders, *Ninth Life* (1994); Barnett, *The Ninth Amendment: It Means What It Says* (2006)

When the founders wanted a mechanism to ensure the protection of natural rights, the Ninth Amendment became the solution.[22] As this Amendment says: "The enumeration in the Constitution, of certain rights, shall not be construed to deny or disparage others retained by the people."

No doubt, then, this is the amendment that to the greatest extent protects first principles.[23] As seen from the perspective of principled law it is the one that carries the greatest weight, for while the first eight amendments were to guard against obvious threats, this amendment was designed to cover all possible rights-violations.[24] The Ninth Amendment was unanimously decided, and while the rest of the Bill of Rights resulted from a compromise in the debates, the Ninth Amendment did not.[25] To the founders its importance was self-evident, and their only concern was that it would fail to hold the forces of despotism at bay.[26] They were well aware that sinister forces were bent on undermining the American experiment and their foremost concern was to prevent the new government of falling prey to the factions that had enslaved the people of Europe.[27] They were no less naïve about the corruptibility of their own

---

[22] Barnett, *The Ninth Amendment: It Means What It Says* (2006); Barnett, *The Golden Mean Between Kurt & Dan: A Moderate Reading of the Ninth Amendment* (2008)

[23] Tribe & Dorf, *Levels of Generality in the Definition of Rights* (1990) 1100-1001 ("Ninth Amendment . . . affirmatively acts as a presumption in favor of generalizing at higher levels of abstraction.")

[24] A majority of the Ninth Amendment scholars have concluded that these unenumerated rights were no less important than those enumerated. See Barnett, *The Ninth Amendment: It Means What It Says* (2006) 13-14 ("the purpose of the Ninth Amendment was to ensure the equal protection of unenumerated individual natural rights on a par with those individual natural rights that came to be listed "for greater caution" in the Bill of Rights."); Richards, *Liberalism, Public Morality, and Constitutional Law* (1988); Sanders, *Ninth Life* (1994); Niles, *Ninth Amendment Adjudication* (2000); Sweet & Harris, *Moral and Constitutional Considerations in Support of the Decriminalization of Drugs*, in FISH (ED.), *HOW TO LEGALIZE DRUGS* (1998); Grey, *The Uses of an Unwritten Constitution* (1988); Sherry, *The Ninth Amendment: Righting an Unwritten Constitution* (1988); Solum, *Originalism and the Unwritten Constitution* (2013)

[25] Sanders, *Ninth Life: An Interpretive Theory of the Ninth Amendment* (1994) 789

[26] Barnett, *The Ninth Amendment: It Means What It Says* (2006) 48-50

[27] Many founders were conspiracy theorists. They were convinced that there was a monstrous conspiracy afoot to subvert the American project and the liberty of the people. Jefferson, for instance, believed that there was "a deliberate and systemical plan of reducing us to slavery,"

government,[28] and the powers that ruled Europe rightly feared the American experiment. It was (and probably remains) humanity's most successful attempt at controlling the oppressive tendencies inherent in the NC State, and the founders recognized that the success of the American project depended on the ability to protect the Constitution against those "violent and oppressive factions which embitter the blessings of liberty."[29]

The Ninth Amendment was of principal importance as a bulwark against these factions. Hence, to deny the Ninth Amendment its rightful position as a central tenet of the U.S Constitution would not only degrade it to the status of a NC document, but it would pave the way for tyranny.

Perhaps, then, it should come as no surprise that this is what the U.S. Supreme Court has done. As we shall see, this Amendment has generally been avoided altogether on the excuse that it is too vague and open-ended to work with, but it is just as likely that the Court's disdain can be ascribed to political priorities rather than mere ignorance. The dynamics that define NC systems dictate that those who govern will construe laws and constitutions most favorably for increasing their own powers and as we saw in part one, there will be a tremendous pressure on the individual to conform to the expectations of the status quo. Hence, as the Court consistently has downgraded all FC aspects of the Constitution to NC status, only the most naïve would outright deny the possibility of this dynamic at play. After all, to FC scholars the meaning of the Ninth Amendment is easy to deduce, and it is no more vague or open-ended than it must be to do the job that the founders intended.

We must never forget that the thinking behind our constitutional order was simple. The idea was, as far as possible, to empower the individual and to restrict government, and with that in mind the content of the Ninth Amendment should be less elusive. It simply means what it says, and it is there to make sure that the proponents of state power have

---

(MCDONALD, *NOVUS ORDO SECLORUM,* 78) and Washington was no less convinced that the British were "endeavoring by every piece of art and despotism to fix the shackles of slavery upon us." (Ibid.) This belief in conspiracies did not end with the revolution.

[28] As Samuel Osgood wrote to John Adams "Our danger lies in this—That . . . the aristo-cratical influence, which predominates in more than a Major part of the United States will finally establish an arbitrary Government in the United States." Ibid.171

[29] Madison in THE FEDERALIST PAPERS (2010) at 176. See also Madison, *the Federalist no. 14* Ibid; BAILYN, *THE IDEOLOGICAL ORIGINS OF THE AMERICAN REVOLUTION* (1967) 56-69

no fig leaf behind which to hide authoritarian ambitions. Put in its proper frame therefore its implications (at the very least for criminal policy) are clear and as a general conception of the rights it reserves, we can say that in all those areas in which the state cannot claim, justify, and prove that an infringement on our personal freedom is *absolutely necessary* for the protection of society, the state shall refrain from such interference—and this Amendment protects the activity, *whatever* it is.

Now, it is in the nature of things that NC individuals are burdened with an authoritarian bent. As we have seen, they will either have an urge to rule others or to be ruled by others, and so they have great difficulty accepting this premise. This, most likely, is the reason why the Ninth Amendment has been put to sleep by the Supreme Court. The large majority of Ninth Amendment scholars, however, are FC individuals and to them this interpretation is uncontroversial.[30] There is agreement among these scholars that the framers understood the unenumerated rights referred to in the Ninth to be fundamental rights,[31] and that they devised not only the Ninth but also the Tenth Amendment[32] to bar against undue infringement on individual liberty.[33] They see these amendments as two

---

[30] Niles, *Ninth Amendment Adjudication:* (2000) 122 ("The available information concerning the reason for its proposal and passage indicates that the Ninth Amendment is about the right to personal freedom and autonomy. Ninth Amendment rights are rights to act freely to the extent that the actions do not harm others or the society as a whole. And they are rights to be free from the illegitimate expression of governmental power that seeks to restrict personal freedom for any reason other than the protection of the public good."); Sweet & Harris, *Moral and Constitutional Considerations in Support of the Decriminalization of Drugs*, in. FISH (ED.), *HOW TO LEGALIZE DRUGS* (1998) 454 ("Those interpretations that support the conclusion that the Ninth Amendment was intended by the Framers to be given substantive effect as a repository of unenumerated but identifiable rights that are justiciable in federal courts against both state and federal governments seems to us to be the most consistent with the historical evidence surrounding the adoption of the amendment and the most appropriate in securing the overall coherence of the constitutional scheme.")

[31] Ibid. 453

[32] The Tenth Amendment declares: "The powers not delegated to the United States by the Constitution, nor prohibited by it to the states, are reserved to the States respectively, or to the people."

[33] The Bill of rights, as Professors Lash and Barnett have observed, can be seen as a twofold strategy for controlling the expansion of government. The primary strategy was to declare the principle of limited (enumerated) government power, and the secondary strategy was to control the interpretation of this enumerated power. In other words, by drafting the Bill of Rights the framers did what they could to keep the government from unduly interfering with our lives, and the Ninth and the Tenth Amendments were the mechanisms that they relied on to accomplish this feat. Barnett, *The Ninth Amendment: It Means What It Says* (2006) 42-46; Lash, *The Lost History of the Ninth Amendment* (2004) 25-27

parts of a greater whole, the former reserving rights and the latter limiting powers.[34]

This greater whole is the background presumption of a right to liberty. Indeed, as seen from the FC perspective these amendments are but two sides on the same coin, and as Barnett has noted:

> "Going back to the 18th century, there is a mode of interpretation that properly takes the presumption of liberty into account. According to it, constitutional enactments that empower the government are to be narrowly construed when they potentially encroach on the liberty rights of individuals, while they are to be broadly construed when they protect the liberty rights of individuals. As St. George Tucker, a leading constitutional scholar at the time of the founding, said when he discussed the interpretive connotation of the Ninth and Tenth Amendments: 'every power which concerns the right of the citizen, must be construed strictly, where it may operate to infringe or impair his liberty; and liberally, and for his benefit, where it may operate to his security and happiness.'"[35]

Unless we are to reject everything the founders stood for, and unless our purpose is to deny the American people their unalienable rights, we must accept this constitutional construction. The Ninth dictates that in *absolutely all* areas of activity the individual has a right to do with his life, liberty, and property as he wills, unless sufficiently weighty social considerations justify a limit to his freedoms.[36] This means that there must be principled limitation to the police power. For a law to validly infringe

---

[34] "A paramount concern for the Framers was that an imperfect enumeration in a bill of rights would endanger unenumerated substantive rights. Thus, the Ninth and Tenth Amendments, the former reserving rights and the latter limiting powers, were specifically designed to protect fundamental substantive rights of the individual by explicitly limiting the government's powers." Sweet & Harris, *Moral and Constitutional Considerations in Support of the Decriminalization of Drugs*, in FISH (ED.), *HOW TO LEGALIZE DRUGS* (1998) 453

[35] Barnett, *Constitutional Clichés* (2008) 498; See also Bilionis, *On the Significance of Constitutional Spirit* (1992) 1824 ("Keeping faith with the constitutional spirit means interpreting individual rights liberally and enforcing them unflinchingly.")

[36] "The available information concerning the reason for its proposal and passage indicates that the Ninth Amendment is about the right to personal freedom and autonomy. Ninth Amendment rights are rights to act freely to the extent that the actions do not harm others or the society as a whole. And they are rights to be free from the illegitimate expression of governmental power that seeks to restrict personal freedom for any reason other than the protection of the public good." Niles, *Ninth Amendment Adjudication* (2000) 122

our liberty it must be neither arbitrary, disproportional nor discriminatory. It must represent a proper balancing of the interests of the individual and society, and as Barnett reminds us:

> "A conception of the police power that is consistent with this principle would have the following components: (1) a prohibition of an act is proper when the act violates the rights of others (e.g., murder, rape, robbery, theft, trespass)—because such an act wrongfully violates the rights of another person, it is not properly called a 'liberty'; (2) a regulation of liberty is proper when it is necessary to protect the rights of others from the risk of violation—for example, health and safety laws; and (3) to establish that a regulation of liberty is 'necessary' would require the government to show some degree of fit between means and ends and that the measure is not simply a pretext for restricting the exercise of liberties of which the legislature disapproves.
>
> This approach to protecting liberty generally resembles how courts now protect the enumerated natural rights of speech, press, and assembly. The prohibition of wrongful acts, such as fraud, defamation or trespass are constitutional notwithstanding that the acts being prohibited are speech or assembly. Regulations of rightful exercises of speech or assembly in the form of rules governing "time, place, and manner" are proper insofar as there is an appropriate fit between means and ends, they do not place an undue burden on the exercise of these rights, and they are not pretexts for prohibiting speech of which the government disapproves."[37]

In other words, to find out whether an activity can be properly prohibited, it does not matter if it is an enumerated or unenumerated right. In all cases the law must conform to certain criteria of reasonableness, and these criteria are well-known to constitutional lawyers.

Now, originally, the Ninth Amendment (like the rest of the U.S. Constitution) applied only to the federal government. It was only with the passage of the Fourteenth Amendment in 1868 that the federal government obtained jurisdiction to protect the people from rights violations by state governments and this amendment is of great

---

[37] Barnett, *Scrutiny Land* (2008) 1499

significance when it comes to the U.S. Constitution fulfilling its role as a FC document. As it held in part: "No State shall make or enforce any law which shall abridge the privileges and immunities of citizens of the United States; nor shall any State deprive any person of life, liberty, or property, without due process of law; nor deny to any person within its jurisdiction the equal protection of the laws."

This Amendment came into being shortly after the Civil War and its ratification was obligatory before the Confederate States were allowed to rejoin the Union. In the period of the Founding slavery had been so deeply embedded in the social fabric that it proved impossible to write it out of the Constitution. It was this fateful compromise that resulted in the Civil War, but with this amendment Congress redeemed itself and the Constitution officially came to recognize the truth that the Declaration of Independence nearly a century before had deemed "self-evident." America, however, was still being run by racist white men, and this Amendment alone could not bridge theory and practice. With the Slaughter-House Cases, in what scholars have called the "the sorriest opinion ever written,"[38] the Supreme Court effectively reduced it to something more tolerable to the men in charge, but we are here concerned with its true meaning and as for its Equal Protection and Due Process Clauses FC scholars and justices agree that they codified a natural law version of these concepts.[39] As to the Privileges and Immunities Clause,

---

[38] BLACK, *A NEW BIRTH FOR FREEDOM* (1999) 39. In 1873 the Court effectively nullifies the Privileges or Immunities Clause (and what President Lincoln had called "a new birth of freedom") when it held that "nothing was set up, or added, or created or even newly recognized by the Fourteenth Amendment's 'privileges and immunities' clause." FC scholars recognize this as an act of unfathomable mischief, as its framers intended "the Privilege or Immunities Clause . . . to be the Amendment's major source for constitutional protection of both civil liberty and civil equality." Balkin, *Abortion and Original Meaning* (2007) 317. See also Balkin at 313 ("The Slaughter-House Cases severely limited the Privileges or Immunities Clause, mangled the constitutional text and caused enormous mischief in subsequent years."); Tribe, *On Reading the Constitution* (1986) 55 ("The history makes quite clear that the 'privileges or immunities' of United States citizenship were not meant to be limited to rights bearing peculiarly on one's relationship to the national government. They were supposed to refer to some set of fundamental human rights, and we still have to decide what those are."); TRIBE, *AMERICAN CONSTITUTIONAL LAW*, §7-2, 548-53

[39] As John Bingham, the principal author of Section One of the Fourteenth Amendment, said: "Your Constitution provides that no man, no matter what his color, no matter beneath what sky he may have been born, no matter in what disastrous conflict or by what tyrannical hand his liberty may have been cloven down, no matter how poor, no matter how friendless, no matter how ignorant, shall be deprived of life or liberty or property without due process of law—law in its highest sense, that law which is the perfection of human reason, and which is impartial, equal, exact justice; that justice which requires that every man shall have his right; that justice

they also agree that its original meaning "included [not only] the same natural rights retained by the people to which the Ninth Amendment referred, but also the additional enumerated rights contained in the Bill of Rights,"[40] and that "[w]hen the Privileges or Immunities Clause of the Fourteenth Amendment is combined with the Ninth, the unenumerated liberty rights retained by the people were expressly protected against infringement by both federal and state governments."[41]

The Fourteenth Amendment, then, was a giant step forward for the U.S. Constitution. The Amendment completed the Constitution as a FC document by making it applicable to the states—and so, in theory at least, everything was as it should be. The people now had a fully formed mechanism that could "secure the Blessings of Liberty." First, the Constitution's Preamble and Article One set out the perimeters of a limited government, establishing that its power to infringe natural rights was restricted to those laws which were "necessary and proper"[42] to "promote the general Welfare." Second, the Constitution being a "logical extension of the Declaration of Independence,"[43] one that "completed and perfected the revolution,"[44] there was no doubt as to the natural rights principles and values it embodied. Third, the Ninth Amendment were there to remind the government that the enumeration of certain rights should not be construed to "deny or disparage" all the other natural rights retained by the people. Fourth, the background presumption of liberty made it clear that when interpreting the Constitution "all language must be construed 'strictly' in favor of natural rights."[45] And fifth, if the people

---

which is the highest duty of nations as it is the imperishable attribute of the God of nations." Williams, *The One and Only Substantive Due Process Clause* (2010) 480; See also Thomas, *Toward a Plain Reading of the Constitution* (1987); O'Scannlain, *The Natural Law in the American Tradition* (2011); Sabo, *The Higher Law Background of the Constitution* (2009); GERBER, *TO SECURE THESE RIGHTS* (1995) 170

[40] Barnett, *Is the Constitution Libertarian?* (2008) 17

[41] Ibid. 17. See also CURTIS, *NO STATE SHALL ABRIDGE: THE FOURTEENTH AMENDMENT AND THE BILL OF RIGHTS* (1986); BARNETT, *RESTORING THE LOST CONSTITUTION* (2014); BLACK, *A NEW BIRTH FOR FREEDOM* (1999)

[42] For the meaning of this clause, see Barnett, *The Original Meaning of the Necessary and Proper Clause* (2003)

[43] GERBER, *TO SECURE THESE RIGHTS* (1995) 3

[44] McDONALD, *NOVUS ORDO SECLORUM* (1985) 282

[45] Barnett, *The Misconceived Assumption about Constitutional Assumption*s (2008) 36

had any grievances, they were guaranteed "due process of law" and "the equal protection of the laws" by the Fifth and the Fourteenth Amendment.

"Due process of law" means that the government must treat its citizens according to established procedures (that it must abide by the rule of law), and affirms that the law must conform to the principles of natural law—the higher law.[46] This means that the law shall not be "unreasonable, arbitrary or capricious, and that the means selected shall have a real and substantial relation to the object sought to be attained,"[47] which would be the protection of the general welfare. As Justice Harlan put it, due process is the result of a balance between "respect for the liberty of the individual" and "the demands of organized society."[48]

In essence, then, the due process doctrine can be viewed as a vehicle for protecting personal autonomy, and this can only be done by ensuring that the citizens are provided an effective remedy whenever they contest the validity of a law. The doctrine of judicial review is there to provide this remedy, and as this has been accepted as a basic ingredient of the rule of law since the Founding[49] the liberties of the American people should have been secure—provided that constitutional construction was left to competent individuals.

---

[46] For more on due process, see Sanders, *Ninth Life* (1994); Balkin, *Abortion and Original Meaning* (2007); Barnett, *The Original Meaning of the Judicial Power* (2003)

[47] *Nebbia v. New York*, 291 U.S. 502 (1934) 525

[48] *Poe v. Ullman*, 367 U.S. 497 (1961) 542 (Harlan J., dissenting). Barnett elaborates: "A law restricting conduct is consistent with a right to liberty, therefore, if it is prohibiting wrongful acts that violate the rights of others or regulating rightful acts in such a way as to coordinate conduct or prevent the violation of rights that might accidentally occur. A law is inconsistent with liberty if it is either prohibiting rightful acts, or regulating unnecessarily or improperly. A regulation is improper when it imposes an undue burden on rightful conduct, or when its justification is merely a pretext for restricting a liberty of which others disapprove. And one way of identifying a regulation as pretextual is to assess whether the regulatory means it employs do not effectively fit its purported health and safety ends." Barnett, *Is the Constitution Libertarian?* (2008) 9

[49] Barnett, *The Original Meaning of the Judicial Power* (2003); Rubin, *Judicial Review and the Right to Resist* (2008)

5.1.2 "A Frequent Recurrence to Fundamental Principles"

As we have seen, the founders did what they could to ensure that the American legal system was one of principled law. The Constitution may have been a compromise between diverse factions and interests but its principles were clear. They were firmly established at the heart of the Constitution. They were its true lifeblood and the founders expected them to guide America forward on its path towards Utopia. The framers, for instance, may have compromised on slavery, but they knew very well that its very existence undermined the legitimacy of the American project. Many of them were haunted by this compromise but assumed that the principles embodied in the Constitution would work on the social fabric until a more just order could be established. As President Lincoln said:

> "[The founders] did not mean to assert the obvious untruth, that all men were then actually enjoying equality, nor yet, that they were about to confer it immediately upon them. In fact they had no power to confer such a boon. They meant simply to declare the right, so that the enforcement of it might follow as circumstances should permit. They meant to set up a standard maxim for free society, which could be familiar to all, and revered by all, constantly looked to, constantly labored for, and even though never perfectly attained, constantly approximated, and thereby constantly spreading and deepening its influence and augmenting the happiness and value of life to all people of all colors everywhere."[50]

Remember that FC individuals, having the ability to connect with the light of first principles, also have the ability to see their day and age in a historical context. They are the frontrunners, the avant-garde of humanity, and this is both a blessing and a curse. The blessing is that they have a sense of direction (and a sense of connection) that others do not. They know that the principles and values that follow from the Wholeness perspective will become more integrated into the social fabric as humanity matures and that they are privileged to be in a position to aid in

---

[50] Gerber, *Liberal Originalism* (2014) 10

this process. It is a curse, however, in the sense that it is tiresome work. They are born into a society where the majority has little regard or understanding for the bigger picture, where most are happy to embrace collectively shared prejudices, and where people with a vested interest in the status quo will forcefully oppose them.

To those who do not suffer fools gladly this is frustrating, for on the one hand they see how humanity's problems can be solved easily and on the other they see the horrors of the status quo like no others. They see through the lies and the deceit that NC individuals embrace, they see the reality of oppression and injustice where others fail to see anything wrong, and they must learn to be infinitely patient with their fellow men and women.

To the extent the founders were FC individuals, they were in this position. Some, like Hamilton and Washington, were more content to play the game of politics with the expectation that the greater good would prevail, while others, like Jefferson and Paine, had a harder time accepting the status quo.[51] Even so, the distance between theory and practice was obvious to them all (or else they would not have been FC individuals), and it was for this reason that they emphasized the importance of going back to first principles in times of controversy.

First of all, this was the only way America could fulfill its destiny. The idea of America was that of progress, of gradually overcoming challenges so that a more perfect world could emerge. As the Constitution proclaimed, its purpose was to "form a more perfect Union," and this was the essence of the American project; to keep adjusting whatever imbalance remained in the relationship between the individual and the state in order for us to enjoy progressively greater blessings of liberty. First principles were the guiding lights of this process. They were the starry heavens under which the great ship of America would stake out its course, and only by a frequent return to these principles could its

---

[51] It was for this reason that Thomas Paine bitterly attacked Washington for compromising the ideals of the American Revolution and it was also for this reason that Jefferson had a falling out with Hamilton. Powerful factions wanted some sort of aristocracy, monarchy, or hereditary rule established, and when Jefferson returned from France to become Secretary of State in 1790, he found that the corruption of government was already underway. He believed Hamilton's financial system was under the control of sinister forces and that it functioned "as a machine for the corruption of the legislature." JEFFERSON, *THE ANAS* (Online book) 271

visionaries measure and recalibrate a distance between theory and practice.

Secondly, not only would it advance the progress of society from NC to FC status; it would bar against the corrupting dynamics inherent in NC societies. To the extent that the founders represented FC values they were of invaluable service to their country, but there were only so much a few good men could do. The great majority of their contemporaries being NC individuals, it was inevitable that self-serving factions would come to control the machinery of government and the founders feared this like nothing else. They saw this dynamic at play, and they knew that if anything could keep these factions from destroying the foundations of America it was the principles embodied in the Declaration of Independence and the Constitution. Thus, as William Hooper, one of North Virginia's delegates to the Continental Congress in Philadelphia, reminded his fellow delegates, it was "necessary that recurrence should often be had to original principles to prevent those evils which in a course of years must creep in and vitiate every human institution."[52]

Hooper was not the only voice in this choir. To the extent that the framers were FC individuals, they knew that as time progressed, first principles would be the only check on agents of tyranny, and their legacy is seen in at least eleven state constitutions which warned that "no free government, nor the blessings of liberty, can be preserved to any people, but by . . . frequent recurrence to fundamental principles."[53]

Had the courts stood by these principles they would have avoided many an embarrassment over the years. They would also have provided the people with the only reliable means of keeping the American experiment on that path staked out by the Founding Fathers, and this, I believe, is why Justice Thomas urged the American people "to be ever vigilant in reminding us—me and everyone else who has the privilege of serving our nation through public office—of the principles of our founding and how they apply to the controversies of our time."[54]

---

[52] Bilionis, *On the Significance of Constitutional Spirit* (1992) 1811

[53] Article 1, section 35 of the North Carolina Constitution. (completed on September 28, 1776). See Bilionis, *On the Significance of Constitutional Spirit* (1992) 1810-11; see also Snure, *A Frequent Recurrence to Fundamental Principles* (1992)

[54] Gerber, *Liberal Originalism* (2014) 14

However, neither the people nor the courts have given this issue much attention. It has been hundreds of years, and they have consistently ignored the light of first principles, letting government roam free. For this reason, the system of law became increasingly corrupted, and we shall now trace this process.

6

THE CORRUPTION OF AMERICA

"We are walking around in the spaces of a nation which we believe to guarantee 'liberty and justice for all,' as a matter of constitutional law. But outside the realms of free expression and religion . . . our original constitutional text, even including the Bill of Rights, protects only a few limited and special substantive human rights. That is not a slight variation on the principles of the Declaration of Independence, but very nearly antipodal to them."[55]

—Charles L. Black—

AS SEEN THE CONSTITUTION was a FC document. The founders' moral theory, conception of rights, consent theory and doctrine of revolution were all purebred FC thinking, and to a large extent the Declaration of Independence, the state constitutions, and the U.S. Constitution came into being as a reflection of the ideals and values expounded by this era. I say, "to a large extent", as Americans had no other choice. They were under the tyranny of a king whose unjust demands claimed an ever-increasing toll, and the only way they could be free from this burden was by applying FC reasoning. This was the key to their liberty. And this being the case, it is small wonder that it was an auspicious time for such elevated reasoning. As intellectual elites, politicians, and regular citizens all had a vested interest in achieving sovereignty, the circumstances would breed it forth, but as their aims were achieved a different dynamic began—one that would prove the downfall of the founders' project.

---

[55] BLACK, *A NEW BIRTH FOR FREEDOM* (1999) 90

Even though the leading framers, no doubt, believed in their vision and above all sought to ensure its success, society did not go from NC to FC status overnight. When dealing with social dynamics there are no clean breaks; it is just a slow progression towards either end, and so the new government was at the basic level (i.e. the psychological) not much better than before the revolution. The old rule may have been deposed and a FC foundation put in its place. But as the American psyche did not go from NC to FC status in the same period much was still the same—and after the old rule was gone, new rulers emerged victorious.

These new rulers had little use of FC reasoning. In fact, to the extent they were more concerned with protecting their own ambitions than promoting justice, the founder's system of law would be their biggest problem. And so, to successfully play their game of power-politics, they had to abolish the very foundation upon which America was created.

So it was that a system of NC law emerged. Individuals will interpret the Constitution according to their own nature. And while FC individuals will concentrate on the principles and values it intended to protect, NC individuals will interpret it according to their own dispositions. Thus, after the new government was constituted, less noble, more "practical" concerns came into play. To the extent that the American psyche conformed to NC standards, there would be a social dynamic which ensured that the most self-serving, cunning, and ruthless individuals would rise to positions of power and these people had no interest in FC values. Quite the contrary; to whatever extent the ideal of self-governing, responsible, and independent individuals materialized, it would mean the death of the old hierarchical, dominance-oriented way of government, and this is not what NC rulers want. Instead, what they want is the power to shape society according to their own calculations of self-interest. Their goal will always be a strong government that caters to their ambitions, one that proves more responsive to their will than FC ideals, and the new rulers of America were no different. The sum of their perceived self-interest, ambition and avarice therefore provided for a bureaucratic thrust which ensured that the government parted ways with the principles and ideals on which it was founded.

As the framers had noted, this process was well underway at the time of the Founding and by the beginning of the 20th century the American project had been properly derailed. The ruling elites now had complete control of the political process and if the United States had ever been a government of the people, by the people, for the people this clearly was no longer the case. Instead, the United States had become something out of the founders' worst nightmares; an Orwellian state-project that paid homage to FC ideals while secretly doing everything it could to undermine first principles. The courts would prove willing instruments in this process. Siding with the rulers, they would ignore the founders' call for a frequent recurrence to first principles, and so a jurisprudence evolved that undermined the ideals of the Founding.

6.2 THE INFLUENCE OF FACTIONS AND IGNORANCE

Now, while I have pointed out the obvious as to the inherent dynamics of NC societies, this summary may be troubling to some. We all know that the founders were extremely worried about the influence of those forces that sought to "separate the people from their government,"[56] but we tend to forget or deny that they are equally present in our day and age.[57]

This "forgetfulness" is psychologically expedient, as it is one of those defense mechanisms that make life much more bearable. Just like some people, in fear of having to face reality, will ignore all symptoms that there is a cancerous substance growing inside their body, so others will disregard the influence of these forces upon our body of law. However, if we are to make sense of the distance between theory and practice, we must be open to the possibility that these factions did not simply wither away after the Founding. Instead, it would be sensible to assume that such factions, since those days, to the best of their ability have tried to bend

---

[56] George Washington warned against a secret society group adhering to "the diabolical tenets of the Illuminati" that wished "to separate the people from their government" in a letter to Reverend George Washington Snyder, October 24, 1798

[57] For those who are inclined to deny that such factions still exist I refer to my former book, REASON IS, where I trace their influence on the American social fabric since the Founding. See also MIKALSEN, HUMAN RISING (2020)

the fabric of American justice to their own ends, and a student of power politics will have to conclude that they have been rather successful.

At the very least, books have been written by whistleblowers who are familiar with these factions.[58] Their stories speak for themselves as to the disturbing reality behind the façade. And when it comes to the distance between theory and practice, the influence of these factions on the machinery of state can hardly be overestimated. The present state of power-political rivalries is a living testimony to their enduring presence—and so is the zeal with which all governments have fought the progress of human rights law. Our leaders may solemnly declare their commitment to human rights in speeches at the UN and elsewhere, but reality betrays a different picture.

When dealing with NC dynamics power never abdicates willingly. Only a collective increase in FC traits can arrest the ambitions of the individuals in charge, and as nothing threatens the state's hegemony of power more than human rights law, they have effectively kept it at bay. Internationally, we saw how this was done in the aftermath of the Second World War. Before and during the war Western leaders used human rights rhetoric for mobilization of public opinion and after the war the enthusiasm for human rights was so great that a series of human rights initiatives were orchestrated by NGOs. Had things been different—i.e., had humanity matured to the point where a system of FC law could be accepted by government leaders—the world would have been a very different place. Our rulers, however, had no intention of holding themselves accountable for human rights violations. They therefore made

---

[58] See for instance LINDAUER, *EXTREME PREJUDICE* (2010); DECAMP, *THE FRANKLIN COVER-UP* (1992); GRITZ, *A NATION BETRAYED* (1989); PROUTY, *THE SECRET TEAM* (2008); MENASHE, *PROFITS OF WAR* (1998); REED & CUMMINGS, *COMPROMISED* (1994); MARTIN, *THE CONSPIRATORS* (2002); PERKINS, *CONFESSIONS OF AN ECONOMIC HITMAN* (2004); O'BRIEN, *TRANCE-FORMATION OF AMERICA* (1995). For investigations into behind-the-scenes politics: MIKALSEN, *REASON IS* (2014); STICH, *DEFRAUDING AMERICA* (1988); STILL, *THE NEW WORLD ORDER* (1990); SUTTON, *AMERICA'S SECRET ESTABLISHMENT* (1986); COLBY, *DU PONT DYNASTY* (1984); GRIFFIN, *THE CREATURE FROM JEKYLL ISLAND* (2002); RUSSELL, *DRUG WAR* (2000); MAZUR, *THE INFILTRATOR* (2009); KWITNY, *THE CRIMES OF PATRIOTS* (1987); RUPPERT, *CROSSING THE RUBICON* (2004); BENNETT, *SHELL GAME* (2013); TARPLEY, *911 SYNTHETIC TERROR* (2007) STONE, *THE MAN WHO KILLED KENNEDY* (2013); VENTURA, *THEY KILLED OUR PRESIDENT* (2013)

sure that the UN human rights conventions were given no legal status and no system for enforceability.[59]

Domestically, something similar took place in the period after the Founding, as the new rulers had no intention of abiding by the FC standard. Instead, the Constitution would have to be interpreted in ways that appealed to those in power and as a result its most important parts had to go. Looking back, we see that the U.S. Supreme Court has been a most willing servant of power in this process, gradually ensuring that the Constitution became sufficiently void of protective clauses to allow for a return to tyranny.[60] As we shall see, by relying on purebred NC reasoning, the justices at the Supreme Court have done to America what no British king could successfully do; they have effectively stripped its people of all but a handful of rights, they have subjected Americans to the tyranny of arbitrary rule, and tens of millions of Americans have suffered terribly for it.[61]

It would be extremely naïve to discount or deny the influence of behind-the-scenes politics. We have just seen that the first American President warned about the influence of a secret society that wished "to separate the people from their government," and that other founders

---

[59] Together with a handful of countries Americans do not want to be associated with, the U.S. has been at the forefront of denying and disparaging human rights worldwide. It is quite a feat of social engineering—a bureaucratic marvel of Orwellian scope—that the U.S. state apparatus has been able to do this while at the same time retaining its reputation as a defender of those very rights. See NORMAND & ZAIDI, *HUMAN RIGHTS AT THE UN* (2008)

[60] Professor Barnett has described this process: "[Covering] one constitutional clause after another, [I found that] passages that sounded great to me were drained by the Court of their obviously power-containing meanings. First was the Necessary and Proper Clause in *McCulloch v. Maryland* (1819), then the Commerce Clause (a bit) in *Gibbons v. Ogden* (1824), then the Privileges or Immunities Clause of the Fourteenth Amendment in the *Slaughter-House Cases* (1873), then the Commerce Clause (this time in earnest) in *Wickard v. Filburn* (1942), and the Ninth Amendment in *United Public Workers v. Mitchell* (1947). Nor were these landmark decisions isolated cases. In countless other opinions, the Supreme Court justices affirmed they meant it when they said the Constitution did not mean what it apparently said." BARNETT, *RESTORING THE LOST CONSTITUTION* (2014) ix

[61] Jefferson noted this process at work already in his lifetime: "At the establishment of our constitutions, the judiciary bodies were supposed to be the most helpless and harmless members of the government. Experience, however, soon showed in what way they were to become the most dangerous; that the insufficiency of the means provided for their removal gave them a freehold and irresponsibility in office; that their decisions, seeming to concern individual suitors only, pass silent and unheeded by the public at large; that these decisions, nevertheless, become law by precedent, sapping, by little and little, the foundations of the constitution, and working its change by construction, before any one has perceived that that invisible and helpless worm has been busily employed in consuming its substance." Thomas Jefferson, letter to Monsieur A. Coray, Oct 31, 1823

noted similar concerns.[62] Modern people tend to scoff at such notions. Even so, according to the Knights Templar Order—a secret society grouping which presided over the English legal system at the time of the Magna Carta:

> "The real problem, and the ultimate root cause of corruption of the legal system, is the practice of infiltration and fraternal control by secret societies from the 15th century, whose agendas became even more aggressive from the 18th century, and escalated to being shamelessly obvious by the 21st century. Whenever enough of their members occupy enough key positions to control the legal profession, their immoral egotistical arrogance makes them certain they can get away with flagrant violations of the Rule of Law."[63]

The Templars describe Masonic influence as the source of the problem. According to them, the top levels of Freemasonry are "infiltrated by another secret society of 'elites' with highly negative agendas against humanity."[64] While most Masons remain unaware of this, Washington, who himself was a Mason, must have known, as the group named by the Knights Templar is the same group as that was specifically named by Washington— the Illuminati. As most historians believe that this group was dissolved at the end of the 18th century, many people will reject this notion. However, the Knights Templar fraternity, which holds the same legal status as the Vatican State, claims to be fighting the undue influence of this secret society to ensure that our system of law is upgraded to FC status.[65]

It is beyond the scope of this book to pursue the matter in any academic fashion. But leaving aside the question of whether the Masonic Order, at the top level, has been infiltrated by a group with evil intentions, it is indisputable that we, the past 200 years, have witnessed the systematic dismantling of the founders' system of law—and this has happened on the Masons' watch.[66]

---

[62] *Supra*, notes 27 & 56

[63] http://knightsofsolomon.org/templar-magna-carta/

[64] Ibid.

[65] See their website at http://knightstemplarorder.org

[66] The European system of law has been under Masonic control for more than 300 years and by the 1830s the same was true for the American system of law. See Ibid; FINNEY, *THE CHARACTER, CLAIMS, AND PRACTICAL WORKINGS OF FREEMASONRY* (1998); FISHER, *BEHIND THE LODGE DOOR* (1989); ANKERBERG & WELDON, *THE SECRET TEACHINGS OF THE MASONIC LODGE* (1990); SCHNOEBELEN, *MASONRY: BEYOND THE LIGHT* (1991)

However, while the influence of secret societies is beyond dispute, the manipulations of factions are not the only reason why the American legal system has failed to represent the ideal of justice. Far from it. Its institutions, after all, are filled with mere mortals and like other mortals they tend to be moved by passion. Indeed, in the NC society this is the trait that most fully defines human interaction—and it is for this reason that the system of justice has failed to perfect a canon of law worthy of its name.

We have already seen the power of situational factors on our minds. It is difficult to overcome the group-mind and the fact that we are a NC society explains why a majority, even in scholarly circles, have no idea that the Constitution is a FC document, enacted to ensure a reign of first principles. Living in a NC society, the system is rigged in favor of the NC version of events; and with our law schools designed to produce NC lawyers, only a few have the faculty to grasp the essence of the Constitution. As already discussed, the collective unconscious will have sufficient impact to make a majority of those who would otherwise be capable of FC reasoning submit to the status quo. As NC jurisprudence throughout the centuries has attained an aura of respectability, those who drink from the well of judicial precedent are likely to be drawn in by its seductive authority. Like a poisoned fountain it clouds lawyers' minds, muddles their vision, and confounds their logic, leaving them dazed and ill prepared to grasp the inherent contradictions of their trade. It is unfortunate, but by the time they have finished law school most have become so subdued by the pressure to conform that principled reasoning escapes them. In order to fit in they must comply with certain expectations, and in eagerness to adjust they end up too entangled in the web of jurisprudence to see its inconsistencies and inadequacies.

So it is that only a few, those who are further advanced, are able to connect the dots, see the bigger picture, and grasp its essence. Even among this percentage, however, only a few will dedicate themselves to bringing integrity to law. For reasons of convenience, most will accept the status quo and only those even further advanced at the FC-end will have the integrity to speak truth to power, standing up for FC ideals, values, and principles.

Thus, we find that for the last 200 years the discipline of law has fallen into disrepute. In a debate firmly set within the parameters of NC reasoning, the majority of scholars have become trapped by cultural indoctrination and contemporary constraints and fail to see further. This explains the absence of a viable account of criminal law. FC scholars have tried to establish principled limits to its scope, but as most of their peers are at the NC level their impact has been inconsequential. They may have been awed by "the glaring failure of penal theory as it has developed on both sides of the Atlantic;"[67] and they may have been "baffled" why so few care about the integrity of their profession.[68] But there it is. The simple answer is found in the powerful psychological effect of living in NC societies, and not until their peers grow some integrity will their discipline present itself as a respectable endeavor.

This tendency to fall in line is also why constitutional interpretation hardly evolved as a discipline for 200 years. It was left to the justices at the Court to advance the doctrines most suitable to their needs, and not until the latter half of the 20th century did serious scholarship begin. What really sparked it off was a movement of judicial conservatives in the 1980s who argued that the Supreme Court's drift towards protecting unenumerated rights was unconstitutional. In a series of cases the Court had given protection to privacy rights that were not explicitly mentioned in the Constitution and these conservatives claimed that this was an errant doctrine—a doctrine incompatible with the founders' intent.

These scholars claimed (erroneously) that the founders wanted only the enumerated rights protected and (rightly) that the Constitution had to be interpreted as originally intended. They therefore became known as Originalists. As a result of their efforts, other scholars began examining this issue and one of the pioneers was Randy Barnett. When he began researching the Ninth Amendment, he discovered that it had gone virtually unnoticed until that point in time,[69] and his studies led to one surprise after another. It did not take long to discover that the Originalists were wrong and that the founders wanted all rights equally protected. He also found "that the Ninth Amendment was inextricably linked to the other clauses that the Supreme Court had redacted from the text: the

---

[67] HUSAK, *OVERCRIMINALIZATION* (2008) 58

[68] Ibid.

[69] As he said, "so little had been written about the Ninth Amendment that I could read it *all* and almost instantly become an expert in the field." BARNETT, *RESTORING THE LOST CONSTITUTION* (2014) xii

Necessary and Proper Clause, the Commerce Clause, the Privileges and Immunities Clause, and the Tenth Amendment. They all had to go if Congress and state legislators were going to be given the discretion to pass laws 'in the public interest' unconstrained by any limits on their powers besides a few judicially favored rights."[70]

In other words, Professor Barnett discovered that the activities of the Supreme Court were part of a bigger picture, one that predictably conformed to the dynamics inherent in NC societies. In looking at this from an isolated perspective it will be impossible to say what kind of motivations the justices may have had to move the Court in this direction. However, as seen from the bigger perspective, what we can say for sure is that individuals can be counted on to interpret the Constitution according to their own inclinations—and that today's doctrines are the result of leaving interpretation to NC individuals.

[70] Ibid.

6.3 TRACING THE CORRUPTION OF LAW

"The assumption would engage itself slowly, but steadily, that the things written down were far more important as rights than the things left unmentioned. In this subtle shift we find the essential move from natural rights to positive rights, from rights grounded in the nature of human beings as 'moral agents,' to the sense rather of rights that have standing as rights because we have decided, as a people, to confer them to one another. In the age of relativism so portable and facile, so deeply absorbed that it is rarely even noticed, many people by now have made the shift to the latter understanding without being aware that they had made any shift at all. Much less are they aware that they had made a decisive moral break from the premises of the American Founders."[71]

—Hadley Arkes—

As the American society (in every other sense than in its Founding documents) remained a NC society, its system of law would primarily be formed by two forces: (1) the need of rulers to justify their ambitions and (2) the impact of the collective consciousness. The former would be a symptom of the latter, and we have discussed the impact of factions and ignorance on the body of law. It is pointless for our purposes to speculate to what extent the status quo results from one or the other, but these two forces, to a great extent, have shaped law into being. I say, "to a great extent," as being an advanced NC society, there is also the influence of FC reasoning.

In looking at the big picture, we can see that it was most influential at the time of the Founding. Law, in this period, was a very different endeavor than today and there was no "system" as we think of it. Justice had not yet become bureaucratized; there were no urban police forces; and politicians posed little treat to the people's private domain. The system was decentralized. There was no power trip to be afforded by a

---

[71] ARKES, *CONSTITUTIONAL ILLUSIONS & ANCHORING TRUTHS* (2010) 7-8

career in the criminal justice system and crime victims would themselves prosecute most criminal cases.[72]

The doctrine of judicial review was firmly in place and the people, as jurors, exercised absolute power on a case-by-case basis.[73] Natural law reasoning was the name of the game, even though most people had little understanding of FC values and principles. As others have noted, the "[t]he government [that the framers] devised was defective from the start,"[74] for when they spoke of "We the People" they excluded the majority of the population. At most, it included a narrow class of white, property holding men, and less than 20 percent of the populace had any influence on the political process.[75] By and large, these white males had little regard for the rights of blacks, women, and politically weak minorities. These groups had to fend for themselves, but by invoking constitutional principles they would advance on the path to liberation.

We must also recognize that the principles of the enlightenment were corrupted by puritan spirit. In pre-revolutionary colonial America religion was a way of life and the institutions reflected religious values. The criminal law, therefore, was primarily concerned with protecting religious and moral values and these were often opposed to those of the Enlightenment tradition.[76] This was one reason why the founders sought to separate state from church, but even though the American revolution brought profound changes in attitudes toward crime (prosecutions for various sorts of immorality nearly ceased)[77] puritanism lingered.

---

[72] For more on this, see STUNTZ, *THE COLLAPSE OF AMERICAN CRIMINAL JUSTICE* (2013)

[73] As Stuntz noted: "Jurors at the time of the Founding were not the mere lie detectors that they have since become. They were moral arbiters; their job was to decide both what the defendant did and whether his conduct merited punishment. Criminal law meant whatever jurors said it meant; their will trumped even [legal textbooks]." Ibid. 84; see also Edward Rubin, *Judicial Review and the Right to Resist* (2008) 129; MCDONALD, *NOVUS ORDO SECLORUM* (1985) 40; CONRAD, *JURY NULLIFICATION* (1998)

[74] Thurgood Marshall, *Remarks at the Annual Seminar of the San Francisco Patent and Trademark Law Association* (May 6, 1987), see also Brown-Nagin, *The Civil Rights Canon: Above and Below* (2014) 2703

[75] In the period after the founding, roughly one on six were eligible to participate in the political process and far fewer to hold public office. MCDONALD, *NOVUS ORDO SECLORUM* (1985) 162

[76] HASKINS, *LAW AND AUTHORITY IN EARLY MASSACHUSETTS* (1968)

[77] Mark J. Mahoney, *William Trolinger's Memorandum of Law on Ninth and Tenth Amendments* 97-CR-193(A) 4

Even so, decades after the Constitutional Convention, natural rights doctrine were still going strong. As late as 1827 Chief Justice Marshall held in *Ogden v. Saunders*[78] that it is not the state that gives validity and effect to a contract, but a contract that gives validity and effect to the state, and there are many examples of FC reasoning from this period. The courts would frequently trace their analysis back to first principles. Both at the state and federal level they would invalidate statutes that conflicted with unwritten rights,[79] and even Supreme Court justices would do their reasoning by the same reasoning that characterizes FC law, delineating principled limits to the police power and affirming the principle of individual sovereignty.[80]

Looking at this period, however, courts would less and less reliably apply the founders' doctrines, and they fell into the habit of reasoning from the NC perspective. As Gerber observed, by the time "the Court decided *Barron* in 1833, belief in higher law had given way to a view of the written Constitution as the sole source of fundamental principles,"[81] and positive law would become more and more detached from first principles. The presumption of liberty still held sway, as did the limits to the police power, but the state power constantly grew until the founding ideas of America amounted to naught. This shift was slow in coming. Still, it had already begun in the days of the founders and Thomas Jefferson, the author of the Declaration of Independence, commented on the drift towards the English (NC) conception of rights:

> "I join in your reprobation of our merchants, priests, and lawyers, for their adherence to England and monarchy, in preference to their own country and its Constitution. . . . With the lawyers it is a new thing. They have, in the Mother country, been generally the firmest supporters of the free principles of their constitution. But there too they have changed. I ascribe much of this to [the increasing influence of English law, especially] the wily sophistries of a Hume or a

---

[78] 25 U.S. 213 (1827) (Marshall J., dissenting)

[79] Sherry, *The Ninth Amendment: Righting an Unwritten Constitution* (1988) 1003

[80] *Chisholm v. Georgia*, 2 U.S. (2 Dall.) 419 (1793); *Calder v. Bull*, 3 U.S. (3 Dall.) 386 (1798); *Fletcher v. Peck*, 10 U.S. 87 (1810). See also Barnett, *We the People: Each and Every One* (2014); Barnett, *Who's Afraid of Unenumerated Rights* (2006); SIMON, HUMAN RIGHTS OR AMERICAN PRIVILEGES? (2007)

[81] GERBER, TO SECURE THESE RIGHTS (1995) 123

Blackstone. These two books, but especially the former, have done more towards the suppression of the liberties of man, than all the million of men in arms of Bonaparte and the millions of human lives with the sacrifice of which he will stand loaded before the judgment seat of his Maker. *I fear nothing for our liberty from the assaults of force; but I have seen and felt much, and fear more from English books, English prejudices, English manners, and the apes, the dupes, and designs among our professional crafts.*"[82]

Jefferson was not the only founder to lament the increasing influence of NC law. James Wilson, a man who ranked second only to Madison in terms of the contributions he made to the framing and ratification of the Constitution, was explicit in his criticism of English law and while he was professor at the college of Philadelphia, he gave a series of lectures on the subject of natural law and the dangers he attributed to the jurisprudence of Blackstone and Burke. There were others, including John Taylor, who in his work *Construction Construed and Constitutions Vindicated* strongly criticized the increasing use of "sovereignty" as found in Blackstonian positivism.[83] However, the tides of NC law were on the rise, and by the 1830s FC law had become a legal undercurrent, one that would sometimes surface in the opinions of judges, but usually in dissents rather than majority opinions.

Living in a NC society takes its toll, and as time progressed social dynamics would breed forth NC reasoning. Most judges being too blinded by culture to see the bigger picture, they would have to draw upon the authority of precedent rather than first principles and their analysis would be tangled a hapless mixture of FC and NC reasoning. Thus, in its pure form FC reasoning would become exceedingly rare. But in its diluted form it has remained with us to this day, providing some protection against the authoritarian tendencies inherent in the NC State. We see it in the "inherent limitations" approach of the nineteenth century,

---

[82] Letter from Jefferson to Horatio Gates Spafford, March 17, 1814, found in Barnett, *Who's Afraid of Unenumerated Rights?* (2006) 8 (emphasis mine)

[83] Tailor, *Construction Construed and Constitutions Vindicated* (1820) 25

the *Lawton* test,[84] the *Lochner* test,[85] the early alcohol cases, the substantive due process doctrine, the strict scrutiny review, as well as the Court's reasoning in more recent cases such as *Roe, Casey,* and *Lawrence.*

In short, elements of FC reasoning have been present all along, but without sufficient thrust to prevail against the tendencies inherent in NC societies. It is in the nature of things that most people will conform to the expectations of the status quo, and so NC reasoning has continued to inform US legal doctrines.

6.4 FLAWED DOCTRINES AND INCREASING POLICE POWERS

"[T]here have been powerful hydraulic pressures throughout our history that bear heavily on the Court to water down constitutional guarantees and give the police the upper hand."[86]

—Justice Douglas—

The evolving legal doctrines of America were a result of the social dynamics inherent in NC societies. When it comes to these dynamics, that there will be a totalitarian drive inherent in the state. Instead of containing its role, the government will seek an excuse to expand its mandate; instead of confining itself to punishing crime, it will go into the business of preventing crime; and instead of controlling those activities

---

[84] In *Lawton v. Steele*, 152 U.S. 133 (1884) the Supreme Court noted that a legislative "determination as to what is a proper exercise of its police powers is not final or conclusive, but is subject to the supervision of the courts" and emphasized the need to protect against governmental acts "involving an unnecessary invasion of rights" and infringement upon individual acts which are "harmless in themselves, and which might be carried on without detriment to the public interests." (Id. at 138) According to the Court, for a law to be legitimate the state must (1) show that the interests of the public require such interference; (2) that the means are reasonably necessary for the accomplishment of the purpose; and (3) that the law is not unduly oppressive upon individuals. Id. at 137

[85] The *Lochner* Court held that "In every case that comes before this court . . . the question necessarily arises: Is this a fair, reasonable and appropriate exercise of the police power of the state, or is it an unreasonable, unnecessary and arbitrary interference with the right of the individual to his personal liberty?" 198 U.S. at 56 (Peckham, J.)

[86] *Terry v. Ohio*, 392 U.S. 1 (1968) 39 (Douglas J., dissenting)

that directly threaten the rights of others, it will seek to expand the definition of harm.

This is the predictable result of living in a NC State. It will always seek to expand in scope, and as its only recognized function is to maintain the public welfare, these are obvious way to proceed. To expand its reach, the state must find an excuse, a threat from which the "social interest" must be protected, and so the ever-present threat against individual liberty will be the call to sacrifice rights for the public good.[87]

Needless to say, the evolution of law will be informed by this tendency of the state. To the extent that NC individuals are in charge, the legal system will become an instrument of class rule, as they embody exactly the same qualities that fuel the system's force of inertia. This force, after all, is nothing but the result of collective NC traits, and we shall now see how modern doctrines result from such factors.

6.4.1 THE EVOLVING POLICE POWER

In the NC society, special interest groups will be in control of the state apparatus. This includes the legal system, and so the courts will be more concerned with protecting elite interests than individual rights. To the extent that the U.S. legal system has been shaped by NC forces, we can observe this tendency in the evolution of law—and it is plain to see.[88] Indeed, as we are dealing with a system that consistently puts corporate

---

[87] In the NC State "community interest" will more likely be an aphorism for "state interest," for as Dubber reminds us: "Most often, the public is simply the dominant group in society, the ingroup. The state, however, may also come to identify itself with the public and confuse the public's welfare with the state's. The first case results in intrasocial conflict, the second in consternation among members of the (normally) dominant social group who saw the state as the extension of their community. Oppression occurs in both cases, either of outsiders by the dominant social group (via the state) or of the community at large by the state directly." Dubber, *Policing Possession: The War on Crime and the End of Criminal Law* (2001) 956

[88] As Brian Snure observed: "by 1889, instead of preserving life, liberty, and the pursuit of happiness, natural rights primarily served as a conservative check on the progressive measures emanating from state legislatures in response to the rapidly advancing industrial age. Often this use of natural rights resulted in the expansion of corporate power at the expense of social progress and individual rights." Snure, *A Frequent Recurrence to Fundamental Principles* (1992) 675

profits over human lives, it is difficult to conclude otherwise[89] and another symptom is the expansion of the police power.

This common trait of NC states is connected to the first, for to the extent that the state apparatus will be influenced by elites, these factions will be control-oriented and they will want a strong government to satisfy their ambitions. These forces, however, can only account for so much. As a responsible citizenry would do away with authorities who sought to deprive rights, the limits on the police power will depend on the people and its expansion will mirror the extent to which they satisfy NC criteria.

Hence, as the limits on the police power have been expanding, this trend must be attributed to an increasingly infantilized mindset on part of the average citizen. Part three and four shall have more to say on this, but the pressure on individual freedom is apparent everywhere, not least in the history of morals legislation. Beginning with the early alcohol cases, the state expanded its reach into what had previously been considered the individual's private domain. The first alcohol cases were tried in the mid-1800s but, at this time, intoxicating liquors were regarded as property and property rights were fundamental.[90] Thus, possession and use could only

---

[89] After comparing *Lockyer v. Andrade* and *Ewing v. California* to *State Farm Mutual Automobile Insurance Co. v. Campbell* and *Romo v. Ford Motor Company* this is clear. In the first case Andrade was sentenced to life imprisonment with no possibility for parole for stealing $153 worth of videotapes but the Supreme Court refused to intervene; in the second case Ewing was given a life sentence for stealing $1200 worth of golf clubs, but the Court refused to intervene; in the third case damages had originally been awarded in State court after the company had shown bad faith in refusing to settle a suit against a policyholder, but the U.S. Supreme Court accepted the company's appeal and lowered damages; in the fourth case plaintiffs sued Ford for damages after a car accident that killed three people and left three more injured. Ford had rushed a car to market despite its knowledge that the car had a propensity to roll over, lacked a rollover bar to protect occupants, and had a flimsy roof that was sure to collapse in a rollover. Even so, damages were awarded in State court but was lowered after the Supreme Court accepted Ford's appeal. After comparing these cases Professor Chemerinsky commented thus: "There is a cruel irony when these cases are compared. The principle that emerges is that too many years in prison for shoplifting does not violate the Constitution but too much money in punitive damages against a business for "manslaughter" is unconstitutional. . . . There is something just wrong with a Court that has no problem with putting a person in prison for life, with no possibility of parole for 50 years, for stealing $ 153 worth of videotapes, but is outraged when too much is taken from a company in punitive damages when it defrauds its customers." Chemerinsky, *The Constitution and Punishment* (2004) 1051, 1080

[90] In *People v. Gallagher*, Justice Pratt reasoned: "Liquors, then, whether produced by fermentation or distillation, do legally constitute property of use and value; and the owner of this species of personal property, when lawfully acquired, is, upon every principle, . . . entitled to the possession and use of it. This legally includes the right of keeping, selling, or giving it away, as the owner may deem proper. This is a natural primary right incident to ownership." *People v. Gallagher*, 4 Mich. 244, 263 (1856); accord, *Wynehamer v. People*, 13 N.Y. 378, 396-98 (1856) (Comstock, J.)

be prohibited to promote public health, safety, and morals. The state would argue that a prohibition was necessary for exactly these reasons but lost its case again and again as "the keeping of liquors in his possession by a person, whether for himself or for another . . . can by no possibility injure or affect the health, morals, or safety of the public."[91] Harm to the public interest, in other words, had to be more than mere theoretical or indirect. And as alcohol possession or use was "without direct injury to the public, [it was] one of the citizen's natural and inalienable rights."[92]

This conception of harm held sway until 1915 and defendants who challenged laws prohibiting the possession of alcohol had period had a fair shot at invalidating the law as it deprived them of property without due process of law.[93] Only in narcotics cases did the courts reason otherwise and defer to the legislature whenever this issue was brought to their attention.[94] Scholars, however, have documented that the first drug laws were the result of racism, corruption, empire building and ignorance.[95] The proscribed drugs were most commonly used by politically marginalized groups and this explains why government, at the state level, was free to use these laws as means of social control.

Even so, when the first federal narcotics legislation was enacted things were a little different. The Constitution did not provide the federal government with police powers, but as it was formulated as a tax act, its

---

[91] *State v. Gilman*, 33 W. Va. 146, 147, 10 S.E. 283, 284 (1889)

[92] *Commonwealth v. Campbell*, 133 Ky. 50, 117 S.W. 383 (1909)

[93] See Doss Jr. & Doss, *On Morals, Privacy, and the Constitution* (1971); Dubber, *Policing Possession* (2001); Bonnie & Whitebread, *The Forbidden Fruit and the Tree of Knowledge* (1970)

[94] After reviewing the judiciary's deliberations on the prohibition of cannabis, Bonnie and Whitebread conclude: "The nonchalance with which . . . courts cited sensationalistic, non-scientific sources to support the proposition that marijuana produced crime and insanity suggests how widely accepted this hypothesis was among decision-makers, both judicial and legislative, prior to 1931. Given the prevalence of this attitude, the noninvolvement of the middle class, and the precedent established in the earlier alcohol and narcotics cases, it is not surprising that constitutional challenges were either not made or easily rebuffed. . . . The courts, like the legislatures, assumed marijuana caused crime and insanity, and assumed that had public opinion crystallized on the question, it would have favored the suppression of a drug with such evil effects." Ibid.1026

[95] MUSTO, *THE AMERICAN DISEASE* (1973); PROVINE, *UNEQUAL UNDER LAW* (2007); GRAY, *WHY OUR DRUG LAWS HAVE FAILED AND WHAT WE CAN DO ABOUT IT* (2001); Bonnie & Whitebread, *The Forbidden Fruit and the Tree of Knowledge* (1970)

lawfulness survived judicial review.[96] The justices suspected that the Harrison Tax Act was a pretext "to exert . . . the reserved police power of the States,"[97] and at this time the Court was mindful of allotting such power to the federal government. However, the legislation survived by a 4 to 5 decision, and by the time it had become obvious that it really was a springboard for more repressive actions the courts had come to accept its legality. Over the next decades therefore, increasingly punitive measures would be allowed—and whenever the constitutionality of these laws came under attack, the courts would reverse the reasoning they had applied in the alcohol cases: It did not matter if no actual or direct harm to the public interest was involved, prejudice alone would suffice, and the courts would leave these matters to the legislature.[98]

Furthermore, the NC State's drive towards expansion is not only seen in drug cases and the alcohol cases after 1915. It is also seen in other cases, as it was in this period that the Court did away with the right to property altogether;[99] it was in this period that the right to contract was nullified; it was in this period that the presumption of liberty was overturned; it was in this period that the right to self-medicate went out the window; it was in this period that a rational connection between means and ends would no longer be required; and it was in this period

---

[96] *United States v. Doremus*, 249 U.S. 86 (1919); *Nigro v. United States*, 276 U.S. 332, 353 (1928)

[97] *Doremus*, 249 U.S. 95 (White, C.J., dissenting)

[98] The first opiate laws were racist measures directed at the Chinese and the burden of proof were nonexistent. Nobody really cared whether or not the legislation was necessary or reasonable, and as Bonnie and Whitebread noted: "The only astounding thing about the opium possession cases is that there was at least one dissenting opinion. In the Washington case, *Ah Lim v. Territory*, Judge Scott, for himself and another judge, insisted on either a more conclusive demonstration that the private act of smoking opium 'directly and clearly affected the public in some manner' or a more narrowly drawn statute. He catalogued the alleged public justifications [and] after noting the insufficiency of all of the justifications including the argument that the moderate desires of some must be sacrificed to prevent abuse by others, the judge concluded: '[The Act] is altogether too sweeping in its terms. . . . If this act must be held valid it is hard to conceive of any legislative action affecting the personal conduct, or privileges of the individual citizen that must not be upheld. . . . The prohibited act cannot affect the public in any way except through the primary personal injury to the individual, if it occasions him any injury. It looks like a new and extreme step under our government in the field of legislation.'" Bonnie & Whitebread, *The Forbidden Fruit and the Tree of Knowledge* (1970) 1004-05

[99] *Crane v. Campbell*, 245 U.S. 304 (1917) (No private property rights in intoxicants such as alcohol)

that any meaningful restraint on the police power vaporized.[100] Since this period, everything could be criminalized in the pursuit of the public interest and whether or not a legislation actually fulfilled its intended function would be irrelevant. From 1915 and onwards everything would count as "harm," and the legal reasoning of the founders was not only abandoned—it was turned on its ear. The founders' fear of big government not only had no bearing, but the very idea of principled limits to the police power was anathema to the emerging legal mindset.[101] Indeed, this was a period when the answer to all perceived social ills was a call for more state power, and it should come as no surprise that positivism had become the ruling ideology. It was, after all, the only philosophy that would provide the agents of the state with the tools needed to perfect their vision—and so the 20th century would become the bloodiest, most murderous in the history of mankind.[102]

First principles having been properly done away with, there was nothing to keep government from expanding its reach, and this period would continue to the mid-1950s. After this, the Court had its most liberal period (lasting until 1969) where civil rights were recognized as never before. This, however, is not saying much. As Professor Stuntz noted, the protections provided by the founders' legal thinking "were inconsequential before the mid-twentieth century, and have been mostly

---

[100] SIMON, *HUMAN RIGHTS OR AMERICAN PRIVILEGES?* (2007) 254 ("By the late 1930s, the Court's approach had become so deferential to legislatures that it ceased to act as a significant check.")

[101] Professor Charles Burdick wrote in 1922: "Until the latter part of the nineteenth century the public mind was suspicious of governmental encroachment, hostile to governmental regulation, and bent upon the preservation of the largest possible degree of individual freedom. . . . [T]he opinions of the Supreme Court . . . have in recent years shown a change of emphasis, as a result of which the constitutional limitations upon state action have been liberally construed in favor of a wide power of governmental control." BURDICK, *THE LAW OF THE AMERICAN CONSTITUTION* (1922) 469

[102] As Professors Reynolds and Kopel summarized the dynamics between the individual and the state: "The twentieth century was the century of governmental power expanded to a maximum. It is perhaps no coincidence that it was also the century that saw more war, and more governmental-sponsored genocide and slaughter, than any other in memory. As Assistant Secretary of State for Human Rights John Shattuck notes, in the twentieth century 'the number of people killed by their own governments under authoritarian regimes is four times the number killed in all this century's wars combined.' As Neil Stephenson reminds us the twentieth century was one in which limits on state power was removed to let 'intellectuals run with the ball, and they screwed everything up and turned the century into an abattoir.'" Reynolds & Kopel, *The Evolving Police Power: Some Observations for a New Century* (2000) 536

perverse since,"[103] and to this day the Supreme Court have recognized only a dozen or so rights outside those explicitly granted in the Bill of Rights. They include the right to marry,[104] to have children,[105] to direct the education and upbringing of one's children,[106] to marital privacy,[107] to use contraception,[108] to bodily integrity,[109] to abortion,[110] and to refuse unwanted lifesaving medical treatment.[111]

All these rights fall under the "privacy" umbrella, and no new rights have been recognized since the Supreme Court in 2003 accepted it to include a right to engage in personal relationships.[112] These are the crumbs of freedom that the Supreme Court has left us. And it is obvious, as Professor Black noted, "[t]hat is not a slight variation on the principles of the Declaration of Independence, but very nearly antipodal to them."[113]

6.4.2 The Equality and Fundamental Rights Doctrine

The scheme that has made this heist possible is the Supreme Court's NC mode of constitutional construction, one that interprets individual rights narrowly and government powers broadly. Its most central feature is the equality and fundamental rights doctrine that evolved out of the 1930s legal environment. It was in this period the presumption of liberty was overturned and a presumption of constitutionality would be applied to constitutional challenges.[114]

---

[103] STUNTZ, *THE COLLAPSE OF AMERICAN CRIMINAL JUSTICE* (2013) 67-68

[104] *Loving v. Virginia*, 388 U.S. 1 (1967)

[105] *Skinner v. Oklahoma ex rel. Williamson*, 316 U.S. 535 (1942)

[106] *Meyer v. Nebraska*, 262 U.S. 390 (1923); *Pierce v. Society of Sisters*, 268 U.S. 510 (1925)

[107] *Griswold v. Connecticut*, 381 U.S. 479 (1965)

[108] *Eisenstadt v. Baird*, 405 U.S. 438 (1972)

[109] *Rochin v. California*, 342 U. S. 165 (1952)

[110] *Planned Parenthood v. Casey*, 505 U.S. 833 (1992)

[111] *Cruzan v. Director*, Missouri Dept. of Health, 497 U.S. 261 (1990)

[112] *Lawrence v. Texas*, 539 U.S. 558 (2003)

[113] BLACK, *A NEW BIRTH FOR FREEDOM* (1999) 90

[114] The first case was *O'Gorman & Young, Inc. v. Hartford Fire Insurance Co.*, 282 U.S. 251 (1931). This was a slippery slope and from first being applied to constitutional challenges

The positivist spirit that the Court embraced so fully proclaimed that the Court should recognize no more rights than necessary and, unless an act of the legislature burdened an enumerated right, the judges would defer to the legislature. This, however, would reduce the protection of rights to those of free speech and religion and there were noticeable problems with this approach. It was obvious even to positivists that the Constitution had to protect *at least some* unenumerated rights; the Ninth Amendment explicitly said so, and so the task was to separate those unenumerated rights that deserved protection from those that did not.

Thus, to carve out a sphere of protection that could deal somewhat satisfactorily with the most blatant human rights abuses on American soil, the Court would rely on two sets of guidelines: (1) In the area of equal protection challenges, it would apply a suspect classification analysis whereby legislation attacking specifically chosen groups would be subjected to closer scrutiny, and (2), in the area of due process challenges, the fundamental rights doctrine emerged as a solution.[115]

When reviewing equal protection challenges, the Court would only review legislation that discriminated on basis of traits such as race, national origin, alienage, sex, and nonmarital parentage, while all other discriminatory practices would go unheeded. And when it came to due process challenges, the Court would protect only those liberties that were deemed to be "fundamental." No more than a very few liberties would

---

regarding the economic sphere, deference to the legislature grew until in the 1950s it became a doctrine that applied to all but a very few liberties. See Barnett, *Scrutiny Land* (2008)

[115] When a litigant wants to try the constitutionality of a law, he or she will either claim a due process or equality rights violation—or sometimes both. While the Due Process Clause focuses on matters of liberty, ensuring that the state abides by its obligations to the principle of autonomy/human dignity, and that the balance of power between the individual and state is properly calibrated, the Equality Clause protects the liberty interest of individuals vis-à-vis each other, ensuring that no legislation that arbitrarily makes one class of citizens bear the brunt of the law passes constitutional scrutiny. To NC lawyers they may appear separate, but they are fundamentally entwined. Each brings to light important evidence of unconstitutional practices, one providing a limiting principle on state power, the other invalidating all differential treatment on arbitrary grounds. Together these clauses provide the ultimate frame of reference when a law is to be scrutinized. See Tribe, *Lawrence v. Texas: The Fundamental Right that Dare Not Speak its Name* (2004) 1898 ("far from having separate missions and entailing different inquiries, [they] are profoundly interlocked in a legal double helix. It is a single, unfolding tale of equal liberty and increasingly universal dignity."); Karlan, *Equal Protection, Due Process and the Stereoscopic Fourteenth Amendment* (2002) 477 ("Like the two hands that emerge from the sheet of paper to draw one another in M.C. Escher's famous lithograph, Drawing Hands, the ideas of equality and liberty expressed in equal protection and due process clauses each emerge from and reinforce the other.")

receive this honor, and to find out if an infringement on liberty was sufficiently important to rebut a presumption of constitutionality the Court would ask if a right is "so rooted in the traditions and conscience of our people as to be ranked as fundamental;"[116] if it is "of such a character that it cannot be denied without violating those fundamental principles of liberty and justice which lie at the base of all our civil and political institutions;"[117] and if it must be "implicit in the concept of ordered liberty."[118]

Furthermore, to provide another barrier against meaningful review, the Court would not accept a broad definition of rights, such as a right to "autonomy," "privacy," or "liberty." It is no surprise that NC individuals, having everything backwards (i.e., mistaking shadow for light), will fail to see how these concepts connect to the letter of the Constitution, and so the Court decided that it would only examine the right in question at the most specific level that could be identified. It would narrow down the asserted right to the point where it would appear at its most trivial, a doctrine more thoughtful scholars have recognized as "a fraud on the public"[119] and "a gambit toward hacking away not just at substantive due process but also at the nature of liberty itself"[120]—a "gambit [that] should not be allowed to succeed."[121]

As these criteria represent an all-out assault on the founders' conception of rights, they have done so with good reason. For one, the more narrowly we define a right, the more likely the Court is to deny that the asserted right is constitutionally protected.[122] For instance, if the right in question is specified as "a right to engage in sodomy" (as it was in *Bowers*) NC judges, failing to reason from first principles, will quickly find that no such right exist (as they did in *Bowers*), whereas if it is specified as "a right to engage in personal relationships" (as it was in

---

[116] *Snyder v. Massachusetts*, 291 U.S. 97, 105 (1934)

[117] *Powell v. Alabama*, 287 U.S. 45, 67 (1932)

[118] *Palko v. Connecticut*, 302 U.S. 319, 325 (1937)

[119] Barnett, *The Golden Mean Between Kurt & Dan* (2008) 898

[120] Tribe, *Lawrence v. Texas* (2004) 1923

[121] Ibid. 1924

[122] Tribe & Dorf, *Levels of Generality in the Definition of Rights* (1990); Barnett, *Scrutiny Land* (2008); Barnett, *The Presumption of Liberty and the Public Interest: Medical Marijuana and Fundamental Rights* (2006)

Lawrence) they are likely to find that it does (as they did in *Lawrence*). In any event it is the same activity, just defined at different levels of specificity. And as Barnett noted, "[t]he fact that courts can come out any way they want, depending on which of the accurate characterizations of the liberty they choose shows that there is something seriously wrong with current doctrine."[123]

Second, the Court's equality jurisprudence does not make any sense. The Court has not recognized any new groups worthy of suspect classification status since 1977, and even if it had it would still leave other groups unprotected. Hence, it is a senseless endeavor no matter how many groups of "suspect classifications" it will include, as *all* individuals have the same right to be protected from unjustifiable discriminatory practices.[124]

Third, the Court's fundamental rights test is so malleable that judges are likely to arrive at a conclusion based on nothing but their own prejudices.[125] It goes without saying that its criteria, to NC individuals, will not amount to much protection, as only FC scholars have the wits to perform a rights analysis at its most abstract level. Only they can reason from first principles and from a general presumption of liberty. Only they can see why such a wide-ranging conception of rights is "so rooted in the traditions and conscience of our people as to be ranked as fundamental;" why it is "of such a character that it cannot be denied without violating those fundamental principles of liberty and justice which lie at the base

---

[123] Ibid. 43

[124] As Justice Stevens said, "[t]here is only one Equal Protection Clause. It requires every State to govern impartially. It does not direct the courts to apply one standard of review in some cases and a different standard in other cases." *Craig v. Boren*, 429 U.S. 190 (1976) 211-12 (Stevens, J., concurring). See also GERBER, *TO SECURE THESE RIGHTS* (1995) 175; Ball, *Why Liberty Judicial Review is as Legitimate as Equality Review* (2011); Goldberg, *Equality Without Tiers* (2004); Maguire & Nourse, *The Lost History of Governance and Equal Protection* (2009); Karlan, *Equal Protection, Due Process and the Stereoscopic Fourteenth Amendment* (2002); Jackson, *Putting Rationality Back Into the Rational Basis Test* (2011); Massey, *The New Formalism: Requiem for Tiered Scrutiny?* (2004); Tussman & tenBroek, *The Equal Protection of the Laws* (1949)

[125] Preiser, *Rediscovering a Coherent Rationale for Substantive Due Process* (2003) 4 ("the history-and-tradition or conscience-of-our-people test is completely arbitrary, and the provisions of the Bill of Rights as expanded by the Court too often are interpreted in ways that disregard the historical record and/or the 'tradition' of our people. . . . [T]he tests actually function as masks legitimatizing the virtually naked preferences of the justices."). See also Farrell, *Justice Kennedy's Idiosyncratic Understanding of Equal Protection and Due Process, and its Costs* (2014)

of all our civil and political institutions;" and why it must be "implicit in the concept of ordered liberty."

To NC individuals none of this is obvious. Lacking the capacity to reason from first principles all they have is their own idea of what these criteria imply—and it is for this reason that the fundamental rights test only protects traditional forms of liberty. While NC individuals tend to think that this is the best they can do, FC individuals will know that such an endeavor is not only unfruitful but dangerously misguided. After all, we have no guarantee that traditional values are rooted in reason, and—not surprisingly—this test has a proven record of falsely authenticating arbitrary laws.[126]

Another problem with the fundamental rights test is an all-or-nothing approach to rights protection that does not make sense. Even the most "fundamental" of rights (the enumerated ones) must be subject to some sort of proportionality analysis, and, as Tribe noted, "any such exercise in enumeration is a fool's errand that misconceives the structure of liberty and of the constitutional doctrines that provide its contents."[127]

The reason for this is that no matter what kind of activities appellants want vindicated, we are not dealing with isolated events. We are dealing with a set of principles about the role of government, principles derived from higher law—from the unwritten Constitution—which defines the parameters of individual freedom, and we should never forget to see constitutional challenges in this light. We must remember that in the world of constitutional interpretation the micro and macro is ultimately one—and that the Whole exceeds the sum of its component parts. This Whole is the idea of autonomy, of individual self-rule and expression. It is a concept that is all-encompassing and fully embracive. It cuts through undue infringements across the board and its very design is rendered meaningless by the fragmented hollow-out approach to constitutional law advocated by current doctrine.

That much would have been obvious to the founders and it is a great shame that that the American legal system has been formed into being by individuals with so narrow a focus that this greater frame of reference has

---

[126] *Bowers v. Hardwick*, 478 U.S. 186 (1986) (The Court declined to hold unconstitutional laws that threatened individuals with twenty years imprisonment for engaging in adult consensual homosexual conduct)

[127] Tribe, *Lawrence v. Texas* (2004) 1934-35

gone lost. However, FC scholars have rightfully rejected "the foolishness of attempting to define the dimensions of human liberty . . . by enumerating a catalog of private actions that might (or might not) fall on the protected side of [an imaginatively drawn] constitutional line."[128] They know "the claim that a unique body of law applies to each medium of expression is descriptively and normatively false,"[129] and that the Constitution provides a protection by degrees *of every conceivable human endeavor.*

This being too obvious to ignore, even a few justices have taken issue with this way of doing things.[130] We shall see more in part three, but the second Justice Harlan noticed as much when he said that the liberty protected by the Constitution "is not a series of isolated points pricked out in terms of the taking of property, the freedom of speech, press, and religion; the right to keep and bear arms; the freedom from unreasonable searches and seizures; and so on. It is a rational continuum which, broadly speaking, includes *a freedom from all substantial arbitrary impositions and purposeless restraints.*"[131]

Last, and not least, this is all *unconstitutional.* We now know that the founders not only wanted *all rights equally protected,*[132] but that a presumption of liberty would be the main barrier against unlawful rights transgressions.[133] By adopting a presumption of constitutionality and

---

[128] Ibid. 1934; Sweet, *All Things in Proportion?* (2010) 45 ("We think it is a bad strategic move for the Court . . . to treat a rights provision as either de facto absolute or de facto without force. It is also indefensible, as a formal matter, to excise a right from a Constitution. Yet that is what the Court has done, in this and many other cases, to its discredit.")

[129] Tribe & Dorf, *Levels of Generality in the Definition of Rights* (1990) 1070

[130] Justice Marshall has advocated for abandoning the dichotomy between fundamental and nonfundamental rights, see *Dandridge v. Williams,* 397 U.S. 471,520-23 (1970) (Marshall, J., dissenting) and *San Antonio v. Rodriguez,* 411 U.S. 1, 98-99 (1973) (Marshall, J., dissenting)

[131] *Poe v. Ullman,* 367 U.S. 497 (1961) 543 (Harlan, J., dissenting) (emphasis mine)

[132] Sanders, *Ninth Life* (1994) 798-99 ("So long as one continues to embrace a constitutional mindset that reads a fundamentality hurdle into group-two rights, one will systematically ignore the Ninth Amendment's message and commit precisely the imperfect enumeration error that all the Framers feared."); Barnett, *The Ninth Amendment: It Means What It Says* (2006) 77 ("the judicial protection of liberty . . . which reverses the presumption of constitutionality only when enumerated rights are infringed, is unconstitutional. . . . Indeed, [it] would seem to be the epitome of a constitutional construction that is expressly barred by the original meaning of the Ninth Amendment.")

[133] Tribe & Dorf, *Levels of Generality in the Definition of Rights* (1990) 1102 ("The Ninth Amendment, in our view, places the justificatory burden on those who would deny the existence of a given right.")

making it effectively irrebuttable the Court has successfully derailed the founders' project, for according to the most used standard of review, the rational basis test, the government bears no burden of proof. Instead, it is the defendant that must rebut *every conceivable* basis for the statutory classification, and there is no need for the government to respond to the charges.[134] As long as a judge cannot discount the possibility that a legislation was motivated by some concern for the public welfare, it will pass constitutional muster. It is completely irrelevant whether the legislation actually does protect the public interest and, using this standard of review, there are no limits to the state's power to criminalize behavior. As scholars have noted, even the criminalization of pizza, doughnuts, or Beethoven music on pain of lifetime imprisonment would pass the Court's rational basis test.[135] This alone speaks to its merits, and another problem is that it overturns the adversarial principle, which is vital to the legitimacy of the legal process.[136]

For these reasons, scholars have criticized the Court's doctrines for a failure to protect rights[137] and they are clear that the burden of evidence

---

[134] "[T]hose attacking the rationality of the legislative classification have the burden to negative every conceivable basis which might support it. Moreover, because we never require a legislature to articulate its reasons for enacting a statute, it is entirely irrelevant for constitutional purposes whether the conceived reason for the challenged distinction actually motivated the legislature. Thus, the absence of legislative facts explaining the distinction on the record has no significance in rational-basis analysis. In other words, a legislative choice is not subject to courtroom fact-finding and may be based on rational speculation unsupported by evidence or empirical data." *F.C.C. v. Beach Commc'ns, Inc.*, 508 U.S. 307, 313–15 (1993) (Thomas J.)

[135] HUSAK, *OVERCRIMINALIZATION* (2008) 124-25; Oteri & Silvergate, *The Pursuit of Pleasure: Constitutional Dimensions of the Marihuana Problem* (1968) 56

[136] Ward, *The Rational Basis Test Violates Due Process* (2014) 726, 729 ("the rational-basis test makes state's attorneys out of judges . . . and [it] does not just violate Due Process. It likewise violates the ABA's Model Code of Judicial Conduct, the source of nearly every state code of judicial conduct, which requires disqualification when 'the judge's impartiality might reasonably be questioned' including when the 'judge has a personal bias or prejudice concerning a party.'")

[137] Dubber, *Toward a Constitutional Law of Crime and Punishment* (2004) 1 ("It has become a commonplace that there are no meaningful constitutional constraints on substantive criminal law."); Conkle, *The Second Death of Substantive Due Process* (1987) 216 ("it is difficult to maintain that there is a doctrine of substantive due process. Instead, the Court's decision-making appears to rest on little more than ad hoc policymaking, hardly a defensible practice in the exercise of judicial review."); Preiser, *Rediscovering a Coherent Rationale for Substantive Due Process* (2003) 1 ("the Supreme Court's classification of our various freedoms, by assigning greater value to some and lesser to others, lacks an objective foundation or even a coherent rationale."); Tribe, *On Reading the Constitution* (1986) 61 (describing the Court's jurisprudence "a largely arbitrary fiat."); Niles, *Ninth Amendment Adjudication* (2000) 135 ("Substantive due process is a weak and flawed doctrine."); Kadish, *Fifty Years of Criminal Law: An Opinionated*

must be placed on government whenever the constitutionality of a criminal law is challenged.[138] This is the only way to honor fundamental principles of justice; this is the only way to bring integrity to law; and this is the only way for the justices to honor their pledge to the Constitution.

This being so one would expect the Court to act on their criticisms, either by refuting their argument or abandoning the NC system of law. To this day, however, these scholars have been ignored.

Review (1999) (lamenting the failure to constitutionalize the general part of the criminal law.); Buchhandler-Raphael, *Drugs, Dignity, and Danger* (2012) 293 ("the broken criminal justice system is in tension with one of the fundamental principles of American constitutional jurisprudence, namely, constitutional protection of individual liberties and freedom from government intrusion into the private lives of individuals."); Finkelstein, *Positivism and the Notion of an Offense* (2000) 337 ("the Court has been unwilling to constitutionalize the basic doctrines of the criminal law."); Erlinder, *Mens Rea, Due Process, and the Supreme Court: Toward a Constitutional Doctrine of Substantive Criminal Law* (1989); Ashworth, *Is the Criminal Law a Lost Cause?*(2000); HUSAK, OVERCRIMINALIZATION (2008); Colb, *Freedom from Incarceration* (1994); Jackson, *Putting Rationality Back Into the Rational Basis Test* (2011); Borgmann, *Rethinking Judicial Deference to Legislation Fact-Finding* (2009); Hessick, *Rethinking the Presumption of Constitutionality* (2010); Fallon, *Individual Rights and Governmental Powers* (1993); Sweet, *All Things in Proportion?* (2010); Goldberg, *Equality Without Tiers* (2004); Treiman, *Equal Protection and Fundamental Rights—A Judicial Shell Game* (1979); Brown, *Liberty, the New Equality* (2002); Materni, *The 100-plus Year old Case for a Minimalist Criminal Law* (2015)

[138] Finkelstein, *Positivism and the Notion of an Offense* (2000) 335, 369 ("[W]e have a presumption against the use of the criminal sanction, stemming from the commitment to a background right to liberty our constitutional jurisprudence contains. The use of the criminal sanction is justified only if the infringement of liberty it imposes is sufficient to overcome that presumption. . . . From this it follows that the decision to criminalize is one that stands in need of justification."). See also Moore, *Liberty and Drugs*, in DE GREIFF (ED.), DRUGS AND THE LIMITS OF LIBERALISM (1999) 61-109; BARNETT, RESTORING THE LOST CONSTITUTION (2014); Doss Jr. & Doss, *On Morals, Privacy, and the Constitution* (1971) 404; Nowak, *Realizing the Standards of Review Under the Equal Protection Guarantee* (1974) 1081-82; Gunther, *Foreword: In Search of Evolving Doctrine on a Changing Court: A Model for a Newer Equal Protection* (1972) 20-24; McGinnis & Mulaney, *Judging Facts Like Law* (2008) 35; Preiser, *Rediscovering a Coherent Rationale for Substantive Due Process* (2003) 51, 53; Brashear, *Marijuana Prohibition and the Constitutional Right of Privacy* (1975) 573; Tribe & Dorf, *Levels of Generality in the Definition of Rights* (1990) 1102; Borgmann, *Rethinking Judicial Deference to Legislative Fact-Finding* (2009) 47; Torke, *the Judicial Process in Equal Protection Cases* (1982); Roach, *The Primacy of Liberty and Proportionality, Not Human Dignity, When Subjecting Criminal Law to Constitutional Control* (2011) 107

6.5 THE EVOLUTION OF LAW: A SYMPTOM OF THE NC PSYCHE

"[T]he amorality of modern constitutional questions and answers is in part a psychologically, as opposed to legally, mandated author- itarian reaction to the diseased state of the modern political theory that underlies our constitutional framework. . . .[C]ourts and commentators are presently inclined toward an authoritarian and hence amoral resolution of our constitutional questions in part because modern interpretations of our underlying political theories . . . reflect our anxieties about ourselves, fears about others, and our asocial and even psychopathological tendencies, rather than our social aspirations."[139]

—Robin West, Professor of Law and Philosophy—

The American system of law is the predictable result of leaving law to NC lawyers, and we shall here explore the psychological component of these doctrines—the NC mindset.

We know that NC individuals will see the world from a fragmented and isolated perspective. They have not yet developed the integrity to free themselves from contemporary prejudices and restraints and so they (1) cannot connect with the light of first principles and (2) fail to see their day and age in a historical context. They may care deeply about opinions of right and wrong, but what they primarily care about is *their own idea* and not its merits. Therefore, they will take great pride in their morality, even though their moral stance is detrimental to fellow human beings.

Furthermore, even if they had sufficient humility to question basic presumptions, they would not be much better off. Only to the extent that their inner world connects and coheres with FC values will their ideas about right and wrong prove to the betterment for society but failing to grasp the implications of first principles, NC individuals have no means of checking whether this is so. Instead, they must point to tradition or authority figures in search for a basis of opinion, and this will not help.

---

[139] West, *The Authoritarian Impulse in Constitutional Law* (1988) 534, 539

In addition, NC individuals will have an authoritarian proclivity. They will either (1) want to rule others or (2) be ruled by others, and as they in any case will see the world as a treacherous place, they easily fall prey to enemy images. Thus, they will constantly be looking for ways to guard against perceived ills, and the dynamics of NC societies ensure that those who most clearly demonstrate these traits will be drawn to positions of power. The further we go towards the NC-end, the more this holds true, and it is easy to see what kind of social dynamics and law that will result.

First of all, NC jurists will not be able to draw upon the resources found in the depth of law—i.e., FC law. Only those who can connect with the light of first principles can grasp the Wholeness of law, the essence of the Constitution, and as they fail to connect with this "depth" they will be operating on the surface, oblivious to the greater picture and how it comes together. As they fail to connect with this depth, they also fail to connect fact and value, and they can neither bring coherence nor integrity to the system of law. As Thomas Paine, one of the great minds of the Enlightenment put it:

> "When a man in a long cause attempts to steer his course by anything else than some polar truth or principle, he is sure to be lost. It is beyond the compass of his capacity to keep all the parts of an argument together, and make them unite in one issue, by any other means than having this guide always in view. Neither memory nor invention will supply the want of it. The former fails him, and the latter betrays him."[140]

Nowhere is this better seen than in the evolution of U.S. doctrines, for these are just as fragmented and incoherent as their proponents' mindset. Lacking the analytical capability needed to operate on the waters of law, both above and below its surface, NC individuals are like people who cannot swim. They will therefore be looking for whatever driftwood (i.e., precedent) they may find and cling on to it.

As a result, they have a fear for deep waters; they will never trace an argument back to first principles and they will never begin their analysis

---

[140] PAINE, *RIGHTS OF MAN* (1996) 78

with them. Being firmly set within the parameters of NC law they will instead be psychologically predisposed to disregard the founders' call for a frequent return to first principles, either for reasons of political expediency or ignorance. Psychologically speaking, there are good reasons for this, for should they bring these principles into the equation— should they now, after 200 years of a steady drift off course, suddenly begin to look at the map—it would be an intolerable wake-up call.

For one, it takes a certain amount of courage to face that they have been navigating without a functional compass for 200 years and that, as a result, those defenses that the founders put in place to bar against tyranny have been laid to waste. It is much easier to ignore all evidence of failure, hoping that not too many people will see the mess they have made of law in this period.

Secondly, there is no way that they can do their math with first principles and arrive at a conclusion that is tolerable to the status quo. For 200 years the government has been allowed to trespass on our catalogue of rights whenever its agents deemed it expedient. To the extent that society is defined by NC traits, power will not yield willingly, and our leaders will not voluntarily let their "lust for self-aggrandizement"[141] be checked by principled limits. Thus, to whatever extent the Court accepts its role as a tool for tyrants in the engineering of society, we can expect it to keep ignoring the founders' call for a return to first principles.

In addition to this, there is a sincere concern that trusting the guidance of first principles will prove a recipe for disaster. Failing to connect the bigger picture, they do not see how these principles provide a perfect frame of reference—one that on a case-by-case basis can calibrate all variables into a coherent and consistent body of law. The lack of understanding makes conservatives fear that if natural rights be recognized, the barricade that keeps anarchy in check will be gone and society will perish. Consequently, as they cannot see how everything connects below the surface, they will go with precedent rather than think things through.

Psychologically speaking, these are the most obvious reasons why the justices at the Court have paid little attention to the principles of

---

[141] BAILYN, *THE IDEOLOGICAL ORIGINS OF THE AMERICAN REVOLUTION* (1967) 56-69

law.[142] Their disregard for first principles, however, is not the only predictable characteristic of NC jurists. For them to pull off their coup the bigger picture must be ignored all together, and so they must deny the implications of the founders' political theory as well as the obvious connection to the Declaration of Independence. Isolating the Constitution from its historical, political, and moral context is of paramount importance, for only in doing so can they turn the Constitution into a NC document.

Having done this, they can attribute to the Constitution any meaning they want, and true to their character they will read the text as a recipe for tyranny. The most obvious FC parts of the document, like the implications of the preamble and the Ninth Amendment, will be ignored. The Fifth Amendment's Due Process Clause will be taken to mean that for a person to be deprived of his life, liberty or property, a certain protocol must be followed—but this protocol will not include questioning the premises of the legislation. Likewise, as the concept of human dignity will carry no weight, the Eighth Amendment's prohibition of cruel and unusual punishment will have no substantive meaning. The Fourteenth Amendment's Privileges or Immunities clause, the most obvious candidate for grounding American law in human rights jurisprudence,[143] will mean little more than a right to travel to Washington to petition the government. The Necessary and Proper Clause will be perceived as a carte blanche to prohibit whatever they like, and so on, and so on.

Only one thing is more terrifying to NC individuals than freedom and that is the freedom of others. They will therefore construe freedoms narrowly and government powers broadly. When it comes to individual freedoms, they will ask: "Does the Constitution explicitly allow such behaviors?" and if it does not, they believe that they have a right to

---

[142] As Professor Stuntz observed: "Curiously, those legal principles made little difference before the 1960s . . . [and the] constitutional language [was interpreted] narrowly. Madison's iconic legal rights . . . were inconsequential before the mid-twentieth century, and have been mostly perverse since. . . . America's justice system suffers from a mismatch of individual rights and criminal justice machinery, between legal ideals and political institutions." STUNTZ, THE COLLAPSE OF AMERICAN CRIMINAL JUSTICE (2013) 67-68

[143] Tribe, *On Reading the Constitution*, (1986) 55 ("The history makes quite clear that the "privileges or immunities" of United States citizenship were not meant to be limited to rights bearing peculiarly on one's relationship to the national government. They were supposed to refer to some set of fundamental human rights, and we still have to decide what those are."); see also TRIBE, AMERICAN CONSTITUTIONAL LAW, §7-2, 548-53

prohibit the activity. When it comes to government powers, on the other hand, they will be asking: "Does the Constitution explicitly forbid such an act of government?" and if it does not, the state is be free to expand its sphere of influence.

To the extent that there are exceptions to this rule it will be due to the lingering influence of FC traits, as these are still with us. However, we are here concerned with the NC mindset and this reading is extremely common among scholars. As they cannot grasp the bigger picture—the Whole of law—they isolate and narrow down all aspects of the Constitution until it is void of substantive meaning. Furthermore, lacking a proper compass for navigating these waters they will seek to abstract themselves from the reading of the document. To the extent they engage the text wholeheartedly, there is a fear of applying their own subjective values, and so they prefer to leave it to the legislature to define the parameters for the rule of law. Their thinking is that, at the very least, the system of law will follow the prevailing trends and opinions of society— and this is good enough for them. Somehow, they fail to recognize that "it is emphatically the province and duty of the judicial department to say what the law is,"[144] and that neither public opinion nor tradition are reliable guideposts.

The problem with this narrowed-down and wishfully objective reading of the Constitution is obvious to FC individuals. For one, majority rule is not the solution but the problem that the Constitution is to remedy,[145] and secondly, to the extent we look to text and tradition for answers, these sources can blind us to the prejudice and ignorance of our predecessors. Only the light of first principles can help us see past internal contradictions and conflicting textual sources; only they can help us discover the folly of tradition; and only they can guide us beyond the present-day mental horizon. Jurists like Tribe and Dorf[146] have demonstrated the fallacy of beginning in the other end—and as those who

---

[144] *Marbury v. Madison*, 5 U.S. 137, 2 L. Ed. 60 (1803) (Marshall J.)

[145] "Madison saw the potential tyranny of the majority as posing an even greater threat to liberty than either of the main branches of government—and we have seen how much the Framers feared government. Thomas Jefferson observed similarly: '[A]ll, too, will bear in mind the sacred principle that, though the will of the majority is in all cases to prevail, that will, to be rightful, must be reasonable. Let the minority possess their equal rights which equal law must protect . . . and to violate would be oppression.'" Sanders, *Ninth Life* (1994) 809

[146] Tribe & Dorf, *Levels of Generality in the Definition of Rights* (1990)

agitate for the NC approach will be the most small-minded and prejudice-laden of all lawyers, society would be ill-served by following their lead.

It just so happens that such jurists, despite their assurances to the contrary, are the ones who to the greatest extent are trapped within the prison of their own minds. They think that "objectivity" is best achieved by withdrawing completely from the equation; that only in looking at the founders' writings, history, tradition, and textual sources can the meaning of the Constitution be objectively interpreted. And it is true. Even so, they fail to understand that *everything they do* is subjectively motivated; that the textual sources require their interpretation and that no matter what textual and historical sources they examine, they must choose what period to look to and what importance to attribute to the data. Like other positivistic-oriented scientists they fail to realize that no matter what they cannot separate themselves from their studies; that their inner world still shapes everything they do, and that their search for meaning and answers will be informed by their own preconceptions, values, and belief structures.

This, of course, also goes for the rest of us. But psychologists have found that to the extent there is a meaningful measure of objectivity, it will be found at the FC-end.[147] Therefore, in recognizing our own limitations and trusting the principles of justice to guide us, we can compensate for our own subjective shortcomings—and in following the light of these principles we can erect a greater framework, one that helps us overcome inherent contradictions.

Psychologically speaking, this is why the most subjectively driven and misguided lawyers are the ones with the greatest fear of principled reasoning. While FC individuals have a sense of identity that is rooted in something deeper, NC individuals have a sense of identity that is fundamentally entwined with their beliefs. Thus, nobody is more set on preserving their own notions of morality than NC individuals; nobody is more protective of their prejudices. To the extent that their concerns are sincere, their fear of principled reasoning must be attributed to the fact that they do not understand it and that they lack the capacity to operate within law's greater framework. However, the arguments they put forth to bar against principled reasoning (i.e., operating at the highest level of

---

[147] MASLOW, *RELIGIONS, VALUES, AND PEAK-EXPERIENCES* (1994) 61-62

generality) can be so obviously flawed that it looks more like a desire to shield their own preconceived notions. An example was provided by Judge Bork when, in discussing the constitutionality of homosexuality, he charged that "[t]here is no apparent reason why the Court should manipulate the level of generality to protect unconventional sexual behavior any more than liberty should be taken at a high enough level of abstraction to protect kleptomania."[148]

When he speaks of "manipulating the level of generality," what Bork refers to is the Supreme Court's doctrine of operating with the most narrowed-down conception of an asserted right. As seen, this is a sure way to disparage rights, for it is much easier for the Court to deny that there is a constitutionally protected right to have anal intercourse than it is to deny that there is a right to self-determination. It is the same activity, but the more specifically defined the easier it will be for the Court to conclude that the founders never intended exactly this activity to be protected.

As previously discussed, NC individuals have a natural bent towards recognizing as few rights as possible while reserving for the government the broadest latitude in legislating for the public welfare, and this is one way they do this. Bork himself is a strong supporter of this doctrine. He is one of America's most controversial judges, both admired and detested for his stance against the wave of so-called immorality that has flushed away the "old" America. It bears emphasis that we are not speaking about the "old" America of the founders, the one built on reason, but the one that religious conservatives, racists, and homophobes remember with so much fondness. If it were up to Bork, America today would be more like America in the early 1900s, and this may be the real reason for his fear of principled reasoning.

It is, after all, the most value-neutral method that can be employed when it comes to the quest of giving specific content to the Constitution's terms. It will limit the influence of subjective sympathies better than any other method, for to the extent that we familiarize ourselves with its implications we will transcend the boundaries of time and the cultural baggage that clouds our vision. Hence, conservatives like Bork will reject such reasoning for the fear that it may show them more than they want to

---

[148] Tribe & Dorf, *Levels of Generality in the Definition of Rights* (1990) 1099-1100

see of our misguided ways; that it may uncloak prejudice and falsehoods they are not yet prepared to correct; and that it will expose their "moral concern" for what it really is—as unwarranted meddling with other people's lives.

In any case, whatever Bork's rationale may be, his fear of first principles is not motivated by reason. The light of first principles provides us with *the only* objective measure for carving out a reasonable and valid body of law, and anyone equipped with the moral compass needed to maneuver by their lights will know that they will no more protect thievery than murder and mayhem. All they do is draw a line that protects the individual against undue infringements on his life, liberty, and property—and this makes Bork's and others opposition highly suspect.

Ideally, this would have been clear if they would only recognize that they themselves, by their standard of reasoning, (i.e., by sticking to tradition, positive law, and the will of power as guideposts for constitutional interpretation) would have been exactly the kind of judges Hitler needed to build his Third Reich. It is clear that only those capable of principled reasoning could have exposed the Nazis' system of arbitrary law for what it was—and the same applies to our age.

However, as NC individuals cannot conceive of normative development, this is not likely to deter faith in a system of arbitrary law. To them, there is no universal standard of ethics that can measure such growth, and so Hitler's reign was no more immoral or ethically flawed than any other. The evidence they will produce to support this claim is that because people disagree on morality, there can be no true moral principles—and no true principles of law. However, to quote Leo Strauss, it should be obvious that "[b]y proving that there is no principle of justice that has not been denied somewhere or at some time, one has not yet proved that any given denial was justified or reasonable."[149]

To the contrary, diversity of opinion only provides us with a true basis for morality. Words like "greatness", "courage", "wisdom", and "integrity" are pretty much defined by their negation, and so a true standard of ethics would be meaningless if it were not possible to depart from a loftier ideal. To those who live in darkness therefore, (those at the

---

[149] Sabo, *The Higher Law Background of the Constitution* (2009) 18

NC-end) it will appear to be no universal morality. But for those at the other end—those who have emerged from the darkness—behind the apparent fragmentation of existence and the relativity of morals and values that comes with it, there is always a greater Wholeness, complete in itself. And once we begin to tap into this understanding, once we begin to merge with this Wholeness and the values that follow, it is clear that a universal standard of morality does exist—but that we must be further evolved to see it.

Most NC individuals, no doubt, will remain unconvinced until they wise up to the greater picture. In the world of NC, double standards are the name of the game, there is no solid ground, and another interesting feature that goes to prove the inconsistency of their position is that even though NC jurists reject any true standard of justice, they themselves will appeal to first principles in their decision to deny first principles.

As mentioned in part one, any legal argument will begin with the premise that a law derives its authority from the state or from some deeper moral foundation. Positivists reason from the former position while natural law theorists reason from the latter, and so the two begin their argument from the exact opposite starting point: FC individuals accept as their anchoring principle the preposition that whenever there is a conflict between higher law and positive law, the latter must yield, while jurists like Bork accept the premise that if there is a conflict, the higher law must yield. Even so, whereas FC individuals understand that their legal reasoning is grounded in something deeper than positive law, positivists like Bork fail to understand that their reasoning is itself comparable to the tenets of natural law, only with an authoritarian bent. As Arkes and others have noted,[150] the preposition that higher law must yield whenever there is a conflict between the two is itself a principle of construction that is nowhere to be found in the Constitution nor any other source of law, and so its "claim to fame" must be derived from the assumption that it is some kind of axiom—a self-evident *primary* truth, just like the first principles of natural law.

In this sense, both natural lawyers and positivists can be said to build their argument on "first principles." Even so, this is where any similarity ends, for while the principles of natural law are self-evident (any

---

[150] ARKES, *CONSTITUTIONAL ILLUSIONS & ANCHORING TRUTHS* (2010) 228

argument that proceeds from them will be harmonious with reason and advance the sense of justice) the principle that positive law must always take precedence is impossible to take seriously. After all, if we accept its premise, the connection between morality and law falls apart. The most heinous crimes against humanity would become legalized and there would be no end to the misery that could be inflicted in the name of law. To accept such a rationale would be preposterous. It would leave us at the bottom NC-end, and the incongruity of this preposition leaves us with no other conclusion but a moral obligation to accept the premise that positive law derives its legitimacy from higher law.[151]

Thus, the problem for NC jurists should be evident: positive law is itself only partial but pretending it to be whole its proponents fail to see the point where their reasoning collapses, landing them in disrepute. This failure to connect wholes is evident in everything they do, and we shall now expand on the problematics of a system of arbitrary law, studying the result of the NC mindset writ large.

---

[151] To paraphrase Arkes, "natural law must be the matrix or foundation of positive law, being that any propositions that are at odds with those deep axioms of natural law cannot present a coherent claim to be regarded as law." Ibid. 229

PART THREE

THE DRUG LAW:
A CASE STUDY

7

THE LAW & CONSTITUTIONAL CHALLENGES

"To rob the public, it is necessary to deceive it. To deceive it, it is necessary to persuade it that it is being robbed for its own benefit, and to induce it to accept, in exchange for its property, services that are fictitious or often even worse."[1]

—Frederic Bastiat—

BEING FAMILIAR WITH THE downfall of American law and the basic difference between FC and NC jurisprudence, it is time for a more in-depth view of how the system of arbitrary law works to deny justice. We have seen that when a litigant wants to try the constitutionality of a law, he or she will either claim a due process or equality rights violation—or sometimes both. In the area of Due Process challenges we have seen that the doctrines of American law separate between fundamental rights and mere liberty interests; the fundamental rights will be those rights explicitly mentioned in the Bill of Rights and those dozen or so unenumerated rights that the Court has recognized as being of such importance that they qualify for protection anyway. In the area of equal protection challenges we have seen that the Court has targeted laws that attack groups of people on the basis of traits such as race, alienage, national origin, or sex; if a litigant claims an equal protection violation on these grounds the Court will review the matter, but not else.

Thus, we find that the Court's doctrines will provide certain people with protection against discriminatory practices and that they will provide protection against infringements of certain rights deemed

---

[1] SCHALER (ED.), *DRUGS: SHOULD WE LEGALIZE, DECRIMINALIZE OR DEREGULATE?* (1998) 198

fundamental. If these criteria are met, strict scrutiny will apply, and the appellant will find herself well protected. The burden of evidence will be on the government to show that the legislation is a reasonable and necessary enterprise. This means that it will be for the state to demonstrate that it serves a compelling interest, that it is narrowly tailored to serve this interest, and that its objectives could not be met by relying on less restrictive means. If the Court, however, decides that these criteria are not met, then a presumption of constitutionality will apply, and the burden of evidence will be on the appellant to convince the Court that there can be no conceivable legitimate reason for the law. In reality, this burden of proof has proven impossible to shoulder and the government wins no matter what.

While this is a simplification,[2] this is the essence of the Supreme Court's approach to constitutional challenges, and we shall now, by example of drug policy, see how it makes a mockery of law.

7.1 THE WAY FORWARD IN A FC SYSTEM OF LAW

In the history of the drug laws there have been more than a hundred constitutional challenges.[3] The majority has focused on the legality of laws criminalizing the production, possession, use, or sale of the marijuana plant (or derivatives thereof) and together these challenges cover a broad spectrum of constitutional protections. In the area of equal protection challenges, appellants have argued that the scheduling system that categorizes illegal drugs is arbitrary and irrational. As regards to marijuana its status as a Schedule I drug has been challenged on the premise that neither the plant nor its derivatives satisfy the three statutory criteria necessary for inclusion in this category: (a) high potential for abuse; (b) no currently accepted medical use; and (c) lack of accepted

---

[2] Due to obvious problems, the Court has abandoned this all-or-nothing approach to rights protection. In order to fill in the blanks left by these two options, it can apply forms of scrutiny that can be placed somewhere in between these two extremes. This will be what has been called "rational basis review with bite," intermediate, or heightened review. Even so, as we shall see, the Courts will use its fundamental rights doctrine to get the results that it wants.

[3] See list, page 361.

safety for use of the drug under medical supervision. Litigants have provided substantial scientific evidence showing that none of these criteria apply and they have noted that the drug law was not properly framed. They claim that it is overinclusive because the law punishes cannabis users as harshly as it punishes more harmful substances, like cocaine and heroin, and that it is underinclusive because the law fails to define similar punishments for comparable substances, like tobacco and alcohol. The essence of their charge is that the criminalization of drugs must have some scientific basis and that if society is going to permit alcohol and tobacco, two very dangerous drugs with significant attendant harms, then, in light of current knowledge, there is no rational basis for prohibiting marijuana.

Furthermore, the harms associated with marijuana being less significant than those associated with legally regulated substances, they have argued that its prohibition is not a valid exercise of the police power. They have held that their choice in drugs is important to them for religious, medical, and/or recreational reasons, and that unless the state can document that the law is a necessary or reasonable intrusion, drug prohibition constitutes a violation of their right to autonomy, liberty, property, and the pursuit of happiness. They have claimed the protection of the First Amendment because the ingestion of these substances involves the reception of information or ideas (sometimes deeply spiritual in nature) and because "the State cannot, consistently with the spirit of this Amendment, unduly contract the spectrum of available knowledge."[4] They have claimed the protection of the Eighth Amendment because the severity of the sentences for drug law violations is incompatible with its prohibition of cruel and unusual punishment. They have claimed the protection of the Ninth and the Tenth Amendment because these were intended to protect all unenumerated rights and to keep the government off their backs. And they have claimed the protection of the Fifth and the Fourteenth Amendment because the drug laws, failing to reflect a proportionate and reasonable application of the police power, violate the Constitution's Due Process and Equal Protection mandates.

---

[4] *Grisvold v. Connecticut*, 85 U.S. at 484 (paraphrasing)

These charges are by no means unheard-of. We know that under the FC conception of rights it does not matter if a right to use drugs is enumerated in the Constitution.[5] The founders wanted all rights equally protected and the Ninth and Tenth Amendment were intended to ensure that the people retained their freedoms. No doubt, then, drug users—just as everyone else—have a right to challenge the constitutionality of a law that targets them for persecution. An effective remedy is at the core of the courts' mandate, and the issue brought before the courts is not some insignificant matter to be treated lightly—it is not about a "right to get high." As Professor Husak has noted, each year more persons are jailed or imprisoned for drug offenses than were jailed or imprisoned for all other crimes combined in any year from 1920 to 1970.[6] More than 40 million Americans have suffered imprisonment. Every year 1.5 million more are caught in the net of the criminal process, and an additional 40 million annual drug users are up for grabs.[7] The ordeal directly associated with incarceration is just one aspect of the many consequences of the drug law, as violators will have to live the rest of their lives as second-class citizens, being ineligible for social security, student loans, as well as hundreds of other government programs. Many will also lose the right to vote and as a result more than 1.4 million Afro-Americans currently have no say in the electoral process. Add to this the disastrous effects that incarceration and other hardships have on their families (25 percent of African Americans who grew up in the past three decades have had at least one parent locked up) and we may begin to appreciate why philosophers of law have labeled drug prohibition "the worst injustice perpetrated by our system of criminal law in the twentieth century,"[8] why judges have named it "the biggest failed policy in the history of our

---

[5] As Chief Justice Marshall explained, the nature of our Constitution "requires that only its great outlines should be marked, its important objects designated, and the minor ingredients which compose those objects be deduced from the nature of the objects themselves." *McCulloch v. Maryland*, 4 Wheat. 316, 407 (1819)

[6] Husak, *Liberal Neutrality, Autonomy, and Drug Prohibitions* (2000)

[7] Even though blacks and other minority groups use these drugs no more often than white people, blacks are six times more likely to be the victims of these laws. As a result the United States, per capita, imprisons seven times as many of its black citizens as South Africa, the most racist regime in modern history, did under Apartheid. BECKER, *TO END THE WAR ON DRUGS* (2014) 18

[8] HUSAK, *LEGALIZE THIS!* (2002) 5

country, second only to slavery,"[9] and why also policemen have held the same.[10]

The consequences at the level of society underscores this point as drug prohibition has left a market worth more than $300 billion to be exploited by organized crime. Because this force cannot exist without a comparable corruption of government,[11] it is difficult to overestimate the corruptive influence of the drugs economy. According to law enforcement experts, the political leadership in more than 30 countries is actively involved in the drugs economy.[12] There is much to suggest that this includes the leadership in America,[13] and that even in Washington DC. "no aspirant wins a high elective office today without depending, directly or indirectly, knowingly or not, on crime-generated funds."[14]

It is beyond the scope of this book to describe the destructive consequences of drug prohibition. However, its constitutionality has been contested in academic circles since the 1960s,[15] and so one would expect

---

[9] Judge James P. Gray in BECKER, *TO END THE WAR ON DRUGS* (2014) 36

[10] Norm Stamper, *Legalize Drugs—all of Them*, LA Times, December 4, 2005 ("It is not a stretch to conclude that our Draconian approach to drug use is the most injurious domestic policy since slavery.")

[11] As U.S. Chief Justice Earl Warren noted: "Organized crime can never exist to any marked degree in any large community unless one or more of the law-enforcement agencies have been corrupted. This is a harsh statement, but I know that close scrutiny of conditions wherever such crime exists will show that it is protected. . . . The narcotics traffic . . . could never be as pervasive and open as it is unless there was connivance between authorities and criminals." Earl Warren, addressing the Milton S. Eisenhower Symposium, Johns Hopkins University, Baltimore, Maryland, Nov. 13, 1970

[12] MILLS, *THE UNDERGROUND EMPIRE* (1986)

[13] SCOTT, *AMERICAN WAR MACHINE* (2014); MARTIN, *THE CONSPIRATORS* (2002); GRITZ, *A NATION BETRAYED* (1989); MENASHE, *PROFITS OF WAR* (1998); REED & CUMMINGS, *COMPROMISED: CLINTON, BUSH AND THE CIA* (1994); STICH, *DEFRAUDING AMERICA* (1988); KWITNY, *THE CRIMES OF PATRIOTS* (1987); RUPPERT, *CROSSING THE RUBICON* (2004); O'BRIEN, *TRANCE-FORMATION OF AMERICA* (1995); RUSSELL, *DRUG WAR* (2000); MAZUR, *THE INFILTRATOR* (2009)

[14] Rufus King said this after having conducted an American Bar Association study on the drug laws (the Committee on Narcotics and Alcohol, Section of Criminal Law). MILLER, *THE CASE FOR LEGALIZING DRUGS* (1991) 71

[15] PACKER, *THE LIMITS OF THE CRIMINAL SANCTION* (1968) 333 ("A clearer case of mis-application of the criminal sanction would be difficult to imagine."); FULLER, *THE MORALITY OF LAW* (1969) 166 ("There is much reason to believe that our approach to the problem of drug prohibition is wrong, and that more would be achieved through medical and rehabilitative measures than through the criminal law."); Dichter, *Marijuana and the Law* (1968) 862 ("Since the use of marijuana, even for the mere enjoyment of the experience, is a form of expression dealing solely with the mind, a strong argument can be made for bringing this extremely private form of expression within the ambit of the zone of privacy surrounding the freedom of

the courts to give the issue its due consideration. Drug policy historians, after all, have carefully documented the trail of lies, deceit, prejudice and misconceptions that preceded, enveloped, and followed the legislative process in this period. It has been established that before the drug laws there was no real drug problem in America (except alcohol);[16] that the first drug laws were the result of powerful lobby interests,[17] moral panic, and a deeply flawed political process;[18] that it was motivated primarily by racism, ignorance and empire building, and that things have not improved since then.[19] They have documented how bureaucratic thrust

---

expression."); King, *Wild Shots in the War on Crime* (1971) 100-01 ("If a single folly. . . were to be selected as the worst, it would be the federal drug effort. . . . Uncle Sam has no business imposing criminal repressions in this field; what each citizen inhales, ingests, or injects into himself seems so far removed from the legitimate reach of any federal power that it is impossible to come up with a hypothetically *less* appropriate federal incursion."); Bonnie & Whitebread, *The Forbidden Fruit and the Tree of Knowledge* (1970) 1149 ("we believe that our central objection to the marijuana laws is of constitutional dimensions. We believe that those laws are irrational."); KAPLAN, *MARIJUANA: THE NEW PROHIBITION* (1971) 2 ("The costs of the marijuana laws far outweigh their benefits and . . . a drastic change in our whole approach . . . is necessary to avoid a national tragedy of major proportions."); Brashear, *Marijuana Prohibition and the Constitutional Right of Privacy* (1975) 581 ("it could be argued that marijuana use provides new sources of belief and experience and is protected under the first amendment because it supplies these necessary preconditions to speech and expression."); Hindes, *Morality Enforcement Through the Criminal Law and the Modern Doctrine of Substantive Due Process* (1977)

[16] The history of drug prohibition follows this pattern: *First* comes policy of escalating the drug war *and then* comes the escalating drug problems. We have seen this time and again and many scholars have described it: "When the opening shots were fired, and for many of the early years of the war on drugs, there was no publically recognized drug problem. Racism was the prime reason for the initial half-century of the war on drugs. The war on drugs provided a venue for gratuitously punishing selected types of people while providing a rationale that one was really doing good. It enabled sadism without guilt or embarrassment, without legal or public censure." Jerry Mandel, *The Opening Shots of the War on Drugs*, in FISH (ED.), *HOW TO LEGALIZE DRUGS* (1998) 213; ALEXANDER, *THE NEW JIM CROW* (2011) 5-6; BECKER, *TO END THE WAR ON DRUGS* (2014) 55; DUKE & CROSS, *AMERICA'S LONGEST WAR* (1993) 5; WISOTSKY, *BEYOND THE WAR ON DRUGS* (1990) 185

[17] "The elimination of marijuana came from pressures exerted by newly created 'Federal drug control agencies, cotton and timber interests, and chemical industries.'" *Seeley v. State*, 132 Wash. 2d 776, 940 P.2d 604 (1997) Footnote 10 (Sanders J., dissenting)

[18] In their seminal work Professors Bonnie and Whitebread summarizes their findings: "We have found no indication that the legislators consulted scientific data; instead they relied on sensationalistic police and newspaper identification of marijuana with crime. Naturally these assumptions went unchallenged; the only segment of the public likely to challenge them was small and outside the public opinion process." Bonnie & Whitebread, *The Forbidden Fruit and the Tree of Knowledge* (1970) 1166

[19] BAKALAR & GRINSPOON, *DRUG CONTROL IN A FREE SOCIETY* (1998) 68 ("Looked at as a series of incidents, the history of social and legal responses to drug use . . . sometimes seems melancholy and haphazard. It is easy to find inadequate pharmacology, inconsistent ad hoc responses based on poor information, indulgence of passions and prejudices, including racism, in response to drug scares, institutional self-aggrandizement by narcotics police, and a fair

and power-political incentives ensured that the enemy image of drugs became an addiction, one that politicians would embrace to win votes, bureaucrats would employ to enlarge their budgets, and war profiteers would use to claim ever-increasing powers;[20] that because of these incentives public servants have consistently ignored all evidence of failure only to fuel the cycle of failure and escalation;[21] and that this has led to drug policies ever more detached from realities on the ground, ever more hostile to human flourishing, and increasingly opposed by a widening majority of experts.[22] In short, the history of drug prohibition shows that government has followed one imperative: to keep the War on Drugs going (and growing) at any cost, without checks and balances—

---

amount of hypocrisy and corruption."); Christiansen, *A Great Schism: Social Norms and Marijuana Prohibition* (2010) 235 ("A law that millions of Americans already believe to be invalid will be considered even more so as people learn that it was not based on scientific research, but rather racial prejudice and social conditions peculiar to the 1930s.")

[20] WISOTSKY, *BEYOND THE WAR ON DRUGS* (1990) 173-74 ("It is difficult to find in modern American history an obviously defective and destructive policy so rigidly locked in place. A partial explanation for this unique rigidity lies in the fact that the ordinary corrective mechanisms that operate for some other failed governmental policies do not function here. First, the lack of even a minimal standard of performance by which to measure results precludes responsible dialog within the government. Without real goals there can be no accountability. Not once in the history of the War on Drugs . . . has the Government ever stated a realistic objective. . . . Second, the Government has effectively immunized itself from outside criticism, managing to preempt any serious public debate calling into question the premises of drug enforcement policy.") For more on why our public servants ignore all evidence of failure and instead make everything worse, see BERTRAM, ET AL., *DRUG WAR POLITICS: THE PRICE OF DENIAL* (1996) 102-62; WISOTSKY, *BEYOND THE WAR ON DRUGS* (1990) 173-97; BARNETT, *THE STRUCTURE OF LIBERTY: JUSTICE AND THE RULE OF LAW* (2014) 135-337; MILLER, *THE CASE FOR LEGALIZING DRUGS* (1991) 85-107; MILLER, *DRUG WARRIORS AND THEIR PREY* (1996) 164-69; EPSTEIN, *AGENCY OF FEAR* (1990) Husak, *Liberal Neutrality, Autonomy, and Drug Prohibitions*, (2000) 80 ("If the 'war on drugs' is unjustifiable, why does it continue to be waged? No single answer can be given. An important factor, however, is the financial gain to law-enforcement agencies that assign a high priority to the apprehension of drug offenders.")

[21] After looking through the systemic studies compiled by the National Commission on Marijuana and Drug Abuse, Epstein concluded that "none of the available data systematically gathered over a period of fifty years conformed to the . . . way politicians had used and abused the drug problem." EPSTEIN, *AGENCY OF FEAR* (1990) 268

[22] Galliher, Keys & Elsner, *Lindesmith v. Anslinger* (1998) ("Since the 1960s, few criminologists or criminal law professors have supported government drug policies. To this day, those setting American drug policy continue to ignore expert legal, academic, and medical advice. In the academic community there is now a clear recognition of long-standing patterns of both the ineffectiveness of, and racism inherent in American drug law enforcement. Indeed, opposition to contemporary American drug control policy has become normative in the academic community.")

and that the harder this war has been fought, the greater the human causalities in its wake.[23]

While prohibitionists will disagree, all this has been documented. Not only have advocates of prohibition never proven the validity of their premises; reform activists have noted their unwillingness to engage in debate, and the diversity of literature that prohibitionists and reform activists each can draw upon to advance an argument suggests that this is no coincidence. At the very least it attests to the inherent weakness of the prohibition argument; while philosophers of law are at a loss to find anything of substance in this category,[24] scholars have documented how drug prohibition has continued to this day supported by nothing but false premises, distorted data, overt lies, and a massive propaganda effort.[25]

This being so, one would expect the courts to be mindful of their responsibility to the Constitution, individual applicants, and community at large. Considering that politicians have such a poor track

---

[23] FISH (ED.), *HOW TO LEGALIZE DRUGS* (1998) xvi. ("For decades the federal government—the President, the Congress, and the courts—as well as state governments, both political parties, and a wide array of extragovernmental forces have combined to stifle the expression of a simple truth: drug prohibition, and its instrument of oppression, the war on drugs, makes the drug problem worse rather than better by creating a giant black market."); DUKE & CROSS, *AMERICA'S LONGEST WAR* (1993) 159 ("the government goes to great efforts to keep Americans from understanding that most deaths from drug overdoses are the products of prohibition, not the intrinsic qualities of the drugs themselves; that virtually all of the drug-related crime is the result of prohibition, not the pharmacological properties of the drugs; that the drug business as we know it is solely and entirely the consequence of prohibition. As a result, Americans attribute the evils of prohibition to illicit drugs themselves. The government calculatedly promotes such beliefs.")

[24] Husak, *Four Points about Drug Decriminalization* (2003) 23 ("[N]o case for criminalization has been adequately defended. It is utterly astonishing, I think, that no very good argument for drug prohibitions has ever been given. When I am asked to recommend the best book or article that makes a philosophically plausible case for punishing drug users, I am embarrassed to say that I have little to suggest.")

[25] ROBINSON & SCHERLEN, *LIES, DAMN LIES, AND DRUG WAR STATISTICS* (2007); BECKER, *TO END THE WAR ON DRUGS* (2014); SCHALER (ED.), *DRUGS: SHOULD WE LEGALIZE, DECRIMINALIZE OR DEREGULATE?* (1998); ESCOHOTADO, *A BRIEF HISTORY OF DRUGS* (1999); WISOTSKY, *BEYOND THE WAR ON DRUGS* (1990); DUKE & CROSS, *AMERICA'S LONGEST WAR* (1993); HART, *HIGH PRICE* (2014) 288-332; EPSTEIN, *AGENCY OF FEAR* (1990); FISH (ED.), *HOW TO LEGALIZE DRUGS* (1998); MILLER, *DRUG WARRIORS AND THEIR PREY* (1996) 3-33. Professor Barnett summarizes the prohibitionists' quest: "In war, it is said, truth is the first casualty. To be blunt, many committed prohibitionists inside and outside of government who profess to care so much about the morals of others routinely lie or willfully mislead the public about nearly every aspect of both drugs and the policy of prohibition. Our consistent experience with drug prohibition— from marijuana, to heroin, to cocaine—is that when careful empirical studies are eventually performed, they reveal the initial official accounts to be either false or wildly exaggerated. Rarely, if ever, does law enforcement then reverse itself or even moderate its rhetoric." Barnett, *Bad Trip* (1994) 2603. See also MIKALSEN, *TO END A WAR* (2015) endnotes 1, 14, 64, 66, 70

record on this subject, one would expect the judiciary to step in and provide some quality control of a law that criminalizes 20 percent of the citizenry and of a war effort that scholars and law enforcement have described as a "totalitarian solution," a "vehicle for fascism,"[26] and a "lurch towards the police state."[27]

It is after all incontestable that drug prohibition from a liberal perspective is inherently suspect[28] and that there are especially weighty reasons for reviewing legislation that burdens politically marginalized groups. This, no doubt, includes drug users, as it is impossible to find a group against which government has been more antagonistically predisposed. Hence, as the justices at the Supreme Court have reminded us that "the very essence of civil liberty . . . consists in the right of every individual to claim the protection of the laws, whenever he receives an injury;"[29] "that experience teaches us to be most on our guard when the asserted Government purpose is to protect the public welfare";[30] that "it makes sense to scrutinize governmental action more closely when the State stands to benefit;"[31] and that "if it can be shown that one half of the effort has failed, we are at liberty to consider the question of policy with a freedom that was not possible before,"[32] we would expect them to honor their commitment to the rule of law.

The *only way* to do this would be to give the founders' system of principled law due recognition. And to ensure that the drug laws satisfy the criteria for constitutionality under a FC conception of rights the Court must ask if the drug laws represent a necessary and proper application of the police power. To see if this is so, the Court has several modes of analysis available. It could go with the proportionality analysis that has risen to international prominence or it could go with domestically crafted

---

[26] MILLER, *THE CASE FOR LEGALIZING DRUGS* (1991) 118-24. Miller has even written a book on the subject. For more on how the drug warriors have completed four of the five steps in the chain of destruction identified by Holocaust-researchers (Identification—orstracism—confiscation—concentration—annihilation), see MILLER, *DRUG WARRIORS AND THEIR PREY* (1996)

[27] MASTERS, *DRUG WAR ADDICTION* (2001) 29

[28] Buchhandler-Raphael, *Drugs, Dignity, and Danger* (2012)

[29] *Marbury v. Madison*, 5 U.S. 137 (1803) 163

[30] *Olmstead v. U. S.*, 277 U.S. 438 (1928) 479 (Brandeis J., dissenting) (paraphrasing)

[31] *Bradley v. U. S.*, 410 U.S. 605 (1973); *Harmelin v. Michigan*, 501 U.S. 957 (1991) fn. 9

[32] Justice Holmes, *Common Carriers and the Common Law* (1879) 631

models like the Lawton or Strict Scrutiny test. In either case the way forward is much the same: The state must show that the purpose for the law is legitimate; that the means it employs to reach this goal are necessary; that the law reflects a careful balancing of the interests of the individual and society; and that less restrictive means would not do.

To succeed in this endeavor, the state must show that the separation between licit and illicit drugs makes sense and that there are good reasons for criminalizing illicit drug users. The only way this can be done is by first demonstrating in specific fashion the precise nature of the threat (i.e., the illicit drugs). After this, the state must show that the drug law is necessary to combat the threat; that it is effective in doing so; and that it at the same time preserves the interests of the individual and society. This means that the prohibition not only must be effective in curbing the supply and demand of the illicit drugs, but that it must be *the least intrusive* instrument amongst those which might achieve a protective function. *All these criteria must be met*, for only in doing so can it be said that the law strikes a fair balance between the rights of the individual and the interests of the community.

This is the essence of the test of reason, and if the state fails to show that the drug law satisfies these criteria, then we are dealing with an arbitrary, disproportionate, and discriminatory practice—and we have a violation of our catalogue of rights.

7.1.1 CONSIDERATIONS FOR THE COURT

Now, as we shall see, the courts have never looked into the premises of prohibition. Nevertheless, whenever citizens claim that constitutional rights are violated, they have a right to have the issue determined to the satisfaction of an independent, impartial, and competent court, and the first order of business for a court abiding by the rule of law would be to find out what exactly is the drug problem. For the goal of a drug free America to be legitimate, the state must show that the negative consequences of drug use outweigh the positive. The illicit drugs must be shown to pose a threat so tremendous that the world would be clearly better off without them and their alleged benefits must be shown to be trivial and negligible. To find out if this is so the court must examine why people take drugs, what it means to them, their patterns of use, and whether there can be valid reasons. It must investigate drug use from a historical and anthropological perspective as well as from a social and psychological point of view. Expert witnesses must be called upon to testify on these topics and what we can learn from history and common practices.

Traditionally, prohibitionists have had the privilege of defining the problem. However, their version of events has become increasingly contested, and so the court must find out if drug use really is the useless, misguided, dangerous, and inherently worthless pursuit that they claim. Relevant questions for consideration would be: Are drug users the maladjusted misfits they are portrayed to be? Do they use drugs merely for reasons of peer pressure, boredom, alienation, immaturity, depression, or some other pathology? Are they "victims of a plague who, tempted by pushers, peers, and the pleasures of drugs, succumb to the lure and lose control of themselves?"[33]

Is there some truth to this oft-cited prohibition-lore or does it vastly misrepresent the facts? Could the legalizers be correct in perceiving drug users as autonomous agents, people who normally handle themselves responsibly and consequently should be allowed to choose for themselves how to pursue their life-plan? Are they correct in asserting that most users are happy with their drug of choice, that they are functional citizens, and that they find drug use to be of value—a positive contribution to their life?

Supposed that most people do describe their use in these terms, are they misguided? Do they misrepresent the truth, or could there be good reasons for using drugs? Is there evidence to suggest that their use could be a rational pursuit—one having inherent value? Assuming that there are benefits of drug use, what are they and how do they compare to harms? How many drug users experience the positive effects and how many experiences the harms? And when all is said and done, do the negative aspects of drug use overshadow the positive?

Furthermore, how do all of this relate to autonomy, the weightiest factor on the constitutional scale? Does drug use increase autonomy? Does it limit autonomy? Do the properties of certain drugs exact such a

---

[33] SZASZ, *CEREMONIAL CHEMISTRY* (2003) 175 (paraphrasing)

powerful influence that the concept of self-determination loses its meaning? Does drug use normally have a negative bearing on a person's ability to perform or contribute to society? Is it compatible with the rights of non-users to live free and productive lives? If it is not, in what sense does it conflict with the exercise of the fundamental rights of others? If drug use does negatively impact autonomy, what drugs are worse? How representative are the worst-case scenarios? And how do they compare with those instances of asserted/actual autonomy enhancement?

These are important questions to consider, but we have by no means neared the end of our quest. Before we can form an opinion on the drug problem, we must also ask: what part of it is prohibition related and what part is pharmacologically related? We know that many of the harms associated with drug use must be attributed to its criminalization; what are the actual costs of prohibition?

Another area of investigation must be whether the harms related to drug use are greater than the harms associated with other activities that we have learned to live with. After all, there is a risk associated with everything we do. Nothing is more lethal than living and so what is the risk-benefit ratio? When it comes to sports: Is drug use more dangerous than motorcycling, ski jumping, horse riding, mountain climbing, or other activities? When it comes to foods: Are the illicit drugs more harmful than peanuts, sugar, salt, fast-food, etc.? When it comes to the legal drugs: are the illicit drugs more dangerous than tobacco, alcohol, coffee, aspirin, valium, etc.? Are they more prone to be misused? Do their addictive and pharmacological properties render them especially problematic? And what about the user groups: Why exactly is it ok to persecute the former and not the latter? What crimes against fellowmen has a cannabis/cocaine user, producer, transporter, or distributor committed that alcohol drinkers, producers, transporters, or distributors have not? Are the former more prone to mischief? Has their involvement with these drugs stripped them of autonomy rights and human dignity? Have they debased themselves and lost their humanity? Are they no longer worthy of equal protection?

For drug prohibition to be sustained there must be something about the illicit drugs (other than their classified status) that makes their users worthwhile targets for the criminal law. A prime objective for the court therefore must be to find out why this group of people has been selected to bear the burden of the law. Is there a plausible, nonarbitrary explanation for this or does the classification merely reflect disproval, dislike, or stereotyping of the class of persons burdened by the legislation?

If any of these inquiries come up short, prohibitionists will already be on shaky ground. However, assuming that the harmful effects of drugs are unparalleled; assuming that they are vast and weighty compared to whatever positive qualities; assuming that the positive qualities are of little significance—and that we are qualified to make this value judgment on behalf of others: Once we have established that the goal of a drug-free America is a worthy endeavor, it must be shown to be feasible. The relationship between means and ends is profoundly significant whenever the question of constitutionality is addressed, and the state must not only show that drug prohibition serves important governmental objectives but is substantially related to the achievement of those objectives. This means that the price of pursuing the goal of a drug-free America must not be too high and that the law must be properly tailored to deal with the threat. Not only must there be a relationship of proportionality between the importance of reaching the goal and the price we can be expected to pay for pursuing policy. There must also be a reasonable relationship of proportionality between the ways we deal with different threats—alcohol, tobacco, cocaine, marijuana, etc.

So how have the drug laws served society? Has the prohibition experiment functioned as intended? What has been its effect on the supply and demand of illicit drugs? To what extent has the criminal law been an effective deterrent? To what extent has prohibition succeeded in reducing the potential harms caused by drug use? To what extent are other factors important? Has it proven efficient or are there fatal flaws in the strategy that cannot be amended? Is a prohibition the least drastic means available to deal with the problems of drug abuse, or could we achieve the same—or better—results by less despotic means? And what about the societal consequences of prohibition: To what extent has the drugs economy corrupted our social order? Are the good guys and the bad guys clearly defined different groups, or has the illicit economy corrupted society to the point where even governments are in on it?

If the latter is the case, how realistic is the goal of winning a War on Drugs? And if we add up all the negative consequences of drug use with all the negative consequences of prohibition, which one would come out on top? In the final balancing of scales, are the problems generated by drug use sufficiently serious to merit criminalization or is the remedy a bigger evil than the mischief it seeks to eradicate?

All these questions must be contemplated. The answers must be carefully weighed for the court to make sense of the larger picture and arrive at an informed opinion as to if the war effort is necessary. To find out if the law is a proper application of the police power it must always be necessary—and to be necessary, it must never be more invasive than needed to protect the public welfare. It must be effective in dealing with the mischief at hand and represent a careful balancing of the interests of the individual and society. As always, the liberty presumption favors the individual's right to choose her own life-plan and any doubt must be resolved in favor of liberty. This means that if less invasive means could contain the problem, they must be the preferred option and drug prohibition fails the test of reason.

7.2 The Way Forward in a NC System of Law

We have just seen what it would entail if the state would ever have to defend its policies. However, most justices do not think this is necessary and when a constitutional challenge comes their way, they will find a way to disparage the rights claim. Depending on the charges levied against the law, the courts differ in their approach, but the gist of their argument is that "because there is no fundamental constitutional right to import, sell, or possess illegal drugs," they will defer to the legislative and uphold the legislation.[34]

Some courts have been more hostile to the rights claim than others, but the standard approach for denying drug use status as a protected right is simple. The court will begin its analysis by stating that "in ascertaining whether a right is fundamental, a court must determine whether the right

---

[34] For a few representative cases, see *Raich v. Gonzales*, 500 F.3d 850 (9th Cir. 2007); *Nat'l Org. for Reform of Marijuana Laws (NORML) v. Bell*, 488 F. Supp. 123 (D.D.C. 1980); *United States v. Kiffer*, 477 F.2d 349 (2d Cir.); Louisiana Af. of NORML v. Guste, 380 F. Supp. 404 (E.D. La. 1974); *State v. Mallan*, 86 Haw. 440, 950 P.2d 178 (1998)

is explicitly or implicitly guaranteed by the Constitution." Looking at this, drug use is not explicitly protected and so the question becomes: is it implicitly protected?

So far in the analysis both FC and NC individuals agree, and from here on the proper way forward would be to recognize the individual's autonomy and liberty interest and perform a balancing test as to whether the interests of society outweigh the interests of the individual. This is what FC justices would have done. However, because NC justices mistake the spirit of the Constitution with its letter, they must rely on precedent and tradition rather than principled thinking and so they choose another route.

This is what comes naturally. For one, because they remain bound by contemporary constraints, they have no access to the implications of first principles; they cannot fathom their reach nor see how they connect. Second, because they fail to connect with this bigger picture, they cannot see their day and age in a historical context; they cannot access the timeless world of universal morality; and they do not know how to work with a general conception of rights. Third, because they have no access to this greater framework of FC reasoning, they are in the position of blind leading the blind and so they are naturally afraid of doing their job—which is to be moral arbiters and overturn acts of the legislature whenever politicians fail to respect individual boundaries.

Consequently, NC judges continue their analysis on this track: First they will say that because "guideposts for responsible decision-making in this uncharted area are scarce and open-ended," (i.e., "because we do not know how to operate in FC terrain") and "judicial extension of constitutional protection for an asserted right places the matter outside the arena of public debate and legislative action," (i.e., "we have no better guidance than the irrational movements of the masses") they will defer to the legislature whenever possible.

To find out if deference is an option, they must make sure that the asserted right is a liberty interest and not a fundamental right, for if they can conclude with the former their business is done. Never mind that the founders wanted all rights equally protected. Never mind that the separation between liberty interests and fundamental rights is an arbitrary divide. Never mind that this mode of analysis outright defies the rule of construction specifically outlined by the Ninth Amendment. Because they do not know how to maneuver by first principles they will have to go by precedent. The past is the only map they know that will provide them with a sense of direction, and so the task will be to find out if the asserted right is sufficiently similar to other, already accepted rights to merit protection.

True to the NC mindset, they will demand a narrow description of the asserted right, which (depending on the constitutional challenge) will be the smoking of marijuana either for religious, recreational, or medical purposes. And because the smoking of marijuana for these purposes is not explicitly mentioned in the Constitution, NC judges will determine the status of marijuana smoking by asking whether it is so "deeply rooted in this Nation's history and tradition" or so "implicit in the concept of ordered liberty" that neither liberty nor justice would exist if it was sacrificed.

Because this test is not rooted in any objective criteria it will be for the judge to arrive at a conclusion based on his own preferences, and after comparing marijuana smoking to other, already protected activities he is not likely to be impressed with the importance of protecting this right. Colored by many years of prohibitionist propaganda, he is likely to be deeply suspicious (if not openly hostile) to any claim that this activity merits protection and so the way forward is predictable. After looking at the rights claim the judge will simply reaffirm his own preconceptions, stating that "smoking marijuana receives no explicit or implicit constitutional protection;" that "the act of smoking does not involve the important values inherent in questions concerning marriage, procreation, or child rearing" (i.e., the other protected rights); that "its use predominantly as a 'recreational drug' undercuts any argument that its use is as important as, e.g., use of contraceptives;" and that it is neither so deeply rooted in this Nation's history and tradition nor so implicit in the concept of ordered liberty that freedom or justice would seize to exist if it were sacrificed. At this point in the analysis the judge is likely to quote the *Ravin* court's speculation that "few would believe they have been deprived of something of critical importance if deprived of marijuana," and on this basis he will conclude that "private possession of marijuana cannot be deemed fundamental."[35]

In the large majority of constitutional challenges brought before the courts, this is all the effort it takes for a judge to deny the argument any merit. He or she will simply quote previous court decisions while taking for granted that their analysis was properly performed. Only a very few courts have put in some effort on their own and one of them was the *Ravin* court. In the history of constitutional challenges this is one of the most important, as the Alaska Supreme Court held that the Alaska Constitution's right to privacy protects an adult's ability to use and possess a small amount of marijuana in the home for personal use. Unlike all the other courts that put the burden of evidence on the applicants, the *Ravin* court did not disparage marijuana smoking as an utterly insignificant activity. It recognized that the drug law represented a substantial intrusion into the sphere of privacy, and because "the privacy of the individual's home cannot be breached absent a persuasive showing of a close and substantial relationship of the intrusion to a legitimate governmental interest," it put the burden on the state to show that this was the case.[36]

After a careful review, the justices found "no firm evidence that marijuana, as presently used in this country, is generally a danger to the user or to others." And after weighing "the relative insignificance of marijuana consumption as a health problem," the importance of respecting the sanctity of the home, and the importance of personal autonomy to the people of Alaska, the Court did not see the requisite "close and substantial relationship" between the state's asserted interest in protecting the public from marijuana use and the means chosen to advance that interest (a law prohibiting all possession and use of marijuana). Consequently, the Alaska Supreme Court became the first to provide constitutional protection for marijuana users.

Later courts, however, have disregarded this part of the *Ravin* court's analysis. They have explained it away by saying that the Alaska

---

[35] For this line of reasoning, see *United States v. Maas*, 551 F. Supp. 645 (D.N.J. 1982) at 647; *NORML v. Bell*, 488 F. Supp. 123 (D.D.C.1980) at 132-3

[36] As the court said: "Here, mere scientific doubts will not suffice. The state must demonstrate a need based on proof that the public health or welfare will in fact suffer if the controls are not applied." *Ravin v. State*, 537 P.2d 494 (1975) 511

Constitution provides better privacy protection than other state and federal constitutions (as if that is at all possible), and instead of focusing on that aspect of the court's analysis which held privacy to be important and that the state must show some reasonable relationship between means and ends, they have cited *Ravin* for its fundamental rights analysis. This is highly unfortunate, for as we shall see its fundamental rights analysis was misframed and erroneous. Nonetheless, on the basis of its deeply flawed analysis later courts have jumped to the conclusion that no fundamental right to drug use exists, and this has been the end of any Due Process complaint.

In the area of Equal Protection challenges applicants have fared no better, for "in light of the very limited constitutional interests asserted by defendants," the courts think it "clear that they have not been denied equal protection of law."[37] Because most judges see marijuana use as a significant "threat to society as a whole,"[38] they have great difficulty considering the possibility that the Constitution provides such activity with meaningful protection and they see no reason why the state should have to justify its different treatment of marijuana smokers and alcohol drinkers. They make it clear that in this area the legislature has been granted a wide discretion in attacking social ills and that "if Congress decides to regulate or prohibit some harmful substances, it is not thereby constitutionally compelled to regulate or prohibit all."[39]

Due to this policy of legislative freedom in confronting social problems, the courts have declined to investigate if there is a rational basis for treating the different groups of drug users differently. Not only that, but because of the perceived unimportance of the asserted right, courts "do not agree with the defendants that the Legislature is bound to adopt the 'least restrictive alternative' that would fulfill its purpose of protecting the health, safety and welfare of the community."[40] In fact, because the right in question is perceived to be of so little importance, these judges "know of nothing that compels the Legislature to thoroughly investigate the available scientific and medical evidence when enacting a

---

[37] *United States v. Bergdoll*, 412 F. Supp. 1308 (D. Del. 1976) at 1314

[38] *Borras v. State*, 229 So. 2d 244 (1969) at 246

[39] *United States v. Kiffer, supra,* 477 F.2d at 355

[40] *Commonwealth v. Leis*, 355 Mass. 189 (1969) at 195

law. The test of whether an act of the Legislature is rational and reasonable is not whether the records of the Legislature contain a sufficient basis of fact to sustain that act. The Legislature is presumed to have acted rationally and reasonably,"[41] and this is true even if evidence to the contrary exists.

In other words, "every presumption is indulged in favor of the validity of a statute."[42] The legislature's decision to criminalize drug use may be contaminated with prohibitionist prejudice, contradictory logic and demonstratively false presumptions—it does not matter. At this level of scrutiny there is no inquiry into the relationship between means and ends, no second-guessing of Congress's "wisdom, fairness, or logic of legislative choices,"[43] and the burden remains with the contender to show that there can be no conceivable rational basis for the legislative action. This has proven impossible, for as long as the state holds that the classifying measure is necessary no further explanation is needed.[44]

With very few exceptions, the courts that have considered the constitutionality of the drug laws have consistently applied this form of review. As a result, all these constitutional challenges have failed, and we shall now go into detail as to the reasoning that has been used to uphold drug prohibition.

---

[41] Id. 192

[42] Id. 200

[43] *Heller*, 509 U.S. 319

[44] As the *Pickard* court held: "Under the deferential standard of rational basis review . . . as long as there is some conceivable reason for the challenged classification of marijuana, the [drug law] should be upheld. Such a classification comes before the court bearing a strong presumption of validity, and the challenger must negative every conceivable basis which might support it. The asserted rationale may rest on rational speculation unsupported by evidence or empirical data. The law may be overinclusive, underinclusive, illogical, and unscientific and yet pass constitutional muster. In addition, under rational basis review, the government has no obligation to produce evidence to sustain the rationality of a statutory classification." *United States v. Pickard, et. al.*, No. 2:11-CR-0449-KJM (2015) 27-28 (citations and internal quotation marks omitted)

8

MORE ON THE PROBLEMATICS OF NC REASONING

"It is of great importance to observe that the character of every man is, in some degree, formed by his profession. A man of sense may only have a cast of countenance that wears off as you trace his individuality, whilst the weak, common man has scarcely ever any character, but what belongs to the body; at least, all his opinions have been so steeped in the vat consecrated by authority, that the faint spirit which the grape of his own vine yields cannot be distinguished. Society, therefore, as it becomes more enlightened, should be very careful not to establish bodies of men who must necessarily be made foolish or vicious by the very constitution of their profession."[45]

—Mary Wollstonecraft—

THE PROBLEMS WITH THE NC system of law and current U.S. doctrine have already been discussed. The case of the drug laws, however, provides us with a better understanding of the problematics of NC legal reasoning. Nowhere is its illogicality and deceptiveness better exposed, and nowhere is the injustice that follows in its wake more pronounced. We shall now discuss the various ways by which the courts set a challenge up for failure.

---

[45] WOLLSTONECRAFT, *A VINDICATION OF THE RIGHTS OF WOMEN* (1790) 17

8.1 Improper Deference

The first thing we may notice is that the courts use a presumption of legality to sustain the validity of the law. The defendants are never given a chance to defend themselves, as whatever evidence there exists to challenge the constitutionality of the law is ignored. This, as Judge Shangler of the Michigan Supreme Court noted, "contradict[s] the principle that the constitutionality of a criminal statute predicated upon the existence of a particular state of facts may be challenged by showing to the court that those facts have ceased to exist."[46] In every challenge to the drug laws the appellants seek an opportunity to show that the present state of facts no longer support prohibitionist assumptions, and as "[t]he determination that the classification remains justified . . . can only come after full consideration of the most contemporary and informative data,"[47] they are effectively denied their day in court.

The right to an independent, impartial, and competent court is at the very heart of the right to a fair trial. And so, as a person cannot be imprisoned without being accorded a fair hearing in accordance with the Due Process Clause, the extreme prejudice with which these challenges is met is incompatible with constitutional protections.

Furthermore, not only do the courts deny appellants an opportunity to have the true state of facts determined but the courts' faith in the legislature is hardly warranted. Legislatures, after all, rarely act in accord with principle when they enact laws. The laws they enact usually come about as a result of lobbyism, peer pressure, or as a response to majoritarian will, and the principled reasoning that guides human rights thinking has nothing to do with either. In fact, human rights law is there to protect us from the despotism of special interests, bureaucracy, or populism. And so, as the legislature has not been known to examine if the laws they enact and uphold are compatible with its principles, the courts' presumption of legality is highly misplaced.

Another reason why the courts' deference violates the Constitution is that the burden of proving guilt naturally belongs to the state. Hence, as it is a constitutional requirement that the burden of proving guilt is placed

---

[46] *State v. Mitchell*, 563 S.W.2d 18 (Mo. 1978) 34 (Shangler J., dissenting)

[47] Id. 35 (Shangler J.)

squarely on the government, it is only logical that the burden of proving that the criminal law is compatible with constitutional limits should be placed there. After all, the question of guilt does not only depend upon whether a defendant has broken the law. The question of guilt goes further. It is fundamentally entwined with the judicial maxim that all punishment must be deserved, and as the principle of *just desert* (no punishment without moral culpability) reaches into the substantive areas of the law, the question of guilt depends on whether the law conforms to principles of justice.

Thus, the constitutional requirement that the burden of proving guilt remains with the government logically extends to constitutional challenges and the criminal law. As Justices Black and Douglas stated in their *Turner* dissent:

> "It would be a senseless and stupid thing for the Constitution to take all these precautions to protect the accused from governmental abuses if the Government could by some sleight-of-hand trick with presumptions make nullities of those precautions. Such a result would completely frustrate the purpose of the founders to establish a system of criminal justice in which the accused . . . would be able to protect himself from wrongful charges by a big and powerful government. It is little less than fantastic even to imagine that those who wrote our Constitution and the Bill of Rights intended to have a government that could create crimes . . . and then relieve the government of proving a portion of them.
>
> [If] Congress . . . define[s] a crime . . . due process requires the Government to prove *each element* beyond a reasonable doubt before it can convict the accused of the crime it deliberately and clearly defined."[48]

This is especially important in those "crimes" where no person is directly victimized. In instances such as this, where the government to justify punishment refers to such abstract notions as "harm to society," the burden of proving that the law conforms to principles of justice must not only befall the government, but the government must pass the

---

[48] *Turner v. United States*, 396 U.S. 398 (1970) (Black, J., with whom Douglas J. joins, dissenting.) (emphasis mine)

compelling interest/strict scrutiny test. If not, the government will have the power to criminalize any behavior no matter how private or innocent. After all, most of our actions cause some indirect harm to some vaguely defined social interest. For example, sport activities—in fact, *any* activity—can result in physical injuries which again could be said to pose some degree of harm to society. Likewise, much of what we eat contains some harmful substances. Not only that, but all foods can be abused by overeaters, and, as all foods have the potential of making us less than healthy, the government could find an excuse for criminalizing these products. Furthermore, speech is often provocative and every day people say things that have the potential of indirectly harming some social "interest." It may strike at prejudices and biases and have profound unsettling effects. In times of tyranny, for example, simply speaking the truth will be a revolutionary act and the government's interest in self-preservation can be used to justify any infringement on "objectionable" speech.

Now, the "harms" attached to sports, foods, and speech are quite different in nature. The first two are characterized by physical and economic harm, while the latter is usually thought of as a "moral" harm. The NC State is more likely to criminalize the latter, for it is willing to accept a great deal of physical and economic harm if it does not threaten the perceived values of the status quo (which means the power base of authority).

When our leaders talk of "harm to society," therefore, what they usually mean is a threat to their own perceived power base, and history leaves no doubt that this is the common denominator behind the "harms" our leaders are keen to eradicate. While they tend to accept (and encourage) any harmful activity as long as it is seen to promote their interests (power, prestige, and money), we see that any abstract and vaguely defined "harm" is to be dealt with as long as it is deemed threatening to the powers that be. More shall be said on this, but NC leaders are keen to criminalize anything they do not like. Consequently, unless the government bears the burden of showing us that it has a compelling interest in criminalizing such behavior, there is no limit to the laws it may enact.

Now, this improper deference to the legislature is a consequence of the rational basis test, which again is an upshot of the fundamental rights doctrine. We know that FC scholars have criticized both for being incompatible with the spirit of the Constitution and in drug cases several judges have joined the choir. As Justice Sanders put it in his *Seeley* dissent:

> "This two-tiered classification system of strict scrutiny and rational basis has proven problematic and subject to criticism because it shoehorns what in reality exists on a continuum into absolute but artificial categories. While the 14th Amendment simply references 'liberty,' the question posed by the majority is whether there is a 'fundamental interest' to smoke marijuana. I disagree with this formulation because the constitution speaks of principles, not specifics. Freedom from needless suffering; the right to individual autonomy; the right to bodily integrity . . . and freedom from arbitrary, privacy-invading restraints are the principles applicable here.
>
> Better we should question the predicate which supposedly justifies state intervention in the first place than shift the burden to the private citizen to show why he should be free—which is, or should be, the natural state in a free society."[49]

This, of course, is pure FC reasoning, and to FC justices like Sanders it is clear that laws prohibiting the sale, use, and/or ingestion of marijuana are in violation of the Constitution. They have long held that First Amendment, Fifth Amendment, Eighth Amendment,[50] Ninth Amendment and Fourteenth Amendment rights are implicated in drug use. According to them, it is clear that *there is* a "fundamental constitutional right to smoke marijuana;"[51] "that it is founded upon the constitutional rights to personal autonomy and privacy, guaranteed by

---

[49] *Seeley v. State*, 132 Wash. 2d 776, 940 P.2d 604 (1997) 631 (Sanders J., dissenting)

[50] Bonnie & Whitebread, *The Forbidden Fruit and the Tree of Knowledge* (1970) 1153 ("the rationality arm of the eighth amendment should prohibit imprisonment for violation of that legislation, even for five minutes")

[51] Justice Abe of the Hawaiian Supreme Court stated in 1972 that "I do not agree . . . that one does not enjoy the fundamental constitutional right to smoke marijuana. . . . I believe that the right to the 'enjoyment of life, liberty and the pursuit of happiness' includes smoking of marijuana, and one's right to smoke marijuana may not be prohibited or curtailed unless such smoking affects the general welfare." *State v. Kantner*, 493 P.2d 306 (1972) at 312 (Abe J., concurring)

[the state and Federal] Constitution;"[52] that "our present method of regulating marijuana . . . is unreasonable and unconstitutional in violation of the due process and equal protection clauses of the Fourteenth Amendment;"[53] that the drug law therefore "violates the Federal and State Constitutions in that it is an impermissible intrusion on the fundamental rights to liberty and the pursuit of happiness, and is an unwarranted interference with the right to possess and use private property;"[54] and that "where the State endeavors to intrude into the individual's private life and regulate [such] conduct, . . . it is the duty of the courts to offer a haven of refuge where the individual may secure vindication of his right to be let alone."[55]

Hence, the only problem for drug users is that FC individuals are few and far between. In the history of challenges to the drug laws, we find them expressing their judgment in the dissents rather than the majority opinions. But even so, their reasoning speaks for itself and it is clear that "the majority's response is . . . misguided and in error."[56] Furthermore, the self-defeating reasoning relied upon by the majority suggests that it only "seeks a legal shield behind which it can avoid objective inquiry,"[57] and that the rational basis test and fundamental rights analysis is their way of doing so.

For reasons that have already been discussed (and which will be further explained) NC judges have strong objections against letting drug users have their day in court. Reason, however, will not come to their rescue and so, to disparage the rights-claim, they must rely on phony tactics. These shall now be reviewed.

---

[52] Id. 313 (Levinson J., dissenting)

[53] Id. 319 (Kobayashi, J., dissenting)

[54] *People v. Sinclair*, 387 Mich. 91, 194 N.W.2d 878 (1972) 133 (Kavanagh J., concurring)

[55] *Kantner*, 493 P.2d 306 (1972) 317-18 (Levinson J., dissenting)

[56] *State v. Mitchell*, 563 S.W.2d 18 (1978) 29 (Seiler J., dissenting)

[57] Id. 29 (Seiler J., dissenting)

8.2 Mistaking Shadow and Light

The most common way for courts to deny drug users a fair trial is by a failure to recognize that the enumerated rights are a shadow that is cast by the light of more fundamental principles. We have seen that according to the founders' conception of rights, it does not matter if rights are enumerated. The unenumerated rights are just as important as those spelled out, but NC judges, being oblivious to the bigger and how it connects, only focus on the enumerated rights. Thus, they will perform an analysis that betrays an ignorance of the ideas upon which the American system is built. This ignorance is made explicit by such statements:

> "Plaintiffs' claim in the present case rests on bare allegations of a general right to privacy to do what one wishes in his own home and with his own body. Although plaintiff does claim enforcement of this right of privacy through the Fifth and Fourteenth Amendment and through the Ninth Amendment, he does not ground it or even attempt to ground it on any one of the amendments which protect certain guaranteed rights and which in doing so create constitutionally guarded zones of privacy."[58]

As discussed previously, the right to privacy is not explicitly stated in the Constitution. Even so, it is recognized that zones of privacy are created by the penumbras of the first, third, fourth, fifth, and ninth amendments, and the objection in this case was that the appellant did not first attempt to ground his claim in one or more of these. A more telling example of the confused reasoning with which challenges to the drug laws are met is difficult to find, for if the judge did not have it backwards he would have understood that plaintiff's failure to "ground it or even attempt to ground it on any one of the amendments" did not impair the argument at all. How could it? The amendments themselves are grounded in (and validated by) the underlying principles of law. These principles do not care if an activity is enumerated or whether it is similar to other activities already granted "fundamental" status. All they do is establish

---

[58] *Louisiana NORML v. Guste*, 380 F. Supp. 404 (1974) 407

that the individual is to be given a free rein and that any limitation to his domain must be justified by sufficiently weighty considerations. That is all. The central issue is autonomous choice, and whether you, I, or the government, would think it wise is irrelevant.

Looking at the relationship between these principles and the enumerated rights, the right to privacy is more closely connected to these principles than the amendments. The light of these abstract principles is channeled into a more "tangible" right to privacy, which again provides context and substance to the few enumerated rights. Thus, it obviously makes no sense to ask the appellants to ground their claim in the latter. The legalization argument remains firmly grounded in the principle of autonomy—the underlying principle that has given validity all the enumerated rights (as well as the right to privacy), and this being the case, it is absurd to ask the appellants to look for it elsewhere.

The example above was District Judge Comiskey's reply to a legal challenge made by the law reform organization NORML in 1974.[59] Comiskey's response, however, is not unique. It represents the norm, and six years later, when NORML countered the drug law with another challenge, they were met with the same reaction. In an effort to ground the rights-claim in precedent NORML's lawyers had relied on *Stanley v. Georgia*, a case where the Supreme Court had granted constitutional protection to the private possession of obscene materials. The *Stanley* Court had held that "the right to receive information and ideas, regardless of their social worth, . . . is fundamental to our free society,"[60] and had asserted a "right to satisfy [one's] intellectual and emotional needs in the privacy of [one's] own home."[61] For obvious reasons NORML argued that the private possession/use of marijuana deserved no less protection than obscene materials, but Circuit Judge Tamm responded:

"NORML tries to bootstrap the Stanley right of privacy in the home into a fundamental right that protects all activities taking place

---

[59] At the time, other scholars also noted the NORML court's backwards approach. As Brashear observed: "the opinions suggest that the courts were influenced more by the absence of an express amendment protecting marijuana use than by the inapplicability of the right of privacy." Brashear, *Marijuana Prohibition and the Constitutional Right of Privacy* (1975) 581

[60] *Stanley v. Georgia*, 394 U.S. at 564

[61] Id. at 565

therein. This reading reverses the proper analysis. The home offers refuge for activities grounded in other protected rights. The right protected in Stanley was the first amendment right to read and receive information even if the information itself was not constitutionally protected. Without that first amendment right at issue, Stanley would have no right to privacy in the home."[62]

Again, we see the same backwards reasoning in effect. If the founders' conception of rights is brought to bear it is Judge Tamm that "reverses the proper analysis," as the home *does not* merely "offer refuge for activities grounded in other protected rights." Instead, it offers refuge for *activities grounded in the principles from which other constitutionally protected rights are derived.* These are the principles of fundamental justice, principles such as those of dignity, autonomy, proportionality, equality, non-arbitrariness, limited government, and the liberty presumption. They are all connected and while unenumerated, they are the principles that breathe life and substance into the enumerated rights.

Apropos first principles, the courts' flawed natural rights reasoning, mirrors the same mistake. In *Seeley*, the plaintiff asserted that the legislature's placement of marijuana in schedule I of controlled substances violated article I, § 32 of the Washington Constitution, which provides "[a] frequent recurrence to fundamental principles is essential to the security of individual right and the perpetuity of free government." In this case, Ralph Seeley, a man diagnosed with a rare form of bone cancer (as well as being an able lawyer), argued that the phrase "frequent recurrence to fundamental principles" suggested that the framers retained the notion that natural rights should be considered when protecting individual rights. Defending himself, he claimed that this section of the Washington Constitution designated "extra-constitutional fundamental principles as essential to the security of individual rights," and that it was evidence of the framers' belief in natural law. He brought forth evidence that the notion of fundamental principles was central to natural law theories when the Constitution was adopted and that by adopting art. I, § 32 the framers intended to expand the scope of rights protected by the Constitution. On this basis, he held that the Constitution granted him a

---

[62] *NORML v. Bell*, 488 F. Supp. 123 (D.D.C. 1980)

right to have marijuana prescribed as medical treatment for the nausea and vomiting associated with chemotherapy.

The courts' analysis is worth noting, as it is another testimony to the intellectual barrenness of NC reasoning. As discussed in part two, the Constitution was a natural rights document, one by which the founders positivized the higher, unwritten natural law. The "frequent recurrence" Clause was an offshoot of this thinking and it was to be a reminder from the founders of the importance of anchoring the body of law to first principles. They knew that powerful forces would conspire to deprive the people of their government and that a system of arbitrary law was the means by which this would be done. Thus, the purpose of this section of the Washington Constitution was to guard against the influence of these forces and the NC system of law that would be their crowning achievement.

As seen from the FC perspective, this is the only sensible interpretation of the "frequent recurrence" Clause. Just like the Ninth Amendment it means exactly what it says, and its purpose was to ensure that the relationship between the individual and state were constantly recalibrated to align with first principles.

Just like the Ninth Amendment, however, this Clause would prove difficult for NC individuals to come to terms with, and as soon as a system of arbitrary law was in place they would join ranks to protect it. We have already seen why. Because NC individuals fail to see the bigger picture, their psychology is to support the status quo—and because they have an authoritarian bent, this status quo will favor the agents of tyranny rather than liberty. It goes without saying that to these people the very idea of a return to first principles will be anathema. One way or another it will have to be discouraged and whether it be for reasons of ignorance or political expediency, this is what most jurists have done.

Hence, as the majority of justices are NC individuals, it should come as no surprise that the Washington Court chose this route. As if they were interpreting ancient hieroglyphs whose meaning was long since lost, the justices made no real effort to decipher the true meaning of the "frequent recurrence to fundamental principles" Clause. Instead, the majority simply noted that it had been used infrequently by the judiciary and that Washington jurisprudence had yet to see a consistent approach to this clause. From there on, following their authoritarian proclivity, they jumped to the conclusion that the framers must have intended to leave it to the government to legislate as it saw fit. And to support this thesis, so out of step with the founders' temperament, they laid bare an equally blemished understanding of natural law. As the majority put it: "Respondent fails to identify a natural right, in existence at the time of the constitution's adoption, to use marijuana or to choose a particular medical treatment." And because "[n]either constitutional history [n]or pre-existing state law indicate that using marijuana is a right that the Washington Constitution was designed to protect," the court deduced that "art. I, § 32 was not meant to provide a substantive right to use marijuana for medical treatment."[63]

Again, we are provided with an extraordinary example of the cognitive despondency that defines NC reasoning. For one, the court's decision smacks of insincerity and bias. Humans have for tens of thousands of years used different substances to experience different states of consciousness[64] and only the last hundred years have we had laws restricting the use of some of these substances. As pertains to the medical use of marijuana, which was the court's inquiry, it has been used in Asian and Middle Eastern countries for at least 2,600 years for these purposes. It first appeared in Western medicine in 60 A.D. in the pharmacopoeia of Dioscorides and it has been listed in subsequent pharmacopoeias since that time. In the 19th century, marijuana was widely used for a variety of ailments, including muscle spasms, and cannabis was still to be found in the British Pharmaceutical Codex as late as 1949. While the *Seeley* court didn't mention any of this, other courts have recognized the historical use of marijuana for medicinal purposes, and as the Ninth Circuit held in *Raich v. Gonzales*, "[i]t is beyond dispute that marijuana has a long history of use—medically and otherwise—in this country."[65] As the *Raich* court recognized, it was only with the passage of the Controlled

---

[63] *Seeley v. State*, 132 Wash. 2d 776, 940 P.2d 604 (1997) 622

[64] "The use of psychoactive plants or fungi to alter consciousness is probably a nearly universal human cultural activity. Ethological evidence of the consumption of psychoactive plants among a variety of animal species, as well as archaeological evidence of early human substance use, suggests that the roots of such practices are a longstanding part of the cultural history of humanity and cannot be reduced to some degenerate or delinquent modern phenomenon." Tupper & Labate, *Plants, Psychoactive Substances and the International Narcotics Control Board* (2012) 18

[65] *Raich v. Gonzales, et al.*, 500 F.3d. 864 (9th Cir. 2007)

Substances Act in 1970 that Congress placed marijuana on Schedule I, taking it outside of the realm of all uses, including medical, under federal law.

In the history of man, then, it was not until the 20th century that the right to self-medicate was no longer taken for granted, and so it is difficult to see how the Washington Court earnestly could have believed that there was no "natural right, in existence at the time of the constitution's adoption, to use marijuana or to choose a particular medical treatment." The right to self-medicate was at this time incontestable, and the court's opinion is made even more suspect by the fact that this right is a subset of an (if possible) even more fundamental right, the right to bodily integrity. This right has deep roots in American history and legal tradition. There is a wealth of jurisprudence to draw upon, and it is indisputable that the right to be free of government intrusion with respect to one's body has roots in natural rights principles and the philosophy of individual autonomy. American legal precedent has consistently upheld legal protection for this individual right, and even before the Founding it was a firmly established basis of Anglo-American law.[66]

Aside from the denial of historical evidence, the court's claim that the applicant "fails to identify a natural right, in existence at the time of the constitution's adoption, to use marijuana or to choose a particular medical treatment," indicates that the justices either (1) knew nothing of the founders' natural law reasoning or (2) willfully ignored it. It suggests that they were looking for a textual source explicitly stating that "We, the framers of the U.S. Constitution, hold marijuana use to be a natural right," when in fact the framers could be counted upon to do no such thing. First of all, they saw no need to enumerate natural rights as their existence had nothing to do with textual basis. We have already seen that there is a written *and an unwritten* constitution of the United States. The former draws its legitimacy from the latter, and as the natural law belongs to the realm of unwritten law, the court's attack makes no sense. It might as well deny a right to have children, to wear a hat, to farm lands, or to go

---

[66] Blackstone recognized a right to personal security that "consists in a person's legal and uninterrupted enjoyment of his life, his limbs, his body, his health, and his reputation." He extended protection to the "preservation of a man's health from such practices as may prejudice or annoy it." 1 BLACKSTONE, *COMMENTARIES* 128, 133 (1765)

to sleep because the founders did not explicitly articulate these natural rights.[67]

Furthermore, in 1889, at the time of the adoption of the Washington Constitution, cannabis was a freely sold and frequently used medicine[68] and the framers could not see any reason for stating the obvious—that it was a natural right. Unlike modern day justices, they abided by a presumption of liberty, and unless marijuana use somehow violated the rights of others to live free and productive lives, there was no question in their mind that it was a natural right. When it comes to this, Seeley's right to use marijuana for palliative relief from terminal illness can hardly be said to violate the rights of non-users to administer their own affairs as they see fit. And as Seeley's medicinal choice is "theoretically and practically consistent with the exercise of the fundamental rights of others," it is plainly "inferable from the axioms of natural law theory."[69]

Thus, Seeley's claim was firmly grounded in the principles of natural law. One does not have to look further than across the border to find a Supreme Court decision declaring it to be so,[70] and as Rufus King put it, "If people have no freedom to make such choices as cannabis over nicotine for their preferred lung irritant, what did the Constitution leave them?"[71]

8.3 Ignoring the Bigger-Picture Implications

We would do well to ponder King's question, for as seen from the FC perspective drug prohibition does implicate important rights. As seen

---

[67] Considering that the Eighth Circuit, in *U.S. v. White Plume*, actually denied farming status as a protected right, the irony is complete. As it stands the state can now deny people a right to live off their land without offering a reasonable (much less compelling) justification.

[68] In the period between 1840 and 1900 more than 100 articles about the therapeutic value of cannabis were published in Europe and North America. See MATHRE, *CANNABIS IN MEDICAL PRACTICE* (1997)

[69] Sweet & Harris, *Moral and Constitutional Considerations in Support of the Decriminalization of Drugs*, in FISH (ED.), *HOW TO LEGALIZE DRUGS* (1998) 455

[70] In *Regina v. Smith*, 2015 SCC 34, the Canadian Supreme Court held that Canadians have a fundamental right to use medical marijuana and that this liberty includes taking THC in whatever form the patient chooses.

[71] KING, *THE DRUG HANG UP* (1972) chapter 30

from this perspective, the War on Drugs is an authoritarian attempt to control consciousness and it is not so much a war on drugs as a war on autonomous choice. As Graham Hancock noted, the fundamental premise of this war effort is that "we as adults do not have the right or maturity to make sovereign decisions about our own consciousness and about the states of consciousness we wish to explore and embrace. This extraordinary imposition on adult cognitive liberty is justified by the idea that our brain activity, disturbed by drugs, will adversely impact our behavior toward others. Yet anyone who pauses to think seriously for even a moment must realize that we already have adequate laws that govern adverse behavior toward others and that the real purpose of the 'war on drugs' must therefore be to bear down on consciousness itself."[72]

The fact that is so obvious from the FC perspective, that the right to drugs is a right to control one's consciousness, the most intimate, elemental, and personal there is, has been lost on NC individuals. This is because they are born into a world where prohibitionist propaganda has defined the drug policy debate for nearly a century. And because they have been raised to believe in the one-sided and untruthful image of drugs as a source of all our problems, they have fallen victim to an exaggerated enemy image. To them, therefore, drugs are simply bad. They are an evil to be eradicated by whatever means necessary, and only to the extent that this is done can our children be safe.

We shall have more to say on the enemy image of drugs and how it fails to mirror reality. However, leaving aside the question of whether drugs are "bad," it is undeniable that the whole point of taking drugs is to alter the chemical balance of the brain, leading to changes in a person's cognitive process, and it follows that fundamental rights necessarily *are* involved. As Professor Richards noted "the right of drug use, if it is a right, is a right associated with the control of consciousness, and thus with the right of conscience itself, and should be understood accordingly."[73]

The U.S. Supreme Court has already recognized that "the right to receive information and ideas, regardless of their social worth, . . . is fundamental to our free society,"[74] and that, except in very limited cases,

---

[72] HANCOCK (ED.), *THE DIVINE SPARK* (2015) 30-31

[73] RICHARDS, *TOLERATION AND THE CONSTITUTION* (1989) 281

[74] *Stanley v. Georgia*, 394 U.S. 557 (1969) 564

the right to be free from unwanted government intrusion in one's privacy is fundamental. The Court has also acknowledged that "the State may not, consistently with the spirit of the First Amendment, contract the spectrum of available knowledge,"[75] and that the "right to receive" recognized in *Stanley* is "a right to a protective zone ensuring the freedom of a man's inner life, be it rich or sordid."[76] Furthermore, the Court has acknowledged that people have a fundamental right to make certain "intimate and personal choices,"[77] and that "[a]t the heart of liberty is the right to define one's own concept of existence, of meaning, of the universe, and of the mystery of human life."[78] The Court has also noted that "[b]eliefs about these matters could not define the attributes of personhood were they formed under compulsion of the State,"[79] and that the First Amendment secures a "right of the individual to be free from governmental programs of thought control, however such programs might be justified in terms of permissible state objectives."[80]

All this applies to the drug law, for the War on Drugs is nothing if not an attempt to control our thought processes. It may be for our own good or for the good of society; this is a question that remains to be addressed, and it can only be properly addressed under the auspices of an independent, impartial, and competent tribunal. However, thought processes are, at the deepest level, *what we are*, and as Hancock noted, "to the extent that we are not sovereign over our own consciousness, then we cannot in any meaningful sense be sovereign over anything else either."[81]

Also, as seen from the FC perspective, drug use implicates another important right—the right to liberty. Because the state uses the criminal law to address the "problem" of drug use, drug law violators, if caught, will be subjected to arrest and imprisonment. We have already seen FC scholars insist that these people "have every right to demand a

---

[75] *Griswold*, 381 U.S. 479 (1965)

[76] *United States v. Reidel*, 402 U.S. 351 (1971) 360 (Harlan J., concurring)

[77] *Casey*, 505 U.S., at 851

[78] Id. at 851

[79] Id.

[80] *Reidel*, 402 U.S. 351 (1971) 359 (Harlan J., concurring)

[81] HANCOCK (ED.), *THE DIVINE SPARK* (2015) 3

justification for how they have been treated,"[82] and according to these scholars, criminal law must be subject to unique scrutiny to ensure that no punishment is unjust. There is a rule of law that the more severe the sanction, the greater will be the burden of overcoming the liberty presumption. And as the drug law imprisons millions of people and threatens to imprison many millions more, it should be uncontroversial that the government must have very good reasons for doing so. This is the only way to honor the fundamental principles of law, and because liberty, as Husak and other scholars have noted, "is a fundamental interest," it "should be subject to deprivation only by a compelling state interest."[83]

As the drug law clearly implicates autonomy and liberty rights, FC justices will insist that the government proves that this is the case. Judge Sweet, for instance, has argued forcefully that the right to drugs is a constitutionally protected autonomy right, and that "[b]ecause the right to self-determination is a fundamental right, any governmental action that encroaches upon it must be justified by a 'substantial' state interest and be tailored in the narrowest manner possible."[84] As he continued: "governmental action encroaching on the right to self-determination faces a scale that is tipped heavily against it before the balancing analysis

---

[82] HUSAK, *OVERCRIMINALIZATION* (2008) 94-103

[83] Husak, *Two Rationales For Drug Policy*, in FISH (ED.), *HOW TO LEGALIZE DRUGS* (1998) 58. See also Colb, *Freedom from Incarceration* (1994) 812 ("The eighth amendment requires scrutiny of every form of punishment, with a concomitant determination of whether it is cruel and unusual. Substantive due process additionally requires strict scrutiny of every deprivation of a fundamental fight. Because incarceration involves both punishment and the deprivation of a fundamental right, incarceration must accordingly withstand scrutiny under both the eighth amendment and the due process clause of the fourteenth (or fifth) amendment."); Materni, *The 100-plus Year old Case for a Minimalist Criminal Law* (2015) 27 ("when the government wants to regulate conduct through the most restrictive means at its disposal, and in such a way that the very core of liberty is affected, it needs to have a compelling interest to do so, coupled with the absence of less restrictive means to achieve that interest—in other words, criminal legislation should be subject to strict scrutiny.")

[84] Sweet & Harris, *Moral and Constitutional Considerations in Support of the Decriminalization of Drugs*, in FISH (ED.), *HOW TO LEGALIZE DRUGS* (1998) 483. To substantiate this claim the authors refer to *United States v. O'Brien*, 391 U.S. 367, 377 (1968); *Young v. New York City Transit Authority*, 903 F.2d 146, 157 (2d Cir), cert. denied, 498 U.S. (1990); *Simon & Schuster, Inc. v. Members of New York State Crime Victims Bd.*, 112 S. Ct. 501, 514 (1991) (Kennedy J., concurring); *Loper v. New York City Police Department*, 802 F. Supp. 1029, 1041 (S.D.N.Y. 1992), aff'd, 999 F. 2d 699 (2d Cir. 1993)

even begins,"[85] and pertaining to the liberty encroachment other justices have also noted the need for strict scrutiny.[86]

8.3.1 HOW THE BIGGER-PICTURE IMPLICATIONS ARE IGNORED

To NC justices however, none of this is obvious. As far as they are concerned drug use has no inherent value and neither does the freedom of the drug using population. Some will be more frank about admitting this than others. Nonetheless, their actions speak for themselves, for whenever challenges to the drug law are brought before the courts they will protect the law from critical review and drug users' autonomy and liberty rights will carry no weight in their analysis.

This is their modus operandi: In order to sustain the law, they have to steer clear of the bigger picture and any coherent analysis. They must ignore the fundamental principles of justice, discount the factual picture, and narrow their focus to the point where their twisted and self-refuting logic is not too obvious. This is done by the following sleight-of-hand: They will define the right narrowly, look to precedent for guidance, and begin analysis with the assumption that the enumerated rights and a handful of others are the only worthy of protection. This approach to constitutional interpretation obviously connects with their failure to understand the difference between shadow and light, but because of this backwards methodology challenges to the drug laws fail again and again. Medical marijuana challenges are disparaged because "the liberty interest specially protected by the Due Process Clause [does not] embrace a right to make a life-shaping decision on a physician's advice to use medical marijuana to preserve bodily integrity, avoid intolerable pain, and

---

[85] Ibid. 483

[86] As Justice Levinson of the Hawaii Supreme Court held, "[a]ny criticism which attempts to deter courts from inquiring into the constitutionality of laws must distinguish between legislation which seeks to regulate economic and social relationships and that which intrudes into the purely private sphere of human life. In the former instance courts rightfully grant the legislature wide latitude for experimentation in the promotion of the general good. But, where the State endeavors to intrude into the individual's private life and regulate conduct having no public significance, it is the duty of the courts to offer a haven of refuge where the individual may secure vindication of his right to be let alone." *State v. Kantner*, 493 P.2d 306 (1972) 317-18 (Levinson J., dissenting)

preserve life, when all other prescribed medications and remedies have failed."[87] Traffickers and distributors will be denied their right to a fair trial "[b]ecause there is no colorable claim of a fundamental constitutional right to import or to distribute marihuana."[88] And even hemp farmers will be denied their day in court because, "[t]he Supreme Court has not declared 'farming' to be a fundamental right."[89]

The reasoning is, of course, false on all accounts because the rule of narrowing blinds the justices to the real issue, which is the law's relation to the fundamental principles of justice. To know if there is a right to use cannabis for medical, recreational, or religious reasons; to know if there is a right to produce or distribute marijuana commercially; and to know if there is a right to grow hemp, the court must first look at this underlying issue—but this is never done. Because NC individuals fail to operate at a more abstract level of generality, they will cling on to what little they can grasp and so they begin in the other end, with the few enumerated rights. These textual sources will be used to consider the issue, and because drug use, possession, production, trafficking, distribution, etc., is not explicitly granted by the Constitution, they will look to the unenumerated right to privacy to see if it can contain the asserted right in question.

Now, the only way this could be done with some sincerity would be *first* to formulate a general conception of the right to privacy and *then* determine whether the possession/use/sale of cannabis was fit to be included. In the history of the drug laws, however, only one court has ever done so. This was the *Ravin* court, and it found it impossible to formulate a general idea of privacy which did not include drug use. In its general outline of privacy, it was defined as "a right of personal autonomy in relation to choices affecting an individual's personal life" and "a right to be let alone." From this characterization it followed quite naturally that the use of cannabis in the privacy of one's home had to be included in such a right, and this is what the court confirmed. Perhaps for this reason no other courts have followed the *Ravin* court's example. Instead, they will skip this part and go directly to the fundamental rights test already discussed; they will ask if cannabis use is of such importance that it is

---

[87] *Raich v. Gonzales, et al.*, 500 F.3d. 864 (9th Cir. 2007)

[88] *United States v. Bergdoll*, 412 F. Supp. 1308 (D. Del. 1976) 1313

[89] *United States v. White Plume*, 447 F.3d 1067 (2005)

"implicit in the concept of ordered liberty," and as this test is flexible enough to accommodate any bias, no court has found drug use deserving of constitutional protection.

When it comes to this, we have already seen that the fundamental rights analysis, the rule of narrowing, and the presumption of constitutionality are not only interconnected and symptomatic of the justices' closed mindset. As we have seen they are also unconstitutional, for while the presumption of liberty and the equal treatment of all rights claims are inferable from first principles, these doctrines are not. In truth, they are merely helpful means of divesting with proper thinking and frowned upon constitutional challenges, and nowhere is this better seen than in drug cases. By narrowing their focus NC justices somehow manage to escape the inevitable conclusion that autonomy and liberty rights are important rights worthy of strict scrutiny. This can only be achieved by applying a frame of reference so detached from reality that it becomes possible to ignore the logic that dictates otherwise; that the rights at issue are not only about a right to bodily integrity and to control our own thought processes, but a right also not to be imprisoned for doing so—rights that must be called fundamental if the word is to have any meaning at all.[90]

It is also interesting to note that in the NC state of affairs, the game is always rigged in favor of the state. As pertains to the rule of narrowing, therefore, it is no coincidence that constitutional challenges must be defined at its most specific level, whereas this rule is not applied to the state. The courts, for instance, do not demand that the state justifies its aggression by narrowing down the issue as to whether "a state has a right to persecute and imprison non-violent citizens for exercising their autonomy rights in ways that directly hurt no one." They do not insist that the state justifies its assault on liberty by narrowing down the issue as to whether "a state has a right to harass and incarcerate individuals for trying to experience their connection to God more directly in ways that truthfully harm no one." And they do not ask the state to justify its violent onslaught against citizens by narrowing down the issue as to whether "it has a right to hunt down and lock away individuals for striving towards

---

[90] As Tribe dryly noted, "I would suppose that protecting your ability to control your own body would have to be on anyone's short list of basic liberties or privileges and immunities in our system of government." Tribe, *On Reading the Constitution* (1986) 63

greater levels of well-being and happiness in ways that directly affect no one—not even themselves—negatively."

At least 90 percent of all drug use conforms to these criteria and yet the courts would never think to ask the state to defend its hostility to autonomous choice in this way. True to their authoritarian inclination, the justices would never even consider looking for exactly where in the Constitution such a right could be granted to the state. Instead, it is the individual that must vindicate his choice of drugs and every conceivable doubt benefits the state. The presumption of liberty being effectively reversed, what we are dealing with is, of course, a presumption of guilt, and so it is that the American system does sneakily what fascist jurists did openly.[91]

To summarize, this is the problem with current doctrines. Aside from being unconstitutional, they are the result of the isolated, fragmented, and freedom-fearing perspective that defines the NC mindset, and it comes as no surprise that they are well tailored to help the justices ignore the bigger-picture implications. The courts' restricted focus effectively defines away the right we want to validate, as the judge is free to draw upon his personal bias to conclude that drug use is not important enough to merit protection. Never mind that many people and religious groups attest to the ability of some drugs to communicate with the Divine;[92] never mind that some of these drugs have been used by wisdom seekers for millennia; never mind that some of them have a proven record for facilitating physical and psychological healing;[93] never mind that they are

---

[91] To quote Vincenzo Manzini, a leading jurist in Mussolini's Italy: "nothing more incongruous and paradoxical can be imagined than the presumption of innocence . . . if a presumption indeed needs be, that should be a presumption of guilt." Materni, *The 100-plus Year old Case for a Minimalist Criminal Law* (2015) 22

[92] See *infra* notes 93, 106, 167

[93] Clinical research on psychedelic drugs has yielded positive results in the following areas: Criminal recidivism, relationship counseling, treatment of substance abuse and addiction, PTSD, depression, end-stage psychotherapy with the dying, and obsessive-compulsive disorder, as well as being unique tools for stimulation of the meditative state and elicitation of mystical experience. See WINKELMAN & ROBERTS (EDS.), *PSYCHEDELIC MEDICINE* (2007); Grob, et al., *Pilot Study of Psilocybin Treatment for Anxiety in Patients with Advanced-stage Cancer* (2011) 71-78; Mash, *Ibogaine Therapy for Substance Abuse Disorders* in BRIZER & CASTANEDA (EDS.), *CLINICAL ADDICTION PSYCHIATRY* (2010) 50-60; Vollenweider & Kometer, *The Neurobiology of Psychedelic Drugs: Implications for the Treatment of Mood Disorders* (2010) 642-651. Anthropologists generally agree that the use of these psychedelic drugs is beneficial to the cultures that use them. See Ibid and SZASZ, *CEREMONIAL CHEMISTRY* (2003) 126. See also notes 106, 167

important tools for personal growth; never mind that most drug use is personally rewarding and socially unproblematic;[94] never mind that people with a history of moderate drug use on average are better functioning than non-drug users;[95] never mind that there is evidence to suggest that drug use *enhances* self-control and autonomy, whereas prohibition undermines conditions of autonomy;[96] never mind that 1.5 million Americans are arrested every year for violating this law; never mind that their use doesn't directly harm anyone else; never mind that prohibition has failed to reduce the supply and demand of drugs;[97] never mind that there are less invasive means of dealing with any social problems arising from their use; and never mind that the destructive consequences of prohibition are tearing the fabric of society apart.[98] None of this matter. In fact, it is consistently ignored because of the courts' narrow focus.

8.4 REASONING FROM THE NARROWED-DOWN PERSPECTIVE

We have seen that there are autonomy and liberty interests at stake in challenges to the drug laws and there is more to say on how they are

---

[94] Scholars have pointed out that drug use is a natural part of life, an important aide to the full development of individual potential. See DUKE & CROSS, *AMERICA'S LONGEST WAR* (1993) 153-54; WISOTSKY, *BEYOND THE WAR ON DRUGS* (1990) 201-02; MILLER, *THE CASE FOR LEGALIZING DRUGS* (1991) 152-57; MILLER, *DRUG WARRIORS AND THEIR PREY* (1996) 1-7

[95] Longitudinal studies of drug users indicate that adults who once had been moderate drug users are presently "the psychologically healthiest subjects, healthier than either abstainers or frequent users." Compared to moderate users, abstainers "show some signs of relative maladjustment." Shedler & Block, *Adolescent Drug Use and Psychological Health: A Longitudinal Inquiry* (1990) 612, 625

[96] Husak, *Liberal Neutrality, Autonomy, and Drug Prohibitions* (2000) 69-70

[97] This is well known. For example, *Analysis of Marijuana Policy* (June 1982) prepared by the National Research Council's Committee concluded that: "It can no longer be argued that use would be much more widespread and the problematic effects greater today if the policy of complete prohibition did not exist." 29-30

[98] To quote the UNDP: "evidence shows that in many countries, policies and related enforcement activities focused on reducing supply and demand have had little effect in eradicating production or problematic drug use. As various UN organizations have observed, these efforts have had harmful collateral consequences: creating a criminal black market; fuelling corruption, violence, and instability; threatening public health and safety; generating large-scale human rights abuses, including abusive and inhumane punishments; and discrimination and marginalization of people who use drugs, indigenous peoples, women, and youth." UNDP, *Perspectives on the Development Dimensions of Drug Control Policy* (2015) 2

disparaged. We have already discussed how the rule of narrowing dissociates the right in question from the bigger picture, making it possible to ignore the bigger context and the fundamental issues at play. Furthermore, we can count on the courts to deny the plaintiff's rights claim any merit by (1) belittling the rights claim, (2) focusing on precedent and refusing to expand the area of protection, (3) misframing the issue, (4) relying on falsehoods and an exaggerated enemy image, (5) applying different kinds of logic to otherwise similar cases, (6) applying the same logic to otherwise dissimilar cases, and (7) emptying words of their essential meaning.

8.4.1 BELITTLING THE RIGHTS CLAIM

This tactic takes many forms. The *NORML* court, for instance, in discussing if smoking marijuana was worthy of constitutional protection, concluded in the negative by comparing the use of cannabis to previously accepted activities. First, it took for granted that "the act of smoking does not involve the important values inherent in questions concerning marriage, procreation, or child rearing."[99] Then, referring to previous decisions where the courts had recognized the use of contraceptives as constitutionally protected, the court stated that "its use predominantly as a 'recreational drug' undercuts any argument that its use is as important as [such objectives]."[100] It bears noticing that FC scholars and justices have refuted this part of the argument.[101] Nevertheless, to support the

---

[99] *NORML*, 488 F.Supp. 133

[100] Id.

[101] Judge Sweet and Edward Harris comments on this part of the NORML court's analysis: "In its analysis the court not only dismisses the value of 'recreational' activity but actually counts the recreational aspect of the activity against the significance of the activity. In doing so, however, the court necessarily fails to grasp both the recreational aspect of nonprocreational sexual relations implicitly recognized in *Griswold* and the significance of the fundamental right to recreation that individuals have in their pursuit of life, liberty, and happiness." Sweet & Harris, *Moral and Constitutional Considerations in Support of the Decriminalization of Drugs*, in FISH (ED.), *HOW TO LEGALIZE DRUGS* (1998) 482. The Authors continue on this footnote: "The right to recreation is implied in the concepts of liberty and happiness set forth in the Declaration of Independence. In *Olff v. East Side Union High Sch. Dist.*, 404 U.S. 1042 (1972), Justice Douglas identifies recreation as a fundamental right implied in the concept of liberty: "The word 'liberty' is not defined in the Constitution. But, as we held in *Griswold v. Connecticut*, it includes at least the fundamental rights 'retained by the people' under the Ninth Amendment. One's hair style, like one's taste for food, or one's liking for certain kinds of music, art, reading, recreation,

validity of this conclusion, the court quoted the *Ravin* court's assumption that "few would believe they have been deprived of something of critical importance if deprived of marijuana."[102]

Just like the *Ravin* court, the *NORML* court provided no evidence that this was so. It merely took this for granted. However, perhaps this is not really true. After all, drug users will go through extraordinary difficulties to pursue their habits. Even though government agents have done everything in their power to make life a living hell for them, they have had no success in deterring drug use. Today, hundreds of millions of people around the world will risk the hassles of the criminal sanction to experience their preferred states of consciousness and drug use persists even in those countries where the death penalty is provided.

This being so, the eagerness with which we pursue a choice in drugs could be seen as a testimony to the legitimate interest in question. At the very least, scholars have pointed out that the judgment of individual drug users is far more reliable than that of the state,[103] and as Bakalar and Grinspoon noted:

"If it ever became necessary for the government to use vast amounts of money and personnel to curb an organized illicit traffic in [some] other commodity forbidden by consumer protection laws, the law would probably be repealed. If people wanted the commodities so much, we might conclude that they have a legitimate interest and value strong enough to outweigh any argument for prohibition. In other words, we would handle the problem as we handle mountain climbing, hang-gliding, or motorcycle racing: We would treat it as a

---

is certainly fundamental in our constitutional scheme—a scheme designed to keep government off the backs of people." (481)

Justice Levinson of the Hawaii Supreme Court had this to say on the constitutional right to privacy: "[It] encompasses more than just freedom from government surveillance. It guarantees to the individual the full measure of control over his own personality consistent with the security of himself and others. This freedom to choose one's own plan of life is essential to the pursuit of happiness and the enjoyment of life and thus finds additional protection in article I, section 2 of the Hawaii Constitution. In the instant case, the State's infringement upon this right of personal autonomy becomes apparent when one understands the nature of marihuana and the reasons for its use." *State v. Kantner*, 493 P.2d 306 (1972) at 315 (Levinson J., dissenting) (references omitted)

[102] *Ravin v. State*, 537 P.2d at 502

[103] DUKE & CROSS, *AMERICA'S LONGEST WAR* (1993) 152

matter of preferred tastes and activities (however questionable) rather than consumer error."[104]

The *NORML* and the *Ravin* courts are not the only ones that have failed to add any importance to people's choice in drugs. Later courts have basically copied the *NORML* court's analysis,[105] and to this day they have all excepted drug use from those personal rights that can be deemed "fundamental" or "implicit in the concept of ordered liberty." To them, accepting drug use as a right to autonomy or privacy seems so contrary to the values upon which society is erected that even "obscene materials" have better protection. This is the case even though drugs have more potential to bring about new insights and mental discoveries of any real value, but this aspect of drug use has gone neglected.

The bias against drug use is so great that no court has attributed any weight to the positive aspects of drug use.[106] Even though most drug use is unproblematic to society and rewarding to the users, it is portrayed as an evil to be eradicated. Hence, autonomy and liberty rights are easily disparaged, for if drugs are "bad" what interest could be at stake in prohibition? If drug use is a menace to society, why should we not imprison the people who ensure its continuation? Why should we think twice about this?

To NC judges, no further thinking is needed. However, they must find a way to deny drug users a fair trial, and this is how it is done.

8.4.2 DISPARAGING AUTONOMY RIGHTS

When defending drug users' autonomy rights, many lawyers have argued the First Amendment. To reason with the courts this has been a traditional way forward, as the courts will consistently mistake text for principle, thinking the text to be the source of a right. Whether it be for reasons of

---

[104] BAKALAR & GRINSPOON, *DRUG CONTROL IN A FREE SOCIETY* (1998) 19

[105] E.g., *United States v. Maas*, 551 F. Supp. 645 (D.N.J. 1982) 647

[106] Some of the benefits of drug use are artistic creativity, spiritual enlightenment, and consciousness expansion. See WEIL, *THE NATURAL MIND* (1986); SHULGIN, *PIKHAL: A CHEMICAL LOVE STORY* (1992); STOLAROFF, *THANATOS TO EROS* (1994); notes 93, 167

ignorance or convenience, therefore, many lawyers have accepted this false premise and held that drug use comes under the protection of the First Amendment.

Leaving aside the fact that there is no need to anchor drug users' autonomy rights in the First Amendment to determine if drug use is a protected activity, their thinking is understandable. First, the courts expect the appellant to hang his rights-claim on one or more enumerated rights, and secondly, autonomy is recognized as being at the heart of the First Amendment.[107] Thus, as scholars of law and philosophy have noted that the concept of autonomy by necessity includes the right to choose which drugs are to be ingested,[108] one would think that the courts would be interested to see if this is in fact so.

After all, without a freedom to experience the whole range of thought, emotion, and sensation connected to the human experience, we are being deprived sources of insight. And as drug use *does* provide "new sources of belief and experience,"[109] it follows that it must be "protected under the first amendment because it supplies these necessary preconditions to speech and expression."[110] According to this reasoning, just as the Constitution treats restrictions upon speech, press, and religion as a substantial harm, so the judiciary should recognize that the Constitution applies the same protection for infringements on our freedom to think. It should recognize that our freedom to form opinions, to gain new perspectives, and to develop and exercise our thought processes *as we see fit* is not merely a prerequisite for constitutional protections, but that without it the avowed right to "life, liberty and the pursuit of happiness" becomes an Orwellian ruse.

---

[107] Husak, *Two Rationales for Drug Policy*, in FISH (ED.), *HOW TO LEGALIZE DRUGS* (1998) 45-47

[108] Husak, *Liberal Neutrality, Autonomy, and Drug Prohibitions* (2000) 64 ("Feinberg for example, writes that 'the kernel of the idea of autonomy is the right to make choices and decisions—what to put into my body, what contacts with my body to permit, where and how to move my body through public space, how to use my chattels and physical property, what personal information to disclose to others, what information to conceal, and more.' Since drugs are 'put into [the] body,' drug use is unquestionably autonomous on this conception."); DUKE & CROSS, *AMERICA'S LONGEST WAR* (1993) 152; Michael Moore, *Liberty and Drugs*, in DE GREIFF (ED.), *DRUGS AND THE LIMITS OF LIBERALISM* (1999) 61-109

[109] Brashear, *Marijuana Prohibition and the Constitutional Right of Privacy* (1975) 581

[110] Ibid.

As thought precedes verbal communication the freedom of speech would be meaningless without us first recognizing a fundamental right to cognitive liberty. Recognizing this right is equally central to our freedom of religion: without an absolute freedom to connect with our inner world by whatever means we deem fit, it would mean little more than a freedom to accept established authority.[111] Provided therefore that the use of drugs can be shown to help us grasp new concepts, to access new ideas, to gain spiritual insight, and to rediscover and illuminate the majesty of our inner landscape, it follows that our right to use drugs, while enumerated, is an integral part of the Constitution. As Justice Brandeis described the founders' quest:

> "The makers of our Constitution undertook to secure conditions favorable to the pursuit of happiness. They recognized the significance of man's spiritual nature, of his feelings and of his intellect. They knew that only a part of the pain, pleasure and satisfactions of life are to be found in material things. They sought to protect Americans in their beliefs, their thoughts, their emotions and their sensations. They conferred, as against the Government, the right to be let alone—the most comprehensive of rights and the right most valued by civilized men."[112]

The fact that drug use should be included in the right to be let alone is obvious to those that reason from the FC perspective. Since the 1960s scholars have made the connection between drug use and the rights protected by the First Amendment,[113] and Justice Levinson of the Hawaii Supreme Court recognized as much when he said that:

---

[111] As Tribe and Dorf noted, "the freedom of speech, the freedom of religion, and so forth make sense only if connected by a broader and underlying principle of freedom of thought and conscience. . . . Free speech is an empty freedom if not possessed by a free mind." Tribe & Dorf, *Levels of Generality in the Definition of Rights* (1990) 1069 (referring to Justice Harlan's conception of liberty)

[112] *Olmstead v. United States*, 277 U.S. at 478 (1928) (Brandeis, J., dissenting)

[113] Dichter, *Marijuana and the Law* (1968) 862 ("Since the use of marijuana, even for the mere enjoyment of the experience, is a form of expression dealing solely with the mind, a strong argument can be made for bringing this extremely private form of expression within the ambit of the zone of privacy surrounding the freedom of expression.")

"The individual who uses marihuana does so from choice, in the pursuit of various goals which may include the relief from tension, the heightening of perceptions, and the desire for personal and spiritual insights. In short, marihuana produces experiences affecting the thoughts, emotions and sensations of the user. These experiences being mental in nature are thus among the most personal and private experiences possible. For this reason I believe that the right to be let alone protects the individual in private conduct which is designed to affect these areas of his personality."[114]

As I have said, the question of whether there are good reasons for a prohibition is not being addressed here. Perhaps there is evidence that some drugs are so "bad" that we cannot be allowed to choose for ourselves if we want to use them; we do not know because the issue has never been seriously reviewed. Nonetheless, *they can* be used for these purposes,[115] and so First Amendment rights *are* implicated in drug use.

The reason why so many lawyers have tried to get the courts to accept the idea that drug users' autonomy is protected by the First Amendment is that, if this is so, the state must show a compelling interest in denying drugs. The burden of evidence befalls prohibitionists, for as the U.S. Supreme Court once held, all rights must be construed liberally[116] and "[a] State's interest must be 'compelling' or 'paramount' to justify even an indirect burden on First Amendment rights."[117]

---

[114] *State v. Kantner*, 493 P.2d 306 (1972) 315 (Levinson J., dissenting)

[115] Certain drugs can be said to bring about states of mind in which new ideas and often profound information is attained. This is especially true of the psychedelic drugs—and this information can even be said to be of great importance to us as a society. See notes 93, 106, 167

[116] "It has been repeatedly decided that these Amendments should receive a liberal construction, so as to prevent stealthy encroachment upon or 'gradual depreciation' of the rights secured by them, by imperceptible practice of courts or by well-intentioned but mistakenly over-zealous executive officers." *Gouled v. United States*, 255 U.S. 304

[117] *Brazenburg v. Hayes et al.*, 408 U.S. 665 (1972); see also *Griswold* 381 U.S at 497 (Goldberg J., concurring) ("Where there is a significant encroachment upon personal liberty, the State may prevail only upon showing a subordinating interest which is compelling.")

Now, this connection between drug use and the First Amendment, while compelling for those who reason from the bigger perspective, have not persuaded NC individuals. They must find a way to ensure that the drug law escapes scrutiny, and so, where the religious use of drugs is not at issue,[118] the courts will deny that First Amendment rights are involved. As one may expect, they have never cared to bolster their position by countering the argument above or by offering any convincing analysis in support of their thesis. All they have done is refer to the *Stanley* Court, where the justices, after holding that the possession of obscene materials was protected because the First Amendment right to receive information was involved, continued to say that:

> "What we have said in no way infringes upon the power of the State or Federal Government to make possession of other items, such as narcotics, firearms, or stolen goods, a crime. Our holding in the present case turns upon the Georgia statute's infringement of fundamental liberties protected by the First and Fourteenth Amendments. No First Amendment rights are involved in most statutes making mere possession criminal."[119]

On this basis the courts have denied that First Amendment rights are implicated in drug use. A proper constitutional interpretation, however, leaves us with another conclusion, for while the principles of justice "in no way infringes upon the power of the State or Federal Government to make possession of other items such as narcotics, firearms, or stolen

---

[118] In those cases where appellants claim a right to use drugs on religious grounds the courts will accept that First Amendment rights are involved. However, except for a few cases regarding indigenous tribes' shamanic use of psychedelic drugs, (e.g., *People v. Woody*, 1964) courts will reject the appeal for strict scrutiny. In essence, they will simply assume that the appellants' claims are not sincere, and that even if they are, the requirements for a compelling interest are fulfilled if the legislature believes it has a compelling interest in prohibiting these drugs. See *Leary v. United States*, 383 F.2d 851 (1967); *United States v. Kuch*, 288 F. Supp. 439 (1968); *Gaskin v. State*, 490 S.W.2d 521 (1973); *United States v. Middleton*, 690 F.2d 820 (1982). For a fuller discussion of the issue, see Finer, *Psychedelics and Religious Freedom* (1968); Comment, *Free Exercise: Religion Goes to "Pot"* (1968); Doss & Doss, *On Morals, Privacy, and the Constitution* (1971); Mazur, *Marijuana as a Holy Sacrament* (1991); Tupper & Labate, *Plants, Psychoactive Substances and the International Narcotics Control Board* (2012)

[119] *Stanley*, 394 U.S. at 568 (footnote 11)

goods, a crime," they do demand that no such activity can be made a crime unless the proposed legislation passes a proper balancing test—one that, as natural rights theorists would put it, can separate license from liberty. Such a test weighs the individual's autonomy and liberty interests against society's need for protection, and the extent to which the scales are tipped in favor of the individual depends on the facts. In this regard, criminalizing the possession of stolen goods will pass with flying colors whereas the criminalization of narcotics possession is less likely to succeed. Whether we ground drug users' autonomy rights in the First or the Ninth Amendment is irrelevant. In either case, weighty individual interests are involved, and as the Supreme Court traditionally has reserved its heightened scrutiny for "values grounded in equality and personal autonomy,"[120] the state must show that even weightier considerations speak in favor of denying people a choice in drugs.

From a perspective of principled law, this is uncontestable. And unless the state can show that the drug law survives a proper analysis, the *Stanley* Court's oft-cited quote on the protection of privacy, properly modified, should read: "If the First Amendment means any-thing, it means that a State has no business telling a man . . . what books he may read, what films he may watch, *or what drugs he may take*. Our whole constitutional heritage rebels at the thought of giving government the power to control men's minds."[121]

---

[120] Bilionis, *The New Scrutiny* (2002) 103. Professor Bilionis referred to these cases: "See, e.g., *Cleburne*, 473 U.S. at 440 (noting that laws that classify by 'race, alienage, or national origin . . . are subjected to strict scrutiny and will be sustained only if they are suitably tailored to serve a compelling state interest,' that '[s]imilar oversight by the courts is due when state laws impinge on personal rights protected by the Constitution,' and that '[l]egislative classifications based on gender also call for a heightened standard of review'); *Carey v. Population Servs. Int'l*, 431 U.S. 678, 684-86 (1977) (espousing strict scrutiny for intrusions upon fundamental privacy rights as a matter of substantive due process); *Craig v. Boren*, 429 U.S. 190, 218 (1976) (espousing intermediate scrutiny under the Equal Protection Clause for laws that classify on the basis of sex); *Harper v. Va. State Bd. of Elections*, 383 U.S. 663, 669-70 (1966) (espousing strict scrutiny under the Equal Protection Clause for discriminatory infringements of fundamental interests); *McLaughlin v. Florida*, 379 U.S. 184, 192-93 (1964) (espousing strict scrutiny under the Equal Protection Clause for laws that classify on the basis of race)."

[121] *Stanley*, 394 U.S. at 565

8.4.3 Disparaging Liberty Rights

As seen, the courts have consistently refused to recognize drug users' autonomy rights and their liberty rights have not fared much better. The fact that many millions have been imprisoned because of the drug law and that the freedoms of millions more is at risk has never prompted the court to demand a justification.[122] In fact, in the American system of law, the freedom of drug users have no value, and economic and other regulations are more carefully scrutinized. As Judge Spiegel of the *Leis* court held:

> "We do not agree with the defendants that the Legislature is bound to adopt the 'least restrictive alternative' that would fulfill its purpose of protecting the health, safety and welfare of the community. The least restrictive alternative doctrine does not apply to the instant case. It has been limited to regulations affecting interstate commerce, constitutionally sheltered activity, and economic regulations. The Narcotic Drugs Law is not an economic regulation. It affects neither interstate commerce nor constitutionally sheltered activity."[123]

Also in *Schmitt*, the Michigan Court of Appeals attested to the perceived unimportance of drug users' liberty rights.[124] The defendant argued that, instead of the rational basis test, the court should use the substantial-relation-to-the-object test used in *Manistee Bank & Trust Co v. McGowan*.[125] In that case petitioner claimed a decision by the legislature to carve out a discrete exception to a general rule (such as requiring a showing of gross negligence by a guest passenger to recover for loss or injury from his host while all others recover on a showing of mere negligence) was unconstitutional. One would be hard pressed to argue that the liberty rights of 40 million Americans should count for less than the financial interests of a few people, but that did not discourage the Michigan court. As it said: "We do not find defendant's arguments

---

[122] In *Ravin* and a few cases concerning the religious use of peyote and ayahuasca the state has had to defend its policy (and lost), but none of them focused on the liberty interest of drug users.

[123] *Commonwealth v. Leis*, 355 Mass. 189 (1969) 195-96 (references omitted)

[124] *People v. Schmidt, 86 Mich. App. 574 (1978)*

[125] *Manistee Bank & Trust Co v. McGowan*, 394 Mich. 655; 232 N.W.2d 636 *(1975)*

on these points persuasive. The legislative decision to place controls on marijuana, from among the galaxy of substances, does not compare with the legislative decision to single out guest passengers for special treatment in recovering for a loss resulting from an automobile accident."[126] That was it, and so the court decided that the rational basis test would do fine.

Now, not only are economic rights more important than drug users' liberty rights, but the courts provide enhanced protection for commercial speech. Hence, laws prohibiting the advertising of prices for prescription drugs[127] and laws restricting the advertising of liquor, tobacco, and other harmful products[128] also receive heightened scrutiny. Any such restriction on commercial speech will be subjected to the substantial interest test where the government must prove that it directly advances the government's objective and that it is no more extensive than necessary to achieve that purpose. All this, while drug users are being imprisoned en masse for laws that we have reason to suspect would fail any type of meaningful scrutiny, and that the judiciary to has shielded from review.

When it comes to this, the *Pickard* court[129] provides us with an example of how drug law violators' liberty rights are disparaged. The defendants had argued that strict scrutiny should be applied because their fundamental right to liberty was at stake, and the court confirmed this by stating that "[e]very person has a fundamental right to liberty in the sense that the government may not punish him unless and until it proves his guilt beyond a reasonable doubt at a criminal trial conducted in accordance with the relevant constitutional guarantees."[130] As seen from the bigger perspective, the "relevant constitutional guarantees" means that no one shall ever be imprisoned for violating laws that do not conform to the criteria laid out by the fundamental principles of justice. The defendants, however, should have suspected that something was amiss when the judge continued: "But substantive due process requires a 'careful description of the asserted fundamental liberty interest.' Hence,

---

[126] *86 Mich. App. at 578*

[127] *Pharm. Bd. v. Va. Consumer Council*, 425 U.S. 748 (1976)

[128] *Liquor mart, Inc. v. Rhode Island*, 517 U.S. 484 (1996); *Lorillard Tobacco Co. v. Reilly*, 533 U.S. 525 (2001)

[129] *Pickard, et. al.*, No. 2:11-CR-0449-KJM (2015)

[130] Id. at 24

the right asserted in this case cannot be the broad fundamental liberty interest defendants claim."[131]

According to Judge Mueller, a general right to freedom from imprisonment did not define the right in question. More specifically defined, the right in question was if *marijuana producers* had a right to freedom from imprisonment and this notion was easily dismissed by the court. In support of her ruling the judge referenced a series of court decisions holding that there was "no fundamental right" to use, import, sell, or possess marijuana in any context, and that was all it took to deny a proper hearing.

The lack of analysis betrays an eagerness not to reflect on the subject. Indeed, the lack of coherence is palpable to anyone who cares to think about things, so let us see how the court jumped from a true premise to a false conclusion.

First, the judge accepted the premise that all individuals enjoy a fundamental right to be free from undue incarceration. The appellants having made this claim, the court could not simply deny that this is not so—especially after the prosecution, in its supplemental brief, had admitted that:

> "Defendants enjoy a fundamental right to liberty, [but the statute] does not encroach on that liberty interest. The only way it could would be if there were a constitutional right to manufacture marijuana, which of course there is not. If there were a constitutional right to manufacture marijuana, then the government would have to concede that the statute encroaches on that right, and the statute could only be sustained via proof that the law was narrowly tailored in support of a compelling governmental interest (strict scrutiny)."[132]

Now, we have established beyond contention that a constitutional right to be free from undue liberty deprivation exists, and from here the right thing to do would be to apply strict scrutiny and see if the drug law violated drug users'/producers' autonomy and liberty rights. A proper balancing test would have provided the answer to this question and the

---

[131] Id.

[132] *United States v. Schweder, et al.*, Supplemental Brief (May 21, 2014) 14

court could not, like the prosecution, simply take for granted that the law was beyond reproach. Remember that the Constitution "is cut out of one cloth" and that its purpose is to protect the individual from all undue interference. The light of first principles shines in *all* directions and it is impossible to determine if marijuana production constitutes a fundamental right before these principles have been applied.

When it comes to this, the light of first principles is all we need to establish that the state must have good reasons to punish the individual for exercising his liberty/autonomy rights. And as the state has enacted such punishment for violations of the drug law, the law *must survive* a balancing test, one that shows compelling reasons for criminalizing such conduct. This means that a restriction must either (1) be in place to protect the rights of others in their individual capacity or (2) to protect the rights of others in a communal capacity. There are certain minimum criteria that a law must comply with to be lawful, and to determine if the drug law fulfills these criteria it must be subjected to the test of reason. Unless this is so, the right to be free from undue incarceration is rendered meaningless, as the state will be free to throw coffee drinkers, sugar consumers, pizza eaters, football players, and anti-war activists in prison simply by prohibiting such activities.

We must never forget that these laws would pass the rational basis test. Only a more searching review like the Lawton, strict scrutiny, or the internationally recognized proportionality analysis would stop them dead. And if we accept the premise (which human rights law does) that for a system of law to have legitimacy, it must provide protection against wanton infringements on our autonomy/liberty rights, we must also concede that the legitimacy of the U.S. justice system depends on the extent to which it ensures that its criminal law survives these more demanding types of scrutiny.

The failure of the *Pickard* court, then, becomes plain to see. For by accepting the doctrine that fundamental liberty interests must be narrowly defined and quoting previous court decisions that have held the use of cannabis not to be a fundamental right, the court quashed any meaningful application of the appellants' unalienable rights. It simply makes no sense to accept the premise that one has a fundamental right not to be unduly incarcerated and then use a rational basis test to see if this fundamental right is violated—and yet this is what the court did.

Now some, like Judge Spiegel of the *Leis* court,[133] may say that drug law violators are not "unduly" incarcerated. They have, after all, chosen to exhibit behavior they know is prohibited. However, as Professor Colb points out, the fact that people can avoid punishment by conforming to the demands of a law does not "eliminate concerns about depriving an individual of a fundamental right when that deprivation is not necessary to serve a compelling governmental interest. . . . [E]ven people on notice of the consequences of their actions are entitled to a searching review of whether it is constitutionally appropriate to permit those consequences to follow."[134]

In challenges to the drug law therefore there are two issues before the court: (1) if drug use, production, distribution, etc., are constitutionally protected autonomy rights, and (2) if the incarceration of those who are engaged in these activities serves a compelling state interest.[135] None of these questions can be answered without bringing first principles into play and in both cases strict scrutiny must be applied. However, no matter what the court may decide as to the autonomy rights, it still must deal separately with the liberty rights at stake. It may, after all, be that some drugs are so harmful that the state can show a compelling interest in reducing their use, but even so the fourteenth and fifth amendment right to liberty from undue incarceration is a fundamentally protected right, putting constrains on how government may pursue an otherwise acceptable end.[136]

---

[133] *Commonwealth v. Leis,* 355 Mass. 189 (1969) 199 ("The defendants are not charged with having a 'status' over which they have no control.")

[134] Colb, *Freedom from Incarceration* (1994) 796, 803

[135] Already 40 years ago, professors of law pointed out the confusion on this issue, but the courts have neglected their duty to provide a proper analysis. As Hindes stated in 1977: "Courts are not being asked to decide whether the Constitution implicitly says anything about smoking marijuana; they are being asked if there is any good reason for putting someone in jail for smoking marijuana. No principled evaluation of these cases can avoid reference to the broader social purpose of a criminal prosecution." Hindes, *Morality Enforcement Through the Criminal Law and the Modern Doctrine of Substantive Due Process* (1977) 381

[136] Colb, *Freedom from Incarceration* (1994) 812 ("The eighth amendment requires scrutiny of every form of punishment, with a concomitant determination of whether it is cruel and unusual. Substantive due process additionally requires strict scrutiny of every deprivation of a fundamental right. Because incarceration involves both punishment and the deprivation of a fundamental right, incarceration must accordingly withstand scrutiny under both the eighth amendment and the due process clause of the fourteenth (or fifth) amendment.")

Because of this, all confinement must be justified according to the compelling interest test, and as Sherry Colb noted: "If incarceration is not necessary to a compelling interest, then the state does not confront the 'enemy' when it incarcerates the criminal; it confronts decent individuals and strips them of their most prized freedom—their liberty from confinement."[137]

8.4.4. Denigrating Equal Protection Challenges

The tendency to belittle drug users' rights claims is seen in the courts' equal protection analysis. The Equal Protection Clause requires "that criminal statutory classification schemes cover all persons or things related to each other reasonably, logically or scientifically."[138] A criminal statute therefore violates equal protection if it treats similarly situated persons differently for reasons not rationally related to the purpose of the statute.[139] Consequently, to the extent that we are dealing with the same supply and demand factors when it comes to licit and illicit drugs; to the extent that there are the same varying patterns of use associated with the different groups of drugs; and to the extent that comparisons of licit and illicit drugs indicate that there is no meaningful difference between those groups singled out for persecution and those we tolerate, there is evidence to suggest that the different categories of drugs lack a rational basis and that the illicit drug users are being denied the equal protection of the law. A fundamental premise of the social contract is that we all have a right to be treated with equal respect and concern. Hence, if the government has created two classes of drug users, it better have good reasons for using the criminal law against one group; and as always, the burden is on the government to show a compelling interest in treating the two classes of people differently.

---

[137] Ibid. 820

[138] *State v. Kantner*, 493 P.2d 306 (1972) at 319 (Kobayashi, J., dissenting). See also *McLaughlin v. Florida*, 379 U.S. 184, 85 S. Ct. 283, 13 L. Ed. 2d 222 (1964); *Skinner v. Oklahoma*, 316 U.S. 535, 62 S. Ct. 1110, 86 L. Ed. 1655 (1942); *Lindsley v Natural Carbonic Gas Co*, 220 US 61; 55 L Ed 369; 31 S Ct 337 (1911)

[139] *Reed v. State*, 264 Ga. 466, 448 S.E.2d 189 (1994)

What this means is that the government must show that cannabis users, for instance, cannot enjoy the same liberty and autonomy rights as alcohol drinkers; that they for some reason represent a bigger social problem; that weighty social considerations necessitate that the criminal law be used against them; that the criminal law is an effective means to an end; that it is the least restrictive means available for dealing with the problems associated with cannabis use; and that the law reflects a proper balancing of the rights at stake. Because fundamental interests are involved, the law must be narrowly tailored to achieve its stated purpose. This means that both over- and under-inclusiveness is frowned upon, so let us see how the drug law conforms to these criteria.

8.4.4.1 EQUALITY ANALYSIS 101

As far as the Equal Protection Clause is concerned, assuming that the purpose of the drug law is to promote the general welfare, we can say that for the law to be a 100 percent reasonable application of the police power, two criteria must be met: (1) all those to whom the law applies must be morally blameworthy for acts against the public welfare, and (2) their transgressions must be more pronounced than the acts of individuals who are not singled out for persecution.

To the extent these criteria are fulfilled, the law can be said to treat similarly situated people the same. This is a prime tenet of the Equal Protection Clause but, looking closer, the classification does a poor job in this regard.[140] First of all, as the purpose of the law is to protect the public welfare, it can only seriously concern itself with drug abuse—only drug abusers, to some extent, put the public welfare at risk. When the drug laws were enacted it was assumed that all drug use equaled abuse. However, there is evidence to presume that roughly 90 percent of all drug consumers use drugs responsibly, that they are functional and well-

---

[140] As Professor Husak noted: "The prior decision to prohibit some drugs while allowing others does not appear to reflect an impartial . . . judgment about their relative dangers. . . . This basis for distinguishing among various drugs poses a genuine threat to equal protection." Husak, *Two Rationales For Drug Policy* in FISH (ED.), *HOW TO LEGALIZE DRUGS* (1998) 43

behaved citizens, and that they represent no problem to the public welfare.[141]

If this is the case, the statute is over-inclusive because it includes many people who have done nothing to deserve persecution. We should never forget that moral blameworthiness is a primary criterion for subjecting people to the criminal law and that any degree of over-inclusiveness is highly problematic.[142] In order for over-inclusiveness to be legitimate, there must be extremely good reasons to maintain the classification. Only in circumstances of genuine emergency, where society is under threat by some imminent evil, can such measures be considered as acceptable.

Prohibitionists, for their part, believe that this is the case. They proceed upon the presumption that (1) drugs are a menace to society; (2) that their use has no intrinsic value; (3) that the threat is so profound that applying the criminal law is necessary for the protection of society; (4) that the law is effective in dealing with this threat; and (5) that less restrictive solutions would be unfit for purpose. In their mind, therefore, everything is as it should be. Even moderate prohibitionists believe drugs to be so bad that an over-inclusive law is justifiable. According to them, this collateral damage is the price society must pay for survival. More fanatical prohibitionists, however, insist that the law is not over-inclusive at all. Because drugs are so dangerous, they will claim that *every* drug user is morally blameworthy for his or her choice in drugs; that even though they appear to be functional and well-behaved citizens they are a part of a greater problem; and that they deserve whatever punishment they get. As Daryl Gates, the chief of LAPD, once told Congress: "Casual drug users should be taken out and shot; we are at war and drug use is treason."[143]

Prohibitionists, of course, are entitled to their opinions. However, we are in a situation where we must accept on faith that such wartime

---

[141] The United Nations estimates that there are 250 million drug users worldwide, of which less than 10 percent are problem drug users. Report of the Global Commission on Drug Policy (June 2011) 13

[142] As Professors Tussman and tenBroek remind us, "such classifications fly squarely in the face of our traditional antipathy to assertions of mass guilt and guilt by association. Guilt, we believe, is individual, and to act otherwise is to deprive the individual of due process of law." Tussman & tenBroek, *The Equal Protection of the Laws* (1949) 352

[143] Gates testifying before the Senate Judiciary Committee 5. September, 1990

measures are necessary, as these opinions have yet to be empirically confirmed.

Furthermore, the problematic nature of the drug law becomes even more apparent when we consider that not only is it over-inclusive; it is also under-inclusive as it fails to include substances that pose an even greater threat to the general welfare. When it comes to social harms, both alcohol drinkers and tobacco smokers represent a bigger threat to society.[144] And as professors Tussman and tenBroek noted: "Since the classification does not include all who are similarly situated with respect to the purpose of the law, there is a prima facie violation of the equal protection requirement of reasonable classification."[145]

To conclude, we find that the traits singled out are not synonymous with being offenses against the public welfare and that there are other, more obvious threats traits to society which are not singled out. On this basis, the law does a poor job at arresting offenders against the public welfare. It is both over- and under-inclusive, and to sustain such classification on equal protection grounds the law "requires both the finding of sufficient emergency to justify the imposition of a burden upon a larger class than is believed tainted with the mischief, *and* the establishment of 'fair reasons' for failure to extend the operation of the law to a wider class of potential saboteurs."[146]

This is for the state to show. To this day it has never had to justify its actions on any other terms but its own. But when we recognize that 90 percent of those singled out have done nothing to harm the public welfare and that there are other population groups more deserving of reproach (if crimes against the common welfare is the criteria) it is difficult to escape the conclusion that the law arbitrarily singles out one class of citizens for persecution—and that the law, on Equal Protection terms, is unconstitutional.

It is also important to recognize that the people being persecuted are the least politically influential. We are in other words dealing with class-legislation because politicians have singled out a politically insignificant

---

[144] See DUKE & CROSS, *AMERICA'S LONGEST WAR* (1993) 22-77; WISOTSKY, *BEYOND THE WAR ON DRUGS* (1990) 185-215

[145] Tussman & tenBroek, *The Equal Protection of the Laws* (1949) 348

[146] Ibid. 353

and marginal group for persecution while ignoring more powerful interest groups whose behavior puts the general welfare more at risk. Indeed, this is the sole defining trait for the criminalized group as a whole; people are persecuted not because they are threats to the public welfare, but because they are the scapegoats that must bear the brunt of the ingroup's prejudice and baseless intolerance.

This is even openly admitted. As many prohibitionists are keen to point out, both alcohol and tobacco would be prohibited today, if these substances did not have a long history of use in Western society. In other times and places both alcohol and tobacco have been frowned upon (while some of the illicit drugs have been accepted) and it is well-known that culture, not reason, has been the defining characteristic of drug policy.[147] However, just as "culture" did not justify classifying people on grounds of race, gender, and certain sexual preferences, so it remains irrelevant for drug policy. The essence of the Equal Protection Clause is that people shall not be singled out for disadvantage or privilege based on morally irrelevant traits, and this is always the case when criminal punishment is involved. As Sunstein noted, "a difference is morally irrelevant if it has no relationship to individual entitlement or desert,"[148] and to sustain the criminalization of drug users the state must show that they are more deserving of punishment than alcohol drinkers.

There can be no doubt that the former are at a systemic disadvantage. They live in a state of perpetual subordination without sufficient political power to defend themselves against policies enacted for reasons of prejudice or ill will. To this day they have been easy prey for politicians eager to find scapegoats and problem-areas to attack, and because the Equal Protection guarantee requires that "courts should protect those who

---

[147] As the British Medical Association observed: "[A]lmost every psychoactive drug known to humanity, from alcohol to opium, has been regarded by some government and society as a dire threat to public order and moral standards, and by another government and another society as a source of harmless pleasure. Further, nations and governments sometimes change their views completely. Almost every society has at least one drug whose use is tolerated, while drugs used in other cultures are generally viewed quite differently and with deep suspicion. Mexican Indians may have disapproved of alcohol, but they used mescaline. Most Muslim cultures forbid alcohol, but they tolerate cannabis and opium." *Living with Risk: The British Medical Association Guide*, BMA Professional and Scientific Division (1987) 58

[148] Sunstein, *Homosexuality and the Constitution* (1994) 13

can't protect themselves politically,"[149] drug users clearly deserve their day in court.

8.4.4.2 HOW THE EQUALITY DOCTRINE FAILS TO PROTECT DRUG USERS

The equal protection standard discussed is a doctrine of principled law. It is, however, not the doctrine being applied in the United States. As seen in part two, a suspect classification doctrine has evolved under the auspices of the Supreme Court. Therefore, courts will apply the equal protection standard described above only to legislation affecting a fundamental interest or laws targeting individuals on the basis of race, alienage, national origin, or sex. Hence, because drug use is not accepted as a fundamental right and the drug law makes no distinction relying on any of these categories, American justices will apply the rational basis standard. This means that they do not care if the law is a fit means to an end; they do not care if less invasive means could have been applied; and they do not care if there are no good reasons for treating illicit drug users differently than alcohol drinkers. In the instance of the drug law neither over-inclusiveness nor under-inclusiveness is seen as a problem and the state is free to deal with the illicit drug users as it deems fit. As Justice Coler of the South Dakota Supreme Court held:

> "Normally, the widest discretion is allowed the legislative judgment in determining whether to attack some, rather than all, of the manifestations of the evil aimed at; and normally that judgment is given the benefit of every conceivable circumstance which might suffice to characterize the classification as reasonable rather than arbitrary and invidious. . . . With specific reference to appellant's contention that marijuana is less harmful than tobacco and alcohol, we find support for our holding from the United States Court of Appeals, Second Circuit, which . . . concluded that 'If Congress decides to regulate or prohibit some harmful substances, it is not

---

[149] Goldberg, *Equality Without Tiers* (2004) 553 (quoting Ely)

thereby constitutionally compelled to regulate or prohibit all. It may conclude that half a loaf is better than none.'"[150]

We shall have more to say on the courts' use of such words as "reasonable," "rational," and "arbitrary." Suffice now to say that they are void of meaningful content, for our politicians need only imagine that drug prohibition does some good and it does not matter if this is in fact so. As long as the drug law is "rational" to prohibitionists, the courts will defer to the legislature, and in this regard it is interesting to note the court's "half a loaf" comment. It is frequently used to deny drug users their day in court, but this abused quote stems from Thomas Jefferson and referred to the enumeration of rights in the Constitution. As discussed in part one there was a debate among the founders as to whether rights should be enumerated in the Constitution. Many were against it because it would be impossible to enumerate every one, and as "it would be implying, in the strongest manner, that every right not included in the exception might be impaired by the government without usurpation . . . it would be not only useless, but dangerous, to enumerate" only some.[151] Jefferson, however, felt that the natural rights of the people were too easily infringed without a Bill of Rights, and despite the danger of an imperfect enumeration he held that "half a loaf is better than no bread. If we cannot secure all our rights, let us secure what we can."[152]

It is ironic that this passage, which initially attached to the liberty presumption, has become a tenet for arbitrary government. Orwellian judges have reversed Jefferson's intention; there are now no principled limits to the police power—and as it is employed to justify totalitarian notions, the transformation could not have been more profound.

While ironic, it is also symptomatic of the shift from the FC to the NC conception of law. Following this reasoning, the Equal Protection Clause is rendered meaningless for all but a few fundamental rights and suspect classifications. It is stripped of its very essence, for could a law prohibiting doughnuts while exempting more harmful foods be valid? Would a law seeking to reduce motorcycle accidents be legitimate if it

---

[150] *State v. Strong*, 245 N.W.2d 277 (1976) 279-80 (citations and quotation marks omitted)

[151] James Iredell quoted in Barnett, *The Ninth Amendment: It Means What It Says* (2006) 27-28

[152] Jefferson letter to Madison, March 15, 1789. Found in KURLAND & LERNER, *THE FOUNDERS' CONSTITUTION* (Web edition) Papers 14 at 659-61

targeted only Harley Davidson motorcyclists? Could a law seeking to reduce the negative influence of videogames target only Nintendo users? Is it too much to ask that the state provides us with good reasons before targeting doughnut eaters, Harley Davidson motorcyclists, and Nintendo gamers for persecution?

As scholars and justices have pointed out, all these laws would pass the rational basis test,[153] and they have also noted the parallels between drug taking and such activities.[154] Hence, these examples are relevant. Not only are the drug laws unconstitutional for the exact same reason, but the social burden associated with drug prohibition is worse than the evils that would result from these laws. As other food, motorcycle, and videogame manufacturers have products that can match the experience provided by the proscribed products, few would be likely to break the law to continue eating doughnuts, driving Harleys, or playing Nintendo. Consequently, the illicit economy following such criminalization would not even remotely trouble society to the extent that drug prohibition has done—and gangsters, paramilitary groups and secret services would not start wars to gain control of profits.

Yet this is the case with drug prohibition. Documenting the evils resulting from prohibition is beyond the scope of this book, but in Latin America 150.000 people die every year because of the drugs economy;[155] in America, roughly half of the 15.000 annual violent deaths can be attributed to drug prohibition;[156] and globally, 160.000 of the 200.000

---

[153] *State v. Mallan*, 86 Haw. 440, 950 P.2d 178 (1998) n. 67 (Levinson J., dissenting) (prohibition of the possession of peanuts would pass rational basis)

[154] "As an act of paternalism—protecting us from harming ourselves—drug prohibition is hard to distinguish from coercive governmental prohibition of obesity, excess television viewing, loafing, wasting money on unnecessary luxuries and infinite other ways in which people seem to act contrary to their long-term best interests. Even the nature of the self-harm is similar. The main cost of using drugs excessively is not poor health but an unrewarding life." DUKE & CROSS, *AMERICA'S LONGEST WAR* (1993) 151

[155] Organization of American States, *The Drug Problem in the Americas* (2013) 76

[156] "When I was a prosecutor, over half of the murders I prosecuted were 'drug law related' in the sense that the victim was killed as a result of a drug deal gone bad or a robbery of someone suspected of having either valuable drugs or money from selling drugs." Barnett, *Bad Trip* (1994) 4. This figure is supported by research gathered by Ostrowski in *The Moral and Practical Case for Drug Legalization* (1990) (648-50), where he concludes that some 40 percent of US murders are drug-law related. Professor Duke elaborates on similar findings: "In many cities, such as New Haven, Connecticut, at least half of the killings are drug-business related. Nationwide, between 5,000 and 10,000 murders per year are systemic to the drug business. Thus,

drug-related deaths can be traced back to black-market factors.[157] It is impossible to ponder the trials posed by these factors. Caught between cops and gangsters, users exist between a rock and a hard place, even though substances like alcohol and tobacco are freely available. *This* is a testimony to the importance of their drugs of choice. *This* should tell us that their choice is not to be taken lightly, attributing to it no value or benefit.

Prohibitionists will predictably disagree, but so what? What right have alcohol drinkers, tobacco smokers, or non-drug users to decide on the importance of drug use to others? They have nothing but their own prejudice to support their opinions. Reason has never been brought to the table and so why should their bigotry, chauvinism and distorted worldview merit any consideration? What if we could find a billion people to whom outward appearance such as hair length was of little importance? Would their view in any way be representative for others? The courts have ruled time and again that this is an issue for the individual to decide, so why should drugs be otherwise? Why should alcohol drinkers, tobacco smokers and non-drug users be allowed to throw cannabis or opiate users in jail without ever providing good reasons? Why should the preconceived and deluded notions of fearful minds—of brains muddled by 100 years' worth of prohibitionist propaganda—be allowed to carry the day? What sort of justice system would allow such a travesty to continue decade after decade?

Unfortunately, the honest answer is that *only a society* in which the principle of equal protection carries the same weight as the off-track society portrayed in Orwell's *Animal Farm* would allow such a state of affairs. And the courts, therefore, could just as well, like the pigs in Orwell's classic novel, solemnly have declared that "Of course we are all equal, but some—like alcohol drinkers, tobacco smokers and non-drug users—are more equal than others."

While such analogies are never popularly embraced, the facts speak volumes. The cruel irony of the equality doctrine is that it discriminates

---

more people are killed by the prohibition of drugs than by the drugs them-selves." Duke, *Drug Prohibition: An Unnatural Disaster* (1995) 577 (sources omitted)

[157] Drug analyst James Ostrowski estimates that roughly 80% of the world's 200.000 drug-use-deaths are caused by prohibition while only 20% by the inherent qualities of the drugs. Ostrowski, *The Moral and Practical Case for Drug Legalization* (1990) 654. See also MIKALSEN, *TO END A WAR* (2015) n. 79-80 at 168-73

against people based on irrelevant traits; that its application makes a mockery of law; and that all this is plain to see. "Plain to see," at least for FC justices,[158] and yet, because "some are more alike," this charade can continue.

The inherent absurdity is made evident when we consider that in other situations, when the legislature enacts a law that burdens a segment of the population on basis of race or ethnic background, individuals associated with the group are entitled to a judicial determination that the burden they are asked to bear is precisely tailored to serve a compelling governmental interest. This is the case no matter how negligible the burden they are being asked to bear. Even if no criminal law is applied and the purpose of the legislation is to help a disadvantaged group, the Court will demand that the regulation be justified according to the most exacting criteria of scrutiny.[159] Why, then, are not drug users who risk lifetime imprisonment afforded the same courtesy? Why should the drug law—a law which arguably has had no less disastrous consequences than any race or ethnicity-based law—be exempt from the same level of review? Should not the millions of Americans who are imprisoned because of this law have a right to expect that it be precisely tailored to serve a compelling governmental interest? Or—if this is too much to ask—that, at the very least, it be *somewhat* tailored to achieve a legitimate purpose? What sort of justice system would deny even this? Why should drug users be left with no meaningful quality control? How is this fair?

A reply from prohibitionists is that the "suspect" classified groups are being asked to shoulder a burden based on an inherent trait they can do nothing about, while drug users have chosen to exhibit behavior they know is prohibited. To some extent there is a difference between being

---

[158] As Justice Kobayashi of the Supreme Court of Hawaii noted: "The evidence indicates that the harms produced by the abusive use of marijuana are essentially of the same nature and quality as those produced by the abusive use of alcohol. As such, the failure to include alcohol within the criminally proscribed statutory classification could itself be considered violative of equal protection." *State v. Kantner*, 493 P.2d 306 (1972) at 320 (Kobayashi, J., dissenting). See also *State v. Mitchell*, 563 S.W.2d 18 (Mo. 1978) 37 (Shangler J., dissenting) ("I am convinced on impressive empirical authority that marihuana poses no threat to the public safety and welfare and less a danger to the person than that posed to the user of cigarettes and alcohol. There can be no reasonable basis to classify marihuana with narcotics or to penalize them alike. I would find that [the] classification of marihuana violates the equal protection clause of the Fourteenth Amendment to the United States Constitution and is invalid.")

[159] *Adarand Constructors, Inc. v. Pena*, 515 U.S. 200 (1995), involving a federal affirmative action plan providing a benefit to minority contractors.

criminalized for being black or Hispanic and for being a drug user. However, as seen, that people can avoid punishment by conforming to the demands of a law does not "eliminate concerns" about the importance of ensuring that the law is justified in the first place.

A second reply is that we have a hideous history with legislation that burdens a group based on traits of race or ethnicity, and that, to guard against the mistakes of the past, a law that separates people based on these criteria must pass strict scrutiny. This answer will provide us with proper justification for applying strict scrutiny to race-based legislation. However, it does not explain why drug users should not also be protected against discriminatory practices. After all, as a group they fulfill most criteria for being included in a suspect classification analysis. It is clear that the law directed against them were motivated by racism, ignorance, and prejudice; that it is a fear-based response to a perceived threat against the status quo; and that it burdens a politically inferior group.

Just like previous laws affecting race, the drug law is not only used to control a minority population but it serves to confirm and justify the prejudices and hypocrisies of the ingroup, making it appear legitimate to hate and despise the targeted population. Today, therefore, this class of people is so ostracized that it is politically acceptable to blame them for most evils. The very language that is used in political debates, courts, and media outlets to describe "the problem" leaves no doubt. In our modern-day caste system, they are the "untouchables," the "vermin," the "pushers," and the ones infested by the "plague." They are those designated to the lowest rung on the social ladder and delegated the unbearable task of atoning for the sins of others.

We shall have more to say on this aspect of prohibition, but the sentencing practices clearly reveal that when it comes to these "misfits" anything goes. The horrendous effect that the drug law has had on the lives of tens of millions of people is simply too unfathomable to grasp. But we can begin by acknowledging that these millions are real people; they have names. They are people like Robert Zornes and his wife, Jenice, both 22 years, who were lying on the lawn watching meteors on the night sky when about half a dozen officers raided their home. After uncovering a tiny amount of marijuana on the premises, the government sentenced Robert to 20 years while Jenice "got off" with one year. They are people like David Ciglar, a firefighter credited with saving over 100 lives and also a husband and father of three. Ciglar got a mandatory minimum of 10 years after being caught with a tray of marijuana seedlings in his garage and his family home was confiscated. They are people like James Geddes, who was sentenced to 90 years after police found a small amount of marijuana and five plants in his vegetable garden. They are people like James Cox, who discovered the therapeutic effects of marijuana after struggling with cancer. He was sentenced to 15 years for growing his own medicine; his wife, Pat, got 5 years and they also lost the family house. They are people like Will Foster, a husband and father of three who struggled with crippling rheumatoid arthritis. He was sentenced to 93 years in prison for his attempt to find relief through cannabis—a sentence that was later reduced to 20 years. They are people like Jodie Israel and Calvin Treiber, a couple who belonged to a religious community that used marijuana as a sacrament. Jodie was sentenced to 11 years while Calvin received a 29-year sentence for possessing smaller amounts of the herb. Their four children were orphaned by the government and separated from each other to live in different homes.[160]

While the courts' equal protection doctrine allows for this, the Equal Protection Clause does not. The equality guarantee inherent in the Constitution seeks to remove from existence all laws that serve the interests of a particular class rather than the general public (class legislation) and to eliminate all statutes that subject one class of citizens to a code not applicable to another. The Clause is connected to the fundamental principles of justice and these principles care not one bit if rights are termed "fundamental" or classifications are called "suspect." They simply demand that *all* infringements on liberty be reasonable, and they demand that all groups singled out for persecution shall have their day in court.

Recognizing this, there is no reason why laws directed at drug users should be held to a lesser standard than laws directed at blacks, women, or homosexuals.[161] The right not to be unduly deprived of autonomy and

---

[160] For more on these and many more examples of the victims of the War on Drugs, see CONRAD, NORRIS & RESNER, *HUMAN RIGHTS AND THE US DRUG WAR* (2001)

[161] Justice Marshall has argued that "the level of scrutiny employed in an equal protection case should vary with 'the constitutional and societal importance of the interest adversely affected and the recognized invidiousness of the basis upon which the particular classification is drawn." *City of Cleburne v. Cleburne Living Ctr.*, 473 U.S. 432, 460 (Marshall, J., dissenting in part) (quoting San Antonio Independent School District v. Rodriguez, 411 U.S. 1, 411 U.S. 99 (1973)

liberty is fundamental. And while the examples above may belong to the extreme end, they are certainly not unique. In fact, we can multiply the pain and suffering of these people and their families by a million before we come close to putting the cruelty of the drug law in its proper perspective. Why, then, is the suffering of these people reduced to insignificance? Where in all this is the right to equal respect and concern? The equal protection test is simple: Would we accept alcohol drinkers or tobacco smokers being treated like this?

There is evidence to suggest that we would not. Not only does reason forbid it, but the European Court of Human Rights looked into the issue of depriving alcohol users their liberty rights in *Witold Litwa v. Polen*. The Court concluded that even a couple hours in a holding cell was unconstitutional and so we have an idea of the different measures of decency applied towards the two groups of people. But why is it so difficult to understand that the drug law violators have an equal right to liberty? Why is it impossible to accept to this group the same measure of human dignity?

To find the answer, we must look to the enemy image of drugs.

8.5 THE IMPACT OF AN OVERBLOWN ENEMY IMAGE

Studies reveal that the more we know about illicit drugs, the less scary they become.[162] In fact, in comparing the harms associated with tobacco and alcohol to those of illicit drugs, we find that we have legalized the drugs that are the worst for society (alcohol) and the most addictive and harmful to the individual (tobacco).[163]

According to Duke and Gross, per 100,000 users, tobacco kills 650 people each year, alcohol 150, heroin 80, cocaine 4, and marijuana zero.[164] The most comprehensive study done on the harms associated with the different drugs confirms this picture. In this study the Independent

---

[162] BAKALAR & GRINSPOON, *DRUG CONTROL IN A FREE SOCIETY* (1998) 17

[163] MIKALSEN, *TO END A WAR* (2015) notes 70-72 at 154-62

[164] DUKE & GROSS, *AMERICA'S LONGEST WAR* (1993) 74-77

Scientific Committee on Drugs compared each drug to 16 criteria of harm. On a scale from zero to 100, where zero was the most favourable outcome and 100 was the worst possible, they came up with a ranking that looked like this: Psychedelic mushrooms (6), Buprenorphine (7), LSD (7), Khat (9), Ecstasy (9), Anabolic Steroids (10), Butane (11), Mephedrone (13), Methadone (14), Ketamine (15), Benzodiazepines (15), GHB (19), Cannabis (20), Amphetamine (23), Tobacco (26), Cocaine (27), Methylamphetamine (33), Crack (54), Heroin (55), and Alcohol (72).[165]

As we can see, there is no relation between the overall harmfulness of these drugs and their classification. In fact, in most cases the classification is completely backwards, as some of the least dangerous drugs are the most strictly prohibited.

Predictably, many people will disagree with the conclusions reached by the ISCD. After all, we live in a world where the prohibition ideology has shaped our minds to such an extent that most of us simply cannot accept these findings. That alcohol could be more dangerous than heroin and tobacco more dangerous than LSD is so contradictory to common beliefs that most automatically discard such findings. Nonetheless, the more we learn about drugs, the more likely we are to agree.[166]

The more we know, the more we understand that the same supply and demand mechanisms are involved when it comes to the licit and illicit drugs; that there are the same varying patterns of use; and that the illicit drugs are no worse than the licit. In fact, some of them hold enormous potential for psychological healing/growth and can be of immense value to society.[167] And the more we come to terms with this factual picture, the

---

[165] Nutt et al., *Drug harms in the UK: a Multicriteria Decision Analysis*, LANCET 2010: 376, at 1558–65

[166] As Professor Escohotado noted: "[In the ten-year period after its prohibition] up to twenty million may have been introduced to LSD in the United States and Europe, and the number of crimes or fatal accidents caused by its use in that decade hardly reached that produced by alcohol in one single day." ESCOHOTADO, *A BRIEF HISTORY OF DRUGS* (1999) 123

[167] Not only are the psychedelic drugs unique tools in the rehabilitation of drug addicts but in helping us overcome dysfunctional, deeply flawed, but commonly accepted outlooks on life. They can, in short, help us become full FC individuals. See MIKALSEN, *REASON IS* (2014); FORTE, *ENTHEOGENS AND THE FUTURE OF RELIGION* (2012); GRAY, *THE ACID DIARIES* (2010); SMITH, *CLEANSING THE DOORS OF PERCEPTION* (2000); GROF, *REALMS OF THE HUMAN UNCONSCIOUS* (1975); GROF, *LSD: DOORWAY TO THE NUMINOUS* (2009); GOLDSMITH, *PSYCHEDELIC HEALING* (2010); WINKELMAN & ROBERTS (EDS.), *PSYCHEDELIC MEDICINE* (2007); GRINSPOON & BAKALAR, *PSYCHEDELIC DRUGS RECONSIDERED* (1997); GROF, *THE*

more we also come to grips with its implications—that the classification system that separates licit and illicit drugs makes no sense, and that the basis of the War on Drugs is fundamentally flawed.[168]

Prohibitionists, however, are not there. The enemy image of drugs is deeply ingrained, and, as knowledge brings us closer to the FC level while ignorance and fear drags us down to the NC level, it comes as no surprise where prohibitionist reasoning is found. Due to the exaggerated enemy image, they will apply two diametrically opposed types of reasoning to the two classes of drugs—and while they recognize alcohol and tobacco consumers as autonomous individuals responsible for their lifestyle choices, they see illicit drug consumers as the victims of sinister influences, meaning cynical dope peddlers and the lure of an easy fix.

This is the myth that sustains the ideology of prohibition. Without this foundation, it would be impossible to infantilize adults and persecute them for using their drugs of choice. Without it, the demonization of those involved with the drugs economy would be understood as the mindless endeavor it is. And without it, the cruelty of our sentencing practices would be plain to see.

We shall now see how the courts are colored by this fiction.

8.5.1 PROHIBITIONIST REASONING WRIT LARGE

Prohibitionist reasoning in its pure form was most prevalent in the first half of the 20th century. The narcotics police were the purveyors of information and as neither the legislature nor the courts knew anything about these drugs, they fell prey to the Federal Bureau of Narcotics' misinformation campaigns. According to the *Burke* court, it was "an established fact" that "narcotic drugs are dangerous. Not that they are poisons within themselves, but worse than poisons. Their excessive use

---

COSMIC GAME: EXPLORATIONS OF THE FRONTIERS OF HUMAN CONSCIOUSNESS (1990); STRASSMAN, *DMT: THE SPIRIT MOLECULE* (2001); Tupper & Labate, *Plants, Psychoactive Substances and the International Narcotics Control Board* (2012); Watts, *Psychedelics and Religious Experience* (1968); *supra* note 93

[168] MIKALSEN, *TO END A WAR* (2015) n. 70-75 at 154-65

destroys will power, ambition, self-respect, and in the end, mentality. They make men and women moral perverts."[169]

"Narcotic drugs" included cannabis, and we saw another example of the influence of this enemy image in *Markham*. In this case the defendant sought an opportunity to dispel the myths surrounding marijuana, proving it was no "narcotic" and therefore should not be classified among the hard drugs. Circuit Judge Duffy, however, held that it was a narcotic because Congress had decided it was a narcotic and that it belonged to the class of hard drugs because the legislature had decided it belonged there. As proof of the harmful effects of marijuana, he cited the following text from the legislature's deliberations:

> "Marihuana is . . . used illicitly by smoking it in crudely prepared cigarettes, which are readily procurable in almost all parts of the country at prices ranging from 10 to 25 cents each. Under the influence of this drug the will is destroyed and all power of directing and controlling thought is lost. As a result of these effects many violent crimes have been and are being committed by persons under the influence of the drug. Not only is marihuana used by hardened criminals to steel them to commit violent crimes, but it is also being placed in the hands of high school children in the form of marihuana cigarettes by unscrupulous peddlers. Its continued use results many times in impotency and insanity."[170]

The enemy image of drugs having such an influence, it comes as no surprise that several states made the death penalty available for those who delivered drugs to adolescents. It also comes as no surprise that in *Thomas*, the first challenge raising the issue of cruel and unusual punishment, the Louisiana Supreme Court upheld that state's mandatory minimum sentence of ten years without parole for unlawful possession. As the court said, "[i]n view of the moral degeneration inherent in all aspects of the crime denounced by the Narcotics Act, it cannot be said that the length or severity of the punishment here prescribed is

---

[169] *Burke v. Kansas State Osteopathic Assoc., Inc.*, 111 F.2d 250, 256 (1940)

[170] *United States v. Markham*, C07.126, 191 F.2d 936 (1951)

disproportioned to the offense."[171] Five years later, in *Garcia*, the Texas Supreme Court upheld a life sentence for first offense possession.[172] But even if the moral climate supported the severity of such punishment (and has continued to do so until this day), there were a distinct change in the air. As drug use became more widespread throughout the 1960s, an increasing amount of research and information became available. By 1970, between ten and fifteen percent of the American people had tried marijuana and it was plain to see that prohibitionists had misrepresented the factual picture.

The courts would increasingly draw upon this knowledge to reject the government's version of events. In 1970, in *State v. Zornes*, the Supreme Court of Washington was the first to find marijuana laws unconstitutional on classification grounds.[173] In 1971, in *People v. McCabe*, the Supreme Court of Illinois followed and concluded that the classification of marijuana with the hard drugs violated the equal protection clause of the Fourteenth Amendment. One year later, in *People v. Sinclair*, the Supreme Court of Michigan dealt another blow to the drug law. Delivering the opinion of the court, Justice Swainson affirmed that:

> "Comparison of the effects of marijuana use on both the individual and society with the effects of other drug use demonstrates not only that there is no rational basis for classifying marijuana with the 'hard narcotics', but, also, that there is not even a rational basis for treating marijuana as a more dangerous drug than alcohol. . . . The murky atmosphere of ignorance and misinformation which casts its pall over the state and Federal legislatures' original classification of marijuana with the hard narcotics has been well documented . . . We can no longer allow the residuals of that early misinformation to continue choking off a rational evaluation of marijuana dangers. That a large and increasing number of Americans recognize the truth about

---

[171] *State v. Thomas*, 224 La. 435, 69 So.2d 740 (1953). Seven years later, in *Gallego v. United States*, the Ninth Circuit quoted approvingly this moral denouncement when it decided in favor of a five-year minimum for the possession of drugs.

[172] *Garcia v. State*, 166 Tex. Crim. 482, 316 S.-AV.2d 734 (1958)

[173] The court held that the law was arbitrary and irrational. Before this trial courts in Colorado had twice declared the state's marijuana laws unconstitutional but had been reversed both times. *People v. McKenzie*, 458 P.2d 232 (Colo. 1969); *People v. Stark*, 157 Colo. 59.400 P.2d 923 (1965)

marijuana's relative harmlessness can scarcely be doubted. . . . We agree with the Illinois Supreme Court . . . that marijuana is improperly classified as a narcotic and hold that [the law], in its classification of marijuana violates the equal protection clauses of the [state and Federal Constitution]."[174]

As the 1970s unfolded, more and more courts would recognize the relative harmlessness of cannabis. The pressure for reform was growing and many scholars expected prohibition to yield.[175] However, they underestimated the prohibitionists' will to power and ignorance, and despite the incriminating evidence the enemy image held sway.

The *Sinclair* court, for instance, did not properly digest the implications of the passage above, as the court refused to look into the more important issues. Sinclair, a political activist of regional notoriety, had originally contended that the statute (among other things) violated equal protection, denied due process of law, violated rights of privacy retained by the people, and that the penalty provisions imposed cruel and unusual punishment. In all, he raised ten constitutional objections, but the court dealt only with two. One being whether the classification of marijuana as a narcotic violated the equal protection guarantee of the Constitution and the other being whether the two marijuana cigarettes Sinclair was charged with should have been excluded from evidence on the ground that they constituted evidence obtained as the result of an illegal police entrapment. The court concluded in the affirmative on both accounts and reversed Sinclair's ten-year sentence.

Only one of the justices, T.G. Kavanagh, had the acumen to point out that the court had neglected the obvious—the defective relationship to first principles. As he held:

---

[174] *People v. Sinclair*, 387 Mich. 91, 194 N.W.2d 878 (1972) at 104-115

[175] "A fundamental alteration of drug policy, particularly with regard to marijuana, is inevitable. . . . Yet despite an overwhelming volume of scientific criticism of existing law, legislatures have taken only token action. The source of the law is now its defense—ignorance. Even though independent researchers have disproved all of the old assumptions, the status quo is maintained on the ground that the evidence is not yet in on long-range effects of repeated use. A poor basis for a criminal law in any case, this argument is defectively open-ended. . . . If the legislative process continues to stall . . . we predict that the judiciary will no longer restrain itself. . . . Although we would prefer that the courts not be forced to enter still another political thicket, we do believe . . . that a declaration of unconstitutionality is analytically justifiable." Bonnie & Whitebread, *The Forbidden Fruit and the Tree of Knowledge* (1970) 1170

"Although I am persuaded that our statute is unconstitutional, I cannot agree that my Brothers have ascribed the correct or even permissible reasons for this conclusion. . . . I find that our statute violates the Federal and State Constitutions in that it is an impermissible intrusion on the fundamental rights to liberty and the pursuit of happiness, and is an unwarranted interference with the right to possess and use private property. As I understand our constitutional concept of government, an individual is free to do whatever he pleases, so long as he does not interfere with the rights of his neighbor or of society, and no government state or Federal has been ceded the authority to interfere with that freedom."[176]

Again, we see pure FC reasoning in effect, and from this period we have other examples of this more highly evolved perspective. These justices, however, belonged to a minority and the majority would be too enmeshed in the enemy image of drugs to connect with first principles. Hence, despite the efforts of dissenters, constitutional challenges would fail time and again.

Even so, events would go from bad to worse, for as the 1970s drew to a close the enemy image of drugs was reinflated to its former glory. The Reagan and Bush Administrations militarized the War on Drugs and would use this enemy image for all its worth. To succeed, a revision of history was necessary and 64 different catalogues and information pamphlets from the National Institute of Drug Abuse were removed from public libraries.[177] Drug taking was no longer accepted as a health problem. It was purely a moral problem, one that was explained by a lack of character, social commitment, and decency. Also, there was no longer a difference between soft and hard drugs; they were all the same and *all drug use* equaled abuse.

The government's misinformation machine increased its pressure and a predictable moral panic ensued. Only FC individuals have some measure of immunity against propaganda, and even though drug use rates had dropped for five years consecutively, 1989-polls revealed that 62 percent of the American people were willing to give up more of their freedoms in the War on Drugs. 83 percent responded that reporting drug

---

[176] *People v. Sinclair*, 387 Mich. 91, 194 N.W.2d 878 (1972) at 132-33

[177] BAUM, *SMOKE AND MIRRORS* (1996) 164

taking friends and family members to the police was the proper thing to do,[178] for as America's drug czar William Bennett had told them: "Turning in one's friends, is an act of true loyalty—of true friendship."[179] Bennett, a former professor who used to teach ethics, also confirmed that he had "no moral qualms about beheading convicted drug dealers."[180]

It is not for nothing that Professor Wisotsky has described prohibition as "profoundly totalitarian."[181] Even ministers of the Church would join the choir calling for the death penalty,[182] and the enemy image of drugs being reestablished there was, as we can expect, a marked drop in FC reasoning. As seen in part one, there is a connection between the two in the sense that they are diametrically opposed. On the one hand, the more enlightened we become, the less impact an enemy image will have. However, it is also the other way around, and the more powerful an enemy image becomes, the further we will draw towards the NC-end. Psychologically speaking it is difficult to overestimate the power of enemy images. They appeal to our emotions, not our intellect; they affect us in primordial ways, and their impact is such that people will prefer ignorance to knowledge. A principled review must be avoided at all costs, as the enemy image does not only provide an outlet for subconscious fears—it provides us with an identity.

---

[178] Ibid. 245, 277

[179] Ibid. 280

[180] L.A. Times, *Beheading of Convicted Drug Dealers Discussed by Bennett*, June 16, 1989

[181] DUKE & CROSS, *AMERICA'S LONGEST WAR* (1993) 159

[182] As Reverend Jesse Jackson stated: "Since the flow of drugs into the U.S. is an act of terrorism, antiterrorist policies must be applied. . . . If someone is transmitting the death agent to Americans, that person should face wartime consequences. The line must be drawn." SZASZ, *OUR RIGHT TO DRUGS* (1992) 113

8.5.2 THE PSYCHOLOGICAL DIMENSION

"The fact that drug use can be discussed at the highest levels of government only in metaphorical terms with mythological demonic imagery constitutes an unmistakable warning to us that something is seriously wrong."[183]

—Judge Sweet & Edward Harris—

The language and the confused reasoning that accompanies the prohibition ideology, coupled with the fervency with which the persecution of drug users is administered, betrays that something else is afoot. It suggests that psychological defense mechanisms are at play which are rarely understood and to overcome the power of enemy images, these psychological issues must be clarified.

We have already seen that for those in the grips of an enemy image the suggestion of reevaluating the preconceptions from which they build a worldview is met with great resistance. The reasons will soon be explained, but it is impossible to understand the history of constitutional challenges without adding the psychological dimension. Only this can explain why drug prohibition has endured to this day unsupported by evidence and reason. Only this can explain the doublethink[184] and cognitive dissonance that allows for different kinds of logic to be applied to otherwise similar cases. And only this can explain why judges and

---

[183] Sweet & Harris, *Moral and Constitutional Considerations in Support of the Decriminalization of Drugs*, in FISH (ED.), *HOW TO LEGALIZE DRUGS* (1998) 432

[184] "Doublethink" is the act of simultaneously accepting two mutually contradictory beliefs as correct. It is related to cognitive dissonance but somewhat more serious, for while the latter reflects a condition where contradictory beliefs cause a certain conflict in one's mind, the doublethinker is unaware of any conflict or contradiction. In other words, (to paraphrase Wikipedia) doublethinking is the act of relieving cognitive dissonance by ignoring the contradiction between two incompatible world views—or even of deliberately seeking to relieve cognitive dissonance. As Orwell observed: "To know and not to know, to be conscious of complete truthfulness while telling carefully constructed lies, to hold simultaneously two opinions which cancelled out, knowing them to be contradictory and believing in both of them, to use logic against logic, to repudiate morality while laying claim to it, . . . to forget whatever it was necessary to forget, then to draw it back into memory again at the moment when it was needed, and then promptly to forget it again, and above all, to apply the same process to the process itself—that was the ultimate subtlety: consciously to induce unconsciousness, and then, once again, to become unconscious of the act of hypnosis you had just performed." ORWELL, *NINETEEN EIGHTY-FOUR* (1949) 32

lawyers who normally take great pride in the respectability of their profession will undermine the rule of law rather than let drug users have their day in court.

Now, due to the impact of the enemy image (and the psychological incentives that support it), NC individuals will not perceive it this way. Nonetheless, if the reader is not convinced, further documentation will be provided—and to FC individuals, all this is clear. As Professor Wisotsky summarized the judiciary's treatment of drug cases:

> "What is remarkable is the extent to which the irrationality [of the legislature] is shared by the judicial branch, the branch institutionally committed to knowledge and reason. . . . Judges who have been called upon to answer drug law policy questions . . . have abandoned the method of fact-based, reasoned elaboration that is the essence of thinking like a lawyer or deciding like a judge. In place of careful analysis, judges have attempted to justify drug law decisions with misinformation or inflammatory rhetoric. . . . Few opinions combine careful reasoning and attention to evidence or empirical knowledge; we are left instead with drug law decisions based mainly on metaphors of outrage at drug users and sellers. Courts denounce the 'degeneracy' of 'moral perverts,' and call them 'vampires' or the 'walking dead' engaged in 'ugly' and 'insidious' drug distribution offenses. Generations of scientific research, scholarly analysis, and the reports of learned commissions have been almost completely ignored. The Supreme Court of the United States has never cited . . . any of the classic drug policy studies . . . in opinions concerning drug laws. Instead, [its opinions are] filled with emotionally charged dicta mimicking the political rhetoric that has dominated drug control in the United States since its inception. . . . In this respect, they have damaged the ethical basis of the adversary system, converting it largely into a propaganda tool for the party line."[185]

That the Supreme Court has abandoned all pretense of objectivity in this area is not even denied. As Justice Stevens himself said, "No impartial observer could criticize this Court for hindering the progress of

---

[185] Wisotsky, *Not thinking Like a Lawyer* (1991)

the War on Drugs."[186] He took pride calling the Court a "loyal foot soldier in the Executive's fight,"[187] and to explain why otherwise upright judges embrace populist bias and let prejudice take the place of reason, important psychological factors bear emphasis.

One is what John Stuart Mill called the tyranny of majority opinion. After more than 100 years of prohibition its ideology has transcended the factual realm. The premises behind prohibition have been elevated to the status of myth, and the power of myth is simply too great for NC individuals to resist.[188] Today, therefore, everyone knows that "drugs are bad" and the fact that drug prohibition came into being as a result of irrational fears, racism, and insufficient knowledge is conveniently forgotten. I say "conveniently," for as the prohibition philosophy has shaped society, the officials have developed such vested interest in this ideology (and maintaining the overblown enemy image behind it) that no amount of evidence as to the destructive effects of their crusade has succeeded in changing their minds.

This, however, is only one side of the coin and on the other we must recognize that drug users fulfill an important social role. Throughout history people have had a need to find some outsider-group (1) to use as a measure of their own wholesomeness, and (2) to blame for the ills that befall society. If we look closer, this has been the emotional appeal behind every destructive mass-movement and drug prohibition is no different; it persists because it separates the world into us versus them, providing an outlet for unconscious fears.

The psychological incentive behind our eagerness to separate the world into us and them results from the fact that a person cannot live without having some measure of self-worth. Neither organized religion nor Neo-Darwinism can provide us with a sound footing and so people

---

[186] *California v. Acevedo*, U.S. slip op. 17 (1991) (Stevens J., dissenting)

[187] Id.

[188] If the power of myth is not already apparent in the irrational fears and the incomprehensible logic that drives the War on Drugs, it should be plain to recognize in its end, the dream of a drug free society. Even though the drug war has only succeeded in bringing us further away from this imagined ideal, it is still being held up by prohibitionists as the end of their righteous quest, and just like a mirage in the desert can make deluded men run towards their death, so the pursuit of this ever-elusive ideal has only brought society closer to its demise. In pursuit of this ideal we have thrown the Constitution out the window as the "drug exception" to the Bill of Rights keeps broadening the police power. If it were not for the power of myth, alarm bells would ring out by this unfolding process, but instead it has been accepted as a necessary evil.

will have to look elsewhere to solve this problem. Unless they embrace the FC-view on religion/spirituality, there is one way to do this, and it is finding someone to look down on. Hence, if people are not sufficiently free from the NC Groupmind to go with the FC-option, this is what they will do. It may be homosexuals, drug users, a racial group, whatever. The important thing is that something out there must serve as a measure of lesser-worth so that people can experience themselves as having at least some relative value. The more they are troubled by feelings of inadequate self-worth, the greater will be the psychological incentive to trample others down, and as soon as some group has been targeted for this purpose the process of degradation begins. The moral status of those in the outgroup will be bitterly attacked and their humanity eroded until the moral obligations we sense towards our fellow men no longer apply. All those qualities we refuse to accept within ourselves, all our repressed fears, will be projected onto this outsider group—and to the extent that we can see them at the "other," this something that we are not, we will bring meaning to the image of our own goodness.

This outsider group will be blamed for the problems of society and it becomes self-evident that they must be removed. No matter the time and place, this is the recipe behind any mass-movement gone wrong—and in this sense drug users are the modern equivalent of witches, Jews, and other social outcasts. This is well-known among scholars,[189] and according to this view, owing to our fear of having to accept responsibility for ourselves and our actions as free and rational agents, we have located the source of our problems in drugs.

We have seen that in the NC State there will be a constant pressure from above to deprive us of autonomy. Agents of the state will encourage dependency and paternalistic policies, and while this can be a comfortable solution, it is a Faustian bargain that will come back to haunt us. Not only is it a law of politics that tyrannical government will ensue

---

[189] Professors of law, philosophy, and psychiatry have demonstrated that the drug war in its essence is a religious crusade and that the modern persecution of drugs, drug users, and pushers must be seen against the historical backdrop of the ritual persecution of other scapegoats such as heretics, witches, Jews, and madmen. SEE SZASZ, *CEREMONIAL CHEMISTRY* (2003). See also HUSAK, *DRUGS AND RIGHTS* (1992); MILLER, *THE CASE FOR LEGALIZING DRUGS* (1991) 109-24; Stuart, *War as Metaphor and the Rule of Law in Crisis* (2011); Levine & Reinarman, *The Transition from Prohibition to Regulation: Lessons from Alcohol Policy for Drug Policy*, in FISH (ED.), *HOW TO LEGALIZE DRUGS* (1998); Somerville: *Stigmatization, scapegoating and discrimination in sexually transmitted diseases: overcoming "them" and "us"* (1994)

if we fail to take responsibility for our lives, but dereliction of our duty as adults to take responsibility for our own behaviors and lifestyle choices will undermine our feelings of self-worth. This is inevitable, for to the extent we conform to the NC State's expectations, we must abandon that which makes us individuals—our penchant for autonomy, freedom, and responsibility. To the extent we reject these values we will be less than complete individuals. We will be living on our knees, submitting to the rule of others, and we will be secretly ashamed of ourselves.

I say "secretly," as none of this can be admitted. We will continue to see ourselves as sovereign agents and in no way acknowledge the extent to which we fall short of this ideal. This phenomenon is well-known,[190] and it should come as no surprise that people who reject autonomy in their own life feel deeply threatened by those who take its value more seriously.

Thus, drug users become so deeply despised. For one, drug use is associated with youth culture. Adolescents have an ingrained opposition to false authority, a yearning for freedom, and the courage to act on it. Fretting about all this has always been a favorite pastime of the elder generation for in the youth they are confronted with the reality of their own souls. This is a most difficult encounter. While the elder generation at some point shared the youth's impatience with false authority, their social conditioning and careers have made them cognitively weak and morally corrupt. The price they have paid for conformity is accepting a social contract based on lies, oppression, and injustice, and this is not easily admitted. Therefore, most adults go through life with eyes wide shut, willfully neglecting the obvious. Reality must be avoided at all costs and they will stick with the established paradigm—the idea that (1) the current state of affairs is not that bad; (2) that to the extent there are problems to be solved their authorities are working on it; (3) that improvement takes time (in the sense, who knows when?); (4) that the

---

[190] To paraphrase Miller: "To live what Joseph Campbell calls an 'authentic life' people must consciously choose one of the alternatives—irresponsibility or autonomy. Many people refuse to make a conscious choice. They refuse to admit that their lives repudiate autonomy. Rather than face reality, they choose to live a lie. The result is mental illness, as guilt grows about betrayal of moral ideas. This personal guilt cannot be faced (otherwise people could make a conscious choice). Yet an outlet must be found. Drug addicts become natural scapegoats for wrath; they do freely what their fellow citizens do in shame. Drug addicts personify what Americans hate about themselves." MILLER, *THE CASE FOR LEGALIZING DRUGS* (1991) 111

only responsible way of action is to work within the system to improve things; (5) that rejecting the authority of those in charge is not a sensible option; and (6) that those who do are irresponsible and immature troublemakers.

This is the mindset that goes with being a well-adjusted citizen. And as these citizens do not have the courage to oppose false authority, they fret about the younger generation. This psychological response is only natural, as they themselves, at some level, are aware that something is rotten in the kingdom. Thus, they are deeply uncomfortable when faced with any reminder of the treason they have committed in accepting a social contract on false pretenses. To protect from this embarrassment, they instinctively reject questions or behaviors that rock the boat—and as the youth cannot be blamed for cherishing FC values, they are abused for their drug preferences. Because they have qualms about authority, and still own the integrity to demand some meaningful measure of control over their lives, that percentage of the population who blindly accept the power of authority will side with authority in these perceived acts of rebellion. It is well-known that drug use to many people is an expression of liberation rather than enslavement. By using these drugs responsibly and to their satisfaction they not only dispel the propaganda that authority rely on to keep the populace sedated; they refute the fundamental premise of the crusade—the hilarious notion that authority persecutes them for their own good.[191]

No wonder this act of insolence is deeply frowned upon. Their activities are a reminder that those who side with authority build their lives on a lie, and so they are persecuted for representing those values preached but abandoned by the elder generation. Because this generation cannot face the fact that rebellion, suicide, crime, depression, and misbehavior among the youth are no more than symptoms of the extent to which society fails to live up to wholesome ideals, values, and

---

[191] As Miller noted, "drug users . . . demonstrate the sincerity of their belief in personal freedom by persisting in free choice of drugs even at the risk of arrest and imprisonment. That kind of moral courage contrasts with elders who fear even the right to choose. Youths challenge the validity of orders that other citizens want to obey. Youths who act as they live in a democracy generate hatred among citizens who fear democracy." MILLER, *THE CASE FOR LEGALIZING DRUGS* (1991) 117

principles, they must find some other cause to explain all this—and so drugs, music, and the like, will be blamed.[192]

Thus, scapegoating drug users is intimately connected with these "well-adjusted" citizens' inability to face the Faustian bargain that comes with being compliant members of a deeply unjust society. The problem of "dangerous drugs" becomes the answer, an escape clause, that makes the otherwise unfaceable possible to ignore. Even if drug prohibition has failed in its explicitly stated purpose it has succeeded exceptionally well in this regard. The myth of the "demon drugs" has made it possible for the average citizen to keep a cognitive discord intact by ignoring reality and making the victims bear the oppressor's guilt. No one else—not robbers, rapists, or murderers—is hated as are drug users, and the minimum penalties imposed by U.S. Federal law illustrate this level of fear, as well as the insanity that results: Burglary with a gun—2.0 years; kidnapping—4.2 years; rape—5.8 years; attempted murder—6.5 years; possession of LSD—10.1 years![193]

It is no coincidence that the less we know, the easier it becomes to believe in the demonizing traits that is ascribed to the "other;" the greater impact the enemy image will have on our minds; the more we will despise and fear the perceived "enemy;" and the more efficiently this enemy image will provide its psychological function, which is absolve us from "sin." When it comes to this psychological set-up ignorance, fear, and disgust feed off each other, and for the sake of "sanity" reason cannot be allowed. If prohibitionists were to reconsider the underlying premises of their assumptions, they would no longer have straw men to attack. Instead, they would have to face their fears and inadequacies head on— and they would have to come to terms with the horrible truth of their campaign, which is too disturbing to consider.

---

[192] Hence, as Bakalar and Grinspoon observed, the reason why we prohibit drug use is analogous to the reason why Iranians prohibit Western music. In Iran, listening to Western music is seen as an act of rebellion against the establishment and the way it handles social problems. In the same way, drug use in our society it is taken as a personal threat to those who support the status quo. The people in charge, whether it be of Western or Iranian society, will always see themselves as preservers of all that is decent and worthwhile. Change is regarded as a threat to their powerbase and so, to them, music and drug use represents an objectionable way of life, one that is characterized by unproductive behavior, unreliability, dishonesty, lack of moral values, and anti-authoritarian tendencies. BAKALAR & GRINSPOON, *DRUG CONTROL IN A FREE SOCIETY* (1998) 19

[193] SZASZ, *CEREMONIAL CHEMISTRY* (2003) 188

We must remember that the problem to begin with is an ego unsure of itself and that psychological growth (which always equals more love for self and others) is needed before they can face reality. Consequently, they will strongly reject any attempt to have reality imposed on them or their policies. No matter the historical context this psychological set-up is the same, and it is no easier for a prohibitionist to come to terms with the reality of his campaign than it was for a Nazi or an inquisitionist. This being so, unless we are to look for more sinister motives, the hysteria and absurd reasoning that goes with the prohibition ideology is a testimony to the power of the unconscious, for when the truth becomes unbearable defense mechanisms will intervene to keep us from putting two and two together.

Now, most people are oblivious to such psychological influences. They know that they despise drug users (and hate drug distributors) but they do not know why, and they will look for rational reasons to explain irrational opinions. As we shall see, the enemy image dictates the logic and not the other way around, and so they will be looking for evidence that confirms their opinions: they will reason from worse-case scenarios, they will rely on hearsay and flawed research, and they will ignore all evidence to the contrary. So it is that even today, nearly fifty years after Professor Kaplan, after a two-year study of the drug law, concluded that the arguments relied upon by prohibitionists "are often so transparently flimsy that one can hardly believe they have been put forward seriously,"[194] continue to regurgitate the very same logic, even though the evidence to refute it has grown exponentially.

This is the power of enemy images and the psychological incentives behind them. It is simply taken for granted that one knows what one knows, and as long as they remain in the grip of these influences prohibitionists will degrade any constitutional challenge to the point where, as the Supreme Court held in *Chapman*, "whatever debate there is [will] center around the appropriate sentence and not the criminality of the conduct."[195] It is simply impossible for these judges to take seriously the notion that drug use could be a constitutionally protected activity as it would open the floodgates to self-reflection. Hence, as other

---

[194] KAPLAN, *MARIJUANA: THE NEW PROHIBITION* (1971) 3

[195] *Chapman v. United States*, 500 U.S. 453 (1991)

commentators have noted, the sloppy reasoning that is applied in drug cases is a testimony to the psychological bias that serves to deny users a fair trial,[196] and we shall now explore this bit.

8.5.3 The Problem of Differently Applied Logic

"An extraterrestrial creature who listened to our declarations about the terrible problems created by drugs, and then compared our approach to marijuana with alcohol and tobacco, would have to conclude that we do not quite mean what we are saying."[197]

—James Bakalar & Lester Grinspoon—

From what we have seen, drug prohibition can only be taken seriously by a society firmly established at the NC level. Indeed, from the FC perspective, drug prohibition is seen as a symptom of the psychological traits that define the NC mindset, as only a society scared of embracing the responsibility that comes with being adults would accept the premises of drug prohibition. The reasoning that accompanies the prohibitionist mindset is characteristic of the lower-analytical faculties of those inhabiting the NC-end, and for those inhabiting the FC-end it is seen as the folly it is. For instance, the decision to deny drugs status as property is ridiculous as seen from the FC perspective, for as James Madison said: "In its larger and juster meaning, [property] embraces everything to which a man may attach a value . . . [and includes that] which individuals have in their opinions, their religion, their passions, and their faculties."[198]

On this notion alone, the distinction between licit and illicit drugs is illegitimate. As seen from the bigger perspective, the separation that now exists between recreational, medical, and religious drug use is also

---

[196] Brashear, *Marijuana Prohibition and the Constitutional Right of Privacy* (1975) 575 ("the brevity of the treatment suggests that these courts not only considered the right of privacy in general to be somewhat suspect, but also assumed that the argument was not seriously offered by defendant.")

[197] BAKALAR & GRINSPOON, *DRUG CONTROL IN A FREE SOCIETY* (1998) 131

[198] SCHALER (ED.), *DRUGS: SHOULD WE LEGALIZE, DECRIMINALIZE OR DEREGULATE?* (1998) 181

unreasonable and the same applies to our perception of drug users. Because we have lost our way so completely as a society, this may not be obvious, but as seen from the FC perspective our schizophrenic view on drug users borders on the comical. Psychiatrist Thomas Szasz noted it thus:

> "If the state (official medicine) certifies you as sick and gives you drugs—regardless of whether you need them or not, whether they help you or not, even whether you want them or not—then you are a patient receiving treatment; but if you buy your own drugs and take them on your own initiative—because you feel you need them or, worse, because you want to give yourself peace of mind or pleasure— then you are an addict engaged in drug abuse.
>
> This outlook on life and the policy it engenders rests on a medical imagery that idolizes the therapeutic state as benevolent doctor, and demonizes the autonomous individual as a person who is both a criminal and a patient and whose sole aim in life is to be high on drugs and low on economic productivity."[199]

Because this passage aptly summarizes our view on drug taking, we could easily have solved the "drug problem" by giving all drug users a diagnosis and "medicating" them with their drugs of choice.

This, however, is not the point. The problem goes deeper, and it is not so much that a minority of the drug using population will develop a dysfunctional relationship to their favorite drugs but that we refuse to see them as autonomous agents. In doing so we enable them, for only to the extent that problem-users are perceived as responsible for their lives will they be empowered to change their ways. It is unfortunate therefore that, instead of ascribing responsibility where it is due, we make the mistake of attributing to the drugs some sinister influence. In changing our focus from the autonomous agent to an inanimate object, not only do we increase the likelihood that irresponsible drug relationships will evolve but we nourish an unwholesome enemy image. There will always be users who are eager to buy into the notion that drugs have ruined their

---

[199] Sweet & Harris, *Moral and Constitutional Considerations in Support of the Decriminalization of Drugs*, in FISH (ED.), *HOW TO LEGALIZE DRUGS* (1998) 434

lives, and as our society encourages this rejection of responsibility, fuel is provided for the myth that drugs are "bad."

I say "myth" as it should be obvious that drugs cannot be "bad," any more than knives or axes can be. It all depends on the user, and just as knives and axes can be used for bad as well as good things, so can drugs. In this sense, a fear of drugs is as irrational as a fear of knives or axes. Their ordinary intended purpose is benign and at least 90 percent of all use conforms to this norm. Furthermore, drug taking is volitional and there is no need for "pushers" to push them on to anyone. In fact, drug consumers are exactly like other consumers, and the War on Drugs, as Professor Wisotsky has noted, is actually "a war on the American people—their values, needs, and choices, freely expressed in the marketplace of consumer goods."[200]

When it comes to merchandise such as alcohol, tobacco, coffee, and coca cola, this is all too obvious. But when it comes to the illicit drugs prohibitionists turn this logic on its head. Instead of seeing drug users as autonomous agents, they are perceived as being victims of a plague and it becomes their perceived duty to protect people from themselves. This is where prohibitionists' logic breaks down and they leave reason behind. They will apply two wholly different standards to the world; one for the illicit drug users and one for everyone else; and being caught in the grips of the enemy image, they will not question this differently applied logic nor come to terms with its implications. Instead, they will operate on autopilot, ignoring all evidence of cognitive discord and duplicity. Refusing to see the disconnect that gives meaning to their ideology they will eagerly embrace a schizophrenic worldview. They will happily feed and nourish the deception that validates their position, and we shall now see the result of this phenomenon.

---

[200] WISOTSKY, *BEYOND THE WAR ON DRUGS* (1990) 198

8.5.3.1 Different Measures of Harm, Culpability, and Human Dignity

That we are dealing with two different mindsets is evident everywhere, not least in the workings of the U.S. Supreme Court. As Justice Black described the problem of illicit drugs:

> "Commercial traffic in deadly mind-, soul-, and body-destroying drugs is beyond doubt one of the greatest evils of our time. It cripples intellects, dwarfs bodies, paralyzes the progress of a substantial segment of our society, and frequently makes hopeless and sometimes violent and murderous criminals of persons of all ages who become its victims. Such consequences call for the most vigorous laws to suppress the traffic as well as the most powerful efforts to put these vigorous laws into effect."[201]

Would it be conceivable for the justices to describe the trafficking of alcohol in these terms? I think not. It would be difficult to imagine a Court that would label barkeepers and others involved in the distribution chain of alcohol as dealers "in deadly drugs,"[202] and who would describe a young man who on five occasions had sold a can of beer as a "trafficker in human misery."[203] Such terms are reserved for the traffic in illicit drugs, the drugs that are imagined to have no benefits to society, whose users are victims (but still worthy of punishment), and whose distributors are "dealers in death", worthy of the most severe sentences.

These different standards result from an exaggerated enemy image. If it wasn't for this, the folly would be self-evident, but there it is; it has already separated the world into two different ways of thinking and this disconnect is seen in the different perceptions of harm, culpability, and human dignity that is applied to the two classes of users. The facts speak for themselves, for would the Supreme Court have declined to consider

---

[201] *Turner v. United States*, 396 U.S.398 (1970) (Black, J., with whom Douglas, J., joins, dissenting.)

[202] Justice Powell discussing drug dealers in *United States v. Mendenhall*, 446 U.S. 544 (1980) 561-562

[203] *United States v. Markham*, C07.126, 191 F.2d 936 (1951) ("The proof had established five different sales of marihuana cigarettes by the defendant, and we do not think it was prejudicial to refer to him as a trafficker in human misery.")

whether a mandatory lifetime sentence for possession of one beer constituted cruel and unusual punishment? Would it have accepted the premise that a person in possession of one beer were implicitly and partly responsible for all the death, misfortune, and misery that the abuse of alcohol contributed to society?

It is difficult to entertain the idea that they would. Still, that was the position of the Court in *Carmona v. Ward,* when it refused to consider whether two mandatory life sentences, one for possession of an ounce of a substance containing cocaine, and the other for sale of 0.00455 of an ounce of a substance containing cocaine, constituted cruel and unusual punishment.

The different logic that applies to licit and illicit drug users is further exemplified by the Supreme Court in *Hutto v. Davis* and *Harmelin v. Michigan.* In the former, the Court approved of imposing 40 years in prison for the possession of 9 ounces of marijuana, while in the latter a young man in possession of 672 grams of cocaine was sentenced to mandatory life. Would the Court, as it did, have attempted to justify such a sentence for barkeepers on account that "a sentence of life imprisonment without parole, while being the second most severe penalty permitted by law, is not grossly disproportionate to the crime of possessing" 100 bottles of vodka? Would it deride his defense by claiming that the "defendant's suggestion that the crime was nonviolent and victimless is false to the point of absurdity"? Would it justify this life sentence by reference to studies that demonstrate the grave threat that alcohol, and particularly strong drink, pose to society in terms of violence, crime, and social displacement?[204]

Again, I think not. While the disastrous consequences of alcohol abuse are factually accurate, it would be difficult to imagine a court which put the responsibility for a minority of alcohol drinkers' excessive use and poor lifestyle choices on the bartender. Still, the Court does not hesitate in comparing Harmelin's crime of possessing 672 grams of cocaine to that of first-degree murder. As Justice Kennedy said: "a rational basis exists . . . to conclude that petitioner's crime is as serious

---

[204] *Harmelin v. Michigan,* 501 U.S. 957 (1991)

and violent as the crime of felony murder without specific intent to kill,[205] a crime for which no sentence of imprisonment would be disproportionate. . . . A professional seller of addictive drugs may inflict greater bodily harm upon members of society than the person who commits a single assault."[206]

More of the different set of reasoning that is applied in drug cases was seen when Kennedy discussed the connection between crime and drugs. As he said:

> "Petitioner's suggestion that his crime was nonviolent and victimless . . . is false to the point of absurdity. To the contrary, petitioner's crime threatened to cause grave harm to society.
>
> Quite apart from the pernicious effects on the individual who consumes illegal drugs, such drugs relate to crime in at least three ways: (1) A drug user may commit crime because of drug-induced changes in physiological functions, cognitive ability, and mood; (2) A drug user may commit crime in order to obtain money to buy drugs; and (3) A violent crime may occur as part of the drug business or culture. Studies bear out these possibilities, and demonstrate a direct nexus between illegal drugs and crimes of violence. To mention but a few examples, 57 percent of a national sample of males arrested in 1989 for homicide tested positive for illegal drugs. The comparable statistics for assault, robbery, and weapons arrests were 55, 73 and 63 percent, respectively. In Detroit, Michigan in 1988, 68 percent of a sample of male arrestees and 81 percent of a sample of female arrestees tested positive for illegal drugs. Fifty-one percent of males and seventy-one percent of females tested positive for cocaine. And last year an estimated 60 percent of the homicides in Detroit were drug-related, primarily cocaine-related. *"[207]*

Again, the exact same reasoning could be applied to alcohol and tobacco. A statistically significant percentage of those who come into

---

[205] "Felony murder" means that the malicious intent inherent in the commission of any crime, however trivial, is considered to apply to any consequences of that crime, however unintended. As of 2008, 46 states in the United States had a felony murder rule, under which felony murder is generally first-degree murder.

[206] Id.

[207] Id. (Kennedy J., with whom O'Connor J., and Souter J., joins) (sources omitted)

contact with the criminal justice system will be users of these drugs and while tobacco is no more associated with killing sprees than cannabis, alcohol most certainly is.[208]

Furthermore, it bears emphasis that none of these statistics prove a causal connection between drug use and crime. Scholars have found no such link[209] and most of the problems Kennedy addresses are in fact attributable to prohibition, not the pharmacological properties of drugs. Professor Steven Duke speaks to it thus:

> "Contrary to what our government told us when it imposed drug prohibition, most illegal recreational drugs have no pharmacological properties that produce violence or other criminal behavior. Heroin and marijuana diminish rather than increase aggressive behavior. Cocaine—or cocaine withdrawal—occasionally triggers violence but usually does not. Very little crime is generated by the mere use of these drugs, especially in comparison to alcohol, which is causally related to thousands of homicides and hundreds of thousands of assaults annually. The major linkages between illegal drugs and crime must be found elsewhere—in prohibition. . . . [In fact,] the drug war as it is currently being waged probably produces at least half of our serious crime. That is, half of our crime (not counting drug crimes, of course) simply would not occur were we not conducting a drug war. No more damning an indictment of our political leaders can be

---

[208] BAKALAR & GRINSPOON, *DRUG CONTROL IN A FREE SOCIETY* (1998) 131 ("Half of all wife abusers in Great Britain are heavy drinkers; more than half of the prisoners have serious drinking problems; half of the homicides are committed by people who have been drinking.")

[209] "Independent researchers say that the causal relationship between drugs and crime is merely a hypothesis that has not been proven true. Two scholars from the Earl Warren Legal Institute of the University of California at Berkeley, Franklin Zimring and Gordon Hawkins, who have published a highly regarded study of drug control problems in 1995, even contend that it is untrue. Indeed, they argue that while 'it is beyond dispute that drug use and crime overlap and interact in a multiplicity of ways,' the higher rate of drug use among offenders could be explained by factors in their personality, such as a higher propensity for taking risks and 'a willingness to ignore the threat of moral condemnation,' that lead them to both commit crimes and take drugs. In this view, both drugs and crime are simultaneous but independent consequences of other variables; in simple terms: it is not drug use that causes crime but rather other factors that lead the vast majority of those who commit crime to also take drugs." Laniel, *The Relationship between Research and Drug Policy in the United States* (1999); see also MILLER, *DRUG WARRIORS AND THEIR PREY* (1996) 16-17

imagined than that they have affirmatively created half the crime under which we suffer."[210]

The mythical link between crime and drugs was dispelled half a century ago.[211] However, it is a central tenet of prohibitionist reasoning and crops up again and again. A curious example is provided by Justice Boyd of the Florida Supreme Court. The litigant had argued that because *Stanley* protected the private possession of obscene materials, so also the smoking of marijuana in the home should be constitutionally protected. On behalf of the majority, Boyd responded:

"Reprehensible as the possession of obscene material may be, the possession and use of marijuana poses a much greater potential threat to society. Appellant states that the primary purpose of smoking marijuana is the 'psychological reaction' it produces in the user and that by smoking marijuana he was 'merely asserting the right to satisfy his intellectual and emotional needs in the privacy of his own home.' This Court is aware that commission of other types of crime, particularly violent crimes, has an emotional effect on the perpetrator. This, however, does not give a constitutional right to commit the crime.

Marijuana does not enjoy the protection of the First Amendment. Its use does not constitute 'private consumption of ideas or information.' Neither are Fourteenth Amendment rights abridged nor the right of privacy violated. Marijuana is a harmful, mind-altering drug. An individual might restrict his possession of marijuana to the privacy of his home, but the effects of the drug are not so

---

[210] Duke, *Drug Prohibition: An Unnatural Disaster* (1995) 575, 581 (sources omitted.) For more on how and why prohibition generates crime and other negative externalities, see Benson, *The War on Drugs: A Public Bad* (2008) 4-36; Ostrowski, *Answering the Critics of Drug Legalization* (1991) 12-13; Rasmussen and Benson, *Rationalizing Drug Policy under Federalism* (2003) 685-711; Werb et al., *Effect of Drug Law Enforcement on Drug-Related Violence: Evidence from a Scientific Review* (2010). For more on why prohibition is not justified to prevent crime, see HUSAK, LEGALIZE THIS! (2002) 82-93 and BAKALAR & GRINSPOON, *DRUG CONTROL IN A FREE SOCIETY* (1998) 133. For other scholars who have pointed out that most drug related deaths and problems are in fact prohibition related, see Barrios & Curtis, *The Impact of the War on Drugs on Puerto Ricans: A Lost Generation,* in FISH (ED.), HOW TO LEGALIZE DRUGS (1998) 125; Majoor, *Drug Policy in the Netherlands: Waiting for a Change,* in FISH (ED.), HOW TO LEGALIZE DRUGS (1998) 152-53

[211] See for instance Bonnie & Whitebread, *The Forbidden Fruit and the Tree of Knowledge* (1970) 1105; KAPLAN, MARIJUANA: THE NEW PROHIBITION (1971)

restricted. The interest of the state in preventing harm to the individual and to the public at large amply justifies the outlawing of marijuana, in private and elsewhere.

Recently . . . [we recognized] that 'it is to the interest of the state to have strong, robust, healthy citizens, capable of self-support, of bearing arms, and of adding to the resources of the country.' Since marijuana, in addition to harming the individual, is a threat to society as a whole, we have no difficulty in upholding its prohibition by the state."[212]

We see how the court describes the high of a marijuana cigarette as comparable to the high of violent crimes, and with this image in mind it is easy to understand why marijuana users are denied constitutional protection. That marijuana users directly harm no one (except themselves) and that the law itself poses a much greater threat to users and society is completely ignored. Ignored is also that the justices' fundamental premise—the premise that the government has a right to take whatever measures it deems fit in its battle against imagined social problems—is inherently flawed. Reasoning by analogy the court could just as well have compared the high of runners, chocolate eaters, coca cola drinkers, and tobacco smokers with the psychopathic high of the violent offender, and on this basis justified the criminalization of such individuals.

The Florida Supreme Court, however, does not merely grant the government full authority to deal with perceived evils; it takes its reasoning to its logical conclusion, and by implication extends to the government a right to healthy citizens.

The government, of course, has no such right. Only in totalitarian states like Hitler's Germany do the state have an imagined right to citizens who are "strong, robust, healthy, capable of self-support, of bearing arms, and of adding to the resources of the country." The idea belongs to the extreme NC-end, and the founders' America is the very antithesis to this notion. As Professor Fuller pointed out 50 years ago, *the essence of the modern state project is the distinction between a morality of duty and a morality of aspiration.* The morality of duty concerns our duties to our fellowmen: We shall, in short, not infringe on each other's

---

[212] *Borras v. State*, 229 So. 2d 244 (1969) 246

autonomy or liberty rights, and the state is there to ensure that we do not violate the rights of other persons. The morality of duty, then, concerns *the very least* that we can expect from each other; it sets the bar where we cannot lower it further, not without unduly infringing the rights of others to the same liberties as ourselves. This threshold equals the parameter of justice. Not only can it not be lowered; it cannot be heightened, as the idea of freedom would become meaningless.

In other words, it is *only* if we fail to live up to the morality of duty as it is defined by this threshold that the state may rightfully intervene. *Any unwanted state meddling in our private affairs must be because we have failed to abide by the morality of duty*, and while we can all do better—be more compassionate, altruistic, and service-oriented—the state has no right to expect this from us. This is where the morality of aspiration kicks in, and it is entirely up to the individual to figure out how he/she will honor his/her FC aspirations.

Drug users therefore cannot be expected to conform to any other standard than the morality of duty. However, if they fail to do so, there are already laws to deal with those misbehaviors that affect the rights of others and the drug law cannot be justified on such grounds. It is merely another testimony to the different standards we apply to drug users that the Florida Court would embrace such reasoning. For as Husak noted, "[a]part from the context of drug use, no one believes that anyone possesses a right to mandate that persons be healthy, that workers be productive, that parents be good, that neighbors be reliable, or that students be attentive."[213] If this were the case, most of how we organize our lives would be subject to restrictions and the idea of liberty would be void of all content.

Another area where we see the application of the different standards is in those courts where the criterion for upholding the prohibition is whether marijuana is a harmless drug. Several courts have ruled in favor of the state because the appellant has not succeeded in convincing the judges that marijuana is a completely harmless substance.[214] In doing so,

---

[213] Husak, *Two Rationales For Drug Policy* in FISH (ED.), *HOW TO LEGALIZE DRUGS* (1998) 52

[214] *Commonwealth v. Leis,* 355 Mass. 189, 243 N.E.2d 898 (1969); *Marcoux v. Attorney General*, 375 Mass. 63, (1978); *United States v. Maas*, 551 F. Supp. 645 (D.N.J. 1982) 648 ("Defendants could not prove that it has been established conclusively that use of marijuana is

they are misframing the issue, for the question is not whether marijuana is a harmless recreational drug. The question is whether the possible harms are significant enough to merit prohibition; whether prohibition is the least intrusive means available; whether prohibition is suited to deal with the alleged harms; and whether the harms associated with the drug are less significant than the harms attributed to prohibition.[215]

Furthermore, we see the different standards being applied on the eagerness with which the courts defer to the legislature because of the "unknown" harms associated with illicit drugs. The argument is that "alcohol is susceptible to a less restrictive alternative means of control," because "there are recognized, accurate means of determining its use and its abuse" and "the effects of alcohol upon the user are known."[216] However, these are not viable reasons for imprisoning drug users. As Justice Seiler of the Missouri Supreme Court noted:

> "This contention is unresponsive for two reasons. The first is that however 'incomplete' our knowledge may be or how 'debatable' the 'medical issue' concerning marijuana may be or how much 'disagreement or controversy' may surround any discussion concerning the drug, this grants no legislative license to violate one's constitutional right to be free from cruel and unusual punishment. There is surely less 'debate' and 'controversy' concerning the assuredly harmful effects of cigarette smoking. Yet were the legislature to prohibit the sale of cigarettes as a crime, I question whether this court would be as deferential were the legislature to mandate a penalty of imprisonment from five years to life for the sale of less than half a pack.
>
> The second reason [why this] view is unresponsive is that [the court] has shielded itself behind alleged factual uncertainty which is the relic of an earlier day. No longer can we realistically claim, as once we could, that the data upon which to judge the effects of

---

harmless, yet only such proof could alter this court's determination that the legislation is supported by a rational justification.")

[215] As Justice Abe of the Hawaii Supreme Court stated "the finding that marijuana is harmful to the user does not authorize the State under its police power to prohibit its use under threat of punishment. Under the doctrine . . . the State must prove that the use of marijuana is not only harmful to the user but also to the general public before it can prohibit its use." *State v. Kantner*, 493 P.2d 306 (1972) at 313 (Abe J., concurring)

[216] *Leis 355 Mass.* 189 (1969) 198

marijuana is either unreliable, crudely assembled, or considerably outdated. Substantial private research . . . has been joined by . . . comprehensive government supported efforts, well-financed studies utilizing advanced scientific analysis. These studies demonstrably, effectively, categorically, and reliably show that there is no firm evidence that marijuana as presently used in this country is attended with danger to the user or to others."[217]

Regarding Seiler's first point, the different measures of human dignity attributed to tobacco and cannabis smokers and the different measure of harm we attach to the products, it is made evident in *RJR-MacDonald Inc.*, where the Canadian Supreme Court investigated the possibility of prohibiting tobacco. Despite the Court's finding that "the detrimental health effects of tobacco consumption are both dramatic and substantial," the Court held that the government was justified in not criminalizing tobacco consumption. The reason for this decision was that criminalizing tobacco products "would likely lead many smokers to resort to alternative, and illegal, sources of supply," rendering such an approach "unfeasible."[218]

Now again, the exact same thing can be said of the criminalization of other drugs and the only relevant difference is that the potential harms associated with cannabis consumption pale in comparison to the harms caused by tobacco consumption. Why, then, do our officials come to opposite conclusions? Why is prohibition a valid endeavor when it comes to one type of drugs but not the other? How can we reconcile the use of two divergent scales of harm and human dignity?

An answer is yet to be provided.

8.5.3.2 DIFFERENT MEASURES OF RATIONALITY

When asked to defend their policies, prohibitionists will say that drug use is a disaster to society and that it is not compatible with a rational conception of the good life. According to them, drug use is construed as

---

[217] *State v. Michell*, 563 S.W.2d 18 (1978) 29-30 (Seiler, J., dissenting)

[218] *RJR-MacDonald Inc. v. Canada (Attorney General)*, (1995) 3 S.C.R. 199

pathological behavior, as an objectionable activity that deserves no recognition, and to legalize drugs would be to "send the wrong message."

As other scholars have noted, however, it is a myth that drug use is necessarily pathological and in reality it is indistinguishable from other pleasure-giving activities such as eating, sex, and falling in love.[219] Even addicts can be said to "have chosen to follow a way of life which offers them the rewards of activity, company and a recognized identity,"[220] and to "single out drug use as necessarily and uniquely harmful to reason (and so specifically worthy of prohibition) is to fall for the 'myth of the demon drugs.'"[221]

If we are to paint drug use as an irrational activity, a habit that no sound mind would pursue, we must adopt Jon Elster's definition of rational choice which involves three optimizations: Optimization of action, given desires and beliefs; optimization of beliefs, given the available information; and optimization of information acquisition given desires and beliefs.[222]

Using this standard, we can see that some types of drug use (but not all) could be defined as irrational behavior. But then again, so would the behaviors of the rest of the population. It is all a matter of perspective, and as seen from the FC-end hardly anything we do meets this strict standard of rationality.[223] The footnote provides us with a few examples,

---

[219] Fingarette, *Addiction and Criminal Responsibility* in SCHALER (ED.), *DRUGS: SHOULD WE LEGALIZE, DECRIMINALIZE OR DEREGULATE?* (1998) 306-38; DE GREIFF (ED.), *DRUGS AND THE LIMITS OF LIBERALISM* (1999) at 46-58, 102-06, 123-27, 144-52; HUSAK, *DRUGS AND RIGHTS* (1996) 81-130

[220] Stevens, *Drug policy, harm and human rights: A rationalist approach* (2011) 235

[221] Ibid.

[222] Elster, *Rationality and Addiction*, in DE GREIFF (ED.), *DRUGS AND THE LIMITS OF LIBERALISM* (1999) 25-45

[223] Let us begin here: If we seek a better world, why are we slowly destroying the planet? Considering the evidence to suggest that the inner and outer world are not separate entities; that our thoughts do have an impact on our surroundings; and that those thoughts that follow from the Wholeness perspective (the psychology of love) create harmony, while those thoughts that are derived from the idea of separation (the psychology of fear) generate all our troubles: Why do we not make a conscious and consistent effort to embrace those thoughts that follow from the position of love? If we want to live happy lives and if we want a better future for our children, why do we choose those thoughts and actions that generate discord rather than harmony? Considering that research from the social sciences indicate that people who live in equality-oriented, freedom-oriented, and collaborative-oriented societies live happier, healthier, and more peaceful lives, why do we choose the opposite? Why do we choose hierarchical, control-oriented, and competition-oriented societies? And not least: Considering that the only sound measure of the integrity among politicians is the extent to which they support human rights—

and when it comes to prohibitionists it is well known that they themselves demonstrate the exact same traits as are associated with the most hardcore drug addicts.[224] The history of drug prohibition, after all, is a history of the extent to which they have denied reality in order to feed an oppressive habit and mistaken sense of moral superiority. And if their irrational behavior is not already apparent, consider this: If disagreement helps us rethink our position, sharpen our intellect, improve our analysis, and see past our own misconceptions, why are prohibitionists not willing to debate the pros and cons of current drug policies? If prohibitionists really want what is best for humanity, why are they unwilling to let these policies be reviewed by an independent, impartial, and competent tribunal?

No one of sound mind would dedicate themselves to a position like this and then refuse to consider if the position is at all defensible—and yet, this is what prohibitionists have done. Hence, they are throwing stones in glass houses whenever they try to paint drug use as an irrational pursuit, and as 90 percent of drug use does not even fit the DSM-IV diagnostic criteria for dependence, we have no reason to regard drug use as an irrational endeavor.

This being so, the courts' willingness to accept the criminalization of drugs due to the legislature's fear of "sending the wrong signal" is misplaced. First of all, as Judge Sweet and Harris pointed out, "the moral question of what laws a government ought to enact and enforce is logically independent of what the individual ought to do."[225] As such, a move away from prohibition does not mean that politicians approve of drug use; it just means that they recognize that there are areas of the

---

and considering that most of them, in action if not words, show a contempt for these rights in the management of our affairs—why do we elect them? Why are they not held to account for the devious wars and double dealings in which they indulge? Why do we let young men and women fight wars of aggression? Why do we time and time again fall victim to our officials' lies and misdirection?

[224] Barnett, *Bad Trip* (1994) 2598 ("It seems that no facts are sufficient to shake the prohibitionists' faith in this tragic policy. As . . . suggested elsewhere, some persons act as though they are addicted to drug laws, with all the connotations of irrationality that term is meant to convey when applied to drug users. Consequently, they are unlikely to be swayed by the copious facts and arguments presented [by reform activists]. . . . [Nonetheless] the case against prohibition is overwhelming, precisely because so many different types of considerations all point to a single solution: the legalization of illicit drugs.")

[225] Sweet & Harris, *Moral and Constitutional Considerations in Support of the Decriminalization of Drugs*, IN FISH (ED.), *HOW TO LEGALIZE DRUGS* (1998) 447

individual domain where they have no business interfering—that's all. Secondly, the message politicians really are sending is not a message that we should listen to. As Sheriff Bill Masters wryly noted:

> "If you want to know the "message" politicians are sending to our children with the drug war, here it is: it's okay for armed enforcers to kill innocent children . . . if they believe drugs to be present. It's okay for police to bust down doors in the middle of the night with submachine guns locked and loaded, if some drugged-up, paid informant said there might be drugs around. It's okay for police to take your property without even charging you with a crime. It's okay for politicians to wipe their feet on the Bill of Rights, as long as they are doing it in the name of getting tough on drug dealers. That's the 'morality' of the War on Drugs."[226]

This is, of course, no true morality. The world of ethics that has spawned a War on Drugs is increasingly being seen for what it is, but prohibitionists have yet to recognize their error.

8.5.3.3 DIFFERENT MEASURES OF WEIGHT

Another area where we see the absurdity of prohibition unfold is in the measurement of drugs before trial. In *Chapman* the Supreme Court held that the punishment for LSD possession should be meted out based on the weight of the carrier medium and not the potency of the substance.[227] This logic also applies to other illicit drugs: "Drugs are drugs" and the punishment is the same whether or not they are of poor or superior quality. By the same logic, possession of a gallon of water containing 0.1 percent alcohol should be met with the same criminal sanction as possession of a gallon containing 98 percent alcohol.

However, while it is unlikely that the Court would have failed to treat the two gallons of alcohol differently, the lack of reason that is attached

---

[226] MASTERS, *DRUG WAR ADDICTION* (2001) 61

[227] LSD is a substance whose dosages are measured in micrograms and pure LSD is usually dissolved in alcohol. Droplets containing LSD crystals are normally applied to a carrier medium like blotter paper or sugar cubes.

to drug cases is even more profound. For instance, in *Fowner*,[228] a man who had been arrested in possession of 79.7 grams of methamphetamine was also charged—*and convicted*—for being in possession of approximately 24 gallons of a liquid mixture containing detectable amounts of a controlled substance. At trial, an expert testified that the liquid was a waste byproduct of methamphetamine manu-facturing and that it was an uningestable waste. Still, the Court of Appeals held that so long as the liquid contained a detectable amount of a controlled substance, its entire weight was properly included in the calculation of the defendant's sentence under the Guidelines.

The Supreme Court accepted this decision.[229]

8.5.3.4 DIFFERENT MEASURES OF BODILY AUTONOMY

Another area which shows the different logic that applies to drug users is the different measures of harm and human dignity that is utilized in abortion cases and drug cases.

Whether or not a fetus counts as a "person," it at least represents a potential human life, and that potential life is extinguished by abortion. A prohibition on abortion therefore protects the life or potential life of human beings. In other words, important rights are at stake, but with *Planned Parenthood v. Casey* the Court determined that a woman's right to bodily autonomy was so fundamental that neither the state nor her husband had a right to interfere with her "interest in deciding whether to bear and beget a child."[230]

There can be no doubt that a woman's decision to have an abortion may have a profound impact on others. Society, not to mention her spouse, family, and unborn child all have an obvious interest at stake, and yet her right to bodily autonomy overrides any other concern. If this is so, it is difficult to see why drug users are denied the same right to bodily

---

[228] *Fowner v. U. S.*, 112 S. Ct. 1998, 118 L. Ed. 2d 594, 60 U.S.L.W. 3778 (1992)

[229] Judge Posner called such judgments "loony," pointing out that "to base punishments on the weight of the carrier medium makes about as much sense as basing punishment on the weight of the defendant." BOWARD, *LOST RIGHTS* (1995) 210

[230] *Casey*, 505 U.S. at 858-59

autonomy. No doubt they, like alcohol drinkers, may make poor lifestyle decisions and no doubt they may suffer for it, but no good reasons have been given for treating drug users' right to bodily autonomy any differently.[231]

8.5.3.5 DIFFERENT STANDARDS FOR EVALUATING BODILY INTEGRITY

In *Washington v. Harper* the Supreme Court "had no doubt" that "a significant liberty interest" was at stake and used heightened review to decide whether the state could administer antipsychotic drugs to a prisoner against his will. Justice Stevens held that:

> "Every violation of a person's bodily integrity is an invasion of his or her liberty. . . . Moreover, any such action is degrading if it overrides a competent person's choice to reject a specific form of medical treatment. And when the purpose or effect of forced drugging is to alter the will and the mind of the subject, it constitutes a deprivation of liberty in the most literal and fundamental sense. . . . The liberty of citizens to resist the administration of mind-altering drugs arises from our Nation's most basic values."[232]

The concern were prisoners' autonomy rights and Justice Stevens defended the right not to be forcibly administered psychotropic drugs. However, speaking in terms of autonomy, it is no less a violation of mental and bodily integrity to be deprived of a choice than to have it forced upon us. Even though the latter is likely to be regarded as a more intrusive violation, the denial of free will is equally present, and there can be no denying that the encroachment of choice itself constitutes a violation of mental/bodily integrity.

---

[231] Relying on *Roe v. Wade* and *Casey*, two abortion cases wherein the Supreme Court majority credited the state's interest to preserve the life of the fetus as 'important' but never-theless insufficient to prohibit the practice when measured against the liberty interests of the mother, Justice Seeley of the Washington Supreme Court held that the drug laws were unconstitutional. As he said: "The majority cannot distinguish these cases. If the state cannot prohibit abortions consistent with due process, it can hardly constitutionally prohibit drug use as its interest to do so is arguably much less important." *Seeley v. State*, 132 Wash. 2d 776, 940 P.2d 604 (1997) 623 (Sanders J., dissenting)

[232] *Washington v. Harper*, 494 U.S. 210 (1990) 239 (Stevens J., dissenting)

Prohibitionists, for their part, have great difficulty in seeing how this is so as they consider drug prohibition to be in everybody's best interest. Nonetheless, we must not forget that drug prohibition itself represents an attempt "to alter the will and the mind of the subject" by the administration of force. *No doubt* also this is experienced by many millions of Americans as an invasion of their liberty, and *no doubt* also this is experienced as a degrading deprivation of autonomy—one that in many cases has even more serious consequences than being force-fed "medication." Consequently, while philosophers may argue whether one or the other constitutes a worse deprivation of autonomy, no one can seriously dispute that both "constitute a deprivation of liberty in the most literal and fundamental sense;" that the same liberty interests are involved whether one is being forcibly deprived of choice or whether one is being forcibly imposed a choice; and that the liberty to be free from both impositions "arises from our Nation's most basic values."

The real issue, then, is in both cases if the government interest is sufficient to overcome an individual's autonomy rights. As we have seen, this issue has yet to be determined by an impartial, independent, and competent court. Nonetheless, as the Washington Supreme Court and other courts have concluded that "a competent individual's right to refuse such medication is a fundamental liberty interest deserving the highest order of protection,"[233] one may wonder what objective reasons the courts can find for denying the same protection to competent individuals being forcibly deprived of their choice in drugs.

8.5.3.6 *MEANINGLESS MODELS OF BLAMEWORTHINESS*

We have already noted the different measures of culpability that attach to licit and illicit drug users. When it comes to the former, responsibility is put where responsibility is due—that is with the individual for those actions and lifestyle choices he himself chooses to pursue. The latter is

---

[233] Id.

not so fortunate, and with *Rodriguez*[234] we are provided with another example of the injustice that drug users must suffer.

In this case, Carlos Rodriguez was sentenced to 18 years for the murder of Susan Hendricks and Fred Bennett. The situation that led to his conviction was the following: Bennett and Hendricks arrived at Rodriguez's apartment to buy cocaine. Immediately after their purchase, the police raided the premises and to avoid persecution Bennett and Hendricks swallowed the cocaine. As a result, they both died and Rodriguez was charged with first degree murder.[235]

This is the logic of prohibition in a nutshell. These deaths were clearly the result of drug policy, but prohibitionists refuse to face reality and blame the victims. Both these deaths, therefore, were listed as overdose deaths and used by the government as examples of the threat that drugs pose to society. Rodriguez, for his part, challenged his conviction, claiming that it constituted cruel and unusual punishment and violated the Eighth Amendment, but the U.S. Supreme Court would not hear of it. We have already seen drug users' liberty or autonomy interests count for naught. And because the drug law, as far as the Court is concerned, does not touch upon important interests, all that is needed is a rational basis. Hence, because the law, in the eyes of prohibitionists, passes this test the Court saw no reason to intervene.

Even so, that the same logic applied to car manufacturers would have survived the rational basis test should have been a warning to the justices that something was amiss. One would clearly expect General Motors to make safer cars if they were held personally accountable for all traffic-related deaths, including those resulting from bad government policies, but no sane person would hold such a statute to be a rational application of law. The question, obviously, is not if the law is "rationally related" to some government purpose, but if it is morally related to the nature of the offense. For punishment to be just, it must be proportional to the moral

---

[234] *New Jersey v. Rodriguez*, 645 A.2d 1165 (1994)

[235] The Comprehensive Drug Reform Act of 1986 holds that "any person who manufactures, distributes, or dispenses . . . any . . . controlled dangerous substance classified in Schedule I or II . . . is liable for a death which results from the injection, inhalation, or ingestion of that substance, and is guilty of a crime of the first degree." At least 14 states impose strict liability for such deaths and two even have capital punishment for those convicted of the crime.

culpability of the offender, and if the concept of blameworthiness is to have any meaning, Rodriguez cannot be blamed for these deaths.

Prohibitionists may think that he got what he deserved but it should be unnecessary to remind them that the same logic applied to alcohol, tobacco, and pharmaceutical drugs would result in imprisonment for life of almost every truck driver, shop clerk, doctor, and bartender in America, along with millions of regular citizens. In fact, by consistently (and more appropriately) applying this logic, one is tempted to ask these justices what punishment they would mete out to the engineers of war. What sort of sentences would be appropriate for the producers of war material, to those who profit from it, and to all those soldiers who do battle? And last but not least, what sort of penalties would be proper for politicians, those pathological liars who have a record of supporting any war, no matter its merits, to satisfy the expectations of war-profiteers?

In all these cases, objectively speaking, punishment would be much more appropriate as *every single one* of them—and to a much greater extent—are morally blameworthy for their actions. I mean, speaking of drug producers, traffickers, and dealers, those in the receiving end of their trade are eager to accept their products; at the very least 90 percent of their consumers use their products responsibly and even the latter 10 percent are thankful. Who can say this about producers of war material and those that put such products to use? How many in the receiving end of a missile, bomb, grenade, or bullet appreciate their contribution to the world?

Anyone with their moral sensibilities intact understands that war profiteers have a personal responsibility for the misfortunes of humanity that extends far beyond that of drug dealers.[236] Morally, it is not even the same ballgame; we are talking the difference between night and day—unless, of course, the prohibitionists can show us that drugs really destroy the mind, rendering users incapable of autonomous choice.

---

[236] To sleep at night, war profiteers say that they are involved in an industry which purpose is to protect society from harm. In their mind, their contribution is to those so-called "just" wars, and their moral compass is guided by the supposition that any government sanctioned activity must be moral. Such naïve thinking do not merit an elaborate response; suffice to say that *no war* the Western powers have fought the last 60 years satisfies the "just war" defense, that any belief to the contrary mirrors a profound unawareness of power-politics, and that this childish, unthinking notion only survives insofar as people are unaware of the propaganda apparatus that is in place to keep their consciousness focused on the surface of events—a surface that is constantly being polished by lies and misdirection. For more on this, see MIKALSEN, *REASON IS* (2014)

Only the undue influence of the collective unconscious may make this comparison unheard-of. To the extent that we are in its grip, we will equal state action with morality, and our moral code will be turned upside down. As we saw in part one, FC ideals and values will have to become NC values and vice versa, and the result is a collective psychosis where our moral compass is obliterated. This is the price we must pay for conforming to the status quo. We simply cannot afford to put two and two together because it would lay bare the profound immorality of state action. Hence, to overcome truth and to preserve the delusion, "all that is needed," to paraphrase Orwell, "is an unending series of victories over our own reason."

Nowhere is this better seen than in drug policy. It is only because of the influence of an enemy image that the injustice of subjecting drug law violators to prohibitionist reasoning is not immediately obvious. Had we thought about things, we would have understood that it being *exactly the same* supply and demand mechanisms involved when it comes to the two classes of drugs, it is clear that drug distributors like Rodriguez are in fact no eviller and more depraved than anyone involved with the supply-chain of alcohol and tobacco.

Accepting this, the next logical step would be to come to grips with its implications—that the drug law enforcers, in fact, are worse than the drug dealers. From a constitutional perspective, the latter have merely provided people with a service they want, while the drug law enforcers have done so much worse. In their enforcement of these laws they have tapped people's phones, opened their mail, spied on them, searched their houses, stripped them naked, performed cavity searches, fined them, demonised them, discriminated against them, stigmatised them, terrorised them, confiscated and destroyed their property and valuables, forced them into "rehabilitation," jailed them, taken their children, destroyed their education and work possibilities, threatened them, humiliated them, beaten them, shot at them, and even killed them. And what is worse, on those occasions when the victims have opposed such abusive behaviours and sought to set things straight in accordance with human rights law, these enforcers—to preserve their pretensions of personal virtue—have denied them every opportunity to meaningfully challenge the law.

As we have seen, under no circumstances can the purveyors of the status quo bear to face reality. It would be too crushing to their self-esteem, and so we continue to live in a society in which each state undertakes to respect and ensure to all individuals—except the drug law violators—the rights recognised in the Constitution; where all persons, except them, shall be equal before the law and be entitled to equal protection of the law; where everybody, except them, shall be recognised as a person before the courts and entitled to a fair hearing by a competent, impartial and independent tribunal to have their rights determined; where everybody, except them, shall have an effective remedy against unlawful detention as well as abusive, discriminatory and degrading policies; and where everyone, except them, shall have an enforceable right to compensation after being the victim of such practices.

We live in a society in which everybody, except them, shall have the right to self-determination and to freely pursue their social, cultural, economic and spiritual development; where every human being, except them, shall have the inherent right to life and to be protected from being arbitrarily deprived of it; where no one, except the drug law violators, shall be subjected to cruel, inhuman, or degrading treatment or punishment; where no one, but them, shall be subjected to arbitrary and unlawful interference with his privacy, family, home or correspondence, and where everyone, but them, have the right to be protected by law against such interferences.

We are supposed to accept a social contract where everyone, except them, have the right to liberty and security of person, and where no one, but them, shall be unlawfully deprived of their liberty; where everyone, but them, shall have the right to freedom of expression and to seek, collect and impart information and ideas of all kinds, regardless of frontiers; where any propaganda for war—except drug war—shall be prohibited by law; where any advocacy of hatred that constitutes incitement to discrimination, hostility or violence shall be prohibited by law—except that which is directed at the drug law violators; and where any family, except theirs, are entitled to protection by society and the state.

These, I am sure, may be tough words for prohibitionists to hear. In their minds, they have sought to rid the world of a terrible plague. They have been soldiers in a crusade that was to be for the betterment of Mankind, and it is difficult to readjust this frame of reference into one more conforming to reality. However, if they wonder whether they are on the side of good, they need only ask drug users whose services they prefer: Do they favour the dealers, those who respect their autonomous choice, or the drug law enforcers, those who infantilize and persecute them?

Prohibitionists should not be surprised to find that the drug users, like alcohol drinkers, tobacco smokers, or chocolate eaters, greatly prefer to interact with that group who cater to their will rather than that group who, by the whims of their own self-asserted authority, threaten them with imprisonment to save them from themselves.

This being so, unless prohibitionists can put forth good reasons why these people have no say in the management of their own affairs, the drug dealers are in fact agents of autonomy. If this is so, it is also clear that the law enforcers must be the agents of tyranny—and that, in matters of blameworthiness, they themselves are much more liable to criminal persecution than violators. Moral culpability, after all, must be the result of a violation of autonomy rights, either in a collective or individual capacity. Because of this thieves, rapists, and murderers are worthy of persecution, but none have shown drug use to violate the rights of others. Instead, as professors of law and philosophy have pointed out, it is drug prohibition that violates autonomy rights,[237] and so—unless prohibitionists can prove this argument wrong—the drug law enforcers are the real "traffickers in human misery."

8.5.3.7 NEGLECTING THE OBVIOUS IMPLICATIONS

No wonder prohibitionists refuse to face reality. Had they been willing to think about things they would, as Miller noted, have understood that "transforming ordinary productive citizens into criminals for conduct having less measurable harm than tolerated conduct, is a sign of religious zealotry rather than public welfare."[238] They would, as Justice Seiler

---

[237] Moore, *Liberty and Drugs*, in DE GREIFF (ED.), *DRUGS AND THE LIMITS OF LIBERALISM* (1999) 89 ("our desires, feeling, and beliefs are not our own . . . if they are simply the product of social coercion or mere conforming imitation of social convention: 'He who lets the world . . . choose his life plan for him has no need for any other faculty than the apelike one of imitation.'"); Husak, *Liberal Neutrality, Autonomy, and Drug Prohibitions* (2000) 69-70

[238] MILLER, *THE CASE FOR LEGALIZING DRUGS* (1991) 126. Other scholars have pointed out that drug prohibition is akin to religious persecution. See DUKE & CROSS, *AMERICA'S LONGEST WAR*

noted, have understood that "[w]hen one generation irrationally uses the criminal sanction to coerce and intimidate another into rejecting a relatively harmless drug, marijuana, while openly promoting the use of what we know to be relatively harmful drugs, alcohol and tobacco, respect for law and the legal process suffers."[239] And they would have seen the parallels between their own crusade and those of earlier days.[240]

The argument presented above is after all exceedingly simple. An unbiased twelve-year old could follow the logic to its conclusion, and so the problem is not a mental incapacity to reflect or understand. The problem is that, psychologically speaking, it is extremely difficult to come to terms with this understanding—and this explains the self-righteous conviction with which the aggressors pursue their prey, as well as the breakdown of logic that always accompanies their reasoning.

We have seen it repeated over and over, and more examples will be provided. We have already discussed the Supreme Court's reasoning in *Harmelin,* where it accepted the constitutionality of mandatory life sentences for those in possession of drugs. The majority opinion was a paragon of prohibitionist reasoning, but the refusal to think about things was also made evident by the dissent. To their credit, White, Blackmun, Marshall, and Stevens acknowledged the erroneous reasoning that the majority used to justify its position and noted the following in their dissent: (1) that "to be constitutionally proportionate, punishment must be tailored to a defendant's personal responsibility and moral guilt;" (2) that "unlike crimes directed against the persons and property of others, possession of drugs affects the criminal who uses the drugs most directly;" (3) that "while the collateral consequences of drugs such as cocaine are indisputably severe, they are not unlike those which flow from the misuse of other, legal, substances;" (4) that "it is inconceivable that a State could rationally choose to penalize one who possesses large

---

(1993) 156; SZASZ, *CEREMONIAL CHEMISTRY* (2003); and Ostrowski, *Drug Prohibition Muddles Along*, in FISH (ED.), *HOW TO LEGALIZE DRUGS* (1998) 366. ("The only civilized way to deal with irreconcilable conflicts in ultimate values is to declare freedom of religion and let each go his or her own way. That is the last thing the prohibitionists have in mind. Rather, their solution to the problem of irreconcilable conflict of values over drugs is to inflict on those who disagree with them all the force and violence they can muster.")

[239] *State v. Mitchell,* 563 S.W.2d 18 (1978) 32 (Seiler J., dissenting, Sp. J., Shangler concurring)

[240] For a comparison with the Inquisition, see SZASZ, *CEREMONIAL CHEMISTRY* (2003) 61-74. For a comparison with Nazism, see MIKALSEN, *REASON IS* (2014) 467-81; MILLER, *THE CASE FOR LEGALIZING DRUGS* (1991) 118-24; MILLER, *DRUG WARRIORS AND THEIR PREY* (1996)

quantities of alcohol in a manner similar to that in which Michigan has chosen to punish petitioner for cocaine possession, because of the tangential effects which might ultimately be traced to the alcohol at issue;" and (5) that "the ripple effect on society caused by possession of drugs, through related crimes, lost productivity, health problems, and the like, is often not the direct consequence of possession, but of the resulting addiction, something which this Court held in *Robinson* cannot be made a crime."[241]

When it comes to drugs, this is the most lucid thinking we have seen from the Supreme Court. This, unfortunately, is not saying much, as the justices did not follow their reasoning through. Had they taken their own calculations seriously, they would have added these five points together and checked how this line of reasoning correlated with the principles of fundamental justice, but no such effort was made. It is regrettable that they neglected this obvious next step, as they would have had to conclude that the Constitution not only invalidated the appellant's life sentence *but that its principles also laid bare the unconstitutionality of drug prohibition*. They noticed the wholly different logic that is being applied to the two classes of drugs and they recognized "that to be constitutionally proportional, punishment must be tailored to a defendant's personal responsibility and moral guilt."[242] Accepting this, the foundation of drug prohibition is crumbling, as a proper equality and proportionality analysis would have found inconsistencies which could only have been remedied by abolishing the law. First, by applying coherent reasoning, the drug law's shaky foundation (which is the different standards it uses to define and to deal with harms) would have been exposed. And secondly, had they looked at reality, they would have seen that the standard applied to the licit drugs (that of personal responsibility) was what reasonable people would agree on. They would have had to conclude that this standard conformed to the principles of

---

[241] *Harmelin v. Michigan*, 501 U.S. 957 (1991) (White J., dissenting)

[242] The Supreme Court also recognized this principle in *Carmona*, where the appeals court had rationalized petitioners' sentences "by invoking all evils attendant on or attributable to widespread drug trafficking." As the Court held, this "is simply not compatible with a fundamental premise of the criminal justice system, that individuals are accountable only for their own criminal acts." *Carmona et al. v. Ward, Correctional Commissioner, et al.*, 439 U.S. 1091, 99 S. Ct. 874, 59 L. Ed. 2d 58 (1979)

justice, while the one that is being applied to illicit drugs would have been found to be as irrational as the fear that ensured its survival.

In the history of the Court, this was the closest the justices ever got to getting it right. They outlined the bigger picture but failed to connect the dots. This is nothing new, as psychological incentives ensure that prohibitionists can never afford to think their argument through. If they did, its incoherence would have to be recalibrated into one of harmony with reason and the principles of justice, and they prefer the status quo.

In the following, we shall further explore the ingenuity with which meaningful review is kept at bay.

8.5.4 RELYING ON PREJUDICE AND FLAWED ANALYSIS

To support the use of conflicting logic prohibitionists will sometimes try to explain why it is reasonable to treat alcohol drinkers differently than illicit drug users. In this passage from *Commonwealth v. Leis*, the trial judge gives it a shot:

> "The ordinary user of marijuana is quite likely to be a marginally adjusted person who turns to the drug to avoid confrontation with and the resolution of his problems. The majority of alcohol users are well adjusted, productively employed individuals who use alcohol for relaxation and as an incident of other social activities."[243]

The problem is that there is no empirical evidence to support this view. There is only prejudice and ignorance to sustain it but because prohibitionists are never asked to validate the premises of their argument, this type of reasoning persists.

Another example was provided by the Appeals Court, when Judge Spiegel said that:

> "There are at least two distinctions between alcohol and the 'mind altering intoxicants' that are defined by the law to be narcotic drugs. First, alcohol is susceptible to a less restrictive alternative means of control. There are recognized, accurate means of determining its use

---

[243] Bonnie & Whitebread, *The Forbidden Fruit and the Tree of Knowledge* (1970) 1131

and its abuse. Second, the effects of alcohol upon the user are known. We think that the Legislature is warranted in treating this known intoxicant differently from marihuana, LSD or heroin, the effects of which are largely still unknown and subject to extensive dispute."[244]

Whatever merit this argument might have had 50 years ago, it is, as Justice Seiler previously remarked, no good today. Since the *Leis* court, no plant has been more carefully studied than cannabis, and still prohibitionists are arguing that we "just do not know enough" to grant the defendant the benefit of the doubt.

Furthermore, another example was provided by the German Constitutional Court when it said that:

"There are also important reasons for the differing treatment of Cannabis products and alcohol. It is indeed accepted that the *abuse* of alcohol brings with it dangers both for the individual and for society which are equal to or even greater than those posed by Cannabis products. However, it must be borne in mind that alcohol can be used in many ways. There are no comparable uses for the products and parts of the Cannabis plant. Products containing alcohol serve as a source of nourishment and pleasure. In the form of wine they are also used in religious ceremonies. In all cases the dominant use of alcohol does not lead to states of intoxication. Its intoxicating effect is generally known and is generally avoided by means of social controls. In contrast, the achievement of an intoxicated state is usually the main aim when Cannabis products are used. Furthermore the legislature finds itself in the situation that it cannot effectively prevent the consumption of alcohol because of traditional patterns of consumption in Germany and the European cultural sphere."[245]

Even though this example is from a foreign court, it so perfectly describes the reasoning that is being used to sustain the status quo that it begged for inclusion. Only very rarely will the courts attempt to justify the different treatment of alcohol and cannabis consumers. I have not found other examples from American courtrooms, and the attempts

---

[244] *Commonwealth v. Leis*, 355 Mass. 189 (1969) 198

[245] BVerfGE 90, 145:197 (1994)

discussed so far should explain why. After all, everything that is said of alcohol can also be said of cannabis, and again we see the court appeal to ignorance rather than reason. To this day, whenever prohibitionists try to enlighten us on the qualitative difference between licit and illicit drugs, this has always been the case. And this being so, it is little wonder that courts usually just defer to the legislature.

Whenever this is done, we find plenty of shoddy reasoning. To divest of the issue, they must look to precedent, and it bears noticing that the courts always refer to irrelevant precedent. To deny appellants their day in court, they will refer to *Lindsley v. Natural Carbonic Gas,*[246] *Williamson v. Lee Optical,*[247] *McLaughlin v. Florida,*[248] *United States v. Carolene Products,*[249] *FCC v. Beach Communications,*[250] *Romer v. Evans,*[251] *Cleburne v. Cleburne Living Center,*[252] *McDonald v. Board of Election Commissioners,*[253] and *New Orleans v. Dukes.*[254]

Thanks to this deferential formula, the drug laws have escaped scrutiny. However, if we look closer, these cases are distinguishable on their facts. To the extent that they were at all dealing with the criminal law none, to my knowledge, were ever imprisoned for failing to abide by their regulations, and as Justice Seiler noted, criticizing the use of *Carolene,*[255] "[t]here is a great difference between a judgment as to whether Congress can declare that a compound of condensed skim milk and coconut oil is 'imitation milk' and a judgment as to whether the legislature can rationally unite marijuana and heroin in a single criminal prohibition."[256] As we have seen, the criminal law is different from all

---

[246] *Lindsley v. Natural Carbonic Gas Co.*, 220 U.S. 61 (1910)

[247] *Williamson v. Lee Optical Co.*, 348 U.S. 483 (1955)

[248] *McLaughlin v. Florida*, 379 U.S. 184 (1964)

[249] *United States v. Carolene Products Co.*, 304 U.S. 144 (1938)

[250] *FCC v. Beach Communications, Inc.*, 508 U.S. 307 (1993)

[251] *Romer v. Evans*, 517 U.S. 620 (1996)

[252] *Cleburne v. Cleburne Living Center, Inc.*, 473 U.S. 432 (1985)

[253] *McDonald v. Board of Election Commissioners*, 394 U.S. 802 (1969)

[254] *New Orleans v. Dukes*, 427 U.S. 297 (1976)

[255] *Carolene Products* upheld the constitutionality of the Filled Milk Act of 1923 and in so doing discredited the judicial interference in the Congressional regulation of interstate commerce to justify deference.

[256] *State v. Mitchell*, 563 S.W.2d 18 (1978) 29 (Seiler J., dissenting)

other regulations, for whenever imprisonment is the preferred option the legislature can no longer be afforded unchecked freedom. The legislature has a wide variety of alternatives to choose from other than the criminal law and when such sanctions are applied the burden of evidence belongs to the government.

Courts, however, have failed to recognize this. Even so, to provide an aura of legitimacy to the status quo, they will sometimes speculate as to the "rational" reasons Congress may have had for its decision. In these instances, we are provided with more examples of futile attempts to legitimize the legislature's actions. The courts, for instance, will hypothesize that "the legislative judgment concerning alcohol and nicotine may well have taken into account . . . the adverse consequences of prohibition, and the economic significance of their production."[257] They will even use reasons of political expediency to explain the legislature's decision,[258] seemingly unaware that a prime basis for the constitutional order is to protect the individual from the undue influence of powerful political factions. And last but not least, they will argue that these drugs are not harmless; that cannabis is more potent today; that politicians may want to criminalize the different drugs in order to fight crime and protect the young; and that legalization would send the wrong message.

But yet again, none of these reasons are sufficient to justify criminalization. What we have been offered as explanations is irrelevant from the perspective of principled law, and the latter examples are not even explanations but merely descriptions of what our officials might have hoped to achieve. As Professor Goldberg points out it is important to separate *descriptions* from *plausible explanations*. Our officials, for example, may say that the drug laws will prevent some degree of possible harm, as they might prevent someone from using a drug and then do something stupid. This, however, is only a description of one of the laws' possible functions and it does not explain why *some* drug users have been chosen to bear the brunt of the legislation. Unfortunately for our officials

---

[257] *State v. Rao*, 171 Conn. 600 (1976) 606

[258] *People v. Schmidt*, 86 Mich. App. 574 (1978) 581 ("In determining whether the legislative decision to classify and control some substances while not taking a like action as to others was arbitrary, we must also recognize that significant political roadblocks exist which preclude regulating some substances which are known to be dangerous.")

this is what is important. The relevant question at issue in an equal protection analysis is not what the government sought to achieve, but if it can explain the different punitive treatment of illicit drug users. Unless the state can explain this bit, we are dealing with a constitutional violation, for as Professor Goldstein reminds us: "Where no reasonable explanation exists for the government's singling out of a trait in a given context, what remains 'is a status-based enactment divorced from any factual context from which we could discern a relationship to legitimate state interests—in other words, class legislation."[259]

8.5.4.1 "Half a Loaf"

As we have seen, all the attempts of justifying why alcohol drinkers deserve different treatment from cannabis smokers have failed, but still the argument that "half a loaf is better than one" must be dealt with. For in a last effort to save the status quo, courts will reason that "[w]hile alcoholism constitutes a major social problem, surely it is not valid to justify the adoption of a new abuse on the basis that it is no worse than a presently existing one. The result could only be added social damage from a new source."[260]

The reasoning is flawed for several reasons. First, there is no evidence for concluding that the legal regulation of other drugs than alcohol and tobacco will lead to more social damage. Variables that come into consideration are the following: (1) The assumption that the criminal law has been a successful mechanism in reducing drug use is not borne out by evidence; (2) other factors than criminalization have proven more effective in regulating the use of different drugs; and (3) the legal availability of a greater array of drugs is likely to reduce the total of harm to society.[261] The reason is that to the extent other drugs will take the

---

[259] Goldberg, *Equality Without Tiers* (2004) 535 (quoting *Romer*)

[260] *NORML v. Bell*, 488 F.Supp. 123, D.D.C. 1980

[261] There is evidence to suggest that drug use will not increase, at least by much. A group of experts concluded thus after looking into the subject matter: "Fairly consistently, the finding has been that changes in penalties for use have little effect on rates of use, or on problems arising from effects of the drug. In general, the attempt at deterrence of use or possession though

place of alcohol and tobacco, the benefit to society and users will ensure a reduction in total harm. Also, the harms associated with prohibition must be taken into consideration, and when the pros and cons of prohibition are weighted in relation to the pros and cons of legal regulation, the harms associated with prohibition clearly outweigh those associated with regulated supply.

These are all factors that must be taken into consideration and finally, provided that the government's reasons for treating the different classes of drug users differently are not convincing, it is irrelevant if more drug users will become problem drug users. The principle of autonomy carries the greatest weight in any rights analysis and unless the government can show that its legislation can stand the test of reason, this is a price that we must be prepared to pay.

8.5.4.2 MISAPPLYING COURT DOCTRINE

The bias against illicit drugs is not only evident in the prejudice and different logic that is applied on a case-by-case basis. It is also evident in the way the justices apply their own doctrines to justify their conclusions. We have seen that the *Ravin* court was unique in that it first delineated a general conception of privacy before determining if cannabis use should be included. For this it deserves credit. However, it should be chastised for not following through with proper analysis, as its fundamental rights reasoning was deeply flawed.

---

criminal laws have failed." (ROOM ET AL., *CANNABIS POLICY* (2010) 148). This finding has been confirmed by a British Government study called *Drugs, International Comparators*. The report found that tough criminal sentences for drug users makes no difference to the rates of drug use, being that use of illegal substances is influenced by factors "more complex and nuanced than legislation and enforcement alone" and "there is no apparent correlation between the 'toughness' of a country's approach and the prevalence of drug use."

Increase in use, however, is not the only measure of success, for we must factor in that the prohibition regime makes use more dangerous. Scholars have calculated that illegal drug use is between five and ten times more dangerous than legal use. This means that even a highly unlikely five-fold increase in drug use under legalization would not increase the current number of drug deaths. See Ostrowski, *The Moral and Practical Case for Drug Legalization* (1990) 669-70; Duke, *Drug Prohibition: An Unnatural Disaster* (1995) 600 ("even if consumption of legalized drugs increased tenfold under a repeal regime, the physical harms associated with drug use could be less than under prohibition"); and MIKALSEN, *TO END A WAR* (2015) endnotes 45, 71, 77, 79, 82

One reason why the *Ravin* court set out to formulate a general conception of a right to privacy was that it had to find a definition that included previous cases where the court had found a violation of privacy rights. One important ruling was *Breese v. Smith*, where the Alaska court had held that a school directive that regulated the hear-length of students was an unlawful invasion of privacy. If drug prohibition was to be a lawful infringement of privacy rights, the task was to formulate a general conception that in a meaningful way incorporated the right to choose one's own hair-length while excluding a right to use cannabis.

The court struggled with this task. In the area of privacy analysis the justices found no way of excluding cannabis use, but in the next step of the examination, the fundamental rights analysis, they found a way to disparage the rights claim. In what scholars have argued was a biased and mistaken analysis, the court held the right to choose one's personal hairstyle to be fundamental while it refused to grant the same status to cannabis use. The reasoning behind this decision was that "hairstyle is a highly personal matter involving the individual and his body," while cannabis use was not. To justify this position, the court simply took for granted that "few would believe they have been deprived of something of critical importance if deprived of marijuana, though they would be if stripped of control over their personal appearances."[262]

It is for good reason that scholars have criticized the *Ravin* court for this analysis. As Professor Husak has pointed out:

"This basis for contrasting the degree of protection offered to hair length in *Breese* from that offered to marijuana use in *Ravin* is deficient. First, no empirical data are cited to support the court's conjecture about what 'few would believe.' Persons who smoke marijuana might feel just as strongly as about their preference as persons who violate the school ordinance governing hair length. Moreover, it is unclear that the degree of protection offered by the right of privacy should depend on the numbers of persons who have or lack the relevant beliefs. Third, and most significant, the question is rigged to enable the court to justify its answer. I concede that more persons would be outraged if 'stripped of control over their personal appearance' than if 'deprived of marijuana.' But the terms of the

---

[262] *Ravin v. State*, 537 P.2d at 502

comparison are flawed and misleading. The first part of the comparison is very general and the second is very specific. Imagine how the question would have been answered if the first part of the comparison were very specific and the second were very general. How would persons feel if 'stripped of control over what they are allowed to put into their bodies' relative to a 'deprivation of shoulder-length hair'? Clearly, the outcome of such a determination would be very different. To be meaningful and unbiased, the examples to be compared must invoke the same level of generality. On that basis it is hard to decide whether persons care more over what they are permitted to put into their bodies than about control over their personal appearance. I see no reason to regard either matter as more important, basic, or fundamental than the other."[263]

8.5.5 EMPTYING WORDS OF MEANING

Having reviewed the many ways by which the courts will deny drug users an effective remedy, we have seen (1) that unprincipled, ad hoc reasoning is offered as an excuse to defer to the legislature and (2) that none of the attempts to justify the status quo are valid from a perspective of principled law. Even so, as long as the courts can hypothesize some reason for the legislature's actions, that is all it takes to close their eyes to the injustice that is our drug laws. In the end, therefore, we find that the root of all this evil is the courts' idea of "rationality" and "arbitrariness," which is so disconnected from reality that it adds insult to injury.

---

[263] Husak, *Two Rationales for Drug Policy*, in FISH (ED.), *HOW TO LEGALIZE DRUGS* (1998) 44-45

We have seen that the enforcement of drug prohibition is highly contested and many scholars[264] and reports[265] conclude that the drug law has failed to protect the welfare of society. According to these sources, prohibition has done the opposite. They affirm that its impact on the supply and demand of illicit drugs has not only been negligible, but that it has generated death, disease, and criminal activity at the individual level while destroying communities and FC values at the collective level. To the most perceptive, this was clear 50 years ago,[266] and the evidence today is overwhelming.[267]

This being so, it should be evident that the courts' rational basis test is worthless. The prohibitionists' presumptions have all been refuted, and yet courts will hold that the drug law meets the rationality criteria. How can this be? Is it not self-evident that "rationally related" must mean something more than a rational relationship between our leaders' assumptions and their actions? No matter what kind of mad hatters we put in charge, this will always be the case. In the 1600s, the burning of witches was rationally related to the goal of ridding the world of evil; in the 1940s, the Nazis' eradication efforts were rationally related to the belief in the superiority of the Aryan race; and in our day, the drug laws are rationally related to the belief that drug users must be persecuted. No

---

[264] The list of professionals is too long, as it includes just about everyone who knows a thing or two about drug policy. However, as examples of collective efforts, a group of 500 luminaries from around the world—including Nobel Laureate Milton Friedman, former Secretary of State George Shultz, and former UN Secretary General Javier Perez de Cueller—have signed an open letter the U.S. President and Congress arguing that the global War on Drugs is causing more harm than good and urging that alternatives be considered. Another group of 770 academics wrote to the UN Secretary General in 1998, declaring that "the global War on Drugs is now causing more harm than drug abuse itself," and asking the bureaucrats "to initiate a truly open and honest dialogue regarding the future of global drug control policies; one in which fear, prejudice and punitive prohibitions yield to common sense, science, public health and human rights." (see http://www.drugpolicy.org/ publications-resources/sign-letters/public-letter-kofi-annan/ungass-public-letter-kofi-annan-signato)

[265] See list in MIKALSEN, *TO END A WAR* (2015) 162-63 (n.73)

[266] See e.g., KAPLAN, *MARIJUANA: THE NEW PROHIBITION* (1971); Kadish, *The Crisis of Overcriminalization* (1968)

[267] MIKALSEN, *TO END A WAR* (2015) at 161-63 (n.72-73) & at 165-77 (n.77-85). See also BERTRAM ET AL., *DRUG WAR POLITICS* (1996) 33-54; BECKER, *TO END THE WAR ON DRUGS* (2014); ALEXANDER, *THE NEW JIM CROW* (2011); ESCOHOTADO, *A BRIEF HISTORY OF DRUGS* (1999); DUKE & CROSS, *AMERICA'S LONGEST WAR* (1993) 78-200; WISOTSKY, *BEYOND THE WAR ON DRUGS* (1990); MILLER, *THE CASE FOR LEGALIZING DRUGS* (1991)

matter the time and place, our leaders' actions will reflect their beliefs—and all these beliefs will be "rational" to the people who hold them. But what kind of justice system will be content with this standard? It has proven utterly useless in preventing the abuse of power, and doesn't this fact—that it is worthless as a standard for protecting human rights—merit consideration?

To put it another way, does not "rationally related," by necessity, imply a certain quality of belief? Does not "rationally related" imply that a law must be *functionally* related to the goal it seeks to obtain? That it must be *morally* related to values that are said to guide us? That it must be *meaningfully* related to the ideals and principles of social contract thinking?

Few would object to this. And so, should not "rationally related", by necessity, imply an opportunity to assess whether in fact our leaders' beliefs are rationally grounded in the first place? What use is this term if it ignores (or rejects as irrelevant) whether policies are enacted on false presumptions? The fact that "rationally related" must imply a certain validity of belief is everywhere insinuated and articulated in American law,[268] and yet we find ourselves in a situation where the drug laws fail this standard—and where the courts for more than fifty years have denied the opportunity to prove this point.

8.5.5.2 THE COURTS' DEFINITION OF "ARBITRARY"

The courts' idea of "rationally related" is intimately connected with their use of "arbitrary," and the problem with the former is brought to light by the latter.

In effect, the courts will hold that if they can imagine some reason for justifying a prohibition it is not arbitrary. Never mind if the reasons

---

[268] *People v. Braun*, 330 N.Y.S.2d 397, 941, 69 Misc. 2d 682 (1972) ("To sustain legislation under the 'police power,' the operation of the law must in some degree tend to prevent offense or evil or preserve public health, morals, or welfare; it should appear that the means used are reasonably necessary for accomplishment of the purpose and not unduly oppressive upon individuals."); Jackson, *Putting Rationality Back Into the Rational Basis Test* (2011) 543 ("Where the legislative enactment infringes on an identified liberty interest, it is not enough that some legislator might have thought that there was a rational relationship. Liberty demands an actual rational link between the means and the ends.")

they imagine are wrong; never mind if the envisioned connection between means and ends is not there; never mind if the facts and the consequences of the law undermine any asserted reason for enacting the law. None of this matter: If they can imagine a rationalization, the law fulfills the criteria to be justified under the rational basis test.

To FC individuals this selective notion of "rationality" and "arbitrariness" is another example of the intellectual despondency that has eaten its way into the heart of American law. It should be a source of worry and contemplation as this is Orwellian Newspeak. The justices are effectively saying that "in this day and age words have no meaning other than that which we put into them. If we like it, then it is 'rational' and if we do not it is irrational and arbitrary—but do not expect us to justify our claims with empiricism. We have no use for reality, we make our own."

This is the outlandish notion that American citizens are expected to endure; this is the contemptible state of affairs that is American law. On this basis 1.5 million people are every year deprived of their freedom; and on this basis 40 million Americans are supposed to live as criminals—all in order to sustain conceited egos and a government that has long since abandoned the rule of law.

These are harsh words, but not unfounded. Everybody knows that "reasonable" and "arbitrary" must refer to some objectively verifiable state of facts. Under the Canadian system, for instance, a law is arbitrary whenever it fails to conform to the criteria set out by the proportionality analysis—that is, whenever it fails to reflect a correct balancing of the individual's right to liberty and society's need for protection.[269] Several justices at the Canadian Supreme Court have held the drug law to be an arbitrary—and therefore unlawful—infringement on these terms,[270] and we find the same definition in international human rights law. At the European Court of Human Rights and in the United Nations system, the terms "unlawful" and "arbitrary" are interchangeable, and as the UN Human Rights Committee stated:

> "In the Committee's view the expression 'arbitrary interference' can also extend to interference provided for under the law. *The*

---

[269] *Carter v. Canada* (Attorney General), 2015 SCC 5, [2015] 1 S.C.R. 331, at para. 83.

[270] *R. v. Malmo-Levine*; *R. v. Caine* 2003 SCC 74, 582, 729 (LeBel & Deschamps dissenting)

introduction of the concept of arbitrariness is intended to guarantee that even interference provided for by law should be in accordance with the provisions, aims and objectives of the Covenant [i.e., first principles] and should be, in any event, reasonable in the particular circumstances."[271]

None of this is controversial. It is the same definition that FC scholars and judges all over the world, including the United States,[272] abide by, and that a majority of American justices reject this definition can only be taken as a testimony to the fact that the system of law has hit rock bottom. After all, what better indication can we find that the U.S. system has left behind all pretense of respectability? To anyone who cares about words and meaning this is, to say the least, an embarrassing state of affairs. Nonetheless, this is the only way that US justices can bridge the gap between theory and practice, and so this is the way it must be until Americans once again take matters of law and government seriously.

---

[271] Ibid. (emphasis mine)

[272] Justice Adkins of the Florida Supreme Court objected to the current state of affairs when he said that "[t]here must be more than a hypothetical rational basis for a classification"; that in the real world "valid and substantial reason for classifications" had to be given; and that this required "a just, fair and practical basis" for the classification—one "based on a real difference which is reasonably related to the subject and purpose of the regulation." He continued to say that "to determine the rationality of a law the Court must look at the purpose the law serves, the facts involved, the impact of the law upon citizens and the relationship between the law and these factors." He made it clear that this was not the case when considering the classification of marijuana and that, therefore, "the statute should be held unconstitutional and the judgment of the trial court reversed." *Hamilton v. State*, 366 So. 2d 8 (1978) 12 (Adkins J., dissenting). See also Fiss, *Groups and the Equal Protection Clause* (1976) 111 ("In most cases it is not a question of whether the criterion and end are related or unrelated, but a question of how well they are related. A criterion may be deemed arbitrary even if it is related to the purpose, but only poorly so.")

9

HAWAII: A MICROCOSM OF THE MACROCOSM

"It has not been shown that consumption of marijuana is any more harmful than a comparable consumption of alcohol and it is doubtful that the presently known effects of marijuana are as adverse as those of alcohol. Until legitimate research indicates otherwise, the harm created by placing a criminal sanction on the activity of a significant percentage of our population who would otherwise be law abiding citizens far outweighs any present benefit to be derived from the effects of classifying marijuana as a narcotic. There is no logical or otherwise rational reason for our society, on the basis of a law that has little or no merit in its application, to continue to make criminals out of and consequently alienate the youth of today."[273]

—Justice Kobayashi—

HAVING REVIEWED THE BIGGER picture and how the dynamic between FC and NC reasoning plays out in the area of drug policy, we shall end this part by focusing on Hawaii. In the history of constitutional challenges this state is unique. Nowhere did FC reasoning come closer to carrying the day in court and nowhere is the dynamic between FC and NC reasoning better exposed. In the following therefore I will rely on the second Justice Levinson's *Mallan* dissent, a noble work which presents the battle between FC and NC reasoning at the Hawai'i Supreme Court as it played out between 1972 and 1998.[274]

---

[273] *State v. Kantner*, 493 P.2d 306 (1972) at 320 (Kobayashi, J., dissenting)

[274] *State v. Mallan*, 86 Haw. 440, 950 P.2d 178 (1998) 193-248 (Levinson J., dissenting)

9.1 The Kantner Court

The story begins with a confusing victory to the proponents of NC reasoning in *State v. Kantner,*[275] where they won even though a majority concluded that marijuana use was a fundamental right.

In this stunning piece of constitutional history, FC reasoning would have proven victorious if not for the event that one of its advocates, Justice Abe, felt compelled to affirm the judgment of the trial court. He, himself, was personally opposed to the result of the ruling, but because the appellants from the outset had accepted the prohibition of marijuana as a reasonable and legitimate exercise of the police power (they only contended that the inclusion of marijuana in the narcotic drug statute was unreasonable and violated the Due Process Clauses of the federal and state Constitution) he found it unreasonable to hold that the state should have met its burden of proof on this point. Levinson and Kobayashi, the other FC reasoners, disagreed, believing it to be sufficiently clear that the merits of the case dictated that the laws prohibiting the possession of marijuana be held unconstitutional. However, because of the failure of the appellants to frame the issue correctly, the extraordinary fact that most of the justices agreed that the prohibition of marijuana possession was unconstitutional did not have much impact.

It is ironic that the only time in the history of drug law challenges when a majority was FC reasoners, the appellants underestimated the unconstitutional nature of the law and the willingness of the justices to deal with it. Be that as it may, the legacy of *Kantner* was three carefully crafted dissenting opinions—opinions that to this day remain among the top five examples of FC reasoning delivered by any American court.

Unfortunately, this was the only time in constitutional history that the stars were sufficiently aligned for FC reasoning to have had an impact on the evolution of drug policy. The year after, in 1973, Justice Abe retired, and Justice Levinson retired in 1974.

---

[275] *Kantner,* 53 Haw. 327, 493 P.2d 306 (1972)

So it came to pass that in 1975, when the next challenge reached the Supreme Court with *State v. Baker,*[276] it was an open question if the new court would honor the analysis put forth in *Kantner*. As it was the only outcome-dispositive and controlling authority on the subject in the jurisdiction, the appellants had every reason to believe that they would—and things started out on a positive vibe. Encouraged by the reasoning of the *Kantner* trio, the district court placed on the state the burden of showing clearly and convincingly that prohibiting the possession of marijuana was a proper exercise of the police power. After carefully reviewing the factual picture, the court held that the state had not met this burden and that the law violated the due process clauses of the state and federal Constitution. The prosecution appealed the decision, and the time came for the new court to show its true colors.

On appeal, the primary question for the majority was if the trial court had been wrong in placing the burden of evidence on the state. Unsurprisingly (if one considers the prevalence of NC reasoning) they held that it had, and their opinion proved to be the traditional display of surrealistic reasoning that inevitably follows from false doctrines. According to the majority, the district court, in beginning with a presumption of liberty, had "approach[ed] the issue . . . with the wrong end of the stick."[277] The right end of the stick, according to the court, would have been to ask whether there was a fundamental right to smoke marijuana and from there on get in the line with the previous decisions which held that no such right existed.

As the problems with this reasoning are spelled out elsewhere, I shall not elaborate on this bit. However, to arrive at this conclusion, the *Baker* court had to perform quite a miscarriage of justice. The quandary for the *Baker* court was that there was a strong precedent in Hawai'i jurisprudence for sustaining the *Kantner* trio's analysis. In a series of

---

[276] 56 Haw. 271, 535 P.2d 1394 (1975)

[277] Id. at 276-82, 535 P.2d at 1398

cases[278] the court had already defined principled limits on the police power, and according to this analysis the state had the burden of proof. To shoulder its burden, it had to (1) show that the interests of the public required such interference, and (2) that the means were reasonably necessary for the accomplishment of the purpose and not unduly oppressive upon individuals.

Taking its own doctrines seriously, then, the court would have had to invalidate the drug law as being an unconstitutional exercise of the police power. The *Baker* court, however, would not be discouraged, and with the injudicious logic that always accompanies such decisions the majority went on a rampage to destroy whatever authority FC reasoning had had. As Justice Levinson himself said on the matter, "the majority opinion . . . effected a deconstruction and reconstruction of this court's jurisprudential 'past' that is utterly Orwellian in its scope and methodology. Indeed, the Baker majority literally 'went by the book.'"[279]

In his dissent Levinson documents how the majority rewrote the past by ignoring reality and reason, but as we have discussed the various ways by which the courts will disparage constitutionally valid rights-claims, the *Baker* court's odyssey to the bottom of the FC/NC scale shall not be rehearsed. Suffice to say that it followed the tired old recipe. And as Levinson noted, so it was that "the *Baker* majority managed to ignore the unignorable: that a mere three years previously, a . . . majority of the *Kantner* court . . . had agreed that, as a matter of constitutional law, the police power of the state did not extend to the criminalization of mere possession of marijuana for personal use."[280]

However, there was still one capable FC reasoner left on the court. This was Justice Kobayashi. A former Attorney General, he stood his ground, reviewed the factual picture, and in a lone dissent was "compelled to conclude that the statute in question constitutes an arbitrary and capricious exercise of police powers by the [state]."[281] As he said:

---

[278] *Territory v. Kraft*, 33 Haw. 397 (1935); *State v. Lee*, 51 Haw.516, 517, 465 P.2d 573, 575 (1970); *State v. Shigematsu*, 52 Haw.604, 607, 483 P.2d 997, 999 (1971); *State v. Cotton*, 55 Haw.138, 516 P.2d 709 (1973)

[279] *Mallan*, 86 Haw. 440, 950 P.2d 178 (1998) 216 (Levinson J., dissenting)

[280] Id.216 (Levinson J., dissenting)

[281] Id.218 (Levinson J., dissenting)

"In my opinion . . . the real purpose of the criminalization of possession of marijuana is simply to perpetuate society's prejudice against marijuana; a prejudice which I believe is based mainly upon inaccurate information. Clearly, the only confirmed harm of marijuana is not in marijuana per se, but the laws which criminalize the possessor. The lives and careers of many thousands of possessors have been damaged or destroyed irrationally and oppressively. The interest of society generally has been seriously harmed by the unnecessary criminalization of a large segment of the people. Organized crime or crimes have been fostered by the act of the [state] in proscribing the possession of marijuana. In the exercise of [the state's] police powers, the law is clear: To justify the state in interposing its authority on behalf of the public, it must appear, first, that the interests of the public require such interference; and, second, that the means are reasonably necessary for the accomplishment of the purpose, and not unduly oppressive upon individuals.

. . . In my opinion, the statute prohibiting the possession of marijuana fails to meet the above test. Mere debatable possible harm of marijuana on the individual user does not justify the [state] in interposing its authority on behalf of the public. Assuming *arguendo* [that] justification exists in proscribing the possession of marijuana, the means used to discourage the individual possession of marijuana is not reasonably necessary. The means used has not only failed to accomplish the purpose, but is irrational and unduly oppressive upon the individual marijuana users. . . . I would affirm the result of the trial court's judgment for the reasons stated."[282]

9.3 THE RENFRO COURT

Six months after *Baker,* with *State v. Renfro,* another constitutional challenge came before the Supreme Court.[283] The appellants, however,

---

[282] Baker, 56 Haw. at 285, 288-92, 535 P.2d at 1402, 1404-06 (Kobayashi, J., concurring and dissenting) (some brackets and ellipsis points in original and some added) (footnotes omitted)

[283] *State v. Renfro,* 56 Haw. 501, 542 P.2d 366 (1975)

stood no chance. Having already rewritten the past into a picture more to its liking, the majority simply referred to *Baker* and left the appellants with the impossible task of convincing a panel of indisposed justices that there were meaningful limits to the police power. In the mind of the majority, this was hardly the case and the appellants lost. As Justice Levinson summarized the proceedings:

"What is particularly striking about the majority opinion in *Renfro* is its mantraesque, rote quality. Although the constitutional constraints established in *Kraft* and *Lee* on the state's police power were acknowledged in theory, they seem essentially to have atrophied to a null set. Indeed, the *Renfro* majority opinion virtually turns the Kraft/Lee analysis on its head. Gone was the proposition, from which 'we start,' 'that where an individual's conduct, or class of individuals' conduct, does not directly harm others, the public interest is not affected and is not properly the subject of the police power of the legislature.' And in the face of a legislative determination 'that the conduct of a particular class of people recklessly affects their physical well-being and that the consequent physical injury and death is so widespread as to be of grave concern to the public,' not only was it no longer required, as a precondition of the state's exercise of the police power, that 'the incidence and severity of the physical harm be statistically demonstrated to the satisfaction of the court,' but the diametric opposite seemed to have become the case: if the incidence and severity of the physical harm was 'inconclusive,' and the state of 'scientific knowledge' was
'incomplete,' then the legislature could exercise the police power in whatever way it wanted.

In short, the *Renfro* majority seemed to have completely forgotten the 'direct harm to others/statistically demonstrated secondary social harm' circumscription of the constitutional exercise the state's police power so carefully explicated in *Kraft* and *Lee*. That being so, it is little wonder that the *Renfro* majority regarded the constitutional right of privacy—if it really believed there was one at all, having never found an instance in which it took precedence over anything else—as being of such minor, non-fundamental importance that individual privacy was invariably obliged to 'give way' to legislative whim and speculation."[284]

Justice Kobayashi, having stated his position with sufficient lucidity in *Kantner* and *Baker*, wrote a one-sentence dissent, holding that he disagreed for the reasons stated in *Baker*.[285] Significantly, however, his opinion in that case had apparently persuaded Judge Sodetani, who joined in the *Renfro* dissent. Accordingly, as in *Kantner*, the marijuana law was found constitutional by a single vote.

Then, on December 29, 1978, Justice Kobayashi retired from the court. For some time there were no more justices capable of principled opposition to the impiety which had eaten its way into the heart of the American legal system. From then on a presumption of constitutionality ruled supreme and the police power was, as far as drug policy goes, boundless. It was under these conditions that a unanimous Hawai'i Supreme Court, on May 21, 1979, handed down a per curiam opinion in *State v. Bachman*.[286] The court simply stated that it found Bachman's contention to be without merit and referred to what it had said in *Baker* and *Renfro*.

9.4 The Mallan Court

It would be 20 years before another justice capable of FC reasoning emerged to challenge the status quo. That honor went to the second Justice Levinson who took on the majority in *Mallan*.

What made this case so interesting was that by the time *Mallan* was decided a right to privacy had been added to the Hawai'i Constitution. In 1978 a Constitutional Convention had gathered in order to provide better constitutional protection against arbitrary infringements on autonomy/liberty rights. As a result, Article I of the State Constitution was amended by adding a new section which read: "The right of the

---

[284] *Mallan*, 86 Haw. 440, 950 P.2d 178 (1998) 221-22 (Levinson J., dissenting) (citations omitted)

[285] *Renfro*, 56 Haw. at 507, 542 P.2d at 370 (Kobayashi, J., dissenting)

[286] 61 Haw. 71, 595 P.2d 287 (1979)

people to privacy is recognized and shall not be infringed without the showing of a compelling state interest. The legislature shall take affirmative steps to implement this right."

The question now was how to interpret this amendment. Could it be, as the proponents of the drug law predictably would argue, that it only referred to a small group of privacy rights, such as those already given preferred protection by the courts? Or could it be that it referred to privacy rights in general—that is, that it protected *any and all* autonomy and liberty rights from undue interference?

Looking at the reports of the Committee that prepared this new amendment, there was no doubt that it meant exactly what it said. The Standing Committee spoke of a "right to personal autonomy," "to be let alone," and continued:

> "It should be emphasized that this right is not an absolute one, but, because similar to the right of free speech, it is so important in value that it can be infringed upon only by the showing of a compelling state interest. If the State is able to show a compelling state interest, the right of the group will prevail over the privacy rights or the right of the individual. However, in view of the important nature of this right, the State must use the least restrictive means should it desire to interfere with the right. Your Committee expects that at times the interests of national security, law enforcement, the interest of the State to protect the lives of citizens or other similar interests will be strong enough to override the right to privacy. *It is not the intent of your Committee to grant a license to individuals to violate the right of others, but rather to grant the individual full control over his life, absent the showing of a compelling state interest to protect his security and that of others.*"[287]

The Constitutional Convention endorsed the Committee's report in its entirety, and so there could be no doubt about the legislature's intent: It was to protect the individual's right to be let alone and to have "*full control over his life*" in the absence of a "*compelling state interest.*" In other words, strict scrutiny would apply, and the government would have to demonstrate that its action had been structured with precision; that it

---

[287] *Mallan*, 86 Haw. 440, 950 P.2d 178 (1998) 225 (Levinson J., dissenting) (emphasis mine)

was narrowly tailored to serve legitimate objectives; and that it had selected the least drastic means for achieving its objectives.

Not only that, but the Standing Committee stated that "the importance of this amendment is that it establishes that certain rights deserve special judicial protection from majority rule. It recognizes that there will always be a dynamic tension between majority rule, which is the basis of a democratic society, and the rights of individuals to do as they choose, which is the basis of freedom, and your Committee believes that this amendment recognizes the high value that individuality has in society. Your Committee, by equating privacy with the first amendment rights, intends that the right be considered a fundamental right and that interference with the activities protected by it be minimal."[288]

As we can see, the legislature most definitely put another act of FC reasoning/legislation on the books and the Supreme Court unanimously recognized all of this in *State v. Kam,*[289] where it held the prohibition of obscene materials in the home unconstitutional.

This being so, the stage was perfectly set for another constitutional challenge to the drug law. Things were looking good for the appellant, Lloyd Mallan, as the court needed only apply its own doctrine with some consistency—then the presumption of liberty would be honored, and the state would have to provide a compelling justification for interfering with his rights. The majority, however, would have none of it. Except for Levinson's powerful dissent, the justices would not include drug use as a protected privacy right and yet again NC reasoning carried the day.

Considering that the legislature so clearly had put an act of FC reasoning on the books, how was this possible?

Again, the answer is found in human psychology. And presuming that more sinister reasons were not involved, the answer is that the minds of NC individuals operate in a closed-loop system whereby the implications of FC reasoning will consistently be ignored. They will ignore the implications of higher-order reasoning because they are not yet ready to expand their horizons—and they are not ready to expand their horizons because it entails an expansion of Self that can be frightening to the ego. Our identity is closely associated with the beliefs

---

[288] Id.

[289] *State v. Kam,* 69 Haw. 483, 748 P.2d 372 (1988)

we hold, and it takes a certain amount of maturity to leave old belief-structures behind. To do so is to leave the old idea of Self behind, and this can only be done when the ego is not too entranced by fear. Fear is the one thing that prevents people from moving forward, as each step is a like a small death to the ego.

It is this "petite-mort" that ensures that so many humans will resist change—and this fear of ego-death is why so many prefer insanity to reason. Following reason, after all, entails a willingness to leave old ideas behind and this is impossible if our identity is too attached to old belief-structures. The further towards the NC-end we operate, the more fervently we will cling on to the old sense of self, and so those at this level will reject reason to escape whatever conclusions they would have to embrace by stepping into a greater, more coherent frame of reference.

The *Mallan* majority was no different. These justices showed no willingness to check the validity of their presumptions, and because the enemy image was beyond reproach the justices could not accept the implications of the legislature's principled position. Something—but not the drug law—had to yield, and we shall see how they solved the problem.

9.4.1 THE MALLAN COURT'S DEFECTIVE PRIVACY ANALYSIS

For an unbiased observer, the *Mallan* court had a huge problem if it were to side with the drug law. To begin with, the Hawai'i Constitution had its own privacy clause, and it left state courts "free to give broader privacy protection than that given by the federal constitution."[290] Now, as we have seen, the premise that privacy rights are better protected by constitutions with an explicit privacy protection clause is itself flawed. It is the underlying principles that determine where the line that separates the individual from the collective's sphere shall be drawn and if the Constitution has an enumerated privacy clause is irrelevant. Be that as it may, the *Mallan* majority recognized that "our case law and the text of our constitution appear to invite this court to look beyond the federal

---

[290] *Kam,* 69 Haw. at 491, 748 P.2d at 377

standards in interpreting the right to privacy,"[291] and the justices went on to the next question, whether there was a constitutionally protected right to possess marijuana for personal use.

In pondering this, the justices looked to the legislature process. It is a long-recognized principle of law that the Constitution must be interpreted with due regard to the intent of the framers and the people adopting it and that the fundamental principle in interpreting a constitutional provision is to give effect to that intent. Hence, the task at hand was to look at the committee reports and debates in the Constitutional Convention where the privacy clause was adopted.

Looking at this, it was clear that the legislature had done its job properly. It was clear that the committee members followed in the founders' footsteps and that their intention was to provide enhanced security against undue government interference. This could only be done by emphasizing the importance of respecting the underlying principles of the constitutional order, and so the committee members sought to set principled limits that protected the privacy of individuals. This was the whole point of the legislature's work—*this was the intention*. However, even though the legislature had made its intentions clear, this did not hinder the majority from refusing to act. Never mind that the right to privacy was *a general* right. Never mind that it only excluded those activities which the government had good reasons for criminalizing. And never mind that the statute explicitly said that *the only* way to determine if this was the case was by the state showing that it had a compelling interest in prohibiting the activity in question.

We have already seen how the impact of an enemy image (and the psychological incentives behind it) will incapacitate those in its grip. Its power takes precedence before all else, and so it is that, to comply with the demands of the enemy image, logic will be turned on its head.[292] We

---

[291] *Mallan*, 86 Haw. 440, 950 P.2d 178 (1998) 186

[292] An interesting example of the self-refuting and paradoxical reasoning that results is found in Tribe and Dorf's essay on levels of generality in the definition of rights. In this article they demonstrate the folly of Justice Scalia's attempt to define rights at the most specific level. However, after first noting the importance of "seek[ing] unifying principles that will push constitutional law toward rationality," and stating that "rationality dictates that one does not segregate the reasoning applicable to one medium from the reasoning that has prevailed with respect to other media," they suddenly, when speaking of drug policy, forget to apply their own rules of construction. Instead, they fall into the same trap as Scalia, claiming that "just as the Constitution's repeated references to private property render fatuous any asserted right to steal,

have seen how this results in different standards of harm, culpability, dignity, decency, as well as other mindless ramblings, and the *Mallan* majority was no different. Even though the legislature had stated that the purpose of the privacy clause was "to grant the individual full control over his life, absent the showing of a compelling state interest," it proved impossible for these justices to cope with the implications. Surely this could not include drug use? Surely it could not mean that the state had to show good reasons for denying people this right? Surely the drug law should not have to be defended?

For some reason, the idea of an effective remedy was repugnant to the majority and they had to ensure that the legislature's exact words and intention was rendered null and void. This was done by resorting to the traditional way of disparaging rights-claims, the fundamental rights analysis. They began by stating that "[t]here is no question that the right of privacy embodied in article I, section 6 is a fundamental right in and of itself. Any infringement of the right to privacy must be subjected to the compelling state interest test. Thus, the only analysis this court need utilize when testing a right to privacy claim such as Mallan's is whether the conduct prohibited by law is entitled to protection under article I, section 6."[293]

When it came to this the answer was easy. The justices did not have to look to any other authority than their own biased notions to find that marijuana use could not possibly be protected by the privacy clause, for even if the legislature had opted for across-the-board protection the court could not imagine that the delegates adopting the privacy provision could foresee the implications of their actions. The justices felt sure that if the committee members' personal preferences (read: prejudices) were allowed to count, they would not have meant what they said. It was simply unthinkable that the legislature would have encouraged a principled application of the law if it meant that the drug laws could be subjected to meaningful scrutiny. And so, interpreting the privacy provision according to their own subjective preferences, the *Mallan*

---

so the concern for the preservation of human life expressed in both the Fifth and Fourteenth Amendments undercuts a fundamental liberty interest in assisting an otherwise healthy individual to poison herself." Tribe & Dorf, *Levels of Generality in the Definition of Rights* (1990) 1070, 1071, 1107

[293] *Mallan*, 86 Haw. 440, 950 P.2d 178 (1998) 247 (JJ., Klein and Nakayama concurring)

majority held that "[i]f the delegates had intended such a result, surely they would have placed an explicit reference in the committee reports. Instead, the committee reports contain no mention of the legalization of illicit drugs."[294]

Such an interpretation is what we can expect from those operating at the NC level. Never mind that this interpretation would undermine the purpose of the constitutional order. Never mind that according to this interpretation the Privacy Clause would be useless, its words void of any objective meaning. Never mind that to arrive at this conclusion they had to rely on the self-refuting logic and incoherent reasoning we have previously discussed. This is a price NC individuals are willing to pay to keep their biased notions intact.

If it were not for the psychological incentives behind the enemy image, however, the justices would have come to grips with the duplicity inherent in such reasoning. They would have understood that it was the mindset of immature individuals at work; individuals who insist on holding two contradictory ideas at the same time, who would like to keep both, and who therefore refused to reconsider the implications of their position. A healthy mind—a mind ready to evolve—could not possibly live with this dissonance. An individual at this level of growth would have understood that a dissonance between two simultaneously held beliefs were an indication of mental sickness. She would have understood that two conflicting ideas could not both be true, that one would have to yield, and that the moral compass of this predicament was found in accepting the implications of principled reasoning. Consequently, she would be open to the light of reason, follow it to its conclusion and discard the incompatible idea. In doing so she would not be worse off. Instead, she would have arrived at a higher, more evolved, and coherent level of reality, one where her sense of self was not entwined with disserving notions and falsely held convictions.

For the *Mallan* majority, however, this was not an option. Relying on the fundamental rights doctrine, they took the coward's way out and opted for the rational basis test. Consequently, it was yet again for the defendant to prove that "the government's action was clearly arbitrary and unreasonable, having no substantial relation to the public health,

---

[294] Id. 186

safety, morals, or general welfare" to a court that already had made up its mind. According to the majority, the idea of using a more demanding test, such as the one advanced by the dissent, was rejected as outmoded and discredited thinking. It belonged to an era of constitutional history from which the court had long departed, and the court had no intention of returning to an age when the presumption of liberty held sway. According to the majority, that would "lead to dangerous and unprecedented results," and "the dissent's general methodology present[ed] a significant danger."[295]

9.4.2 THE MAJORITY'S FEAR OF PRINCIPLED REASONING

To FC individuals it is difficult to imagine the "danger" in abiding by the doctrines of reason. To them it is impossible to see how a state having to justify its criminal laws would be a threat to anything other than arbitrary and unjust laws and the advocates of tyrannical government. But again, NC individuals feel very much threatened by this. The majority admitted as much. To them, the problem with Levinson's reasoning was that it "decriminalizes the use and possession of virtually all contraband drugs used within the home or wherever a person believes he is 'in privacy.'"[296] As Justice Levinson replied in his dissent, this may or may not be the case, depending on whether such a result is the outcome of a properly applied balancing test.

Levinson's response, however, is not persuasive to NC individuals. Being blinded by an exaggerated enemy image, they will resist any urge to follow the implications of principled reasoning. Under no conditions will they double-check the validity of this enemy image, and as the light of reason cannot guide them, they will (1) overcomplicate or (2) oversimplify the issue. In either case their analysis will be off, and they imagine that if FC reasoning proved triumphant, all restrictions on drugs would have to be abandoned and hell would break loose.

---

[295] Id. 192
[296] Id. 189

This is not the case. First of all, we are not talking about an either-or, where we must choose between two extremes. If the prohibition of cannabis should fail to pass constitutional muster it might be that some regulation is still feasible; its sales might be taxed and controlled, its use might be prohibited in public places, and so on. Secondly, even if cannabis prohibition should violate liberty/autonomy rights, it might be that the prohibition of other drugs is constitutional; it all depends on the factual picture and if the state can demonstrate with sufficient evidence that its premises for advocating a prohibition are sound. If the government's argument is sound, prohibition will have no problem with first principles and the law will have proven its validity. But if there is a problem, it will be because the drug law does not serve its stated purpose and because it fails to balance the rights of the individual against the needs of society. *In either case* the best argument wins and the public good will be served—and so, whatever the result, there is *absolutely no need* to fear the outcome.

Prohibitionists' fear of principled reasoning, therefore, is not rational. The majority's warning that it would lead to "dangerous and unprecedented results" is simply a testimony to the power of the enemy images, as we are dealing with emotional resistance. As long as people remain spellbound by the enemy image of drugs no reasoning, no matter how coherent, will make a difference and any objective inquiry will be shunned. History, as well as the pathetic replies to FC reasoning are evidence of this. As we have seen, all the objections raised are proven irrelevant by principled reasoning, and while the *Mallan* majority rehearsed a few of these already refuted objections, they also added another. Explaining why Levinson's reasoning was so "dangerous," the majority not only claimed that its "expansive interpretation circumvents the natural development of the right to privacy in two respects: (1) it removes from the developmental process the voice of the people as expressed by legislative action, and (2) it eschews careful case-by-case development of the right to privacy by the courts."[297]

With respect to the first point, this is of no concern. After all, we are not merely a democracy; we are a democracy governed by the rule of law, and the rule of law dictates that the individual has rights that supersede

---

[297] Id.189

the rule of ignorant and prejudiced beliefs, no matter how commonly or deeply held. As the Hawai'i legislature had reminded the court, "there will always be a dynamic tension between majority rule, which is the basis of a democratic society, and the rights of individuals to do as they choose, which is the basis of freedom," and the right to privacy is one of those fundamental rights that "deserve special judicial protection from majority rule."[298] Hence, what the majority of the voters want does not necessarily matter, and this objection is another of those kneejerk responses that NC judges will use to hide from constitutional responsibilities.[299]

With respect to the second point, this is equally irrelevant. After all, there is nothing in the doctrines of law that speak against a full change of direction whenever rights-violations are discovered. To the contrary, it would be a gross miscarriage of justice to disregard evidence of failure only to retreat from the status quo in incremental steps. The only reason why such an advance would appeal to some is that it would lessen the embarrassment felt by the purveyors and defenders of the drug laws. It is, no doubt, difficult for this lot to face the facts and to confront the reality of their actions. Quite a few would become rabid at the notion of immediate repeal, and so, to sustain their delusive pretenses of virtue, one could argue that we need another 50 years to do away with the drug laws completely.

Indeed, it is small wonder that such a suggestion would come from the *Mallan* majority. The justices belong to that percentage of the populace who are the least keen to face reality, and so it is only natural that they would come up with such a scheme. To thinking people, however, it is nothing but a ploy to escape responsibility for their actions. To maintain a façade of respectability, it is easy to understand why they would want this change of policy to be so slow that no one really is held responsible for crimes against humanity. Even so, this is no good reason for dissolving the drug war effort over a period of decades. The price of

---

[298] Id. 225

[299] "The judiciary is obligated to examine the reasonableness of legislative classifications and to declare them unconstitutional when it finds them to be so. In the words of Chief Justice Marshall, 'It is emphatically the province and duty of the judicial department to say what the law is.' No amount of deference to judicial restraint can discharge this obligation." *People v. Summit*, 517 P.2d 850 (1974) 855 (Lee J., dissenting)

appealing to vanity is bought at the expense of untold human misery, and there can be no justice, no rule of law, before this charade is put to an end.

10

SUMMARY

"The War on Drugs violates the fundamental common law principle of responsibility in its reliance on coercive, preventive laws—prohibition—passed in anticipation of misconduct, whether or not it actually occurs. It thus proceeds from a platform of disrespect for the idea of individual rights and responsibilities; its premises do not harmonize with those of the legal and political systems, and that dissonance may explain much of its futility and destructiveness."[300]

—Steven Wisotsky—

IN THIS PART WE have exposed the American system of arbitrary law. We have also explored the qualitative difference between FC and NC reasoning, and the problem with the latter has been made sufficiently clear. Hence, there is no reason to elaborate. Instead, what I will do in this summary is to give FC reasoners due credit. And in looking at the history of drug law challenges, little more than a handful of justices qualify for this noble status. Justices Abe, Levinson, Kobayashi, and the second Levinson of the Hawaii Supreme Court all passed with flying colors.[301] This honor also goes to Justices Kavanagh of the Michigan Supreme Court[302] and Sanders of the Washington Supreme Court.[303]

---

[300] WISOTSKY, *BEYOND THE WAR ON DRUGS* (1990) 201

[301] *State v. Kantner,* 53 Haw. 327, 493 P.2d 306 (1972); *State v. Baker,* 56 Haw. 271, 535 P.2d 1394 (1975); *State v. Mallan,* 86 Haw. 440, 950 P.2d 178 (1998)

[302] *People v. Lorentzen,* 194 N.W.2d 827 (1972); *People v. Sinclair,* 387 Mich. 91, 194 N.W.2d 878 (1972)

[303] *Seeley v. State,* 132 Wash. 2d 776, 940 P.2d 604 (1997)

In Sanders's case, the issue before the court concerned a right to medical marijuana. However, I have taken the liberty of presuming that he would have applied the same reasoning in matters concerning recreational use. This may not be the case, but his opinion fulfills the necessary criteria. Justices Dolliver, Hicks, and Williams of the same court also voiced an opinion that qualifies,[304] and the same goes for Justices Seiler and Shangler of the Michigan Supreme Court.[305] I will also name Justice Adkins of the Florida Supreme Court for his dissenting opinions. He does, after all, establish that drug use is a protected privacy right,[306] and that the state must have more than a hypothetical rational basis" for its classification. He is clear that there must be a "valid and substantial reason for classifications,"[307] and assuming that he applies the same reasoning consistently, he deserves credit.

In addition to this, there are a few majority opinions that more or less qualify. In *English v. Miller*,[308] *People v. McCabe*,[309] *People v. Sinclair*,[310] *Sam v. State*,[311] and *State v. Zornes*,[312] the court had sufficient integrity to invalidate the marijuana laws on equal protection grounds. However, as the issue before the court was whether the classification of marijuana together with opiates violated the equal protection clause, I believe that these justices would fail the test when push came to shove. Had the appellants raised the bigger issue, whether the different treatment of marijuana and alcohol users violated the equal protection clause, they would most likely, just as every other court faced with this issue, have denied protection on equal protection grounds and so I do not want to reward them with FC status. There are also the justices at the Alaska Supreme Court who, with *Ravin*, found marijuana use to be a protected privacy right and demanded that the state justify its prohibition. Thus,

---

[304] *State v. Smith*, 610 P.2d 869, 93 Wn.2d 329 (1980)

[305] *State v. Mitchell*, 563 S.W.2d 18 (Mo. 1978)

[306] *Laird v. State*, 342 So.2d 962 (Fla. 1977) (Adkins J. dissenting)

[307] *Bourassa v. State*, 366 So. 2d 12 (Fla. 1978)

[308] 341 F. Supp. 714 (E.D. Va. 1972)

[309] 49 Ill. 2d 338, 275 N.E.2d 407 (1971)

[310] 387 Mich. 91, 194 N.W.2d 878 (1972)

[311] 500 P.2d 291 (Okl.Cr.App.)

[312] 78 Wash. 2d 9, 475 P.2d 109

they deserve credit, but the reasoning of the court was so entrenched in the NC paradigm that no FC status shall be awarded.

In addition to the justices summarized, we can add a few from the lower courts. Even so, it is a rather sorry spectacle. We are dealing with more than a hundred constitutional challenges and so we can assume that 90 percent of American justices belong to the NC category. That is, they may from time to time expound the kind of principled reasoning needed to fulfill FC criteria in other areas, but this is easy. It is in the hard cases (as in constitutional challenges to the prohibitions on drugs and prostitution) that they have an opportunity to prove their qualities, and here they fall short. Again and again, we find their reasoning too contaminated by the cultural prejudice of the status quo to correctly apply first principles.

We can also look for the same traits among other legal scholars, such as professors of law. Here the record is also flimsy, but it is unlikely that more than 10 percent will qualify for FC status. All things being equal, this is what we can expect from the general population and I have seen no indication that FC traits are more common among academics. However, even if this should be the case generally speaking, the trend among Ninth Amendment scholars is reversed. Looking at their scholarship, 90 percent could classify as FC individuals. Hence, there is hope for the future. These are the scholars with the firmest grip on constitutional interpretation, and had they been consulted—and their knowledge applied—the American legal system would evolve into FC status.

If we want to get the American system back on track, we need only listen to these individuals. They are the avant-garde, the harbingers of things to come, but they are mostly talking to themselves and have little influence on current events. At the very least, the justices at the U.S. Supreme Court do not seem to have much regard for their criticisms. Just like most politicians, prosecutors, and career bureaucrats at the Justice Department, they remain dedicated to doctrines of arbitrary law and their foremost concern seems to be keeping the status quo intact.

This, again, is as one can expect. As Professor Ervin Staub noted, "being part of a system shapes views, rewards adherence to dominant views, and makes deviation psychologically demanding and difficult."[313] Hence, as the dominant view is the NC mindset, they are representative of this perspective and it comes as no surprise that they have ignored principled reasoning. It is all part of the pattern, and we can expect our body of law to remain in shambles for quite some time, as the system's force of inertia will continue to fight integrity and FC reasoning every step of the way, while the majority of the population remains oblivious.

Even so, we can expect the NC mindset to lose out in the end. As we shall see, we are in the midst of a paradigm shift and the only question is how expensive the funeral will be in terms of lives needlessly lost, millions wrongfully incarcerated, and money unwisely spent promoting organized crime and feeding the totalitarian aspects of the state. The stakes are high. Every year this war continues, the body count and human misery that follows in its wake is comparable to that of conventional wars; as much as 400.000 lives are unnecessarily lost, and one day we will look back and remember the Drug War as one of history's most heinous crimes against humanity.

While prohibitionists will disagree, the evidence is overwhelming. As we have seen, the case against drug prohibition is nearing complete; every aspect of its unconstitutionality has been documented and the problems with the prohibition argument have been exposed in full detail. More and more people are catching up, and it is only a matter of time before prohibitionists will have to recognize our right to an effective remedy. The longer until they do, the more profound will be their denial of responsibility, and the more our officials will go from a position of embarrassment to criminal negligence. To the extent they continue to ignore the evidence, they are depriving the people of basic constitutional rights, and they are, as openly as civil servants ever can be expected to, saying F.U. to the people they are supposed to serve. No one of sound mind would vote for officials such as these and no officials worthy of the people's trust will let this state of affairs continue unchecked. Hence, to the extent that our officials take their duties seriously, they will assist us in ending drug prohibition.

---

[313] ZIMBARDO, *THE LUCIFER EFFECT* (2009) 286. See also ERVIN STAUB, *THE ROOTS OF EVIL: THE ORIGINS OF GENOCIDE AND OTHER GROUP VIOLENCE*

Also, to the extent that the NC doctrines discussed are a sincere attempt to find the best possible instruments for anchoring the light of first principles, of de-abstracting and transfusing this light into a more pliable and concrete form (i.e., something to work with), we can expect judges and lawyers to embrace FC doctrines as soon as their pre-eminence is established. This, no doubt, is the situation today. Indeed, the case for a systemic recalibration towards a state of resonance with FC law is so powerful that impeachment procedures will be the only proper response if the courts fail the people.

This should be uncontroversial. As Professor Gerber noted, "[t]he theory of the Constitution requires that Congress exercise the political courage necessary to perform its constitutional duty of impeaching those justices who seek to 'rewrite' the Constitution rather than interpret it."[314] This is what most justices have done to this day. Under the cover of "objectivity" the courts have never been more subjectively driven,[315] and the flawed reasoning by which they operate ensures the unnecessary, illegitimate, and continued suffering of millions. To the extent the judiciary continues this travesty, they are unlawfully depriving the people of their constitutional rights, and such open hostility is not what the founders intended.

All things considered, therefore, unless their representatives quickly turn things around, Americans will have right to declare the government an enemy of the people and abolish that apparatus which has become so destructive to the principles and ends of the founding. To say this is neither anarchistic hyperbole nor aggravating hate speech: It is simply the idea of America. It should be uncontroversial that American officials are responsible to the people, and that, when betraying their trust, the consequences shall be proportional to their treason. Self-serving, conniving, and dishonest officials should by all rights be fearful of the

---

[314] Gerber, *Liberal Originalism* (2014) 22

[315] "The underlying rationale for choosing selected liberties to be protected from government interference while leaving the rest largely unprotected is to inform us clearly that the Court exercises 'the utmost care whenever asked to break new ground in this field, lest the liberty protected by the Due Process Clause be subtly transformed into the policy preferences of the Members of this Court.' In actuality, however, this has not restrained the Court. Judicial preferences, masked by a glossary of shibboleths, have taken from us the original, rational system of determining whether a governmental restriction bears a substantial relation to the police power." Preiser, *Rediscovering a Coherent Rationale for Substantive Due Process* (2003) 11

people to whom they are beholden—and just like America was an idea whose time had come 250 years ago, so it is time for Americans to embrace the ideas of the Founding.

PART FOUR

A Shifting Paradigm

11

THE ADVANCING PROGRESS OF REASON

"Our world is ruled by inflexible laws which control not only the motions of the heavenly bodies, but the consequences of human conduct. These Universal motions, interpreted politically, are impelling human society out of a state of autocracy and tyranny to democracy and freedom. This motion is inevitable, for the growth of humans is a gradual development of mind over matter, and the motion itself represents the natural and reasonable unfoldment of the potentials within human character."[1]

—Manly P. Hall—

LOOKING BACK AT HISTORY, we see a steady progress of reason. This progress was briefly reviewed in part one where we discussed its implications in fields as diverse as religion and law. It is only in the NC-world that things appear fragmented and apart, but as we evolve towards the FC-end the dissonance and incoherence at the NC level is traversed and the result is a more holistic worldview. To high-end FC individuals therefore law, politics, psychology, religion, physics, and so on, comes together as one, uniting in a coherent superstructure.

To those at a lower level it is difficult to grasp the outline and the internal consistency of this superstructure. It is also difficult to judge the extent to which it is harmonious with reason. However, looking at history the ideals, values, and principles that follow from Wholeness have increasingly come into prominence, and we can intuit that this process will result in a collective recognition of FC traits.

---

[1] HALL, *THE SECRET DESTINY OF AMERICA* (1944) 5

In the field of religion, we can trace this progress in our image of God. 5000 years ago, the NC mindset ruled superior, and the image of God reflected this fact. We can always expect our perception of God to conform to our ideals and understanding, and the Old Testament God proves this point. He was a cruel, jealous, and bitterly vengeful patriarch, one that mirrored the ideals expounded by the outlook of that age. The society model was a strictly hierarchical, dominance-oriented endeavor and the impact of the ideals that follow from the Wholeness perspective was infinitesimal.

2000 years ago, we find a society that had matured. This is reflected in the New Testament God, one that was more forgiving and patient with his herd. Society was still governed by ruthless, self-serving individuals, and it remained firmly entrenched in the extreme NC-end. Nevertheless, we see that the values and ideals that follow from the Wholeness concept were beginning to have an impact. To this day there has been a gulf between theory and practice, but as we have matured this distance has been decreasing. 500 years ago, the idea of human rights would still be unheard of, but 250 years later, with the French and the American Revolution, they became officially recognized. Society, however, had still not advanced to the point where reason would be allowed to triumph and the spirit that breathed life into the French Declaration of Rights and the American Declaration of Independence was quashed by the prevailing way of thinking. Even so, the inherent dissonance between the FC and the NC mindset—and the moral and intellectual superiority of the former—has ensured a gradual calibration of society towards the FC-end.[2]

In the discipline of law, this progress is seen in the advancing appreciation for the dignity of man as found in the increasing recognition of autonomy rights. 2000 years ago, the concept of autonomy had no bearing and there was no shame in dominating or *owning* another human

---

[2] Because of this, we see that religion is in the midst of a paradigm shift where our perception of God is changing from the NC idea of a God "out there" to the FC perception of God "within." Because there is no need for a middleman between us and God in the new paradigm, clerical authorities have been trying to keep the old paradigm in place. Nonetheless, people are moving away from religious dogma to embracing a more experiential spirituality—one that does not insult reason. As this process unfolds, the Christ-Consciousness within (the human potential) awakens, and so it is that the prophesized return of Christ will be a collective Messianic event, a mass-movement into the FC paradigm.

being. Those who did would even take great pride in their achievement, thinking it established manhood. There is still a remnant of such people, but as we draw closer to our age we find that things have changed and at a quicker pace. We still have a way to go before we can call ourselves a FC society, but at the very least we have matured to the point where we do not automatically murder or imprison those who assist in the transformation to this status. Hopefully, therefore, the time will not be long in coming before we also begin *to listen* to those who can observe and understand *the causes* of our problems.

We shall have more to say on this, but before we go into causes we shall continue studying their effects—and studying the progress of history, we see a gradual emergence of the FC mindset. What we are dealing with is two wholly different modes of perception, two opposing lines of reasoning, two different paradigms. One is the source of all our problems and the other is the solution, and as humanity learns from its mistakes the collective psyche is increasingly being influenced by those values, ideals, and principles that follow from the Wholeness. As individuals we will be more or less influenced by one or the other, but collectively speaking the quality of the collective unconscious is changing and the impact of FC reasoning will become dominant. We have not yet reached that point in time. But the increasing polarity is a sure sign that something has got to give, and looking at trends in law there are indications that the NC paradigm is nearing its end.

11.1 THE CLASH OF COMPETING PARADIGMS

In the evolution of American law and society, we have seen two opposing paradigms competing for hegemony. The FC paradigm builds from first principles and proceeds by means of logical argument while the NC paradigm merely satisfies our arbitrary notions of right and wrong. To FC individuals it is self-evident that no law worthy of its name can ignore the principles of justice. It is also obvious that our ideas about right and wrong, if they are to carry any weight, must conform to these principles and that whenever there is discord between the two the light of first principles must be allowed to guide us towards higher understanding and better judgment. However, as we have seen, most people do not care about justice in any meaningful sense. They care deeply about their own opinions of right and wrong, but they have no regard for the principles of justice and whenever there is a conflict between the two, they will go with the former.

We have seen how this is the case when constitutional challenges to socially contested issues are made. In order to make the legal system conform to biased opinions, NC justices must ignore the dictates of reason and the only thing that can help them maintain an aura of respectability is a set of fundamentally flawed doctrines. Because of the need to keep reality at bay, these doctrines must be completely detached from principled reasoning and the result is two different systems of law. We have seen how legal concepts like consent, human rights, the rule of law, popular sovereignty, police power, arbitrariness, rational basis, public good, burden of proof, the limits of the criminal sanction, etc., therefore means different things to different people, and the same goes for the harm principle, equality principle, proportionality principle, and the principle of legality. In other words, depending on which end of the FC/NC model we find ourselves, there will be different theories for justification of the criminal law and the notion of what the Constitution means will be completely different.

What we are dealing with is two wholly different levels of intelligence, different depths of insight, and different reaches of mental faculties. The further we draw towards the NC-end, the more our logic will be colored by faulty belief-systems and an eagerness to preserve a self-righteous and deluded worldview, one that is disconnected from the greater reality, while the nearer we draw towards the FC-end, the greater will be the analytical power involved and the more our world will be harmonious with the ideals, values, and principles that follow from the Wholeness concept.

It is natural that NC individuals will disagree, but we have proven beyond dispute the mental and moral superiority of the FC mindset. We have seen that compared to the reasoning at the FC level, the reasoning coming from the NC-end will be unprincipled, fragmented, disjointed, shallow, trivial, inconsistent, illogical, self-refuting, paradoxical and ad hoc.

We have also seen that psychologically speaking, the NC paradigm is simply a symptom of our willingness to delude ourselves. To those existing at the lower end, the delusion will be too complete for the distance between theory and practice to be perceived. But as we draw nearer to the FC-end, it becomes more difficult to ignore the cognitive dissonance that keeps the status quo in place. At some point we can no longer accept the worldview of those engulfed in the NC Groupmind. The price of conformity will become too great, and so FC reasoning takes the place of NC reasoning.

As a culture we have not advanced to the point where the distance between theory and practice can be officially acknowledged. However, we have advanced to the point where it is plain to see, and we shall now explore some indicators that we are in the midst of a paradigm shift.

11.1.1 THE SHIFTING VIEWS ON DRUG POLICY

At the very core of drug policy, we find a rather simple question. Shall we, to quote Professor Szasz, see the drug user "as a stupid, sick, and helpless child, who, tempted by pushers, peers, and the pleasures of drugs, succumbs to the lure and loses control of himself? Or as a person in control of himself, who, like Adam, chooses the forbidden fruit as the elemental and elementary way of pitting himself against authority?"[3]

Any thinking on drug policy must begin with either of these suppositions. As Szasz noted, "the questions frame two different moral perspectives, and the answers define two different moral strategies: if we side with authority and wish to repress the individual, we shall treat him *as if* he were helpless, the innocent victim of overwhelming temptation; and we shall then 'protect' him from further temptation by treating him as a child, slave, or madman. If we side with the individual and wish to refute the legitimacy and reject the power of authority to infantilize him, we shall treat him *as if* he were in command of himself, the executor of responsible decisions; and we shall then demand that he respect others as

---

[3] SZASZ, *CEREMONIAL CHEMISTRY* (2003) 175-76

he respects himself by treating him as an adult, a free individual, or a 'rational' person."[4]

The former is the preferred NC option while the latter is the favored FC option. In the NC society the concept of individual autonomy will carry no weight, there will be no principled thinking separating the domain of the state and the individual, and the state will be free to transgress upon the latter whenever it is politically expedient. In the FC society, however, the opposite will be the case, and unless it can be shown that drugs deprive the user of autonomous capacity, society will treat him *as if* he "were in command of himself, the executor of responsible decisions." It is as simple as that and policy-wise either supposition makes sense. It all depends on the nature of drug use and if it can be construed as an activity involving autonomous, rational choice.

To this day our drug policies have been rooted in the NC approach. We have taken for granted that drug use equals slavery, that it is motivated by pathological needs and wants, that it has no inherent value, and that it is an irrational and misdirected pursuit. As it turns out none of these assumptions are borne out by the evidence, but that has not stopped us from building drug policy on this ideological foundation.

While it is apparent that current policy is built on a flawed factual foundation, prohibitionists, at the very least, have been doing their reasoning from this premise. This, however, is no longer the case. Since the 1990s, the enemy image of drugs has been waning, and as the moral panic subsides reason is allowed to influence the course of drug policy. Since California in 1996 became the first state to legalize medical marijuana 25 states have followed and now 80 percent of the American people support this policy. With the waning enemy image, we also see that an increasing percentage of the population want to legalize the recreational use of marijuana. In 1990 a mere 16 percent favored legalization, in 2006 it was 32 percent, and today roughly 60 percent want to see this done. As this trend is expected to continue, we can predict that at some point in the near future the prohibition of marijuana will yield. A handful of states have already legalized recreational use and this trend is part of a bigger picture. In the Western hemisphere, we see a movement away from the zero-tolerance ideology that has shaped drug policy. It is

---

[4] Ibid.

an open secret that much of the problems associated with drug use results from prohibition, and as the persecution of drug users is increasingly being perceived as the futile and indecent endeavor it really is, more and more countries are decriminalizing drug use.

With the wave of decriminalization, the foundation of prohibition ideology is crumbling. As we have seen, the only valid foundation for drug prohibition is the perception of drug use as an activity bereft of value, one that cannot be rationally pursued. To support the logic of prohibition the drug user cannot be admitted status as an autonomous agent,[5] and yet, internationally, more and more courts are invoking the right to autonomy to decriminalize drug use. The tension between this view and the prohibition paradigm is evident, for (1) if drug use is granted status as being compatible with the choice of responsible adults the state has no business interfering. And (2) if the state has no business depriving of a choice in drugs, it also follows that there must be a correlative right to purchase such materials for personal use, or else the underlying autonomy right becomes meaningless.[6] As Spooner reminds us, we

---

[5] As Professor Wisotsky noted "Once society shifts from a world view of taking drugs a victimization, helplessness, and aberration to one of conscious regulation of a natural drive, the drug enforcement enterprise will cease to have validity (except for children). Its very premise will have been crushed. The need for the Government's 'protection' from an external enemy will vanish. The War on Drugs will emerge in its true character—a war on one-third of the American people, or more accurately, a stupid and futile attack on their satisfaction of a fundamental human drive." WISOTSKY, *BEYOND THE WAR ON DRUGS* (1990) 214

[6] *People v. Lorentzen*, 194 N.W.2d 827 (1972) 182 (Kavanagh J,.concurring in part, dissenting in part) ("I [have] stated the conviction that the government has no constitutional authority to proscribe possession and private use of marijuana. The right to possess and use something, however, has little meaning unless one also has the right to acquire it, and hence *proscription* of sale cannot be reconciled with a right to possess and use. It may be that some legitimate public interest may be served by the *regulation* of traffic in marijuana, but a statute which absolutely forbids the sale of marijuana is as offensive to the right of privacy and the pursuit of happiness as a statute which forbids its possession and use."); *State v. Baker*, 56 Haw. 271, 535 P.2d 1394 (1975) (Majority opinion) ("An assured right of possession would necessarily imply some adequate method to obtain not subject to destruction at the will of the State."); *Crane v. Campbell*, 245 U.S. 304 (1917) 308 ("An assured right of possession would neces-sarily imply some adequate method to obtain not subject to destruction at the will of the State."); Hindes, *Morality Enforcement Through the Criminal Law and the Modern Doctrine of Substantive Due Process* (1977) 383 ("It is absurd to talk about a right to use a product when it remains illegal to purchase the product and illegal to transport it to the place where it may rightfully be consumed."); Grosman, *Drugs under the Constitution* (2011) 14 ("If we believe there is a right to use drugs as part of our autonomy, we cannot prosecute drug provision, which is instrumentally necessary to perform the conduct protected by such right. The fact that drugs can be found all the same is no valid answer for the State, since that is so despite its attempts to prevent it. Moreover, it could not be claimed that the State adequately protects this right if it pushes the user to the illegal market as the only way to access the drug.")

should also keep in mind that the seller, producer, smuggler, etc., is at most merely an accomplice to the drug user. And that it is a "rule of law as well as reason that if the principal in any act is not punishable, the accomplice cannot be."[7]

As of yet, however, society has not evolved to the point where it is possible for most people to apply reason to drug policy. As previously demonstrated, it is not logic that dictates the enemy image but the enemy image that dictates the logic, and reason must yield. After a century's worth of propaganda, we have not only learned to see the drug user as the victim of a plague, but the prohibition ideology has instilled an image of the drug pusher as being the lowliest, most terrible type of criminal. It does not matter if the ideological foundation (that of turning the context of supply and demand into one of victim and aggressor) is purely mythical. Myth is often more authoritative than reality and this fictitious conception has a power too immense for reason to penetrate. Hence, as the era of dehumanizing drug users draws to an end, we see that while they are being granted status as human beings, worthy of the same respect and legal protection that we ourselves take for granted, drug distributors are not that fortunate.

For the prohibition ideology to sustain itself—and prohibitionists to maintain an aura of respectability—these people must still bear the brunt of our collective guilt. They must fulfill the function of the scapegoat, for without them the prohibitionists would have no demons to fight. Without them, the nature of the prohibitionist crusade would become too obvious; it would begin to dawn on people what a misdirected plot drug prohibition really is, and we would have to "live with ourselves in the wee hours of the morning when we must realize that we savagely persecute pushers, who like abortionists of such recent past, have merely offered a product or a service for which there is intense demand, while we indecisively indulge those who commit countless acts of direct violence against their fellow citizens."[8]

It goes without saying that it is difficult to come to terms with this realization. Coming to grips with the reality of drug prohibition necessitates a reorganization of our moral universe that is not complete

---

[7] Lysander Spooner, *Vices Are Not Crimes* (1875) at 11

[8] SZASZ, *CEREMONIAL CHEMISTRY* (2003) 73 (paraphrasing)

until we fully acknowledge the perversity of society's official moral codes. What we have before us is a psychological process, a cleansing of the national psyche on par with that of South-Africa in the post-Apartheid period and Germany after the Second World War, but as of yet we have not matured to the point where can experience this healing moment, this catharsis of the soul. Collectively speaking, we are still in denial of reality—still unwilling to face the fact that the "bad guys" are simply agents of autonomy, while the "good guys" are really agents of tyranny. As such, as Miller noted, the drug laws can be seen as "a metaphor for pretensions of personal virtue and their repeal a metaphor for confessing the sin of pride."[9]

This is one important reason why prohibitionists resist legalization. The act of repeal would not only be a confession of error; it would be an admittance of guilt, something that is psychologically painful to bear for officials who have brutalized fellow citizens for so long.[10] Hence, to preserve a sense of pride, it remains taboo to think things through. As a result, the ideology of prohibition muddles along, despite the fact that its foundation is not only proven factually inaccurate (this was also the case while our approach to drug policy remained firmly rooted in the NC paradigm), but even though its ideological premise is increasingly being abandoned by courts and officials.

Prohibitionists' will to power and ignorance aside, this new trend is a sure sign that we are in the midst of a paradigm shift. As a civilization we have one foot in the NC-world and another in the FC-world, and the uncanny result is that when FC individuals thought that their psychosis could not become worse, prohibitionists have taken it up another notch. Remember that a symptom of psychosis is to hold two contradictory beliefs at the same time while accepting both. We have already seen how prohibitionists will present themselves as believers in human rights on the one hand while positioning themselves as defenders of the drug law on the other and that they will space out into an incoherent frame of mind (and law) when they are confronted with evidence of a disconnect. If

---

[9] Miller, *The Case for Legalizing Drugs* (1991) 126

[10] As Jim Attie, a law enforcer who had the integrity to leave the NC paradigm behind, said: "I am not proud of what I did. It was a dirty job. It was a form of amorality, and to this day I feel tremendous guilt and have unending nightmares as a result of what I did as a narcotics agent." Valentine, *The Strength of the Wolf* (2004) 292

denying reality is the only way to preserve their beliefs, this is what they will do. In our day, however, prohibitionists have taken it one step further, and to preserve their ideology they now picture the drug user as being *both* autonomous and non-autonomous at the same time. Professor Grosman noted this perplexing new trend in prohibitionist reasoning:

> "Courts and scholars have invoked the right to autonomy to decriminalize drug use, but have advocated for severe punishment of provision and for compulsory detoxification treatments. To justify this approach, they have oscillated between two images of the drug user which, in fact, are inconsistent: on the one hand, an autonomous agent who pursues her freely chosen life plan; on the other, a sort of automaton with no will who gives in to the influence exerted by the person who shares or sells drugs. This ambiguity is hard to maintain, and forces us to re-evaluate the regime in force."[11]

Reevaluating the regime in force, however, is not on the prohibitionist agenda. They have a vested interest in the status quo, and whether this perceived interest is emotional, political, or economic, they will hold on to the prohibition ideology for dear life. Hence, this is the paradox they must embrace: To conform to the changing standards of decency, they must on the one hand accept the drug user as an autonomous agent, but on the other they are unwilling to embrace its implications as doing so will inevitably confront them with the reality of prohibition. So it is that public officials embrace the idea of decriminalization. As a matter of reason and principle it makes no sense, but like children they will have their cake and eat it too—and because

---

[11] Grosman, *Drugs under the Constitution* (2011) 1. Commenting on the Arriola decision of the Argentine Supreme Court, Grossman noted the logical inconsistency associated with the modern prohibitionist doctrine which has become popular in "progressive" countries: "A drug user who has followed the preceding discussion might experience some perplexity. On the one hand, he has heard that his conduct is inherent to his right to autonomy, and is therefore constitutionally protected from 'any legal interference.' On the other, he finds out he can only use drugs in private, or else he might end up in jail; and he must obtain drugs in a black market dominated by mafias, with all the risks and costs this implies, for any form of provision deserves harsh punishment. Moreover, since the State is under the duty to seize all goods illegally acquired, if it finds a drug user in possession of a drug, it should necessarily deprive him of that drug and proceed to destroy it. In fact, our disconcerted user will find out that few actions are persecuted by the State's apparatus with as much eagerness as drug provision. He might find some consolation in the fact that he can get drugs all the same, but he cannot forget that this is so despite the State, which devotes vast resources to prevent it." Ibid. 9

committing to reason is politically and emotionally unpalatable, they embrace half-wit logic to justify their position.

Nevertheless, despite the worsening psychosis, the changing debate on drug policy is an important step to becoming a FC society. What we see unfolding is the natural tension between FC and NC reasoning, and the fact that more and more public officials will admit that drug users are autonomous agents who choose their life plan with a reasonable degree of freedom is a sign that the NC paradigm is nearing its end.

11.1.2 THE GLOBAL MOVEMENT TOWARDS FC LAW

"What we need, in short, is a fresh start. . . .[W]e need to set out principles ourselves, and follow their implications throughout the criminal law."[12]

—Markus D. Dubber—

The changing debate on drug policy is part of a bigger picture. It is the result of a legal revolution that has been gaining ground for some time, for since the 1950s the legal profession has become more international in scope, more calibrated towards a resonance with first principles. This is a natural consequence of FC reasoning, for while fragmentation and disorder are a trademark of NC societies, the impact of the FC mindset will reorganize whatever dissonance into states of higher coherence.

The proof, as they say, is in the pudding. Looking back some 250 years ago, when the political theorists of the Enlightenment established the intellectual foundation for modern governments, a FC system of law was established in both the Old and the New World. The French Declaration of Rights mirrored the American Constitution, and the legal and political theory embodied in these documents were identical. While

---

[12] Dubber, *Toward a Constitutional Law of Crime and Punishment* (2004) 25

their solution to political problems was different,[13] they both built on first principles and their spirit was one and the same.[14]

However, as we have seen, society was still governed by the NC mindset, and it did not take long before this spirit was corrupted and the legal system of both the Old and the New World became one of arbitrary law. Already in 1799, the French Constitution was rewritten to become a model for authoritarian regimes and the American system of law would develop its own doctrines, increasingly detached from the fundamental principles of justice. By 1950, this process was complete. The legal systems of the Old and the New World had evolved into purebred NC systems—systems where the State was the perceived sovereign and the individual was its property.

It is no coincidence that the positivist ideology of these times gave birth to a myriad of oppressive regimes, two world wars, and human misery on an untold scale. It is also no coincidence that out of the horrors of the Second World War, after being confronted with the result of the NC State run amuck, the spirit of humanity would rise again. From what can only be called a legal Dark Age, the light of FC reasoning would once more emerge, and to this day it has continued to grow more powerful. As a result we find that, in Europe, a system of human rights law came into being. It was inspired by the principled thinking that gave birth to America but blessed with not having the doctrinal baggage that had evolved under the American system. Hence, modern human rights law became a system of law much more in touch with the intent of the Founding Fathers.

This is noncontroversial. As the light of FC reasoning shines brighter, it is increasingly recognized that American law has evolved into a system that does not conform to the principles of justice. With the passing of time, the disconnect is only becoming more palpable, and there is no shortage of scholars who have scorned the rational basis test, the fundamental rights doctrine, the presumption of legality, and the suspect

---

[13] In the French system, natural rights were meant to be interpreted and implemented exclusively through the legislative process.

[14] STUNTZ, *THE COLLAPSE OF AMERICAN CRIMINAL JUSTICE* (2013) 77; Kumm, *Democracy is not enough* (2009)

classification analysis as being inherently opposed to the principles put in place by the founders.[15]

The major difference between the two systems is that the American system has come to focus on the shadow that was cast from the light of first principles, whereas is the light itself is modern human rights law's primary focus.[16] Needless to say, this is the only way to meaningfully balance the autonomy interests of the individual against those of the collective—this is the only way to appeal to reason.[17] Because of this, Canadians went with the international human rights system rather than the American when they established their Charter. And because of this more and more American scholars are in favor of a remodeling of the American system in an overhaul inspired by human rights law.[18]

This debate and the increasing discontent with current doctrines and interpretations is indicative of the emerging FC mindset. In all areas of law, we see a new awareness beginning to surface, one that understands the central purpose uniting all law to be the protection of the person as such, of his or her integrity, autonomy, and dignity. We see it in political philosophy where the contractarian approach, since the 1950s, has been the dominant influence. We see it in the Ninth Amendment scholarship that has materialized these past 30 years. We see it in the growing call for a constitutionalization of the criminal law.[19] We see it in the upsurge of

---

[15] See part two, *supra* notes 137, 138

[16] As Kai Möller noted "The point and purpose of constitutional rights under the global model is . . . not to single out certain especially important interests for heightened protection but to ensure that *all* autonomy interests of a person are *adequately protected* at all times." MÖLLER, THE GLOBAL MODEL OF CONSTITUTIONAL RIGHTS (2012) 24

[17] As Dubber observed, a comprehensive account of constitutional criminal law can only "arise from considering the implications of the basic principle of justice that underlies a constitutional system of government, i.e. human dignity based on the capacity for autonomy." And "[w]hile the United States deserves considerable credit, as a historical matter, for the establishment of a constitutional system . . . based on certain minimum guarantees of personal rights, the world has long since caught up with American constitutional law in the protection of human rights." Dubber, *Toward a Constitutional Law of Crime and Punishment* (2004) 22, 4

[18] Sweet, *All Things in Proportion?* (2010); Dubber, *Toward a Constitutional Law of Crime and Punishment* (2004); Jackson, *Constitutional Law in an Age of Proportionality* (2015)

[19] Dubber, *A Political Theory of Criminal Law* (2004) 7 ("A legitimation gap remains, as a perverse sort of exceptionalism has exempted this, the most extreme, form of state governance from principled scrutiny."); Dubber, *Toward a Constitutional Law of Crime and Punishment* (2004); Dubber, *Policing Possession* (2001); Stuntz, *The Pathological Politics of Criminal Law* (2001); Kadish, *Fifty Years of Criminal Law: An Opinionated Review* (1999); Finkelstein, *Positivism and the Notion of an Offense* (2000)

academic research into comparative constitutional law, and what scholars have called the "gradual manifestation of an underlying universal, ultimate rule of law."[20]

The U.S. Supreme Court's increasing reliance on international and comparative law[21] is symptomatic of this global convergence around constitutional principles. So is the growing popularity of proportionality analysis in constitutional adjudication, not to mention the ever-expanding reach of the right to privacy. This expansion is a sure sign of the increasing acceptance of natural rights, and the evolving conception of rights is another indicator.

The past 100 years American law has gone from understanding rights as either absolute or non-existent towards an interpretation more in line with the Global Model of Constitutional Rights, where they are understood as "optimization requirements."[22] Because American lawyers remain constrained by the precedent that has accumulated under a system of arbitrary law, the authority of the fundamental rights doctrine still lingers. But even if the American system has a way to go before it catches up with international trends there is most definitely a movement in this direction. A certain indicator is those occasions when the Supreme Court will abandon its own doctrines to provide some meaningful standard of protection, like it did *in Casey*[23] and *Lawrence*.[24] In cases like these, we

---

[20] Bomhoff, *Genealogies of Balancing as Discourse* (2010) 109

[21] See, e.g., *Roper v. Simmons*, 543 U.S. 551, 576-77 (2005); *Lawrence v. Texas*, 539 U.S. 558, 576–77 (2003); *Atkins v. Virginia*, 536 U.S. 304, 317 n.21 (2002). See also Hirschl, *The Rise of Comparative Constitutional Law* (2008); Huhn, *The Jurisprudential Revolution* (2004) 20-21 ("The language of the *Casey* plurality, adopted by a majority of the Court in *Lawrence*, implies a universal understanding of human dignity that would turn the Constitution from a being a social contract with specific, determinative meanings into a statement of universal fundamental principles which are nevertheless binding upon our government.")

[22] The idea is that rights are comparable to principles and that the goal of rights is to provide as much autonomy, liberty, etc., as possible when weighed against the government's obligation to advance and protect the rights and interests of others. The term "optimization requirements" originated with Robert Alexy. See ALEXY, *A THEORY OF CONSTITUTIONAL RIGHTS* (2002); MÖLLER, *THE GLOBAL MODEL OF CONSTITUTIONAL RIGHTS* (2012)

[23] The *Casey* Court held that the balancing approach was superior to the two-tiered approach because the liberty protected by the Fourteenth Amendment must be viewed on a continuum which balances the citizen's need for freedom of action against the state's justification for intervention. *Planned Parenthood v. Casey*, 505 U.S. 833 (1992)

[24] The *Lawrence* Court ignored the fundamental rights framework and instead, reasoning from a presumption of liberty, concluded that the state interest was insufficient to justify a prohibition on sodomy. *Lawrence v. Texas*, 539 U.S. 558 (2003)

see the Court reconnecting with first principles to provide proper analysis, and we can expect the justices to continue moving forward until they are ready draw consistently on fundamental principles.

Historically we see a contraction and expansion, contraction and expansion. The court may take one step forwards, one step back, one step forward one step back, but we are not at a standstill. In the larger frame, we see that there is an evolution—and that for each cycle, society is calibrated towards a state of harmony with the principles of law.

Over the course of constitutional history, therefore, we see that the substantive core of the Constitution, its objective to protect the inherent and inalienable dignity of the person, is increasingly being recognized. With *Atkins*[25] it was recognized as being at the heart of the Eighth Amendment's Cruel and Unusual Punishments Clause, and with *Lawrence* it was accepted as constituting the essence of the Fifth and Fourteenth Amendments' Due Process Clause. One day we can expect the Court to recognize it as permeating the entire Constitution, for as Dubber noted, the principle of human dignity "underlies not only the protection against cruel and unusual punishments and the guarantee of due process of law, but the Constitution, and in fact the American system of government, as a whole. What is at stake is the basic principle of legitimacy of the American state, and of all modern liberal states: autonomy, or self-determination."[26]

Only to the extent that we recognize the full scope of this principle and work out "its implications for the criminal process in all of its aspects,"[27] will our system of law will be worthy of FC status. In this regard, we are not speaking of a "dignity" that can be defined according to the whims of NC individuals. It is not a social or collective dignity, one that can be defined in terms of "the dignity of living in a drug free world," "the dignity of state," or "the dignity of a superior race."[28] Instead, it is a dignity that speaks to the inviolate nature of each human being, one that is fundamentally entwined with the concept of autonomy and free will. It is the kind of dignity from which follows a right to equal

---

[25] *Atkins v. Virginia*, 536 U.S. 304 (2002)

[26] Dubber, *Toward a Constitutional Law of Crime and Punishment* (2004) 8

[27] Ibid.

[28] For more on why the FC conception of dignity outweighs the competing view of communitarian virtue as dignity, see Buchhandler-Raphael, *Drugs, Dignity, and Danger* (2012)

respect and concern and to be free of all undue infringements. And it is the kind of dignity from which the FC conception of justice and the rule of law draw their meaning. It exists independently of social hierarchy and social institutions, just as it exists independently of state boundaries and state laws. And as Dubber noted, to the extent "we recognize the basis of human dignity in the concept of the person, understood as an individual possessed of the capacity for autonomy, or self-government, the connection between the challenge of constitutional criminal law in the United States and in other legal systems, as well as in international law, becomes clear."[29]

As we become proficient at FC reasoning, we are moving from a fragmented understanding towards one that is holistic, and because of this increasing recognition of the inherent dignity of man, the world's legal systems are being calibrated towards a state of coherence and harmony. It is entirely logical, as the principles, ideals, and values found at the FC-end reflect on each other. They are the larger-than-life conceptions that will transform our society into Utopia if we let them. And as the principles of law are intimately connected with this concept of human dignity, it is only natural that as our understanding and appreciation grows, not only is the concept of dignity being filled with substantive meaning and value, but the principles of law are allowed to inform our legal systems.

Furthermore, the extent to which human dignity is recognized and filled with substantive content being a sign of how far a society has advanced towards the FC-end, it is interesting to note that the American system of law lag behind those that abide by doctrines of international human rights law.[30] The American criminal justice system is qualitatively

---

[29] Dubber, *Toward a Constitutional Law of Crime and Punishment* (2004) 8

[30] Lollini, *The South African Constitutional Court Experience* (2012); Sweet, *All Things in Proportion?* (2010); Gur-Arye & Weigend, *Constitutional Review of Criminal Prohibitions Affecting Human Dignity and Liberty* (2011); Dubber, *Toward a Constitutional Law of Crime and Punishment* (2004); Kumm, *Democracy is not enough* (2009); Kumm, *The Idea of Socratic Contestation and the Right to Justification* (2010); European Commission for Democracy Through Law, *European and U.S. Constitutionalism* (2003) 16 ("although the term "human dignity" is used restrictively by both the U.S. Supreme Court and the European Court of Human Rights, the concept of human dignity seems to play a significantly larger role in Europe."); HUSAK, *OVERCRIMINALIZATION* (2008) 138 ("It is clear . . . that . . . the Canadian Charter of rights and Freedoms . . . has produced more in the way of substantive restrictions on criminalization than anything in the United States Constitution.")

different from not only the European but most civilized countries', and it will comparatively come up short on most FC indicators. While this book has focused on the U.S. system's incompatibility with first principles, the general trend is no less striking. Despite comprising only five percent of the global population, the United States holds one-quarter of the world's incarcerated population. More than 7 million people are under the control of the criminal justice system, with 2, 2 million behind bars. The result is that American rates of imprisonment run at nearly ten times the per capita rate in any other Western country. Not only will Americans punish more often, but they also punish more harshly. Prison sentences are between five to ten times as long as sentences for comparable offences in Germany and France, and almost one in every ten prison inmates in the U.S. is serving a life sentence. In some states, including California and New York, that proportion approximates one in five.[31]

Why this grand scheme of incapacitation?[32] Why this failure to respect the rule of law as envisioned by the Founding Fathers?

The phenomenon of overcriminalization is duly noted by scholars and some will point to the American Constitution as a source of the problem.[33] Professor Stuntz, for instance, has criticized its framers for failing to put clearer limits on the criminal law, noting that they seemed more concerned with procedure than substance. Now, a case can be made that the U.S. Constitution is not flawless in this regard and that Americans would have been better off if the founders, like the framers of the French Declaration of Rights, more visibly had outlined the limits of substantive

---

[31] "Between 1972 and 2003, the national prison population rose by 500%. There were approximately 330,000 individuals in America's prisons and jails in 1973 which amounted to approximately 160 inmates per every 100,000 people in the United States. Over the next three decades, the number of inmates and the rate per 100,000 Americans steadily climbed. In 1985, 313 per 100,000 people were incarcerated. By 1995, the rate had risen to 601 per 100,000 people. In its most recent estimate at mid-year 2005, the Bureau of Justice Statistics placed the rate at 738 prison and jail inmates per 100,000 people. As a result of the increase in the prison population, the United States was required to open the equivalent of one prison per week during the period from 1985 to 2000. The cost of locking up an offender for a single year exceeds $22,000. In some states, the cost is double that amount. All told, the United States spends approximately $60 billion annually on corrections." Gershowitz, *An Informational Approach to the Mass Imprisonment Problem* (2008) 53

[32] Dubber, *Policing Possession* (2001) 958

[33] STUNTZ, *THE COLLAPSE OF AMERICAN CRIMINAL JUSTICE* (2013); Stuntz, *The Pathological Politics of Criminal Law* (2001); Dubber, *Policing Possession* (2001)

law.[34] However, as we have seen, the French Declaration was quickly rewritten into a more "government-friendly" version, and there is no reason to believe that a more substantive-oriented constitution would have saved American law from its embarrassing voyage. There is, after all, no way for a system of principled law to satisfy the ambitions of those in charge of NC societies. And as passion, not reason, is the most influential factor in the shaping of such societies a system of principled law, no matter how carefully designed, could not possibly have survived. One way or another, by constitutional amendment or simply interpreting it to their own liking, the proponents of arbitrary government would have found a way to ensure that the original FC document was turned into one they could use for their own ends.[35]

The proof is in the pudding, as this is what they have done. Any conscientious and informed reading of the Constitution would have interpreted it in light of the founders' political theory, and whenever controversial or difficult issues arose the justices should have "frequently

---

[34] The French Declaration of the Rights of Man and the Citizen did away with the *Ancién Regime* and its provisions were to set the record straight for all time. To begin with its Preamble recognized that "ignorance, neglect, or contempt of the rights of man are the sole cause of public calamities and of the corruption of governments." Therefore, to ensure the happiness of all, a solemn declaration of "the natural, unalienable, and sacred rights of man" was put forth in order to remind all members of the Social Body of their rights and duties, to limit the powers of government, and to provide a platform for "grievances of the citizens, based upon simple and incontestable principles."

These principles should, by now, be familiar. Article 1 held that all "Men are born and remain free and equal in rights," while Article 2 stated that "The aim of all political association is the preservation of the natural and imprescriptible rights of man. These rights are liberty, property, security, and resistance to oppression." When it came to the criminal law, Article 4 held that "Liberty consists in the power to do anything that does not injure others; accordingly, the exercise of the natural rights of each man has no limits except those that secure to the other members of society the enjoyment of these same rights. These limits can be determined only by law." Article 5 emphasized that "the law has the right to forbid only such actions as are injurious to society," while Article 7 made it clear that those officials who failed to honor the natural rights of the citizen by enacting or upholding arbitrary and unjust laws should be punished for their transgressions. To make it clear what kind of laws the Declaration frowned upon, (those who would subject its "procurers, expediters, and executors" to punishment) Article 8 stated that this would be all those criminal codes which were not "strictly and obviously necessary." Furthermore, Article 9 established a presumption of innocence (i.e., liberty) and a principle of proportionality. The principle of equality had already been articulated in Article 1 (and restated in Article 6), and with that the French had put in place a Declaration that would strike fear in the hearts of tyrants.

[35] If this is true—and logic dictates that it is—then, as Stuntz observed, "[t]he Bill of Rights has not endured thanks to its success at the enterprise of constraining government power. More likely, its long legal life stems from its failure." STUNTZ, *THE COLLAPSE OF AMERICAN CRIMINAL JUSTICE* (2013) 85

returned to fundamental principles." Had this been done, it would have been quite clear what kind of limits it provided to the police power, but because this would prove unacceptable to the ruling elites such a reading has been thwarted by the courts.

We can see from this that there is nothing wrong with the American Constitution. It will work just fine if we leave interpretation to FC individuals and whatever problems persist is owed to the fact that it has been left to NC individuals to make sense of things. As long as this is the case, it doesn't matter whether we go with the American or international system of human rights law. NC individuals will take the spirit of both and turn them into authoritarian endeavors—and while the latter has some ideological purity that remains uncorrupted by NC doctrine, there is no shortage of examples that also this system is a ruse.[36]

The legal protection can be no better than that offered by the constitutional courts, committees, and tribunals established in its name, and whenever push comes to shove we find that institutions such as the Canadian Supreme Court, the Norwegian Supreme Court, the German Constitutional Court, the European Court of Human Rights, the United Nation's Human Rights Committee, and so on, will abandon principled reasoning to shield the totalitarian projects of the state from review. Just like American courts have denied drug users a fair trial, so also these institutions can be counted upon to do the same. Thus, while scholars continue to debate whether or not America needs a new constitution, their focus is misdirected. All it takes for the American system of law to provide proper constitutional protection is better judges—and unless we have better judges no amount of remodeling will make a difference.

---

[36] See MIKALSEN, *HUMAN RISING* (2020)

12

THE PROBLEM WITH THE STATUS QUO

"The intrusion of government . . . is symptomatic of the disease of this society. As the years pass the power of government becomes more and more pervasive. It is a power to suffocate both people and causes. Those in power, whatever their politics, want only to perpetuate it."[37]

—Justice Douglas—

SINCE THE 1950S, AN array of FC scholars—Rawls, Dworkin, Gewirth, Sen, Husak, and Barnett, just to name a few—have written lucidly on the demands of a just society. They have provided us with the conceptual framework needed for thriving and their theoretical constructs are within the requirements for FC status. In other words, I am not the first to define the parameters of social interaction in more evolved societies—and yet we have failed to heed their advice.

Looking at this superficially, one could be amazed at our systemic refusal to support and build on those very constructs that would advance the demands of justice. The scholars mentioned are but a fraction of the world's FC scholars and if our officials really wanted to represent the values they swear allegiance to, one would expect them not only to provide lip-service but to *give effect* to the fundamental principles of justice. One would expect them to keep in mind the old adage that that government is best which governs the least; to welcome principled limits on government; to encourage individual autonomy; to support the advance of human rights; to be eager to provide us with an effective remedy whenever allegations of rights-violations were brought to their attention; to provide effective barriers against the undue influence of

---

[37] *United States v. Caldwell*, 408 U.S. 665 (1972); *Branzenburg v. Hayes*, 408 U.S. 665 (1972)

special interest groups; to do away with cultures of impunity; and to ensure that the police power would remain bound by first principles.

One would, in short, expect them to honor those barriers the founders put in place to protect against tyranny. One would expect them to be mindful of their role as civil servants. And one would expect them to be happy to provide a valid justification if constitutional issues such as the legality of the drug laws were disputed. This would, after all, be *the only* way to respond successfully to the problems that plague NC societies—wars, corruption, abuse of power, unjust societal structures, arbitrary law, capricious government, dysfunctional and discriminating policies, and so on. If our officials really wanted what was best for society, if they—as they should be—were always looking for ways to improve the status quo to ensure that that framework which best served human growth and welfare, they would have worked diligently to give this higher version of law its due. They would have welcomed analysis that took a broader view, and, in matters of dispute, they would have gone back to first principles.

This, however, is not what happens. Whenever FC scholars point out the deficiencies of the status quo; whenever they point to the false doctrines of the Supreme Court, the abuse of power, and the extent to which we fail to live by our ideals, they are ignored. And when more vocal critiques of the distance between theory and practice erupt (as when human rights activism proliferates, and the status quo becomes pressed) our officials will respond with brute force. Why is this?

To find the answer we need merely look to our position on the FC/NC model. It is in the nature of things that the quality of our civil servants will reflect the quality of the social fabric. We have already discussed the influence of the collective consciousness and how it holds us in its grip. We have seen psychologists describe the power of situational forces over individual minds, and while a few will have sufficient integrity to go against the grain, the majority will follow the system's force of inertia. They will, in other words, conform to the expectations of the status quo, whatever they might be.

We see from this that the system is rigged towards ensuring its own survival. The prospect will be to preserve the status quo and depending on the quality of the collective consciousness, it will reward FC or NC traits. It will be one or the other and, depending on its quality, the masses will on autopilot embrace one or the other. Indeed, thoughts are like matter; the more mass, the greater their gravitational force. Consequently, the more commonly shared our beliefs, the less we tend to question them and the more difficult it will be for individual minds to leave them behind.

Thus, if we wonder why our system of law is not better than it is; why it fails to live up to its potential; why our government fails to live up to its; and why the justices at the Supreme Court fail to live up to theirs; the reason is simple: It is because we all, collectively speaking, fail to live up to ours. Humanity, after all, is one organism. Our officials respond to the prevailing mindset, and to the extent citizens would take FC ideals and values seriously so would our officials.

Looking at this, it becomes clear that just as humanity would do better with another class of civil servants, so would the principles of justice do better with another people. Our officials' disregard for first principles mirrors our own—and in all cases the problem is a lack of understanding (or respect) for those values, principles, and ideals to which we pay lip-service. Despite our constitutional pledge to the contrary, we live in a society firmly entrenched in the NC mindset, and so every time our officials are faced with an opportunity to help society move forward, they will feel the pressure of conforming to the expectations of the status quo.

Hence, it is clear why public officials tend to fight the natural movement towards the FC State by being loyal to the unprincipled version of law that we are so familiar with. The FC/NC model indicates that the further we go towards the NC-end, the more the psychology of fear will set the standard for their performance and the less they will be guided by the principles, ideals, and values that follow from the Wholeness perspective. It does not matter how pitiful, misleading, or incoherent the logic that sustains the status quo: They will cling on to it no matter what, and to the extent that the status quo is incompatible with reason truth will be their enemy.

We do not need to look to Stalin's Soviet Union, Mao's China, Pol Pot's Cambodia, or Hitler's Germany to see the eagerness with which the majority will abandon reason for madness. We see it clearly in our culture and its mindless embrace of the War on Drugs and the War on Terror. Our officials can be counted on to defend these campaigns no matter what. They will ignore the dictates of reason and the rule of law to shield them from principled review, and no matter how much death and tragedy that may follow in their wake—and no matter how overwhelming the evidence against them—our officials will stand firm with these campaigns in their denial of reality.

It is in the cards that most people will not see this. Only to the extent that the world is seen from the FC perspective will it be obvious. But for those who exist at this level of affairs—and who are committed to the realization of FC ideals, principles, and values—this can be rather frustrating. As seen from this perspective, we live in a state of collective schizophrenia where our officials, on the one hand, talk affectionately about popular sovereignty, rule of law, shared values, human rights, and so on, but whenever we want to ensure that these words are filled with meaning, the very same officials will avoid serious debate. For some reason, if forced to choose between theory and practice, they will work diligently to ensure the survival of the status quo. And while the masses remain too oblivious to care, FC individuals are left pondering if this is for reasons of ignorance or arrogance.

12.1 IGNORANCE AND ARROGANCE: THE PRESERVERS OF THE STATUS QUO

It must be one or the other. Speaking of the drug laws and the tenacity with which our officials have held meaningful review at bay, it is undeniable that they have violated their constitutional oath and official duties. Law, as Lon Fuller noted, is a "purposeful enterprise" and its legality will be measured by the extent to which it fulfills its purpose. As seen there is no shortage of scholars who will testify that the drug law has been to the detriment of humanity, and any official who is not more concerned with protecting the interests of gangsters and war profiteers would want to see the issue resolved. Why then has the state worked to avoid evidentiary hearings? What kind of officials would argue against such a thing? Why would they not want to have the issue properly reviewed? Do they not care whether laws that criminalize 20 percent of the population can be defended? Do they not care if millions of people rot away in the criminal justice system for no good reason? Have they no respect for the morality of the law, the integrity of the Constitution, or the people they serve?

Our officials, no doubt, will assure us that they care deeply about all of this. However, actions speak louder than words—and we can see that the answer is in the negative. Despite the fact that scholars have described the history of the drug law as "a case study in legislative carelessness," one that presents us with "near comic examples of dereliction of legislative responsibility,"[38] the drug law has continued to this day supported by nothing but flawed assumptions, misleading and/or irrelevant statistics, and an amazing dedication to ignorance. Why is this?

At best this irrational and unlawful behavior is explained by the psychological incentives previously described, those which ensure that people will deny reality to protect dysfunctional moral codes and their view of themselves as crusaders for a worthy cause. In all likelihood this—the power of myth and the psychic costs of admitting failure—is the primary reason why drug prohibition is allowed to endure. Ignorance therefore (or more specifically, *the will* to ignorance) is most definitely a factor. However, it is unlikely to account for all the momentum that has ensured the survival of the prohibition ideology. From the social dynamics that define NC societies we know that the further towards the NC-end, the more certain it is that spineless individuals with psychopathic traits will rise to the top. And considering that so many officials privately agree that prohibition has failed while they publicly endorse these policies,[39] we must also factor in a lack of integrity and disregard for the welfare of humanity.

To the extent ignorance is not a factor, the arrogance of power will have to explain their behaviors, as drug prohibition is a NC politician's wet dream.[40] No doubt this must account for the eagerness with which the

---

[38] Bonnie & Whitebread, *The Forbidden Fruit and the Tree of Knowledge* (1970) 1054, 1053

[39] As Julian Chritchley, the former director of the UK Anti-Drug Coordination Unit observed: "What [I think] was truly depressing about my time in the civil service was that the professionals I met from every sector held the same view: the illegality of drugs causes far more problems for society and the individual than it solves. Yet, publicly, all those people were forced to repeat the mantra that the government would be 'tough on drugs,' even though they all knew that the policy was causing harm." MIKALSEN, *TO END A WAR* (2015) 79

[40] As Miller noted: "A goal that cannot be achieved, progress that cannot be measured, results for which no one can be held accountable, and billions of dollars to be gained from the whole thing. Such is the strategy that produces more and more drug warriors. Awesome power is

prohibition ideology is endorsed. No doubt also vested interest must account for the extent to which it has been shielded from review.

However, there is another possibility. This is the possibility that drug prohibition is not merely some badly drawn plan, a capricious and ungainly attempt to do good. Because we live in a NC society, we must be prepared for the eventuality that drug prohibition has functioned *exactly as planned*, and that it works just as those in charge intended. Scholars, after all, have noted that the first drug laws were motivated by the need to control populations, and there is the distinct possibility that the War on Drugs has continued as part of a deliberate scheme of rights demolition.

12.2 SOCIAL ENGINEERING 101

Now, even though most people will have great difficulty imagining this scenario, it cannot be completely ruled out. Like I said, the further we go towards the NC-end, the more certain it is that individuals with psychopathic tendencies will rise to the top and their number one goal will be to work out schemes of control. As Henry Kissinger once noted, "power is the ultimate aphrodisiac", and provided that a network of control-oriented individuals has sufficient influence, they will be interested in social engineering for their own ends. The recipe is simple, for the further towards the NC-end a society is found, the easier it will be for rulers to consolidate power. The closer to this end, the more pliable the populace will be, for the more they will be driven by unconscious fears rather than lucid thinking and the greater and more profound will be their will to denial. As discussed in part one, it is only when power is wedded with chronic fear that it becomes formidable, and it would be extremely naïve to believe that rulers are unaware of this simple equation.[41]

---

wielded by individuals and institutions who would feel harm if the drug problem diminished, who gain by perpetuating policies that strengthen the illicit drug trade." MILLER, *THE CASE FOR LEGALIZING DRUGS* (1991) 107

[41] At the very least, the Founders were well aware of it. As Thomas Paine wrote: "War is the common harvest of all those who participate in the division and expenditure of public money, in all countries. It is the art of conquering at home; the object of it is to increase revenue; and as

Hence, provided that a cabal of elites is sufficiently dedicated to this task, all they have to do is to fill the collective psyche with fear. To the extent this is done, their mission will be successful, and it is for this reason that FC individuals are watchful of enemy images. Without the energy they provide people would follow their natural inclination for cooperation and companionship, and society would become more freedom- than control-oriented. If humanity would follow its natural drive towards the FC-end, the game would be up for those with an agenda of domination, and it is for this reason that elites in NC societies tend to be more interested in social engineering for destructive rather than constructive purposes.

When it comes to this, the FC/NC model is the only map to go by and the choice engineers have to make is whether to move society in one direction or the other. To the extent that we have any interest in the conscious manipulation and formation of society, this is easy to do, and the only question will be to what kind of society we are committed. Do we want a system that values human dignity, respects individual freedom, and breeds responsible, autonomous, and socially concerned citizens? Or do we prefer the opposite; a system breeding weak-minded, fearful, senseless, naïve, and heteronymous individuals, increasingly infantilizing policies, and more and more unlimited state power?

There is no third option. Hence, if social engineers want to create a better world, they need only encourage FC traits through education, media outlets, and the system of law, but if they want to move us towards the NC-end, they must do the opposite. The most efficient way to do this would be to encourage fear, powerlessness, and aggression by (1) promoting the worldview of Neo-Darwinian theory and organized religion, thus making people believe in their hearts that they are worth-less, sinful, depraved, and abandoned beings, left to fend for themselves in a Universe that does not care; (2) by meddling with other countries' internal affairs in pursuit of profits, resources and power-political ambitions; (3) by secretly financing, training, and supporting extremist movements around the world; (4) by rejecting responsibility for the

---

revenue cannot be increased without taxes, a pretence must be made for expenditures. In reviewing the history of . . . Government, its wars and its taxes, a bystander, not blinded by prejudice nor warped by interest, would declare that taxes were not raised to carry on wars, but that wars were raised to carry on taxes." PAINE, *RIGHTS OF MAN* (1996) 42

consequences when a certain percentage of the robbed, occupied, frustrated, and humiliated population (or their own trained and financed extremist groups) lash back with suicide bombings and other violent behavior; and (5) by filling the newspapers and televisions with propaganda, lies, and fear-porn to nourish enemy images and keep the population sedated.

In short, NC leaders need only continue to follow the same old recipe on which they appear to have cooked their sinister brew for hundreds of years. I say "appear," for this has been the way of the world to this day and there are reasons to believe that our society has been engineered for quite some time. As Edward Bernays, Freud's nephew and a social engineer for the elite, wrote in the 1920s:

> "The conscious and intelligent manipulation of the organized habits and opinions of the masses is an important element in democratic society. Those who manipulate this unseen mechanism of society constitute an invisible Government which is the true ruling power of our country. . . . We are governed, our minds are molded, our tastes formed, our ideas suggested, largely by men we have never heard of.
>
> This is a logical result of how our democratic society is organized. Vast numbers of human beings must cooperate in this manner if they are to live together as a smoothly functioning society. . . . In almost every act of our daily lives, whether in the sphere of politics or business, in our social conduct or our ethical thinking, we are dominated by the relatively small number of persons who understand the mental processes and social patterns of the masses. It is they who pull the wires which control the public mind."[42]

To the extent that these people want to control the populace, they only need to keep feeding us the idea that we are the good guys; that our leaders' designated enemies are the bad guys; that our lifestyle and everything we hold dear is threatened by them; and that we need our leaders to protect us. In the world of NC affairs, it is as simple as that, as the majority will eagerly—indeed blindly—accept their authorities' version of events. The reason for this is that NC people are extremely easy to manipulate. Like children need to believe that their parents are

---

[42] BERNAYS, *PROPAGANDA* (1928) Chapter One

good, so NC individuals need to believe in some authority outside themselves. They need to believe that the state is their benevolent protector, the representative of all things good and decent, as the alternative is too terrible to consider.

Hence, they cannot afford to think about things. No matter how perverted, their authorities' moral code will have to be integrated and accepted as their own, and so it is that they will robotically pursue any task, no matter how offensive to reason. This is the power of the collective unconscious. Critical thinking comes at a psychic cost few are willing to pay, and to keep any rational assessment at bay authority will appeal to their sense of patriotism.[43]

To the extent elites succeed in such tactics, the population will be a misinformed, fearful, and easily manipulated breed. Furthermore, their likelihood of success will be proportional to the extent to which a society exists at the NC-end. Just as there is a correlation between freedom and responsibility at the FC-end, so the same goes for trauma and the defense mechanism of denial at the NC-end. There is a dichotomy between freedom/responsibility and trauma/denial, and just as we find a maximum amount of mental health at the FC-end, so we will find an accumulation of pathology at the NC-end. Hence, the ability of control-oriented elites' to define reality on their terms will be proportional to the trauma they can inflict on the individual/collective mind.

All this is well known to social engineers. The science of social control and the working dynamics of mass-psychology is probably thousands of years old, and while it may be difficult to believe that social engineers are active today, manipulating events behind the scenes, it is a possibility that should not be dismissed.

---

[43] As Hermann Goering, Hitler's second in command, said at the Nuremberg trial: "Why of course people don't want war. But after all it's the leaders of the country who determine the policy, and it is always a simple matter to drag the people along, whether it is a democracy, a fascist dictatorship, or a parliament or a communist dictatorship. . . . Voice or no voice, the people can always be brought to the bidding of the leaders. That is easy. All you have to do is to tell them they are being attacked, and denounce the pacifists for lack of patriotism and exposing the country to danger. It works the same in any country." Nuremberg Diary, April 18, 1946

"So, there are questions that need to be posed: Has the government of the United States of America become a criminal enterprise? Is the nation ruled by psychopaths?"[44]

—Professor John Kozy—

Now, as social engineering for destructive purposes can only be successful to the extent that the populace remains unaware, it is self-evident that authority will want to keep it hidden. It is also in the nature of things that NC individuals will not want to hear of it, as the possibility would be too horrendous to consider. Even so, while it may be uncomfortable to contemplate the possibility, the founders them-selves were conspiracy theorists and they feared that control-oriented elite factions would succeed in their mission to "separate the people from their government."[45]

Perhaps their fears were misplaced, perhaps not. In the spirit of the founders, however, we should be open to the possibility. It is evident that something has gone terribly wrong with the American Dream and there is evidence to suggest that it could be by design. In part two we saw that a centuries-old secret society fraternity had gone public, stating that "the real problem, and the ultimate root cause of corruption of the legal system, is the practice of infiltration and fraternal control by secret societies from the 15th century, whose agendas became even more aggressive from the 18th century, and escalated to being shamelessly obvious by the 21st century."[46]

It is indisputable that the American legal system has evolved under the stewardship of the Freemasons for the past 200 years, and according to the Knights Templar Order, the top levels of Freemasonry are "infiltrated by another secret society of 'elites' with highly negative agendas against humanity."[47] Like George Washington, the Templars

---

[44] Kozy, *The Psychopathic Criminal Enterprise Called America*, Global Research, June 4, 2010

[45] George Washington, letter to Reverend George Washington Snyder, October 24, 1798

[46] http://knightsofsolomon.org/templar-magna-carta/

[47] Ibid.

have referred to this group as the Illuminati, and while historians will tell us that this secret society group seized to exist at the end of the 18th century, there remains a distinct possibility that they could be wrong, or that other factions have taken their place. We just saw Edward Bernays discuss "[t]he conscious and intelligent manipulation of the organized habits and opinions of the masses" by "an invisible Government which is the true ruling power of our country," and he is not alone. If we are to believe President Woodrow Wilson, "some of the biggest men in the United States, in the field of commerce and manufacture . . . know that there is a power somewhere so organized, so subtle, so watchful, so interlocked, so complete, so pervasive, that they had better not speak above their breath when they speak in condemnation of it."[48] If we are to believe Caroll Quigley, Bill Clintons mentor and a professor of history at Georgetown University, "there does exist . . . an international Anglophile network which . . . wishes to remain unknown . . . [and whose] far-reaching aim [is] nothing less than to create a world system of financial control in private hands able to dominate the political system of each country and the economy of the world as a whole."[49] If we are to believe Theodore Roosevelt, the 26th President, this "invisible government . . . owe[s] no allegiance and acknowledge[s] no responsibility to the people," and "to destroy this unholy alliance between corrupt business and corrupt politics is the first task of the statesmanship of the day."[50] If we are to believe Winston Churchill, a British Prime minister during the Second World War, the agenda of "this band of extraordinary personalities from the underworld" is a "worldwide conspiracy for the overthrow of civilization and for the reconstitution of society on the basis of arrested development, of envious malevolence."[51]

If we are to believe Franklin Roosevelt, the 32nd President, this "element in the large centers has owned the government ever since the

---

[48] WILSON, *THE NEW FREEDOM* (1913) 13

[49] QUIGLEY, *TRAGEDY AND HOPE* (1966) 950, 324. According to Quigley, he knew of the operations of this network because he had "studied it for twenty years and was permitted for two years, in the early 1960's, to examine its papers and secret records." Ibid. 950

[50] ROOSEVELT, *AN AUTOBIOGRAPHY* (1913) (Appendix B)

[51] W. Churchill, *Zionism versus Bolshevism*, Illustrated Sunday Herald, 8. February 1920, p. 5. See also http://knightstemplarorder.org/secret-societies-debunked/

days of Andrew Jackson,"[52] and there are many others who have spoken in similar terms. At the Iran Contra hearings, for instance, Senator Daniel Inouye spoke of "a shadowy government with its own Air Force, its own Navy, its own fundraising mechanisms, and the ability to pursue its own ideas of the national interest, free from all checks and balances, and free from the law itself."[53] Another important whistleblower is General Fletcher Prouty, first Chief of Special Operations with President Kennedy's Joint Chiefs of Staff, who wrote a book about his interactions with a secret team of operatives. According to him, this "network was ancient and world-wide." It was the "functional element of the dominant power" and would "operate everywhere with the best of all supporting facilities from special weaponry and advanced communications, with the assurance that its members would never be prosecuted." This network would "topple government, create governments, and influence governments almost anywhere in the world;" it was lawless, and would "get the job done whether it had political authorization or not."[54]

Now, it boggles the mind, but let us remain open to the possibility that these people are sincere. Many other whistle-blowers have exposed the activities of this network,[55] so let us suppose that this cabal of elites is real and that they have an interest in manipulating our perception reality. For this to work they would have to control the power centres of society, which includes the secret services, the government apparatus, and the media. The testimony above indicates that this is so, but can we find further corroboration?

---

[52] Franklin D. Roosevelt, letter to Colonel Edward M. House, November 21, 1933

[53] Daniel Inouye, Chairman of the Senate Select Committee on Secret Military Assistance to Iran and the Nicaraguan Opposition, said this during the Iran Contra hearings.

[54] PROUTY, *THE SECRET TEAM* (2008)

[55] See LINDAUER, *EXTREME PREJUDICE* (2010); GRITZ, *A NATION BETRAYED* (1989); MENASHE, *PROFITS OF WAR* (1998); REED & CUMMINGS, *COMPROMISED: CLINTON, BUSH AND THE CIA* (1994); MARTIN, *THE CONSPIRATORS* (2002); PERKINS, *CONFESSIONS OF AN ECONOMIC HITMAN* (2004); O'BRIEN, *TRANCE-FORMATION OF AMERICA* (1995); STICH, *DEFRAUDING AMERICA* (1988); SUTTON, *AMERICA'S SECRET ESTABLISHMENT* (1986); GRIFFIN, *THE CREATURE FROM JEKYLL ISLAND* (2002); RUSSELL, *DRUG WAR: COVERT MONEY, POWER AND POLICY* (2000); MAZUR, *THE INFILTRATOR* (2009); KWITNY, *THE CRIMES OF PATRIOTS* (1987); RUPPERT, *CROSSING THE RUBICON* (2004); BENNETT, *SHELL GAME* (2013); TARPLEY, *911 SYNTHETIC TERROR* (2007); STONE, *THE MAN WHO KILLED KENNEDY: THE CASE AGAINST LBJ* (2013); VENTURA, *THEY KILLED OUR PRESIDENT* (2013); BLUM, *KILLING HOPE* (2003); WILLIAMS, *OPERATION GLADIO* (2015); AGEE, *INSIDE THE COMPANY: A CIA DIARY* (1975)

Again, this is not difficult. If we are to believe John F. Hylan, a former Mayor of New York City, this "coterie of powerful [individuals] virtually run the United States government for their own selfish purposes. They practically control both parties and the majority of the newspapers and magazines in this country. They use the columns of these papers to club into submission or drive out of office public officials who refuse to do the bidding of the powerful corrupt cliques which compose the invisible government. It operates under cover of a self-created screen [and] seizes our executive officers, legislative bodies, schools, courts, newspapers and every agency created for the public protection."[56]

Also from the secret services do we find whistle-blowers who can testify that that they are heavily corrupted by this force, that they are frequently pulling the strings behind the scenes, manipulating the media, training terrorists, arming them, operating as their handlers, etc.[57] And if we are to believe John Stockwell, one of the highest ranking CIA officers to tell his story, "it is the function of the CIA to keep the world unstable, and to propagandize and teach the American people to hate and to fear, so we will let the Establishment spend any amount of money on arms."[58]

Now, supposing that these people are sincere, there would have to be some kind of cover-up unit whose mission was to bury the truth every time it threatened to expose this secret network. Is there any evidence for this?

Yes. If we are to believe Al Martin, a lieutenant Commander attached to the Office of Naval Intelligence, he has written a book detailing the workings of a suppression unit in the Department of Justice that is "so powerful it reaches into all agencies."[59] If we are to believe Senator John DeCamp, he witnessed this cover-up unit in action when his senate committee investigated a corrupt financial institution in Nebraska. When

---

[56] Speech made in Chicago on March 26, 1922 and reported in the New York Times the following day in the article titled *Hylan Takes Stand on National Issues*. See also New York Times, *Hylan Adds Pinchot to Presidency List; Foresees a Revolt*, December 10, 1922

[57] TARPLEY, *911 SYNTHETIC TERROR* (2004); RUPPERT, *CROSSING THE RUBICON* (2004); KWITNY, *THE CRIMES OF PATRIOTS* (1987); MAAS, *MANHUNT* (1986); BENNETT, *SHELL GAME* (2013); WILLIAMS, *OPERATION GLADIO* (2015); AGEE, *INSIDE THE COMPANY: A CIA DIARY* (1975)

[58] Stockwell would state this during speeches. See also STOCKWELL, *THE PRAETORIAN GUARD* (1991); BUTLER, *WAR IS A RACKET* (2010); MELMAN, *THE PERMANENT WAR ECONOMY* (1985); MILLS, *THE POWER ELITE* (1956)

[59] MARTIN, *THE CONSPIRATORS* (2002) 19. More on this unit ibid. at 345-50

it was discovered that certain elites in Nebraska were also involved in drug smuggling, satanic rituals, and the trafficking of children, powerful forces began conspiring against the investigation. And as DeCamp later wrote:

> "Though there are no doubt other branches of the government where corruption flourishes, there is no question in my mind that the stench of evil which emanates from Washington originates in the so-called Department of Justice, particularly in its permanent bureaucracy. . . . In case after notorious case . . . Justice Department personnel appear as liars, perverts, frame-up artists, and even assassins."[60]

Again, it boggles the mind. But suppose that this cover-up unit exists and that it has the power to derail any official investigative effort into the real goings-on. If we take a closer look, we will find much to suggest that the committees which were set up to investigate the most controversial events in American history were either set up to fail or derailed,[61] and if this so, then this cabal of elites is powerful enough to define reality on their terms.

Having the power to manipulate events and define reality, these elites would most likely be interested in social engineering. To the extent that they are NC individuals they would want a society firmly entrenched in the extreme NC-end, and they would have an interest in how it most efficiently could be done. Is there any evidence of this?

Again, the answer is yes. If we are to believe Norman Dodd, the staff director for the 1953 Reece Committee, he found that the elites were very interested in war for social engineering purposes. Dodd gained unlimited access to the Carnegie Foundation's archives and after spending two weeks in the library and following the paper trail back to 1908, he discovered the following:

> "The trustees meeting for the first time, raised a specific question which they discussed throughout the balance of the year in a very

---

[60] DeCamp, *The Franklin Cover-Up* (1992) 293

[61] This includes the attempted fascist coup against Roosevelt in 1934, the assassination of John F. Kennedy and his brother Robert, the Iran Contra affair, the October Surprise, the USS Liberty event, and the 9/11 terrorist attacks.

learned fashion, and the question is: 'is there any means known more effective than war, assuming you wish to alter the life of an entire people?' And they conclude that no more effective means than war is known to humanity. So then, in 1909, they raised a second question and discussed it, namely: 'How do we involve the United States in a war?' . . . and finally they answered that question as follows: 'We must control the State Department.' And that naturally raised the question of how do we do that? And they answered it by saying: 'We must take over and control the diplomatic machinery of this country,' and finally they resolved to aim at that as an objective."[62]

Then came World War I and, despite public opinion to the contrary, America was successfully involved. Let us suppose, then, that this was the result of the elites' manipulation of events. If this is the case, they must be eager to control our perception of history, because, as Orwell once said, "He who controls the past controls the future." According to Dodd, the elites also thought of this. As he said:

"After the war their priorities shifted "over to preventing what they call a reversion of life in the United States to what it was prior to 1914, when World War I broke out. . . . And they come to the conclusion that to prevent a reversion we must control the education in the United States. And they realize that that is a pretty big task.   . . . It is too big to them alone, so they approach the Rockefeller Foundation with the suggestion that that portion of education that which could be considered domestic be handled by the Rockefeller Foundation, and that portion that which is international should be handled by the Endowment. And then they decide that the key to the success of these two operations lay in an alteration of the teaching of American history. So they approach four of the then most prominent teachers of American history in the country, people like Charles and Mary Beard, and their suggestion to them is: Will they alter the manner in which they present their subject? And they get turned down flat. So they then decide that it is necessary for them to do as they say 'build their own stable of historians,' and then they approach the Guggenheim Foundation which specializes in fellowships, and say: 'When we find

---

[62] Norman Dodd interview by Ed Griffin, 1982. Transcript at http://www.realityzone.com/hiddenagenda2.html

young men in the process of studying for doctorates in the field of American history, and we feel that they are the right caliber, will you grant them fellowships on our say so?' And the answer is yes. Under that condition they eventually assembled twenty historians . . . and that group of twenty historians eventually becomes the nucleus of the American Historical Association toward the end of the 1920'ies."[63]

Furthermore, assuming that Dodd is not making all this up and that elites are interested in war for social engineering purposes; if this is so, they would be interested in the production of enemy images. Is there evidence to support this?

Again, this is not difficult to find. If we are to believe Carol Rosin, who was a corporate manager at Fairchild Industries from 1974-77, she was "in a meeting in Fairchild Industries, in a conference room called 'The War Room,' and in that room were a lot of charts on the walls with enemies. Identified enemies, names that people had never heard of, names like Saddam Hussein and Qaddafi, but we were talking then about terrorists, the potential terrorists. No one had ever talked about this before, but this was the next stage after the Russians, of against whom we were going to build . . . weapons—these terrorists."[64]

Yes, it is unheard of. But if elites were contemplating the design of a War on Terror already back in the 1970s, could the events unfolding on 9/11 be part of their plot? Could it be a military false-flag operation

---

[63] Id. It is interesting to note that Beard later criticized the Rockefeller Foundation and its alter ego the Council on Foreign Relations for unduly influencing our perception of WW II events. See his article in the *Saturday Evening Post* for October 4, 1947, *Who's to Write the History of the War*?

As revealed by the Church and Pike Committee, the campaign for the control of our perception has only escalated in scope, and the infiltration of media and academia is well-documented. As pertains to the academia, the Church Committee found that the CIA, by 1975, had paid professors to write at least 1,000 books for propaganda purposes. And when Harvard University in 1980 tried to pass an internal regulation that required professors to report any relationship they had with the CIA, the CIA sued Harvard claiming a violation of the First Amendment and won the right to continue its propaganda operations. As Stockwell summarized the implications: "The result is that if you are researching the Vietnam War, for example, . . . a fair number of the books listed in your bibliography will be CIA propaganda pieces that deliberately misrepresent the facts." STOCKWELL, *THE PRAETORIAN GUARD* (1991) 101. See also GARWOOD, *UNDER COVER: THIRTY-FIVE YEARS OF CIA DECEPTION* (1985); GONZALEZ, *PSYCHOLOGICAL WARFARE AND THE NEW WORLD ORDER* (2010); Bernstein, *The CIA and the Media*, Rolling Stone, October 20, 1977

[64] Interview by Steven Greer. Transcript found at: http://www.bibliotecapleyades.net/exopolitica/esp_exopolitics_ZCab.htm

designed to traumatize the American psyche to the point where denial would be the common reaction? Could it, in other words, have been an intelligence *success* rather than failure?

Again, there is evidence that this could be so. If we are to believe Aaron Russo, a Hollywood producer who became friendly with Nicholas Rockefeller when he was running for Governor of Nevada, Rockefeller told him "eleven months before 9/11 ever happened that there was going to be an event, and out of that event they were going to invade Afghanistan and Iraq . . . that there was going to be this War on Terror, and the whole thing was a giant hoax, a way for the government to take over the American people."[65]

It is beyond the scope of this book to address the topic of 9/11 and the evidence of foul play.[66] Hence, we shall leave it be an open question if the elite factions that the founders so greatly feared have come to control the U.S. Government, just as I shall leave it be an open question whether 9/11 was their doing. However, there is a wealth of evidence that refutes the official story, and the government has sabotaged every effort to find out what really happened. Instead of encouraging truth, we have seen what we can expect from a state firmly entrenched at the NC level. It has used the events of 9/11 as an excuse for grabbing more and more power and for watering down our catalogue of rights. Predictably, government agents have exploited the level of fear that resulted from the attacks for these ends, while the enemy image of terrorism has been nourished and maintained by the media. This enemy image has not only served to legitimize a near doubling of defense expenditures, wars, and a new dawn for the military industrial complex, but it has ensured vast profits for numerous other profiteers, as well as an expansion of fear-driven bureaucracy. The mainstream media has not only aided and abetted by ignoring difficult questions and inconvenient truths, but it has

---

[65] Interview by Alex Jones 2009. Transcript found at http://twochurchesonly.com/volume-1/read.php?page=438

[66] For those who want more information, the website of organizations such as Architects and Engineers for 9/11 Truth (www.ae911truth.org) and Scholars For 9/11 Truth & Justice (www.stj911.org) is a good place to start. For a deeper presentation of behind-the-scenes politics and the events of this day, see www.veteranstoday.com. For well-researched literature, see RUPPERT, *CROSSING THE RUBICON* (2004); SCOTT (ED.), *9/11 AND AMERICAN EMPIRE: INTELLECTUALS SPEAK OUT* (2006); SCOTT, *THE ROAD TO 9/11* (2008); GRIFFIN, *9/11 CONTRADICTIONS* (2008); WOOD, *WHERE DID THE TOWERS GO? EVIDENCE OF DIRECTED FREE-ENERGY TECHNOLOGY ON 9/11* (2010)

helped quell dissent by painting those who question the official narrative as "unpatriotic" and "terrorist sympathizers."

In short, the War on Terror, just like the War on Drugs, has been a boon for the NC State. The parallels between the two campaigns are conspicuous to say the least, as closer scrutiny reveals nothing but smoke and mirrors. For one, the ideological foundation behind these campaigns cannot survive a rational debate. The more one investigates the premises behind both, the more obviously flawed the war mongers' rationale and the more suspicious is the eagerness with which they deny the evidence. Not only is the reality of these enemy images disputed, but even if drugs were all bad and Al-Qaeda terrorists were the sole perpetrators behind 9/11, the strategy is deeply flawed. It is inherent in their very design that these campaigns can never achieve their official objective. Just like the War on Drugs has produced more of the problems it was intended to stop, so the War on Terror has only succeeded in producing more terrorists—and as the official objectives cannot be met, one is bound to wonder if there are other, hidden motives. Secondly, the social dynamics generated by these campaigns are identical. The power of the enemy images tears the social fabric apart by weakening our positive inclinations and empowering our negative. They generate hostility, anxiety, distrust, powerlessness, and fearfulness, making people turn against each other and to their authorities for protection. Hence, it is only logical to be suspicious of the motives behind these campaigns. History, after all, attests that in the NC State control-oriented elites will always be in charge; that enemy images will always be their most efficient tool for keeping an unjust social structure in place; and it would be naïve to believe that the American system proves an exception to this rule.

For this reason, there is a possibility that there is more to these campaigns than meets the eye. Provided that elites are interested in social engineering for NC-ends, the War on Terror and the War on Drugs would be the perfect mechanisms for social control. Hence, responsible citizens will be open to the possibility that this could be one reason why these campaigns—our authorities' holy cows—are so uncritically embraced. When all is said and done, perhaps this is why they continue to be sheltered from meaningful review even though they, by their officially stated ends, are complete and unmitigated disasters.

13

THE AMERICAN PSYCHE: POTENTIAL UNFULFILLED

"You see, the danger is not a single politician with ill intent. Or even a group of them. The most dangerous thing any nation faces is a citizenry capable of trusting a liar to lead them."[67]

—Andy Andrews—

FROM WHAT WE HAVE seen, there are problems in America that not only legal scholars but everyone else should take seriously. The United States today is a wholly different country than the founders envisioned, and the corrupt legal and political system is a symptom of a much bigger problem—the National Psyche.

From the FC/NC model we can see that the quality of a society's body of law and political institutions will mirror the quality of the collective psyche and that a distance between theory and practice at the level of law and government will have its origin in this entity. It is inescapable that a distance between theory and practice at these levels must be a reflection of the extent to which we, collectively, refuse to live by the ideals and values we officially endorse. And this being so, the only reason why the distance between theory and practice escapes our attention is because of our ability to deceive ourselves. After all, if we were to take ourselves seriously, we would also take our ideals and values seriously, and so the disorder at the level of law and government can only endure to the extent that we delude ourselves.

---

[67] ANDY ANDREWS, *HOW DO YOU KILL 11 MILLION PEOPLE?* (2010) 42

Now, as the quip goes, "man's ability to deceive others is only surpassed by his ability to deceive himself" and so, to the extent that we live in denial, the distance between theory and practice will "not exist." Even so, it is clearly seen by those who operate at a higher level of psychological health—those who to a greater degree remain true to FC ideals, principles, and values. As seen from this perspective, this divide is an open wound that must be dealt with if society is to recover. It is, in a very real sense, a sign of mental sickness, and if we are to readjust the body of law and politics into one of conformity with first principles, our primary objective must be the healing of the Nation's psyche. To the extent this is done, all else follows. And we shall here, in closing, have more to say on the challenges facing America.

13.1 A Split Psyche

From the FC/NC model we can see (1) that the NC mindset is the source of humanity's tribulations and (2) that the extent to which this mindset has infected society will be mirrored in its structure. Hence, as the idea of America was a nation founded upon the principles, ideals, and values that attach to the Wholeness concept, the extent to which Americans have betrayed their own values, principles, and ideals is revealed in the structure of society.

Looking at this, the American society is one of the most unequal, hierarchical, authoritarian, and competition-oriented cultures on the planet. And while some will attribute this to the "American Dream," this is another testimony to the sickness that has taken hold of the American psyche. It goes without saying that only those who embrace the NC mindset will equal the promise of America with that of oligarchy, and to the degree that Big Media, politicians, and other snake-oil salesmen will have us believe that the founders' vision was that of an each-man-for-himself, dog-eat-dog world we should not only reevaluate the message but the messenger.

Throughout this book, we have been introduced to the weakness of NC reasoning and the extraordinary poor quality of our civil servants. True to the nature of the NC State their loyalty has been to the status quo rather than reason, and the obvious question becomes: Do we want these people to govern our affairs? Have we seen any indication that they are entitled to our trust? Do we want to see America continue in the direction it has been going? Is this the best that we can do?

A quick glance reveals that, despite the resurgence of FC reasoning, the system has been moving towards the NC-end in this period of time. The budgets for defense, police, and criminal justice programs have been increasing while other sectors are suffering. Not only are negative expenses escalating and positive spending trimmed down. Whatever services the government provides have gradually been transformed into milking cows for the elite, where the point is not so much to provide something of value but to ensure increasing revenue to contractors. As a result, whether it be healthcare, education, defense, or any other area, Americans pay more for poorer services. What we see is a government more and more servient to the expectations of Big Business while the people are left to fend for themselves. As a result, the superrich get richer, the middle class is shrinking, and more struggle to survive.[68] Is this a trend we want to see continue?

It is self-evident that no society can survive this dynamic for long, just as it is self-evident what needs to be done. On the one hand, it is easy to see that unless there is a change of direction what is left of the founders' America will collapse and open tyranny will ensue. On the other, it is equally plain that the problem contains the seeds to its own solution. It is, after all, just a repetition of the timeless scenario that we have seen unfolding so many times. It is the story of a society unguided by the values, principles, and ideals that follow from the Wholeness perspective. It is the tale of a people wildly adrift on the seas of the collective unconscious; of fearful, powerless, and ignorant individuals looking to "others" to save them; of "others" taking control of government; of the psychology of fear running its course; of the totalitarian force inherent in NC government becoming more prominent; of increasing paranoia and despondency; of a control-oriented elite

---

[68] While America's wealthiest 1 percent earned 10 percent of the total income in 1982, they now rake in more than 25 percent. They own more values than 95 percent of the population combined, and they have increased their salaries 275 percent since 1980. According to Forbes/CNBC the 400 richest Americans are now worth a combined $2 trillion, more than the net worth of half of all Americans.

devising devious schemes to stay in power; and of a people willing to embrace ever more desperate measures not to see what is going on. Collectively it is a mass-movement away from integrity, one where the individual "Self" is obliterated as the system's force of inertia becomes more powerful. As its momentum takes over, everything spins out of control, and the downward spiraling continues until the NC mindset has run its course. Then the cycle begins anew, until humanity has learned its lesson and understands the source of its problems.

In a very true sense, the NC mindset serves as a negative catalyst for change, as something new will be born out of the ashes of the old. It is just a question of how bad it will have to get until we wise up, collect ourselves, and embrace FC ideals, principles, and values. And while America is closing in on the point where it will collapse into tyranny, there is also a positive change in the air.

In no other country is the increasing polarity that accompanies end-game scenarios more clearly seen. On the one hand, a significant percentage still has faith in authority. We see their susceptibility to propaganda on surveys revealing that some 50 percent in 2004 believed that Saddam Hussein's regime was involved in the planning, execution, and financing of the 9/11 attacks; that some 50 percent in 2006 believed that weapons of mass destruction were found in Iraq (and that around 40 percent still believe it); that more than 50 percent still believe in the official story of 9/11; and that approximately 50 percent do not even know that a third building, WTC-7, also collapsed that day.

On the other hand, others are beginning to see the writing on the wall, suspecting their government to be a wolf in sheep's clothing. We see this trend in surveys telling us that "28 percent of American voters believe a secretive power elite with a globalist agenda is conspiring to eventually rule the world through an authoritarian world government, or New World Order;"[69] that only 30 percent believe the official story on the Kennedy assassination;[70] that roughly half of all Americans believe their government hides the truth about 9/11;[71] that only 28 percent of those who have seen the collapse of Building 7 believe the official story of that

---

[69] Public Policy Polling survey released in April 2013

[70] 60 Minutes/Vanity Fair poll for May 2015

[71] September 2013 survey by *YouGov Plc.*

event;[72] that 60 percent of Americans would favor an all-inclusive congressional overhaul—i.e., fire every single congressional representative if they could;[73] and that 68 percent of Republicans believe the 2020 election to be stolen by Biden.[74]

For better or worse, polls like these are worth noting. The American psyche is split between those living in denial and those on the alert, and that so many suspect foul play is a sign that the disconnect between theory and practice is becoming increasingly difficult to ignore. Another way to put it is that FC traits are emerging in the populace, as the archetypical NC individual will hardly notice the distance between the two. I say "hardly," as only the most naïve will truly believe that society conforms to the officially recognized standards of decency. Others may recognize that there is room for improvement but will (1) prefer not to think about it; (2) fail to act on it; or (3) actively work to sabotage FC efforts. These are all model NC responses, as they are motivated by ignorance, denial of responsibility, and the will to dominate others.

Now, we all share these traits—some more and some less. However, on some level, we will also be haunted by our acceptance of the status quo, and to the extent that we are, it will be our conscience—the inherent FC aspect of us—that seeks to spur us towards action, towards growth-potentials, and accepting greater responsibilities. We all have this FC voice within, and to the extent that we are willing to listen the road to FC status is quickly traveled. Part one elaborated on this bit. A previous book *Reason Is*, elaborates further, and as it is beyond the scope of this work to provide more detail on the psychological processes that shape NC and FC individuals (and turn the former into the latter), we shall focus on its implications for the American psyche—and the American project.

---

[72] Id.

[73] NBC/Wall Street Journal poll, 2013

[74] https://www.foxnews.com/politics/republicans-president-trump-robbed-poll

13.2 RECLAIMING OUR POTENTIAL

"Call to mind the sentiments which Nature has engraved in the heart of every citizen, and which take on a new force when they are solemnly recognized by all: For a nation to love liberty, it is sufficient that she knows it; and to be free, it is sufficient that she wills it." [75]

—Marquis De LaFayette—

The healing of the American psyche begins at the individual level with a simple choice: Do we want to see the world through FC or NC eyes? If we want to go with the latter, we need only obey any other authority than our own by letting fear, priests, politicians, mainstream media, mainstream scholars, etc., define our reality. Living as we do in a NC society, this is a sure way to continue feeding the energy that keeps the status quo in place. On the other hand, if we want to see the world through FC eyes, this is only possible to the extent that we are willing to question commonly held assumptions. How many people are willing to do this?

It is difficult to say. When it comes to those who still believe that drug prohibition is constitutionally sound; that Saddam Hussein had weapons of mass destruction; that Osama Bin Laden was the mastermind behind 9/11; that the dogmas of organized religion is a path to god or spiritual enlightenment; or that the Neo-Darwinian worldview must be the basis of science, chances are that many will not. Beliefs like these are more than addictive—they provide an existential footing. To abandon them is to let go of that which connects us to the NC Groupmind, and it takes quite an effort to move from this level of understanding to another. A certain percentage of the populace will therefore prefer to stick with what they "know," no matter what evidence exists to the contrary.

It is self-evident that to the extent the American people remains committed to this position, the founders' vision will become an ever more distant dream. These people have effectively abandoned reason and are those Hannah Arendt described as the ideal subjects of tyrannical rule. To the extent the United States is populated by people like this, all hope is lost for the founders' America. However, there are those for whom the

---

[75] PAINE, *RIGHTS OF MAN* (1996)

distinction between fact and fiction, truth and falsehood still holds relevance, and this percentage will question official truths—no matter the ramifications.

The fate of America, therefore, depends on the population that belongs to this category. Only FC traits can solve the Gordian knot that retards healthy progress, and it will be up to them to show others the meaning of integrity. They belong to a proud tradition, for throughout history it is these people who have moved society forward. They are the visionaries that hold up a mirror to society, showing the masses the folly of their ways. They are the ones who are courageous enough to embrace the unknown and to challenge the authority of the old. And they are the protagonists who will pursue the truth, no matter its costs. This is what they must always do, and when it comes to this quest history teaches us that the bigger the taboo, the more important it is to look behind the façade. Taboos indicate trauma, and while they constitute the greatest impediments to reaching the FC state, they also provide valuable opportunities for growth. There can be no healing of trauma unless we have the courage to face our fears—and there can be no achievement of FC status unless this is done.

Speaking of this, we have seen how the War on Drugs qualify as a traumatic event, one that makes people hide from the truth while it continues to inflict pain and misery. Even so, the War on Drugs is not the only wound on the American psyche in need of attention. For healing to be complete, we must also investigate the War on Terror, as the 9/11 attack, quite possibly, is the greatest trauma ever inflicted upon the American psyche. The irrational response that so often accompanies any attempt to bring light to this event is a testimony to the power of denial, for it is obvious that the government has something to hide and that people do not want to think about it. Alert citizens could think of a thousand unanswered questions on the subject of 9/11 alone, not to mention the Kennedy assassinations, Martin Luther King assassination, and the Iran Contra affair. And while only a few have been dedicated to digging into these deep-events, a significant percentage of the population—perhaps 50 percent—suspect that something is amiss.

This gives us a reason to be hopeful for the future. The ability to question authority is a certain indication that they have begun to let go of the NC Groupmind and this is the most difficult part. From there on the road to FC status becomes easier, and if you sit on the fence, not quite sure what to make of this and the questions alluded to above, try these for starters:

If the Government really wanted to eradicate terrorist groups like IS and Al Qaeda, why were Brad Birkenfeld, a UBS banker, imprisoned and gagged after informing US authorities that together with cell phones, hotel rooms, meeting dates, email addresses and other vital information he had solid information on 19,000 bank accounts which were used to finance terrorism?[76] If the War on Terror was a sincere effort to protect the homeland, why did US intelligence services, together with the Department of Justice, the State Department, the Senate Armed Services Committee, and the Senate Permanent Subcommittee on Investigations collude to make sure that none of Birkenfeld's information was passed on to the Army? If President Obama really wanted to win the War on Terror, why was he, as a member of the Senate Permanent Subcommittee in 2007, part of the effort to silence Birkenfeld?

If the Republicans and the Democrats weren't merely two wings of the same bird of prey, why did no one in Congress blow the whistle on these activities after being informed? If the media abided by its watchdog duty, why did CNN, Fox News, Wall Street Journal, USA Today, New York Times, Washington Post, L.A. Times, and other media outlets decide to bury this story? If the Bush Administration merely wanted to liberate Iraq, why was Susan Lindauer, the mediator between the American and Iraqi regime, imprisoned after reporting that Saddam had capitulated and that he would give the Americans anything they wanted—oil, rebuilding contracts, even democratic elections to avoid an invasion? And again, why did Congress and the media, after being contacted by Lindauer, stay silent on this issue?[77]

If the media can be trusted, why have mainstream media for years ignored the criminal enterprise that has become of the Democratic Party? Why have they ignored Tony Bobulinski, a business associate of the Biden family, who held a press conference before the 2020 election talking about Joe Biden's shady dealings with a Chinese spy chief and a business model based on "plausible deniability"? Why have they ignored

---

[76] For more on Birkenfeld and the attempts to silence him, see BENNETT, *SHELL GAME* (2013)

[77] LINDAUER, *EXTREME PREJUDICE* (2010)

Ukrainian officials who have attested to this corruption, and why have they ignored Patrick Byrne, former CEO of Overstock, who have tried to tell the American people that he assisted the FBI in a 2016 sting operation against Hillary Clinton, where she received a $18 million bribe. According to him, this was operation Snow Globe, but it was scrapped by the FBI, because as it was explained to him:

> "President Obama has his people across the federal bureaucracy at this point, but especially at the Department of Justice. Hillary Clinton is going to be President for 8 years and nothing is going to change that, but think of there being a Bunsen burner within the DOJ. That evidence about the bribes you were a part of gathering is going to be sitting on the Bunsen burner. The hand sitting on the burner is going to be one of Barack Obama's people. If Hillary is a "good girl" and defends Obamacare, that flame stays low. If she's a "bad girl" and thinks for herself, that flame is going to get turned up high. That way Barack Obama is going to manage Hillary Clinton for the 8 years she's President, and then when she steps down, Michelle is going to run."[78]

We have just begun scratching the surface. It is only so much a mind can take, and even if this is some of the more "polite" questions, they will be ignored by NC individuals. They open the rabbit hole to a terrifying dimension. Thus, to the extent that the collective unconscious controls and inhibits our reasoning, it will be difficult to contemplate their implications and psychological defense mechanisms ensure that they will be discounted.

---

[78] https://www.israelnationalnews.com/News/News.aspx/293156. According to Byrne, Snow Globe was a plan by CIA Director Brennan and President Obama to control Hillary Clinton's presidency. They were confident that she would win the 2016 election, and panic erupted in Washington when she lost to Trump. His first term, therefore, was a testimony to the power of the unconscious. During this period, the media parroted the Democratic Party and its leaders who had a guilty conscience. From Ukraine to Iraq to Iran to China the trail of corruption ran deep. So did the Clinton machine's influence, and the establishment did everything to protect the status quo. Thus, the more afraid they were that the truth would come out, the more fervently they attacked Trump, and the media assisted by encouraging double standards and spreading fake news. The masses being easy prey for propaganda, a collective psychosis ensued, one that is becoming more evident every day. See www.obamagatescandal.com

Nevertheless, while trauma like the War on Terror and the War on Drugs will be the biggest obstacles to overcome, facing them is *the only* way to get America back on track. If these campaigns are allowed to work their destructive magic, there can be no redemption, and to the extent that they are the manifestations of social engineering, uncovering the reality behind them is of utmost importance. Only in doing so can the cancerous substance that has thrived on NC traits be removed from the body politic—and while questions such as these may be annoying, sensible citizens would demand that they are answered.

At the very least, this is what FC citizens would do. They know that problems do not go away by us ignoring them. On the contrary, they will only get worse, and reflexes that urge us towards denial is a symptom of weakness. Rather than accepting a social contract on false pretenses, therefore, FC individuals adhere to the old trope, "if we can face it, God can fix it." They are serious about social commitments, and not only would they dig deeper until they themselves had uncovered a thousand more questions, but they would ensure that governments responded to their demands. Under no circumstances would they let the truth stay buried for reasons of "national security." They would see such paternalistic concerns as an insult, and they would ensure that those officials who did not assist them in their quest would never hold public office again.

To the extent that Americans do this, they will find that the ultimate authority resides in the people. Civil servants may have let them down, but only because they themselves have denied their inherent FC traits. We have seen that it is a law of politics that we cannot have freedom without responsibility and that we cannot give away our responsibility without also embracing tyranny. The forces of darkness know that this freedom is a terrible burden to bear, and they would love nothing more than to absolve us from it. Likewise, (to paraphrase Voltaire) the FC/NC model shows us that to the extent we continue to believe in absurdities, our leaders will *with a 100 percent certainty* continue their atrocities. These two variables are inextricably entwined and the former controls the other. If we want the founders' project back on track, then, the recipe is simple, and to the extent we collectively move towards the FC-end, the founders' vision will be completed.

Again, we can say this with a 100 percent certainty. Contrary to Neo-Darwinians' beliefs, we do have a say in the creation of reality and our destiny is not in the hands of chance. Also, contrary to religious beliefs, we have never been abandoned by God, and the urge to blame the devil is another symptom of our limited vision and our propensity for denial of responsibility. The reality is the exact opposite, as from the FC perspective the desire of the collective finds a proper expression in contemporary affairs. In looking at this on an individual basis, one can be sick at heart of the events that take place. Bad things certainly happen to good people, but it is only from the NC perspective that it appears to be the work of a universe that does not care. Seeing everything from a too limited perspective, NC individuals will jump to such conclusions. However, in looking at this from the high-end FC perspective, everything is as it must be, and the afflictions befallen humanity have been well deserved. As seen from this perspective, all these unfortunate events—the crime, the poverty, the injustice, drug abuse, the warfare, etc.—is the price we collectively have chosen to pay for embracing NC traits; they have been God's way of showing us our folly; and they have been a lesson we have ignored.[79] Had we been willing to listen to reason, we would have moved on to a more advanced level of being, but to this day we insist on continuing our folly. This being so, the Universe will have to speak louder to its children until we wake up.

However, a perfect storm is brewing. Karma may be tough, but it is also a Master teacher and as more and more people draw nearer to that threshold which separates the NC from the FC paradigm, it is unlikely that humanity will knowingly choose the disgrace that comes with willfully neglecting our potentials much longer. Hence, chances are that the citizens of the United States, as they did 250 years ago, will rise to the occasion once again in a not-too-distant future.

The circle will then be complete. This time, like the last, Americans can expect their struggle for a return to first principles to be an arduous journey. To the extent that the American psyche remains entrenched in the NC paradigm, they can look forward to no help from the judiciary, no help from the executive, and no help from Congress in their epic quest

---

[79] As C.S. Lewis observed, "God whispers to us in our pleasures, speaks to us in our conscience, but shouts in our pains: It's His megaphone to rouse a deaf world." LEWIS, *THE PROBLEM OF PAIN* (1962) 83

for the reestablishment of a system of FC law. To the extent that this is so, they can expect the system's force of inertia to fight them every step of the way. And to the extent that this is so, they will have to outshine the Founding Fathers in their exposure of FC traits. They will have to be prepared for a fight against tyranny that will rank them second to none, and they will have to decide if they want posterity to remember them as cowards, traitors, or champions of liberty.

These are the only options. In the great book of humanity, there can be only one true revolution; this is that revolution which ensures a genuine and lasting transfer from the NC to the FC state of affairs, and this is the revolution at hand. This time, like the last, it will be born out of necessity. It will not merely be a matter of self-fulfillment; it will be a matter of self-preservation, of defending all that is worth fighting for—and while everything hangs in the balance, God *will* Bless America if Americans are worth saving.

CONSTITUTIONAL CHALLENGES TO THE DRUG LAW

Blincoe v. State, 204 S.E.2d 597 (Ga. 1974)

Borras v. State, 229 So. 2d 244 (Fla. 1969)

Boswell v. State, 290 Ala. 349, 276 o. 2d 592, 596[5] (1973)

Bourassa v. State, 366 So. 2d 12 (Fla. 1978)

Commonwealth v. Leis, 355 Mass. 189, 243 N.E.2d 898 (1969)

Daut v. United States, 405 F.2d 312 (9th Cir. 1968), cert. denied, 402 U.S. 945, 91 S.Ct. 1624, 29 L.Ed.2d 114 (1971)

Egan v. Sheriff, Clark County, 88 Nev. 611,503 P.2d 16 (1972);

English v. Miller, 341 F. Supp. 714 (E.D.Va.1972)

English v. Virginia Probation and Parole Bd., 481 F.2d 188 (4 Cir. 1973)

Gaskin v. State, 490 S.W.2d 521 (Tenn. 1973), appeal dismissed, 414 U.S. 886, 94 S.Ct. 221, 38 L.Ed.2d 133 (1973)

Gonzales v. Raich, 545 U.S. 1, 125 S.Ct. 2195, 162 L.Ed.2d 1 (2005)

Gonzales v. State, 373 S.W.2d 249 (Tex. Crim. App. 1963)

Gray v. State, 525 P.2d 524, (Alaska 1974)

Hamilton v. State, 366 So. 2d 8 (Fla. 1979)

Harmash v. United States, 414 U.S. 831, 94 S.Ct. 165, 38 L.Ed.2d 65 (1973)

Harmelin v. Michigan, 501 U.S. 957 (1991)

Illinois NORML v. Scott, 383 N.E.2d 1330, 66 Ill. App.3d 633 (1978)

Joslin v. 14th District Judge, 76 Mich. App. 90,255 N.W.2d 782 (1977)

Kehrli v. Sprinkle, 524 F.2d 328 (10 Cir. 1975), certiorari denied, 426 U.S. 947, 96 S.Ct. 3165,49 L.Ed.2d 1183 (1976)

Kenny v. State, 51 Ala. App. 35,282 So.2d 387, certiorari denied, 291 Ala. 786, 282 So.2d 392 (1973)

Kreisher v. State, 319 A.2d 31 (Del. 1974)

Kuromiya v. United States, 37 F. Supp. 2d 717 (E.D. Pa. 1999)

Laird v. State, 342 So.2d 962 (Fla. 1977)

Leary v. United States, 383 F.2d 851 (5th Cir. 1967), rev'd on other grounds, 395 U.S. 6, 89 S.Ct. 1532, 23 L.Ed.2d 57 (1969)

Louisiana Af. of Nat. Or. for Ref. of Marijuana Laws v. Guste, 380 F. Supp. 404 (E.D. La. 1974), affd mem., 511 F.2d 1400 (5th Cir. 1975), cert. denied, 96 S. Ct. 129 (1975).

Marcoux v Attorney General, 375 N.E.2d 688 (Mass. 1978)

Miller v. State, 458 S.W.2d 680 (Tex.Cr.App. 1970)

Nat'l Org. for Reform of Marijuana Laws (NORML) v. Bell, 488 F. Supp. 123 (D.D.C. 1980)

Oliver v. Udall, 113 U.S.App. D.C. 212, 306 F.2d 819, cert. denied, 372 U.S. 908, 83 S. Ct. 720, 9 L. Ed. 2d 717 (1962).

People v. Aguiar, 257 Cal. App. 2d 597, 65 Cal. Rptr. 171, cert. denied, 393 U.S. 970, 89 S. Ct. 411, 21 L. Ed. 2d 383 (1968)

People v. Alexander, 56 Mich. App. 400, 223 N.W.2d 750 (1974)

People v. Bloom, 270 Cal.App.2d 731, 76 Cal.Rptr. 137 (1969)

People v. Bourg, 552 P.2d 504 (1976)

People v Demers, 42 App Div 2d 634; 345 N.Y.S.2d 184 (1973)

People v. Lorentzen, 387 Mich. 167, 194 N.W.2d 827(1972)

People v. McCabe, 49 Ill. 2d 338, 275 N.E.2d 407 (1971)

People v. McCaffrey, 29 Ill. App.3d 1088,332 N.E.2d 28 (1975)

People v. Morehouse, 80 Misc.2d 406, 364 N.Y.S.2d 108 (Sup.Ct. 1975)

People v. Schmidt, 272 N.W.2d 732 (Ct.App. Mich. 1978)

People v. Sheridan, 271 Cal. App. 2d 429, 76 Cal. Rptr. 655 (1969)

People v. Sinclair, 387 Mich. 91, 194 N.W.2d 878 (1972)

People v. Stark, 157 Colo. 59, 400 P.2d 923 (1965)

People v. Summit, 517 P.2d 850 (Colo. 1974)

People v. Walton, 116 Ill. App.2d 293 (1969)

People v. Woody, 61 Cal. 2d 716, 40 Cal. Rptr. 69, 394 P.2d 813 (1964)

Raich v. Gonzales, 500 F.3d 850 (9th Cir. 2007)

Raines v. State, 225 So. 2d 330 (Fla. 1969)

Ravin v. State, 537 P.2d 494 (Alaska 1975)

Ross v. State, 360 N.E.2d 1015 (Ct.App. Ind. 1977)

Sam v. State, 500 P.2d 291 (Okl.Cr.1972)

Seeley v. State, 132 Wash. 2d 776, 940 P.2d 604 (1997)

Spence v. Sachs, 173 Ohio St. 419, 183 N.E.2d 363

State Rel. Scott v. Conaty, 187 S.E.2d 119 (1972)

State v. Anderson, 558 P.2D 307(Wash. Ct. App. 1976)

State v. Anonymous, 32 Conn. Supp. 324, 355 A.2d 729 (1976)

State v. Baker, 56 Haw. 271, 535 P.2d 1394 (1975)

State v. Carus, 118 N.J.Super. 159, 286 A.2d 740 (1972)

State v Donovan, 344 A.2d 401 (Me, 1975)

State v. Ennis, 334 N.W.2d 827 (N.D.), cert. denied, U.S. 104 S. Ct. 484 (1983)

State v. Hanson, 364 N.W.2d 786 (Minn. 1985)

State v Infante, 199 Neb. 601; 260 N.W.2d 323 (1977)

State v. Kantner, 53 Haw. 327, 493 P.2d 306, cert. denied, 409 U.S. 948 (1972)

State v Kaplan, 23 N.C. App. 410; 209 S.E.2d 325 (1974)

State v. Kells, 259 N.W.2d 19 (Neb. 1977)

State v. Leins, 234 N.W.2d 645 (Iowa 1975)

State v Leppanen, 252 Or. 352; 449 P.2d 447 (1969)

State v. Mallan, 950 P.2d 178 (1998)

State v. Mitchell, 563 S.W.2d 18 (Mo. 1978) (en banc)

State v Murphy, 117 Ariz. 57,570 P.2d 1070 (1977)

State v. Nugent, 125 N.J. Super. 528, 312 A.2d 158 (1973)

State v O'Bryan, 96 Idaho 548; 531 P.2d 1193 (1975),

State v. Olson, 127 Wis. 2d 412, 380 N.W.2d 375 (1985)

State v. Rao, 171 Conn. 600, 370 A.2d 1310 (1976)

State v. Renfro, 56 Haw. 501, 542 P.2d 366 (1975)

State v. Sliger, 261 La. 999, 261 So.2d 643 (1972)

State v. Smith, 93 Wn.2d 329, 610 P.2d 869 (1980)

State v. Stallman, 673 S.W.2d 857 (Ct.App. Mo. 1984)

State v. Stock, 463 S.W.2d 889 (Mo. 1971)

State v. Strong, 245 N.W.2d 277 (S.D. 1976)

State v Tabory, 260 S.C. 355; 196 S.E.2d 111 (1973)

State v. Zornes, 78 Wash. 2d 9, 469 P.2d 552 (banc 1970)

State v. Wadsworth, 109 Ariz. 59, 505 P.2d 230, (banc 1973)

State v. Weidner, 47 Wis. 2d 321, 177 N.W.2d 69 (1970)

State v. White, 153 Mont. 193, 456 P.2d 54 (1969)

State v. Whitney, 637 P.2d 956 (Wash. 1981) (en banc)

United States v. Aguilar, 883 F.2d 662, 692 (9th Cir. 1989)

United States v. Bergdoll, 412 F. Supp. 1308 (D. Del. 1976)

United States v. Castro, 401 F. Supp. 120 (N.D. Ill. 1975)

United States v. Drotar, 416 F.2d 914 (5th Cir. 1969), vacated on other grounds, 402 U.S. 939, 91 S.Ct. 1628, 29 L.Ed.2d 107 (1971)

United States v. Eramdjian, (S.D. Cal. 1957), 155 F. Supp. 914 (S.D. Cal. 1957)

United States v. Fogarty, 692 F.2d 542 (8th Cir. 1982), cert. denied, 460 U.S. 1040 (1983)

United States v. Fry, 787 F.2d 903 (4th Cir. 1986)

United States v. Gaertner, 583 F.2d 308, 312 (7th Cir.1978) (per curiam)

United States v. Gramlich, 551 F.2d 1359 (5 Cir. 1977), certiorari denied, 434 U.S. 866, 98 S.Ct. 201,54 L.Ed.2d 141 (1977)

United States v. Greene, 892 F.2d 453, 456 (6th Cir. 1989)

United States v. Horsley, 519 F.2d 1264 (5th Cir. 1975)

United States v. Kiffer, 477 F.2d 349 (2d Cir.), cert. denied, 414 U.S. 831, 94 S.Ct. 62, 38 L.Ed.2d 65 (1973)

United States v. LaFroscia, 354 F. Supp. 1338 (S.D.N.Y. 1973)

United States v. Maas, 551 F. Supp. 645 (D.N.J. 1982)

United States v. Maiden, 355 F.Supp. 743, 749 (D.Conn.1973)

United States v. Middleton, 690 F.2d 820 (11th Cir. 1982), cert. denied, 460 U.S. 1051 (1983)

United States v. Miroyan, 577 F.2d 489 (9th Cir.), cert. denied, 439 U.S. 896 (1978)

United States v. Oakland Cannabis Buyers' Cooperative, 190 F.3d 1109 (9th Cir. 1999)

United States v. Pickard, et. al., No. 2:11-CR-0449-KJM (2015)

United States v. Pineda-Moreno, 688 F.3d 1087 (9th Cir. 2012)

United States v. Rodriquez-Comacho, 468 F.2d 1220 (9th Cir. 1972), cert. denied, 410 U.S. 985, 93 S.Ct. 1512, 36 L.Ed.2d 182 (1973)

United States v. Rogers, 549 F.2d 107 (1976)

United States v. Thorne, 325 A.2d 764 (1974)

United States v. Ward, 387 F.2d 843 (7th Cir. 1967)

United States v. Washington, 887 F.Supp.2d 1077, 1103 (D. Mont. 2012)

United States v. White Plume, 447 F.3d 1067 (2005)

Wolkind v. Selph, 495 F.Supp. 507, 513 (D.Va.1980), aff'd, 649 F.2d 865 (4th Cir. 1981)

LIST OF FC DISSENTERS:

Bourassa v. State, 366 So. 2d 12 (Fla. 1978). (Adkins J., dissenting)

Hamilton v. State, 366 So. 2d 8 (1978) (Adkins J., dissenting)

Laird v. State, 342 So.2d 962 (Fla. 1977) (Adkins J., dissenting) (Not fully FC but establishes that drug use is a protected privacy right)

People v. Lorentzen, 194 N.W.2d 827 (1972) 182 (Kavanagh J., concurring in part, dissenting in part)

People v. Sinclair, 387 Mich. 91, 194 N.W.2d 878 (1972) (Kavanagh J., concurring)

State v. Baker, 56 Haw. 271, 535 P.2d 1394 (1975) (Kobayashi J., dissenting)

State v. Kantner, 53Haw. 327, 493 P.2d 306 (1972) 311-20 (JJ. Abe, Levinson, and Kobayashi dissenting)

State v. Mallan, 86 Haw. 440, 950 P.2d 178 (1998) (Levinson J., dissenting)

State v. Mitchell, 563 S.W.2d 18 (Mo. 1978) 28-37 (Seiler J. and Shangler Sp.J., dissenting)

State v. Smith, 610 P.2d 869, 93 Wn.2d 329 (1980) 355-367 (Dolliver J., dissenting)

Seeley v. State, 132 Wash. 2d 776, 940 P.2d 604 (1997) (Sanders J., dissenting)

BIBLIOGRAPHY

Ackerman, Bruce, *The Rise of World Constitutionalism*, VIRGINIA LAW REVIEW VOL. 83:771 (1997)

AGEE, PHILIP, *INSIDE THE COMPANY: A CIA DIARY* (Stonehill 1975)

Ahrens, Deborah, *Drug Panics in the Twenty-First Century: Ecstasy, Prescription Drugs, and the Reframing of the War on Drugs*, ALBANY GOVERNMENT LAW REVIEW Vol. 6:397 (2013)

ALEXANDER, MICHELLE, *THE NEW JIM CROW: MASS INCARCERATION IN THE AGE OF COLORBLINDNESS* (New Press 2011)

Alexandre, Michelle, *Sex, Drugs, Rock & Roll and Moral Dirgisme: Toward a Reformation of Drug and Prostitution Regulations*, UMKC LAW REVIEW Vol. 78, No. 1 (2009)

ALEXY, ROBERT, *A THEORY OF CONSTITUTIONAL RIGHTS* (Oxford 2002)

Alexy, Robert, *Constitutional Rights and Proportionality*, JOURNAL FOR CONSTITUTIONAL THEORY AND PHILOSOPHY OF LAW VOL. 22:51 (2014)

AKHIL REED AMAR, *AMERICA'S UNWRITTEN CONSTITUTION: THE PRECEDENTS AND PRINCIPLES WE LIVE BY* (Basic Books 2012)

ANDENÆS, JOHS, *ALMINNELIG STRAFFERETT* (Universitetsforlaget 2004)

ANDENÆS, JOHS., *ETTER OVERVEIELSE: ARTIKLER I UTVALG* (Gyldendal 1992)

ANDENÆS, JOHS, *STRAFFEN SOM PROBLEM* (Exil 1994)

ANDENÆS, MADS & BJØRGE, ERIK, *MENNESKERETTENE OG OSS* (Universitetsforlaget 2012)

Anderson & Rees, *The Legalization of Recreational Marijuana: How Likely Is the Worst-Case Scenario?* JOURNAL OF POLICY ANALYSIS AND MANAGEMENT Vol. 33:221 (2014)

ANDREWS, ANDY, *HOW DO YOU KILL 11 MILLION PEOPLE* (Thomas Nelson 2010)

ANKERBERG, JOHN & WELDON, JOHN, *THE SECRET TEACHINGS OF THE MASONIC LODGE* (Moody 1990)

Araiza, William D., *Deference to Congressional Fact-Finding in Rights-Enforcing and Rights-Limiting Legislation*, NYU LAW REVIEW Vol. 88:878 (2013)

ARENDT, HANNAH, *THE ORIGINS OF TOTALITARIANISM* (Harcourt 1966)

ARKES, HADLEY, *BEYOND THE CONSTITUTION* (Princeton 1990)

ARKES, HADLEY, *CONSTITUTIONAL ILLUSIONS & ANCHORING TRUTHS: THE TOUCHSTONE OF THE NATURAL LAW* (Cambridge 2010)

Ashworth, Andrew, *Is the Criminal Law a Lost Cause?* LAW QUARTERLY REVIEW Vol.116:225 (2000)

ASSAGIOLI, ROBERTO, *TRANSPERSONAL DEVELOPMENT* (Aquarian 1993)

AUROBINDO, SRI, *THE HOUR OF GOD* (Lotus Press 2009)

AUROBINDO, SRI, *THE HUMAN CYCLE* (Pondicherry 2012)

AUROBINDO, SRI, *THE IDEAL OF HUMAN UNITY* (Pondicherry 2012)

AUROBINDO, SRI, *THE LIFE DIVINE* (Pondicherry 1970)

AUROBINDO, SRI, *ON YOGA: THE SYNTHESIS OF YOGA* (Pondicherry 1957)

AUROBINDO, SRI, *WAR AND SELF-DETERMINATION* (Pondicherry 2012)

BAILYN, BERNARD, *THE IDEOLOGICAL ORIGINS OF THE AMERICAN REVOLUTION* (Harvard 1967)

BAKALAR, JAMES B. & GRINSPOON, LESTER, *DRUG CONTROL IN A FREE SOCIETY*, (Cambridge 1998)

Balkin, Jack M., *Abortion and Original Meaning*, CONSTITUTIONAL COMMENTARY Vol. 24:291 (2007)

Ball, Carlos A., *Why Liberty Judicial Review is as Legitimate as Equality Review: The Case of Gay Rights Jurisprudence*, JOURNAL OF CONSTITUTIONAL LAW Vol. 14:1 (2011)

Bandow, Doug, *From Fighting the Drug War to Protecting the Right to Use Drugs: Recognizing a Forgotten Liberty*, FRASER INSTITUTE (2012)

Baradaran, Shima, *Drugs and Violence,* UNIVERSITY OF UTAH COLLEGE OF LAW Research Paper No. 75 (2015)

Barnett, Randy E., *An Originalism for Nonoriginalists*, BOSTON UNIVERSITY SCHOOL OF LAW Working Paper No. 99-14 (1999)

Barnett, Randy, *Bad Trip: Drug Prohibition and the Weakness of Public Policy*, YALE LAW JOURNAL Vol. 103:2593 (1994)

Barnett, Randy E., *Constitutional Clichés*, CAPITAL UNIVERSITY LAW REVIEW Vol. 36:493 (2008)

Barnett, Randy E., *From Antislavery Lawyer to Chief Justice: The Remarkable but Forgotten Career of Salmon P. Chase*, CASE WESTERN RESERVE LAW REVIEW Vol. 63:653 (2013)

Barnett, Randy E., *The Golden Mean Between Kurt & Dan: A Moderate Reading of the Ninth Amendment*, DRAKE LAW REVIEW Vol. 56:897 (2008)

Barnett, Randy E., *The Gravitational Force of Originalism*, GEORGETOWN PUBLIC LAW AND LEGAL THEORY Research Paper No. 13-010 (2013)

Barnett, Randy E., *The Harmful Side Effects of Drug Prohibition*, UTAH LAW REVIEW 11-34 (2009)

Barnett, Randy E., *The Imperative of Natural Rights in Today's World,* BOSTON UNIVERSITY SCHOOL OF LAW, Working Paper No. 03-20 (2003)

Barnett, Randy E., *Is the Constitution Libertarian?* GEORGETOWN PUBLIC LAW Research Paper No. 1432854 (2008)

Barnett, Randy E., *Justice Kennedy's Libertarian Revolution: Lawrence v. Texas*, BOSTON UNIVERSITY SCHOOL OF LAW, Working Paper No. 03-13 (2003)

Barnett, Randy E., *The Misconceived Assumption about Constitutional Assumptions*, GEORGETOWN LAW FACULTY Working Papers (2008)

Barnett, Randy E., *The Ninth Amendment: It Means What It Says*, TEXAS LAW REVIEW Vol. 85:1 (2006)

Barnett, Randy E., *The Original Meaning of the Judicial Power*, BOSTON UNIVERSITY SCHOOL OF LAW Working Paper No. 03-18 (2003)

Barnett, Randy E., *The Original Meaning of the Necessary and Proper Clause*, BOSTON UNIVERSITY SCHOOL OF LAW Working Paper No. 03-11 (2003)

Barnett, Randy E., *The People or the State: Chrisholm v. Georgia and Popular Sovereignty* VIRGINIA LAW REVIEW Vol. 93 (2007)

Barnett, Randy E., *The Presumption of Liberty and the Public Interest: Medical Marijuana and Fundamental Rights*, WASHINGTON UNIVERSITY JOURNAL OF LAW AND POLICY Vol. 22:29 (2006)

Barnett, Randy E., *The Proper Scope of the Police Power*, NOTRE DAME LAW REVIEW Vol. 79:429 (2004)

BARNETT, RANDY E., *RESTORING THE LOST CONSTITUTION: THE PRESUMPTION OF LIBERTY* (Princeton 2014)

Barnett, Randy E., *Scrutiny Land*, MICHIGAN LAW REVIEW Vol. 106:1479 (2008)

BARNETT, RANDY E., *THE STRUCTURE OF LIBERTY: JUSTICE AND THE RULE OF LAW* (Oxford 2014)

Barnett, Randy E., *We the People: Each and Every One*, YALE LAW JOURNAL Vol. 123:2576 (2014)

Barnett, Randy E., *Who's Afraid of Unenumerated Rights?* JOURNAL OF CONSTITUTIONAL LAW Vol. 9:1 (2006)

Barrett, Damon, *Security, Development and Human Rights: Normative, Legal and Policy Challenges for the International Drug Control System*, INTERNATIONAL JOURNAL OF DRUG POLICY 21 (2010)

BAUM, DAN, *SMOKE AND MIRRORS: THE WAR ON DRUGS AND THE POLITICS OF FAILURE* (Little Brown 1996)

Beale, Sara Sun, *What's Law Got To Do With It? The Political, Social, Psychological and Other Non-Legal Factors Influencing the Development of (Federal) Criminal Law*, BUFFALO CRIMINAL LAW REVIEW Vol. 1:23 (1997)

BEATTY, DAVID M., *THE ULTIMATE RULE OF LAW* (Oxford 2004)

BECKER, DEAN, *TO END THE WAR ON DRUGS: POLICYMAKERS' EDITION* (DTN Media 2014)

BENNETT, SCOTT, *SHELL GAME: A WHISTLEBLOWING REPORT TO THE U.S. CONGRESS* (2013) (online book)

Benson, Bruce L., *The War on Drugs: A Public Bad*, NORTHWESTERN UNIVERSITY'S SEARLE CENTER ON LAW (2008)

Bergland, David, *Libertarianism, Natural Rights and the Constitution, A Commentary on Recent Libertarian Literature*, CLEVELAND STATE LAW REVIEW Vol. 44:499 (1996)

BERNAYS, EDWARD, *PROPAGANDA* (Routledge 1928)

BERTRAM, EVA, ET AL., *DRUG WAR POLITICS: THE PRICE OF DENIAL* (University of California 1996)

BEWLEY-TAYLOR, DAVID R.., *INTERNATIONAL DRUG CONTROL: CONSENSUS FRACTURED* (Cambridge 2012)

Bibas, Stephanos & Bierschbach, Richard A., *Constitutionally Tailoring Punishment*, MICHIGAN LAW REVIEW Vol. 112:397 (2013)

Bilionis, Louis D., *The New Scrutiny*, Emory Law Journal Vol. 51:101 (2002)

Bilionis, Louis D., *On the Significance of Constitutional Spirit*, NORTH CAROLINA LAW REVIEW Vol. 70:1803 (1992)

Bilionis, Louis D., *Process, the Constitution, and Substantive Criminal Law,* MICHIGAN LAW REVIEW Vol.96:1269 (1998)

BLACK, CHARLES L., *A NEW BIRTH FOR FREEDOM: HUMAN RIGHTS, NAMED AND UNNAMED* (Yale 1999)

BLAU, JUDITH & MONCADA, ALBERTO, *JUSTICE IN THE UNITED STATES: HUMAN RIGHTS AND THE U.S. CONSTITUTION* (Rowman & Littlefield 2006)

BLAVATSKY, HELENA, *THE SECRET DOCTRINE: THE SYNTHESIS OF SCIENCE, RELIGION AND PHILOSOPHY* (Kessinger1938)

Blickman & Jelsma, *Drug Policy Reform in Practice: Experiences with Alternatives in Europe and the US*, TRANSNATIONAL INSTITUTE (2009)

Block, Walter, *Drug Prohibition: A Legal and Economic Analysis*, JOURNAL OF BUSINESS ETHICS Vol. 12:689 (1993)

BLUM, WILLIAM, *KILLING HOPE: U.S. MILITARY AND C.I.A. INTERVENTIONS SINCE WORLD WAR II* (Common Courage 2003)

Blumenson, Eric, *Recovering from Drugs and the Drug War: An Achievable Public Health Alternative,* JOURNAL OF GENDER, RACE AND JUSTICE Vol. 6, No. 2 (2002)

Blumenson, Eric & Nilsen, Eva, *Policing for Profit: The Drug War's Hidden Economic Agenda*, UNIVERSITY OF CHICAGO LAW REVIEW Vol. 65:35 (1998)

BOLLINGER, LORENTZ (ED.), *CANNABIS SCIENCE: FROM PROHIBITION TO HUMAN RIGHT* (Peter Lang 1997)

Bollinger, Lorentz, *Recent Developments Regarding Drug Law and Policy in Germany and the European Community: The Evolution of Drug Control in Europe*, JOURNAL OF DRUG ISSUES (2002)

Bomhoff, Jacco, *Genealogies of Balancing as Discourse*, LAW & ETHICS OF HUMAN RIGHTS, Vol. 4, Issue 1, Article 6 (2010)

Bonnie, Richard & Whitebread, Charles, *The Forbidden Fruit and the Tree of Knowledge: An Inquiry into the Legal History of American Marijuana Prohibition*, VIRGINIA LAW REVIEW Vol. 56:971 (1970)

Borgmann, Caitlin E., *Rethinking Judicial Deference to Legislative Fact-Finding*, INDIANA LAW JOURNAL Vol. 81:1 (2009)

BOWARD, JAMES, *LOST RIGHTS: THE DESTRUCTION OF AMERICAN LIBERTY* (St. Martin's Griffin 1995)

Boyd, Graham, *Collateral Damage in the War on Drugs*, VILLANOVA LAW REVIEW Vol. 47:839 (2002)

Brandeis, Jason, *The Continuing Vitality of Ravin v. State: Alaskans Still Have a Constitutional Right to Possess Marijuana in the Privacy of their Homes*, ALASKA LAW REVIEW Vol. 29:2 (2012)

Brashear, Bruce, *Marijuana Prohibition and the Constitutional Right of Privacy: An Examination of Ravin v. State*, TULSA LAW JOURNAL Vol. 11:563 (1975)

BROGAN, HUGH, *LONGMAN HISTORY OF THE UNITED STATES OF AMERICA* (Guild 1987)

Brown, Darryl K., *Can Criminal Law Be Controlled?* MICHIGAN LAW REVIEW Vol. 108:971 (2010)

Brown-Nagin, Tomiko, *The Civil Rights Canon: Above and Below*, YALE LAW JOURNAL Vol. 123:2698 (2014)

Brown, Rebecca L., *Liberty, the New Equality*, NYU LAW REVIEW Vol. 77:1491 (2002)

Buchhandler-Raphael, Michal, *Drugs, Dignity, and Danger: Human Dignity as a Constitutional Constraint to Limit Overcriminalization,* TENNESSEE LAW REVIEW, Vol. 80 (2013)

BUCKE, R. M., *COSMIC CONSCIOUSNESS: A STUDY IN THE EVOLUTION OF THE HUMAN MIND* (University Books 1961)

BURDICK, CHARLES K., *THE LAW OF THE AMERICAN CONSTITUTION: ITS ORIGIN AND DEVELOPMENT* (Putnam 1922)

BUTLER, SMEDLEY, *WAR IS A RACKET: THE PROFIT MOTIVE BEHIND WARFARE* (World Library 2010)

CAPRA, FRITJOF, *THE TAO OF PHYSICS: AN EXPLORATION OF THE PARALLELS BETWEEN MODERN PHYSICS AND EASTERN MYSTICISM* (Shambala 2010)

CAREY, GEORGE WASHINGTON, *GOD-MAN: THE WORD MADE FLESH* (1920)

Chemerinsky, Erwin, *The Constitution and Punishment*, STANFORD LAW REVIEW Vol. 56:1049 (2004)

Chemerinsky, Erwin, *Substantive Due Process*, TOURO LAW REVIEW Vol. 15:1501 (1999)

CHOMSKY, NOAM, *POWER AND TERROR: CONFLICT, HEGEMONY, AND THE RULE OF FORCE* (Pluto 2011)

Christiansen, Matthew A., *A Great Schism: Social Norms and Marijuana Prohibition*, HARVARD LAW & POLICY REVIEW Vol. 4:229 (2010)

CLOSE, EDWARD R., *TRANSCENDENTAL PHYSICS* (toExcel Press 2000)

Colb, Sherry, *Freedom from Incarceration: Why is This Right Different from All Other Rights?* NYU LAW REVIEW Vol. 69:781 (1994)

COLBY, GERARD, *DU PONT DYNASTY: BEHIND THE NYLON CURTAIN* (Lyle Stuart 1984)

Cole, David, *Formalism, Realism, and the War on Drugs*, SUFFOLK UNIVERSITY LAW REVIEW Vol. 35: 241 (2001)

Conkle, Daniel O., *The Second Death of Substantive Due Process*, INDIANA LAW JOURNAL Vol. 62:215 (1987)

CONRAD, CLAY S., *JURY NULLIFICATION: THE EVOLUTION OF A DOCTRINE* (Carolina 1998)

CONRAD, NORRIS & RESNER, *HUMAN RIGHTS AND THE US DRUG WAR* (Creative Xpressions 2001)

Csete, Joanne, *From the Mountaintops: What the World Can Learn from Drug Policy Change in Switzerland*, OPEN SOCIETY FOUNDATIONS (2010)

Cunnings, Jordan, *Nonserious Marijuana Offenses and Noncitizens: Uncounseled Pleas and Disproportionate Consequences*, UCLA LAW REVIEW Vol. 62:510 (2015)

CURTIS, MICHAEL, *NO STATE SHALL ABRIDGE: THE FOURTEENTH AMENDMENT AND THE BILL OF RIGHTS* (Duke 1986)

D'Amato, Anthony, *Natural Law: A Libertarian View*, FACULTY WORKING PAPERS, Paper 148 (2008)

DAMON, WILLIAM & COLBY, ANNE, *SOME DO CARE: CONTEMPORARY LIVES OF MORAL COMMITMENT* (New York 1992)

Danovitch, Itai, *Sorting Through the Science on Marijuana: Facts, Fallacies, and Implications for Legalization*, MCGEORGE LAW REVIEW Vol. 43:91 (2013)

DAVIES, PAUL, *THE COSMIC BLUEPRINT: NEW DISCOVERIES IN NATURE'S CREATIVE ABILITY TO ORDER THE UNIVERSE* (Templeton Foundation Press 2004)

DAVIES, PAUL & GRIBBIN, JOHN, *THE MATTER MYTH: DRAMATIC DISCOVERIES THAT CHALLENGE OUR UNDERSTANDING OF PHYSICAL REALITY* (Simon & Schuster 1992)

DEAN, STANLEY R. (ED.), *PSYCHIATRY & MYSTICISM* (Nelson-Hall 1979)

DECAMP, JOHN, *THE FRANKLIN COVER-UP* (AWT. Inc 1992)

DE GREIFF, PABLO (ED.), *DRUGS AND THE LIMITS OF LIBERALISM* (Cornell 1999)

DICE, MARK, *ILLUMINATI: FACTS AND FICTION* (The Resitance 2009)

Dichter, Mark S., *Marijuana and the Law: The Constitutional Challenges to Marijuana Laws in Light of the Social Aspects of Marijuana Use*, VILLANOVA LAW REVIEW Vol. 13:851 (1968)

Dippel, Horst, *Modern Constitutionalism: An Introduction to a History in the Need of Writing*, THE LEGAL HISTORY REVIEW Vol. 73:153 (2005)

Domosławski, Artur, *Drug Policy in Portugal: The Benefits of Decriminalizing Drug Use*, OPEN SOCIETY FOUNDATIONS (2011)

Doss, Arden & Doss, Diane, *On Morals, Privacy, and the Constitution*, UNIVERSITY OF MIAMI LAW REVIEW Vol. 25:395 (1971)

DOSSEY, LARRY, *REINVENTING MEDICINE: BEYOND MIND-BODY TO A NEW ERA OF HEALING* (Harper Collins 1999)

Dubber, Markus D., *A Political Theory of Criminal Law: Autonomy and the Legitimacy of State Punishment*, LEGITIMATING CRIMINAL LAW (2004)

Dubber, Markus D., *The Legality Principle in American and German Criminal Law: An Essay in Comparative Legal History* (2010)

Dubber, Markus D., *New Legal Science: Toward Law as a Global Discipline* (2014)

Dubber, Markus D., *The New Police Science and the Police Power Model of the Criminal Process* (2004)

Dubber, Markus D., *Policing Possession: The War on Crime and the End of Criminal Law*, JOURNAL OF CRIMINAL LAW AND CRIMINOLOGY Vol. 91:829 (2001)

Dubber, Markus D., *Toward a Constitutional Law of Crime and Punishment*, HASTINGS LAW JOURNAL Vol. 55 (2004)

Duke, Steven B., *Drug Prohibition: an Unnatural Disaster*, FACULTY SCHOLARSHIP SERIES, paper 812 (1995)

Duke, Steven B., *The Future of Marijuana in the United States,* YALE LAW SCHOOL, Public Law Working Paper No. 299 (2013)

Duke, Steven B., *Mass Imprisonment, Crime Rates, and the Drug War: A Penological and Humanitarian Disgrace,* FACULTY SCHOLARSHIP SERIES, Paper 826 (2010)

DUKE, STEVEN, B. & CROSS, ALBERT C., *AMERICA'S LONGEST WAR: RETHINKING OUR TRAGIC CRUSADE AGAINST DRUGS* (Tarcher/Putnam 1993)

DWORKIN, RONALD, *A MATTER OF PRINCIPLE* (Harvard 1985)

DWORKIN, RONALD, *LAW'S EMPIRE* (Harvard 1986)

DWORKIN, RONALD, *SOVEREIGN VIRTUE: THE THEORY AND PRACTICE OF EQUALITY* (Harvard 2002)

DWORKIN, RONALD, *TAKING RIGHTS SERIOUSLY* (Harvard 1978)

Ely, John Hart, *Legislative and Administrative Motivation in Constitutional Law*, FACULTY SCHOLARSHIP SERIES, paper 4114 (1970)

EPSTEIN, EDWARD J., *AGENCY OF FEAR: OPIATES AND POLITICAL POWER IN AMERICA* (Verso 1990)

Erlinder, Peter, *Mens Rea, Due Process, and the Supreme Court: Toward a Constitutional Doctrine of Substantive Criminal Law*, AMERICAN JOURNAL OF CRIMINAL LAW Vol. 9:163 (1989)

ESCOHOTADO, ANTONIO, *A BRIEF HISTORY OF DRUGS: FROM THE STONE AGE TO THE STONED AGE* (Park Street 1999)

ESKELAND, STÅLE, *DE MEST ALVORLIGE FORBRYTELSER* (Cappelen Damm 2011)

Eskridge, William N., *Destabilizing Due Process and Evolutive Equal Protection*, UCLA LAW REVIEW Vol. 47:1183 (2000)

European Commission for Democracy through Law, *European and U.S. Constitutionalism*, SCIENCE AND TECHNIQUE OF DEMOCRACY, No. 37 (2003)

Eylon & Harel, *The Right to Judicial Review,* VIRGINIA LAW REVIEW Vol. 92, No. 5 (2006)

Fallon, Richard H., *Individual Rights and Governmental Powers*, GEORGIA LAW REVIEW Vol. 27:343 (1993)

Fallon, Richard H., *Legitimacy and the Constitution*, HARVARD LAW REVIEW Vol. 118:1787 (2005)

Farrell, Robert C., *Justice Kennedy's Idiosyncratic Understanding of Equal Protection and Due Process, and its Costs*, QUINNIPIAC LAW REVIEW Vol. 32:439 (2014)

FEINBERG, JOEL, *HARMLESS WRONGDOING: THE MORAL LIMITS OF THE CRIMINAL LAW* (Oxford 1990)

FEINBERG, JOEL, *HARM TO OTHERS: THE MORAL LIMITS OF THE CRIMINAL LAW* (Oxford 1987)

Finer, Joel J., *Psychedelics and Religious Freedom*, HASTINGS LAW JOURNAL Vol. 19:667 (1968)

Finkelstein, Claire, *Positivism and the Notion of an Offense,* CALIFORNIA LAW REVIEW Vol. 88:335 (2000)

FINNEY, CHARLES, *THE CHARACTER, CLAIMS, AND PRACTICAL WORKINGS OF FREEMASONRY* (DAY 1998)

FINNIS, JOHN, *NATURAL LAW AND NATURAL RIGHTS* (Oxford 2011)

FISH, JEFFERSON (ED.), *HOW TO LEGALIZE DRUGS* (Northvale 1998)

FISHER, PAUL A., *BEHIND THE LODGE DOOR* (Shield 1989)

Fiss, Owen M., *Groups and the Equal Protection Clause*, PHILOSOPHY AND PUBLIC AFFAIRS Vol. 5:107 (1976)

FORST, RAINER, *THE RIGHT TO JUSTIFICATION: A CONSTRUCTIVIST THEORY OF JUSTICE* (Columbia 2011)

FORTE, ROBERT (ED.), *ENTHEOGENS AND THE FUTURE OF RELIGION* (Park Street 2012)

FOWLER, JAMES W., *STAGES OF FAITH: THE PSYCHOLOGY OF HUMAN DEVELOPMENT AND THE QUEST FOR MEANING* (Harper 1981)

FOWLER, JAMES W., *WEAVING THE NEW CREATION: STAGES OF FAITH AND THE PUBLIC CHURCH* (Harper 1991)

FULLER, LON, *THE MORALITY OF LAW* (Yale 1969)

Galliher, Keys & Elsner, *Lindesmith v. Anslinger: An Early Government Victory in the Failed War on Drugs*, JOURNAL OF CRIMINAL LAW AND CRIMINOLOGY Vol. 88:681 (1998)

GARLAND, DAVID, *THE CULTURE OF CONTROL: CRIME AND SOCIAL ORDER IN CONTEMPORARY SOCIETY* (Chicago 2001)

GARWOOD, DARRELL, *UNDER COVER: THIRTY-FIVE YEARS OF CIA DECEPTION* (Grove Press 1985)

GEBSER, JEAN, *THE EVER PRESENT ORIGIN* (Ohio 1997)

GERBER, RICHARD, *VIBRATIONAL MEDICINE* (Bear & Co 2001)

Gerber, Scott D., *Liberal Originalism: The Declaration of Independence and Constitutional Interpretation*, CLEVELAND STATE LAW REVIEW Vol. 63:1 (2014)

GERBER, SCOTT D., *TO SECURE THESE RIGHTS* (New York 1995)

Gershowitz, Adam M., *An Informational Approach to the Mass Imprisonment Problem*, FACULTY PUBLICATIONS, Paper 1264 (2008)

GEWIRTH, ALAN, *THE COMMUNITY OF RIGHTS* (Chicago 1996)

GEWIRTH, ALAN, *REASON AND MORALITY* (Chicago 1981)

GLOVER, JONATHAN, *HUMANITY: A MORAL HISTORY OF THE TWENTIETH CENTURY* (Random House 1999)

Goldberg, Suzanne B., *Equality Without Tiers*, SOUTHERN CALIFORNIA LAW REVIEW Vol. 77:481 (2004)

GONZALEZ, SERVANDO, *PSYCHOLOGICAL WARFARE AND THE NEW WORLD ORDER: THE SECRET WAR AGAINST THE AMERICAN PEOPLE* (Spooks 2010)

GOSWAMI, AMIT, *THE SELF-AWARE UNIVERSE: HOW CONSCIOUSNESS CREATES THE MATERIAL WORLD* (Simon & Schuster 1993)

Gowder, Paul, *Equal Law in an Unequal World*, IOWA LAW REVIEW Vol. 99:1021 (2014)

GRAY, CHRISTOPHER, *THE ACID DIARIES: A PSYCHONAUT'S GUIDE TO THE HISTORY AND USE OF LSD* (Park Street 2010)

GRAY, JAMES P., *WHY OUR DRUG LAWS HAVE FAILED AND WHAT WE CAN DO ABOUT IT: A JUDICIAL INDICTMENT OF THE WAR ON DRUGS* (Temple 2001)

Grey, Thomas C., *The Uses of an Unwritten Constitution*, CHICAGO-KENT LAW REVIEW Vol. 64:211 (1988)

GRIFFIN, DAVID RAY, *9/11 CONTRADICTIONS: AN OPEN LETTER TO CONGRESS AND THE PRESS* (Interlink 2008)

GRIFFIN, G. EDWARD, *THE CREATURE FROM JEKYLL ISLAND* (American Media 2002)

GRINSPOON, LESTER, *MARIJUANA RECONSIDERED* (Harvard 1977)

GRITZ, JAMES BO, *A NATION BETRAYED* (Lazarus 1989)

Grob, Charles et al., *Pilot Study of Psilocybin Treatment for Anxiety in Patients with Advanced-stage Cancer*, ARCHIVES OF GENERAL PSYCHIATRY Vol. 68, no. 1 (2011)

GROF, STANISLAV, *THE COSMIC GAME: EXPLORATIONS OF THE FRONTIERS OF HUMAN CONSCIOUSNESS* (Suny 1998)

GROF, STANISLAV, *LSD: DOORWAY TO THE NUMINOUS* (Park Street 2009)

GROF, STANISLAV, *PSYCHOLOGY OF THE FUTURE* (Suny Press 2000)

GROF, STANISLAV, *REALMS OF THE HUMAN UNCONSCIOUS: OBSERVATIONS FROM LSD RESEARCH* (Souvenir 1979)

GROF, STANISLAV, *WHEN THE IMPOSSIBLE HAPPENS* (Soundstrue 2006)

GROF, STANISLAV & HALIFAX, JOAN, *THE HUMAN ENCOUNTER WITH DEATH* (Dutton 1977)

Grosman, Lucas S., *Drugs under the Constitution*, SELA PAPERS, Paper 108 (2012)

Grund, Jean-Paul & Breeksema, Joost, *Coffee Shops and Compromise: Separated Illicit Drug Markets in the Netherlands*, OPEN SOCIETY FOUNDATIONS (2013)

Gunther, Gerald, Foreword: *In Search of Evolving Doctrine on a Changing Court: A Model for a Newer Equal Protection*, HARVARD LAW REVIEW Vol. 86:1 (1972)

Gur-Arye, Miriam & Weigend, Thomas, *Constitutional Review of Criminal Prohibitions Affecting Human Dignity and Liberty: German and Israeli Perspectives*, ISRAELI LAW REVIEW Vol. 44:63 (2011)

HAGBERG, JANET & GUELICH, ROBERT, *THE CRITICAL JOURNEY: STAGES IN THE LIFE OF FAITH* (Sheffield 2004)

HALL, MANLY P., *THE SECRET DESTINY OF AMERICA* (Philosophical Research Society 1944) (online book)

Hallam, Bewley-Taylor, & Jelsma, *Scheduling in the International Drug Control System*, SERIES ON LEGISLATIVE REFORM OF DRUG POLICIES No. 25 (2014)

Hamburger, Philip A., *Natural Rights, Natural Law & American Constitutions*, YALE LAW JOURNAL Vol. 102: 907 (1993)

HAMEROFF, KASZNIAK & SCOTT (EDS.), *TOWARD A SCIENCE OF CONSCIOUSNESS* (Cambridge 1998)

HANCOCK, GRAHAM (ED.), *THE DIVINE SPARK: PSYCHEDELICS, CONSCIOUSNESS AND THE BIRTH OF CIVILIZATION* (HayHouse 2015)

HART, CARL, *HIGH PRICE* (Harper 2014)

Hart, Henry M., *The Aims of the Criminal Law*, LAW AND CONTEMPORARY PROBLEMS Vol. 23:401 (1958)

HARTSTEIN, MAX, *THE WAR ON DRUGS: THE WORST ADDICTION OF ALL* (2003)

HASKINS, G.L., *LAW AND AUTHORITY IN EARLY MASSACHUSETTS* (Archon 1968)

HEINDEL, MAX, *THE ROSICRUCIAN COSMO-CONCEPTION* (Ulan 2012)

HERBERT, NICK, *QUANTUM REALITY: BEYOND THE NEW PHYSICS* (Doubleday 1985)

Hessick, Andrew, *Rethinking the Presumption of Constitutionality*, NOTRE DAME LAW REVIEW Vol. 85:1447 (2010)

Heyman, Steven J., *The First Duty of Government: Protection, Liberty, and the Fourteenth Amendment*, DUKE LAW JOURNAL 41:507 (1991)

Hindes, Thomas L., *Morality Enforcement Through the Criminal Law and the Modern Doctrine of Substantive Due Process*, UNIVERSITY OF PENNSYLVANIA LAW REVIEW Vol. 126:344 (1977)

Hirschl, Ran, *The Rise of Comparative Constitutional Law: Thoughts on substance and Method*, INDIAN JOURNAL OF CONSTITUTIONAL LAW (2008)

HOBBES, THOMAS, *LEVIATHAN* (Penguin 1982)

Holmes, Justice, *Common Carriers and the Common Law*, THE ANGLO-AMERICAN LAW REVIEW Vol. 13:609 (1879)

HOOD, RALPH, *HANDBOOK OF RELIGIOUS EXPERIENCE* (Religious Education Press 1995)

Hughes, Jula, *Restraint and Proliferation in criminal Law*, REVIEW OF CONSTITUTIONAL STUDIES Vol. 15, Issue 1 (2010)

Huhn, Wilson, *The Jurisprudential Revolution: Unlocking Human Potential in Grutter and Lawrence*, WILLIAM & MARY BILL OF RIGHTS JOURNAL Vol. 12:65 (2004)

Husak, Douglas, *Applying Ultima Ratio: A Skeptical Assessment*, OHIO STATE JOURNAL OF CRIMINAL LAW Vol. 2:535 (2005)

HUSAK, DOUGLAS, *DRUGS AND RIGHTS* (Cambridge 1996)

Husak, Douglas, *Four Points about Drug Decriminalization*, CRIMINAL JUSTICE ETHICS Vol. 22, Issue 1 (2003)

HUSAK, DOUGLAS, *LEGALIZE THIS! THE CASE FOR DECRIMINALIZING DRUGS* (Verso 2002)

Husak, Douglas, *Liberal Neutrality, Autonomy, and Drug Prohibitions*, PHILOSOPHY AND PUBLIC AFFAIRS Vol. 29, No. 1 (2000)

HUSAK, DOUGLAS, *OVERCRIMINALIZATION: THE LIMITS OF THE CRIMINAL LAW* (Oxford 2008)

HUSAK, DOUGLAS & DE MARNEFFE, PETER, *THE LEGALIZATION OF DRUGS: FOR AND AGAINST* (Cambridge 2005)

HØSTMÆLINGEN, NJÅL, *HVA ER MENNESKERETTIGHETER?* (Universitetsforlaget 2010)

Jackson, Jeffrey D., *Putting Rationality Back Into the Rational Basis Test: Saving Substantive Due Process and Redeeming the Promise of the Ninth Amendment*, UNIVERSITY OF RICHMOND LAW REVIEW Vol. 45:491 (2011)

Jackson, Vicki C., *Constitutional Law in an Age of Proportionality*, YALE LAW REVIEW Vol. 124:3094 (2015)

JAHN, ROBERT & DUNNE, BRENDA, *MARGINS OF REALITY: THE ROLE OF CONSCIOUSNESS IN THE PHYSICAL WORLD* (Harcourt 1987)

JAMES, WILLIAM, *THE VARIETIES OF RELIGIOUS EXPERIENCE* (Barnes & Noble 2004)

JEFFERSON, THOMAS, *THE ANAS* (Online book)

Jelsma, Martin, *Drugs in the UN system: the Unwritten History of the 1998 United Nations General Assembly Special Session on Drugs*, INTERNATIONAL JOURNAL OF DRUG POLICY Vol. 14 (2003)

Kadish, Sanford H., *The Crisis of Overcriminalization*, AMERICAN CRIMINAL LAW QUARTERLY Vol.7:17 (1968)

Kadish, Sanford H., *Fifty Years of Criminal Law: An Opinionated Review*, CALIFORNIA LAW REVIEW Vol. 87: 943 (1999)

KAPLAN, JOHN, *MARIJUANA: THE NEW PROHIBITION* (Pocket Books 1971)

Kaplan, John, *The Role of Law in Drug Control: Self-Harming Conduct and Society*, DUKE LAW JOURNAL Vol. 1971:1065 (1971)

Karlan, Pamela S., *Equal Protection, Due Process and the Stereoscopic Fourteenth Amendment*, MCGEORGE LAW REVIEW Vol. 33:473 (2002)

Karst, Kenneth L., *The Liberties of Equal Citizens: Groups and the Due Process Clause*, UCLA LAW REVIEW Vol. 55:99 (2007)

Kesavan & Stokes, *The Interpretive Force of the Constitution's Secret Drafting History*, GEORGIA LAW JOURNAL Vol. 91:1112 (2003)

KING, RUFUS, *THE DRUG HANG UP: AMERICA'S FIFTY-YEAR FOLLY* (Norton 1972)

King, Rufus, *Wild Shots in the War on Crime*, JOURNAL OF PUBLIC LAW Vol. 20:85 (1971)

KRISHNA, GOPI, *KUNDALINI: THE EVOLUTIONARY ENERGY IN MAN* (Shambala 1997)

Kumm, Mattias, *Democracy is not enough: Rights, proportionality and the point of judicial review*, NEW YORK UNIVERSITY PUBLIC LAW AND LEGAL THEORY WORKING PAPERS, Paper 118 (2009)

Kumm, Mattias, *The Idea of Socratic Contestation and the Right to Justification: The Point of Rights-Based Proportionality Review*, LAW & ETHICS OF HUMAN RIGHTS Vol. 4:141 (2010)

KURLAND, PHILIP & LERNER, RALPH, *THE FOUNDERS' CONSTITUTION* (Online book)

KWITNY, JONATHAN, *THE CRIMES OF PATRIOTS: A TRUE TALE OF DOPE, DIRTY MONEY, AND THE CIA* (Norton 1987)

Langer, Ellen & Alexander, Charles, *Higher Stages of Human Development: Perspectives on Adult Growth* (Oxford 1990)

Laniel, Laurent, *The Relationship between Research and Drug Policy in the United States*, Management of Social Transformations, Discussion Paper No. 44 (1999)

Lanza, Robert, *Biocentricism: How Life and Consciousness are the Keys to Understanding the True Nature of the Universe* (Benbella 2009)

Lash, Kurt, *The Lost History of the Ninth Amendment: The Lost Original Meaning*, Loyola Law School, Research Paper No. 2004-5 (2004)

Lee, Donna, *Resuscitating Proportionality in Noncapital Criminal Sentencing*, Arizona State Law Journal Vol. 40:527 (2008)

Lee, Youngjae, *The Constitutional Right Against Excessive Punishment*, New York University Public Law and Legal Theory Working Papers, Paper 3 (2005)

Levinson, Daryl J., *Empire-Building Government in Constitutional Law*, NYU Law School Public Law and Legal Theory Working Paper Series, Working Paper No. 84 (2004)

Levinson, Rosalie Berger, *Reining in Abuses of Executive Power through Substantive Due Process*, Florida Law Review Vol. 60:519 (2008)

Lewis, C. S., *The Problem of Pain* (MacMillan 1962)

Lindauer, Susan, *Extreme Prejudice: The Terrifying Story of the Patriot Act and the Cover Ups of 9/11 and Iraq* (Createspace 2010)

Lipton, Bruce H., *The Biology of Belief: Unleashing the Power of Consciousness, Matter and Miracles* (HayHouse 2010)

Locke, John, *Two Treaties of Government and a Letter Concerning Toleration* (Yale 2003)

Loewald, Hans W., *Papers on Psychoanalysis* (Yale 1980)

Loewald, Hans W., *Sublimation: Inquiries into Theoretical Psychoanalysis* (Yale 1988)

Lollini, Andrea, *The South African Constitutional Court Experience: Reasoning Patterns Based on Foreign Law*, Utrecht Law Review Vol. 8, Issue 2 (2012)

Luna, Erik, *The Overcriminalization Phenomenon*, American University Law Review Vol. 54:703 (2005)

Maas, Peter, *Manhunt* (Randomhouse1986)

MacCoun, Robert & Reuter, Peter, *Drug War Heresies* (Cambridge 2001)

Mackay, Charles, *Extraordinary Popular Delusions and the Madness of Crowds* (Bentley 1841)

Madison, Hamilton & Jay, *the Federalist Papers* (Timeless Classics 2010)

Maguire, Sarah A. & Nourse, V.F, *The Lost History of Governance and Equal Protection*, Duke Law Journal Vol. 58:955 (2009)

Martin, Al, *The Conspirators: Secrets of an Iran-Contra Insider* (National Liberty 2002)

Maslow, Abraham, *Religions, Values, and Peak-Experiences* (Penguin 1994)

Maslow, Abraham, *Toward a Psychology of Being* (Van Nostrand 1982)

Massey, Calvin, *The New Formalism: Requiem for Tiered Scrutiny?* University of Pennsylvania Journal of Constitutional Law Vol. 6:945 (2004)

Masters, Bill, *Drug War Addiction: Notes from the Frontlines of America's No. 1 Policy Disaster* (Accurate 2001)

Materni, Mike C., *The 100-plus Year old Case for a Minimalist Criminal Law*, New Criminal Law Review Vol. 18 issue 3 (2015)

Mathre, M.L., *Cannabis in Medical Practice: A Legal, Historical, and Pharmacological Overview of the Therapeutic Use of Marijuana* (McFarland 1997)

Mazur, Cynthia S., *Marijuana as a Holy Sacrament: Is the Issue of Peyote Constitutionally Distinguishable from That of Marijuana in Bona Fide Religious Ceremonies?* Notre Dame Law Review Vol. 5:693 (1991)

Mazur, Robert, *The Infiltrator* (Little Brown 2009)

McAffee, Thomas B., *The Original Meaning of the Ninth Amendment*, Colombia Law Review Vol. 90:1215 (1990)

McConnell, Michael W., *Natural Rights and the Ninth Amendment: How Does Lockean Legal Theory Assist in Interpretation?* NYU Journal of Law and Liberty Vol. 5:1 (2010)

McDonald, Forrest, *Novus Ordo Seclorum: The Intellectual Origins of the Constitution* (Kansas 1985)

McGinnis, John & Mulaney, Charles, *Judging Facts Like Law: The Courts Versus Congress in Social Fact-Finding*, Constitutional Commentary Vol. 25, Issue 1 (2008)

McTaggart, Lynne, *The Field: the Quest for the Secret Force of the Universe* (Harper 2008)

McWhirter, Darien & Bible, Jon, *Privacy as a Constitutional Right: Sex, Drugs, and the Right to Life* (Quorum 1992)

Melman, Seymour, *The Permanent War Economy: American Capitalism in Decline* (Simon & Schuster 1985)

Menashe, Ari Ben, *Profits of War: Inside the Secret US Israeli Arms Network* (Sheridan 1998)

Mikalsen, Roar, *Human Rising: The Prohibitionist Psychosis and its Constitutional Implications* (Life Liberty Productions 2020)

Mikalsen, Roar, *Reason Is: On the Nature of Consciousness and how Everything is Connected to Everything* (Createspace 2014)

Mikalsen, Roar, *To End a War: A Short History of Human Rights, the Rule of Law, and how Drug Prohibition Violates the Bill of Rights* (Createspace 2015)

Mill, John Stuart, *On Liberty* (Hackett 1978)

Miller, Richard Lawrence, *The Case for Legalizing Drugs* (Praeger 1991)

Miller, Richard Lawrence, *Drug Warriors and Their Prey: From Police Power to Police State* (Praeger 1996)

Miller, William & C'DeBaca, Janet, *Quantum Changes: When Epiphanies and Sudden Insights Transform Ordinary Lives* (Guilford 2001)

Mills, C. Wright, *The Power Elite* (Oxford 1956)

Mills, James, *The Underground Empire: Where Crime and Governments Embrace* (Doubleday 1986)

Moorjani, Anita, *Dying to be Me* (Hay House 2014)

Möller, Kai, *The Global Model of Constitutional Rights* (Oxford 2012)

Möller, Kai, *Proportionality: Challenging the critics*, I.CON Vol. 10: 709 (2012)

Murphy, Michael, *The Future of the Body: Explorations Into the Further Evolution of Human Nature* (Tarcher 1992)

Musto, David, *The American Disease: Origins of Narcotic Control* (Yale 1973)

Nelson, Caleb, *Judicial Review and Legislative Purpose*, New York University Law Review Vol. 83:1784 (2008)

Nelson, William E., *Changing Conceptions of Judicial Review: The Evolution of Constitutional Theory in the United States 1790-1860*, University of Pennsylvania Law Review Vol. 120:1166 (1972)

Niles, Mark C., *Ninth Amendment Adjudication: An Alternative to Substantive Due Process Analysis of Personal Autonomy Rights*, UCLA Law Review Vol. 48:85 (2000)

Nilsen, Eva & Blumenson, Eric, *Liberty Lost: the Moral Case for Marijuana Law Reform*, Suffolk University Law School, Research Paper No. 09-20 (2009)

Nilsen, Eva & Blumenson, Eric, *Policing for Profit: The Drug War's Hidden Economic Agenda*, University of Chicago Law Review Vol. 65:35 (1998)

Normand, Roger & Zaidi, Sarah, *Human Rights at the UN: The Political History of Universal Justice* (Indiana 2008)

Nutt, David, *Drugs—Without the Hot Air: Minimising the Harms of Legal and Illegal Drugs* (Cambridge 2012)

O'Brien, Kathy, *Trance-Formation of America* (Reality 1995)

O'Scannlain, Diarmuid F., *The Natural Law in the American Tradition*, Fordham Law Review Vol. 79:1513 (2011)

Ostrowski, James, *Answering the Critics of Drug Legalization*, Notre Dame Journal of Law, Ethics & Public Policy Vol. 5:823 (1991)

Ostrowski, James, *The Moral and Practical Case for Drug Legalization*, Hofstra Law Review Vol. 18: Issue 3, Article 5 (1990)

Oteri & Silvergate, *The Pursuit of Pleasure: Constitutional Dimensions of the Marihuana Problem*, Suffolk Law Review Vol. 3:55 (1968)

Packer, Herbert L., *The Limits of the Criminal Sanction* (Stanford 1968)

Peikoff, Leonard, *The Ominous Parallels* (New American Library 1982)

Paine, Thomas, *Rights of Man* (WordsWorth 1996)

Perkins, John, *Confessions of an Economic Hitman* (Berrett-Koehler 2004)

PERT, CANDACE B., *MOLECULES OF EMOTION: WHY YOU FEEL THE WAY YOU FEEL* (Pocket Books 1999)

Preiser, Peter, *Rediscovering a Coherent Rationale for Substantive Due Process*, MARQUETTE LAW REVIEW Vol. 87:1 (2003)

PROUTY, L. FLETCHER, *THE SECRET TEAM: THE CIA AND ITS ALLIES IN CONTROL OF THE UNITED STATES AND THE WORLD* (Skyhorse 2008)

PROVINE, DORIS MARIE, *UNEQUAL UNDER LAW: RACE IN THE WAR ON DRUGS* (Chicago 2007)

PURUCKER, G. DE, *WIND OF THE SPIRIT* (Theosophical 1984)

QUIGLEY, CAROLL, *TRAGEDY AND HOPE: A HISTORY OF THE WORLD IN OUR TIME* (Macmillan 1966)

RAWLS, JOHN, *A THEORY OF JUSTICE* (Harvard 2003)

RAWLS, JOHN, *JUSTICE AS FAIRNESS: A RESTATEMENT* (Harvard 2003)

REED, TERRY & CUMMINGS, JOHN, *COMPROMISED: CLINTON, BUSH AND THE CIA* (SPI 1994)

REICH, WILHELM, *THE MASS PSYCHOLOGY OF FASCISM* (Ferrar1970)

Reinarman, Craig, Cohen Peter D. A., & Kaal, Hendrien L., *The Limited Relevance of Drug Policy: Cannabis in Amsterdam and in San Francisco*, AMERICAN JOURNAL OF PUBLIC HEALTH Vol. 94:836 (2004)

Reynolds, Glenn &. Kopel, David, *The Evolving Police Power: Some Observations for a New Century*, HASTINGS CONSTITUTIONAL LAW QUARTERLY Vol. 27:511 (2000)

Richards, David A. J., *Human Rights and the Moral Foundations of the Substantive Criminal Law*, GEORGIA LAW REVIEW 13:1395 (1978)

Richards, David A.J., *Liberalism, Public Morality, and Constitutional Law: Prolegomenon to a Theory of the Constitutional Right to Privacy*, LAW AND CONTEMPORARY PROBLEMS Vol. 51:123 (1988)

RICHARDS, DAVID A.J., *SEX, DRUGS, DEATH, AND THE LAW: AN ESSAY ON HUMAN RIGHTS AND OVERCRIMINALIZATION* (Rowman 1982)

RICHARDS, DAVID A. J., *TOLERATION AND THE CONSTITUTION* (Oxford 1989)

Richards, David A.J., *Unnatural Acts and the Constitutional Right to Privacy: A Moral Theory*, FORDHAM LAW REVIEW Vol. 45:1281 (1977)

Roach, Kent, *The Primacy of Liberty and Proportionality, Not Human Dignity, When Subjecting Criminal Law to Constitutional Control*, ISRAELI LAW REVIEW Vol. 44:91 (2011)

Robinson, Paul H. & Darley, John M., *The Utility of Desert*, NORTHWESTERN UNIVERSITY LAW REVIEW Vol. 91:453 (1997)

ROBINSON, MATTHEW & SCHERLEN, RENEE, *LIES, DAMN LIES, AND DRUG WAR STATISTICS* (SUNY 2007)

ROOM, ROBIN, ET AL., *CANNABIS POLICY: MOVING BEYOND STALEMATE* (Oxford 2010)

Rosenfeld, Michel, *The Rule of Law and the Legitimacy of Constitutional Democracy*, SOUTHERN CALIFORNIA LAW REVIEW Vol. 74:1307 (2001)

ROUSSEAU, JEAN-JACQUES, *THE SOCIAL CONTRACT* (Digireads 2005)

Rubin, Edward L., *Bureaucratic Oppression: It's Causes and Cures*, VANDERBILT UNIVERSITY LAW SCHOOL, Working Paper no. 14-15 (2012)

Rubin, Edward, *Judicial Review and the Right to Resist*, VANDERBILT UNIVERSITY LAW SCHOOL, Working Paper Number 08-11 (2008)

RUPPERT, MIKE, *CROSSING THE RUBICON: THE DECLINE OF THE AMERICAN EMPIRE AT THE END OF THE AGE OF OIL* (NEW SOCIETY 2004)

RUSSELL, DAN, *DRUG WAR: COVERT MONEY, POWER AND POLICY* (Kalyx 2000)

RUSSEL, PETER, *THE GLOBAL BRAIN: SPECULATIONS ON THE EVOLUTIONARY LEAP OF PLANETARY CONSCIOUSNESS* (J. P. Tarcher 1983)

Sabo, Michael, *The Higher Law Background of the Constitution: Justice Clarence Thomas and Constitutional Interpretation*, ASHBROOK STATESMANSHIP THESIS (2009)

Sanders, Chase J., *Ninth Life: An Interpretive Theory of the Ninth Amendment*, INDIANA LAW JOURNAL Vol. 69:759 (1994)

Santiago, Miriam Defensor, *The New Equal Protection*, PHILIPPINE LAW JOURNAL Vol. 58:1 (1983)

SCHALER, JEFFREY (ED.), *DRUGS: SHOULD WE LEGALIZE, DECRIMINALIZE OR DEREGULATE?* (Prometheus 1998)

SCHNOEBELEN, WILLIAM, *MASONRY: BEYOND THE LIGHT* (Chick 1991)

SCHWARTZ, TONY, *WHAT REALLY MATTERS: SEARCHING FOR WISDOM IN AMERICA* (Bantam 1996)

SCOTT, PETER DALE, *AMERICAN WAR MACHINE: DEEP POLITICS, THE CIA GLOBAL DRUG CONNECTION, AND THE ROAD TO AFGHANISTAN* (Rowman 2014)

SCOTT, PETER DALE (ED.), *9/11 AND AMERICAN EMPIRE: INTELLECTUALS SPEAK OUT* (Olive Branch 2006)

SCOTT, PETER DALE, *THE ROAD TO 9/11: WEALTH, EMPIRE, AND THE FUTURE OF AMERICA* (California 2008)

SEN, AMARTYA, *THE IDEA OF JUSTICE* (Harvard 2011)

Shedler, Jonathan & Block, Jack, *Adolescent Drug Use and Psychological Health: A Longitudinal Inquiry*, AMERICAN PSYCHOLOGIST Vol. 45 (1990)

SHELDRAKE, RUPERT, *MORPHIC RESONANCE: THE NATURE OF FORMATIVE CAUSATION* (Park Street 2009)

SHELDRAKE RUPERT, *THE PRESENCE OF THE PAST: MORPHIC RESONANCE AND THE HABITS OF NATURE* (Park Street 1995)

Sherry, Suzana, *The Founders' Unwritten Constitution*, UNIVERSITY OF CHICAGO LAW REVIEW Vol. 54:1127 (1987)

Sherry, Suzanna, *The Ninth Amendment: Righting an Unwritten Constitution*, CHICAGO-KENT LAW REVIEW Vol. 64:1001 (1988)

SHULGIN, ALEXANDER, *PIKHAL: A CHEMICAL LOVE STORY* (Transform 1992)

Siegel, Stephen A., *The Origin of the Compelling State Interest Test and Strict Scrutiny*, AMERICAN JOURNAL OF LEGAL HISTORY Vol. 48:355 (2006)

SIMON, STEPHEN A., *HUMAN RIGHTS OR AMERICAN PRIVILEGES? THE SUPREME COURT'S EVOLVING USE OF UNIVERSAL REASONING* (Doctoral dissertation 2007)

Smith, Annaliese, Comment, *Marijuana as a Schedule I Substance: Political Ploy or Accepted Science?* SANTA CLARA LAW REVIEW Vol. 40:1137 (2000)

SMITH, HUSTON, *CLEANSING THE DOORS OF PERCEPTION: THE RELIGIOUS SIGNIFICANCE OF ENTHEOGENIC PLANTS AND CHEMICALS* (Tarcher/Putnam 2000)

SMOLEY, RICHARD, *INNER CHRISTIANITY: A GUIDE TO THE ESOTERIC TRADITION* (Shambala 2002)

Snure, Brian, *A Frequent Recurrence to Fundamental Principles: Individual Rights, Free Government, and the Washington State Constitution*, WASHINGTON LAW REVIEW Vol. 67:669 (1992)

Solum, Lawrence B., *Originalism and the Unwritten Constitution*, UNIVERSITY OF ILLINOIS LAW REVIEW Vol. 2013:1935 (2013)

Spooner, Lysander, *Vices are Not Crimes: a Vindication of Moral Liberty* (1875) (Online book)

Stevens, Alex, *Drug Policy, Harm and Human Rights: A Rationalist Approach*, INTERNATIONAL JOURNAL OF DRUG POLICY 22 (2011)

STICH, RODNEY, *DEFRAUDING AMERICA* (Diablo 1988)

STILL, WILLIAM T., *NEW WORLD ORDER: THE ANCIENT PLAN OF SECRET SOCIETIES* (Huntington 1990)

STOCKWELL, JOHN, *THE PRAETORIAN GUARD: THE US ROLE IN THE NEW WORLD ORDER* (South End 1991)

STOLAROFF, M.J., *THANATOS TO EROS: THIRTY-FIVE YEARS OF PSYCHEDELIC EXPLORATION* (VWB 1994)

STONE, ROGER, *THE MAN WHO KILLED KENNEDY: THE CASE AGAINST LBJ* (Skyhorse 2013)

STRASSMAN, RICK, *DMT AND THE SOUL OF PROPHECY: A NEW SCIENCE OF SPIRITUAL REVELATION IN THE HEBREW BIBLE* (Park Street 2014)

Stuart, Susan, *War as Metaphor and the Rule of Law in Crisis: The Lessons We Should Have Learned From the War on Drugs*, VALPARASIO UNIVERSITY SCHOOL OF LAW, Legal Studies Research Paper (2011)

STUNTZ, WILLIAM J., *THE COLLAPSE OF AMERICAN CRIMINAL JUSTICE* (Harvard 2013)

Stuntz, William J., *The Pathological Politics of Criminal Law*, HARVARD LAW SCHOOL Public Law Working Paper No. 22 (2001)

Sun, Tammy W., *Equality by Other Means: The Substantive Foundations of the Vagueness Doctrine*, HARVARD CIVIL RIGHTS-CIVIL LIBERTIES LAW REVIEW Vol. 46:150 (2011)

Sunstein, Cass R., *Homosexuality and the Constitution*, INDIANA LAW JOURNAL Vol. 70:1 (1994)

SUTTON, ANTONY, *AMERICA'S SECRET ESTABLISHMENT: AN INTRODUCTION TO THE ORDER OF SKULL AND BONES* (Liberty House 1986)

Sweet, Alec S., *All Things in Proportion? American Rights Doctrine and the Problem of Balancing*, Faculty Scholarship Series Paper 30 (2010)

SZASZ, THOMAS, *CEREMONIAL CHEMISTRY: THE RITUAL PERSECUTION OF DRUGS, ADDICTS, AND PUSHERS* (Syracuse University 2003)

SZASZ, THOMAS, *OUR RIGHT TO DRUGS: THE CASE FOR A FREE MARKET* (Praeger 1992)

TAILOR, JOHN, *CONSTRUCTION CONSTRUED AND CONSTITUTIONS VINDICATED* (1820) (Online book)

TALBOT, MICHAEL, *THE HOLOGRAPHIC UNIVERSE* (Harper 2011)

TALBOT, MICHAEL, *MYSTICISM AND THE NEW PHYSICS* (Routledge 1981)

TARPLEY, WEBSTER, *911 SYNTHETIC TERROR: MADE IN THE USA* (Progressive 2007)

TART, CHARLES L., *TRANSPERSONAL PSYCHOLOGIES: PERSPECTIVES ON THE MIND FROM SEVEN GREAT SPIRITUAL TRADITIONS* (Harper 1992)

TAYLOR, STEVE, *OUT OF THE DARKNESS: FROM TURMOIL TO TRANSFORMATION* (Hay House 2011)

TEASDALE, WAYNE, *THE MYSTIC HEART: DISCOVERING A UNIVERSAL SPIRITUALITY IN THE WORLD'S RELIGIONS* (New World Library 1999)

Tennen, Eric, *Is the Constitution in Harm's Way? Substantive Due Process and Criminal Law*, BOALT JOURNAL OF CRIMINAL LAW Vol. 8: 3 (2004)

Thomas, Clarence, *Judging*, UNIVERSITY OF KANSAS LAW REVIEW Vol. 45:1 (1996)

Thomas, Clarence, Toward a Plain Reading of the Constitution: The Declaration of Independence in Constitutional Interpretation, HOWARD LAW JOURNAL Vol. 30:691 (1987)

Torke, James W., *the Judicial Process in Equal Protection Cases*, HASTINGS CONSTITUTIONAL LAW QUARTERLY Vol. 9:279 (1982)

Treiman, David M., *Equal Protection and Fundamental Rights—A Judicial Shell Game*, TULSA LAW REVIEW Vol. 15:183 (1979)

Tribe, Laurence H., *Lawrence v. Texas: The Fundamental Right that Dare Not Speak its Name*, HARVARD LAW REVIEW Vol. 117:1893 (2004)

Tribe, Laurence H., *On Reading the Constitution*, The Tanner Lectures on Human Values, Delivered at The University of Utah (November 17 and 18, 1986)

Tribe, Laurence H., *Reflections on Unenumerated Rights*, JOURNAL OF CONSTITUTIONAL LAW Vol. 9:483 (2007)

Tribe, Laurence & Dorf, Michael, *Levels of Generality in the Definition of Rights*, UNIVERSITY OF CHICAGO LAW REVIEW Vol. 57:1057 (1990)

Tupper, Kenneth & Labate, Beatriz, *Plants, Psychoactive Substances and the International Narcotics Control Board: The Control of Nature and the Nature of Control*, HUMAN RIGHTS AND DRUGS Vol. 2 No 1 (2012)

Tussman, Jospeh & tenBroek, Jacobus, *The Equal Protection of the Laws*, CALIFORNIA LAW REVIEW Vol. 37:341 (1949)

UNDERHILL, EVELYN, *MYSTICISM: A STUDY IN THE NATURE AND DEVELOPMENT OF MAN'S SPIRITUAL CONSCIOUSNESS* (Methuen 1962)

UNDP, *Perspectives on the Development Dimensions of Drug Control Policy* (March 2015)

VALENTINE, DOUGLAS, *THE STRENGTH OF THE WOLF* (Verso 2004)

VENTURA, JESSE, *THEY KILLED OUR PRESIDENT: 63 REASONS TO BELIEVE THERE WAS A CONSPIRACY TO ASSASSINATE JFK* (Skyhorse 2013)

Vollenweider, Franz X. & Kometer, Michael, *The Neurobiology of Psychedelic Drugs: Implications for the Treatment of Mood Disorders*, NATURE REVIEWS NEUROSCIENCE Vol. 11 (2010)

WADE, JENNY, *CHANGES OF MIND: A HOLONOMIC THEORY OF THE EVOLUTION OF CONSCIOUSNESS* (State university of New York Press 1996)

WALSH, ROGER N., & VAUGHAN, FRANCES, *BEYOND EGO: TRANSPERSONAL DIMENSIONS IN PSYCHOLOGY* (Tarcher 1980)

Ward, Andrew, *The Rational Basis Test Violates Due Process*, NYU JOURNAL OF LAW & LIBERTY Vol. 8:713 (2014)

WATSON, LYALL, *LIFETIDE: A BIOLOGY OF THE UNCONSCIOUS* (Hodder & Stoughton 1979)

Werb et al., *Effect of Drug Law Enforcement on Drug-Related Violence: Evidence from a Scientific Review*, INTERNATIONAL CENTRE FOR SCIENCE IN DRUG POLICY (2010)

West, Robin *The Authoritarian Impulse in Constitutional Law*, UNIVERSITY OF MIAMI LAW REVIEW Vol. 42: 531 (1988)

WHITE, JOHN (ED.), *KUNDALINI: EVOLUTION AND ENLIGHTENMENT* (Paragon 1990)

WILBER, KEN, *THE EYE OF SPIRIT: AN INTEGRAL VISION FOR A WORLD GONE SLIGHTLY MAD* (Shambala 1998).

WILBER, KEN, *EYE TO EYE: THE QUEST FOR THE NEW PARADIGM* (Shambala 1996).

WILBER, KEN, *INTEGRAL SPIRITUALITY: A STARTLING NEW ROLE FOR RELIGION IN THE MODERN AND POSTMODERN WORLD* (Integral Books 2006).

WILBER, KEN, *UP FROM EDEN: A TRANSPERSONAL VIEW OF HUMAN EVOLUTION* (New Science Library 1986).

WILBER, KEN, *QUANTUM QUESTIONS: MYSTICAL WRITINGS OF THE WORLD'S GREATEST PHYSICISTS* (Shambala 2001).

WILCOCK, DAVID, *THE ASCENSION MYSTERIES: REVEALING THE COSMIC BATTLE BETWEEN GOOD AND EVIL* (Dutton 2016)

WILCOCK, DAVID, *THE SOURCE FIELD INVESTIGATIONS: THE HIDDEN SCIENCE AND LOST CIVILIZATIONS BEHIND THE 2012 PROPHECIES* (Dutton 2011)

WILLIAMS, PAUL, *OPERATION GLADIO: THE UNTOLD STORY OF THE UNHOLY ALLIANCE BETWEEN THE VATICAN, THE CIA, AND THE MAFIA* (Prometheus 2015)

WILKINSON, RICHARD & PICKETT, KATE, *THE SPIRIT LEVEL: WHY EQUALITY IS BETTER FOR EVERYONE* (Penguin 2010).

Williams, Ryan C., *The One and Only Substantive Due Process Clause*, THE YALE LAW JOURNAL Vol. 120:408 (2010)

WILSON, WOODROW, *THE NEW FREEDOM* (1913, online book)

WINKELMAN, MICHAEL & ROBERTS, THOMAS (EDS.), *PSYCHEDELIC MEDICINE: NEW EVIDENCE FOR HALLUCINOGENIC SUBSTANCES AS TREATMENTS*, Vol. 2 (Praeger 2007)

Winterbourne, Matt, *United States drug policy: The Scientific, Economic, and Social Issues Surrounding Marijuana* (2012)

Wisotsky, Steven, *A Society of Suspects: The War on Drugs and Civil Liberties*, CATO POLICY ANALYSIS No. 180 (1992)

WISOTSKY, STEVEN, *BEYOND THE WAR ON DRUGS: OVERCOMING A FAILED PUBLIC POLICY* (Prometheus 1990)

Wisotsky, Steven, *Not thinking Like a Lawyer: The Case of Drugs in the Courts*, NOTRE DAME JOURNAL OF LAW, ETHICS AND PUBLIC POLICY, Volume 5, Issue No. 3 (1991)

WOLLSTONECRAFT, MARY, *A VINDICATION OF THE RIGHTS OF MAN* (1792) (Online book)

WOLLSTONECRAFT, MARY, *A VINDICATION OF THE RIGHTS OF WOMAN* (Online Library of Liberty 1790)

WOOD, *WHERE DID THE TOWERS GO? EVIDENCE OF DIRECTED FREE-ENERGY TECHNOLOGY ON 9/11* (New Investigation 2010)

WULFF, DAVID M., *PSYCHOLOGY OF RELIGION: CLASSIC AND CONTEMPORARY VIEWS* (Wiley 1991)

Yankah, Ekow N., *A Paradox in Overcriminalization*, NEW CRIMINAL LAW REVIEW Vol. 14:1 (2011)

Yoshino, Kenji, *The New Equal Protection*, HARVARD LAW REVIEW Vol. 124:747 (2011)

ZIMBARDO, PHILIP, *THE LUCIFER EFFECT: HOW GOOD PEOPLE TURN EVIL* (Rider 2009)

ZUKAV, GARY, *THE DANCING WU LI MASTERS: AN OVERVIEW OF THE NEW PHYSICS* (Morrow & Co 1979)

Roar Mikalsen is the author of six books which are changing the world one at a time. His authorship covers a large area ranging from cosmology, mysticism, self-help, and consciousness research to power politics, human rights law, drug policy, constitutional interpretation, and social engineering. He is the founder of the Alliance for Rights-Oriented Drug Policies (AROD), an organization which addresses drug policy reform from a perspective of human rights and a nominee of two prestigious human rights awards (Vaclav Havel and Martin Ennals).

A platform for his work is Life Liberty Productions, a publishing house and consulting agency dedicated to the Spirit of Freedom. You will find books that are embraced by professionals and have the potential to bring humanity one step further on the online store lifelibertybooks.com